DRAG☆N BALL

FULL COLOR FREEZA ARC

2

STORY AND ART BY
AKIRA TORIYAMA

DRAGON BALL

FULL COLOR FREEZA ARC

CONTENTS

DRAGON BALL FULL COLOR FREEZA ARC

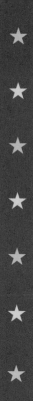

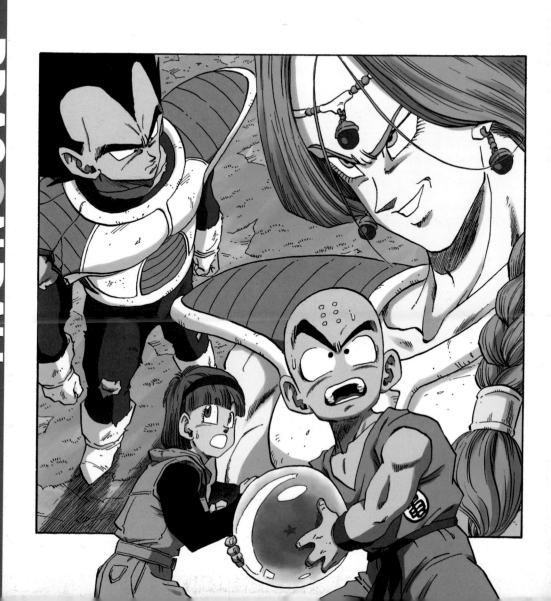

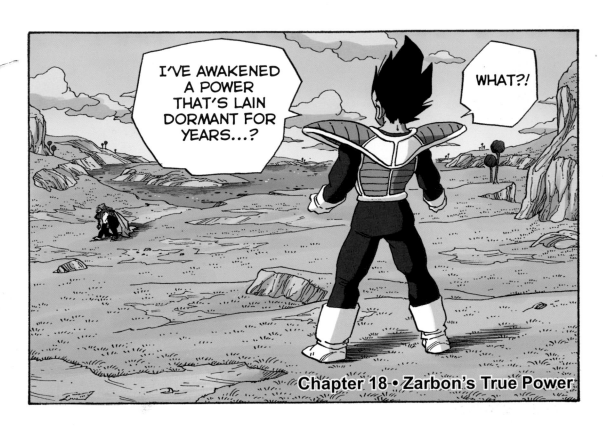

I'VE AWAKENED A POWER THAT'S LAIN DORMANT FOR YEARS...?

WHAT?!

Chapter 18 • Zarbon's True Power

I SEE...

HEH HEH HEH...

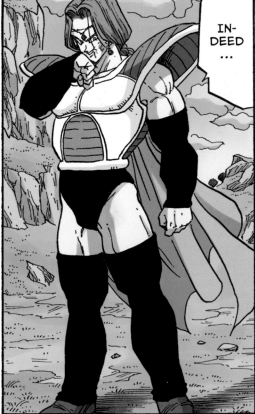

IN-DEED...

HAAH HA HA HA!!

YOU DO KEEP ME ENTER-TAINED, ZARBON!!

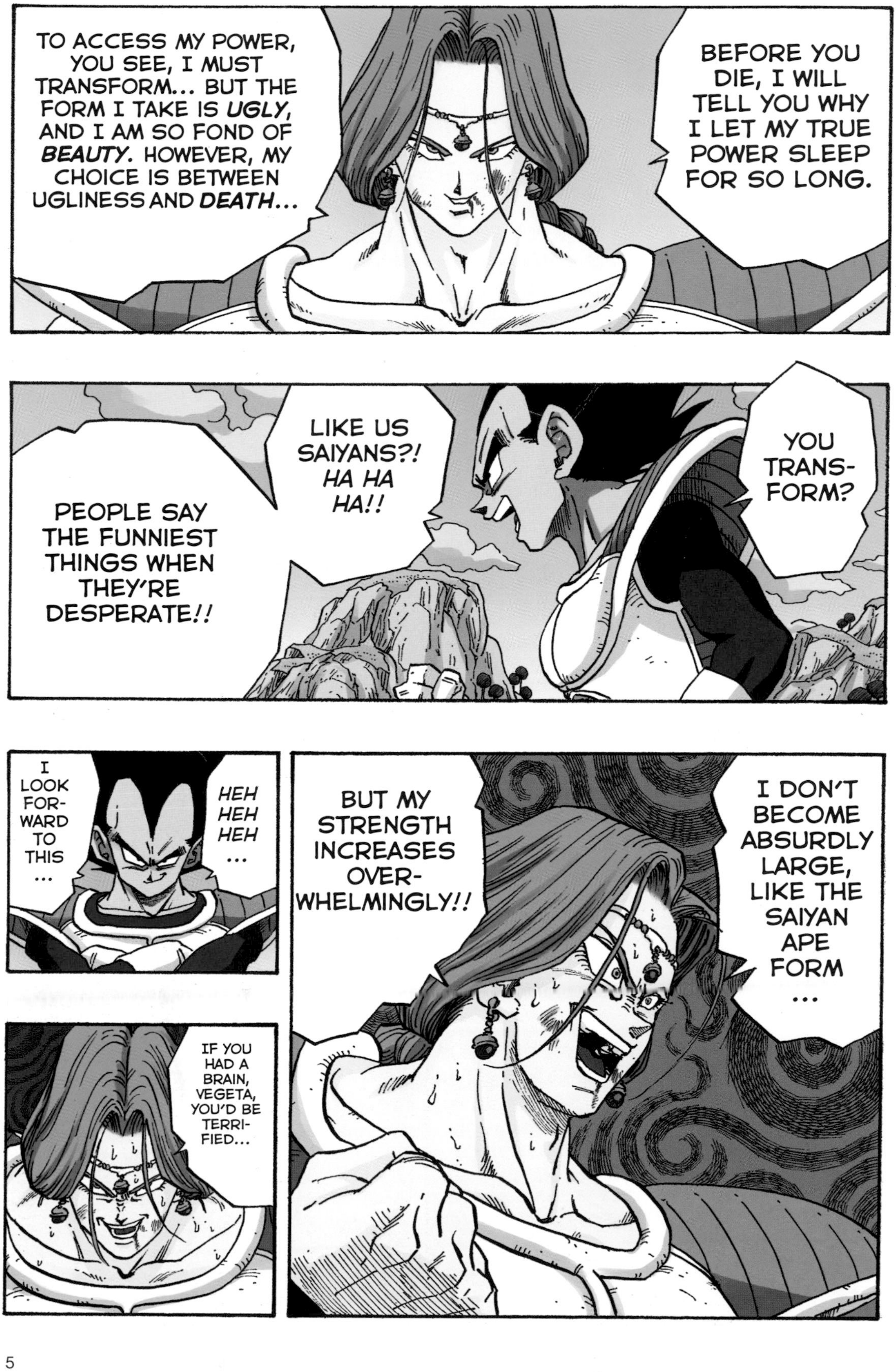
BEFORE YOU DIE, I WILL TELL YOU WHY I LET MY TRUE POWER SLEEP FOR SO LONG.
TO ACCESS MY POWER, YOU SEE, I MUST TRANSFORM... BUT THE FORM I TAKE IS *UGLY*, AND I AM SO FOND OF ***BEAUTY***. HOWEVER, MY CHOICE IS BETWEEN UGLINESS AND ***DEATH***...
YOU TRANS-FORM?
LIKE US SAIYANS?! *HA HA HA!!*
PEOPLE SAY THE FUNNIEST THINGS WHEN THEY'RE DESPERATE!!
I DON'T BECOME ABSURDLY LARGE, LIKE THE SAIYAN APE FORM...
BUT MY STRENGTH INCREASES OVER-WHELMINGLY!!
HEH HEH HEH...
I LOOK FOR-WARD TO THIS...
IF YOU HAD A BRAIN, VEGETA, YOU'D BE TERRI-FIED...

ドン
!!

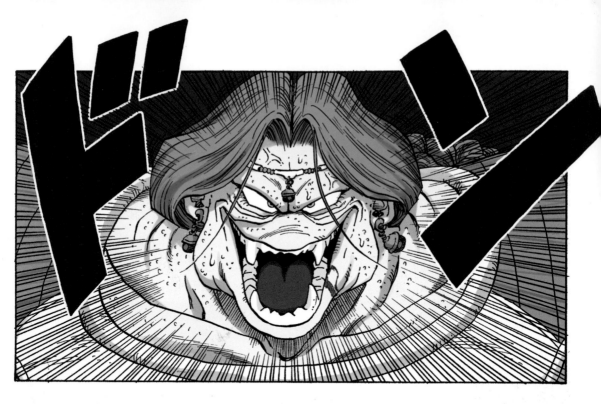

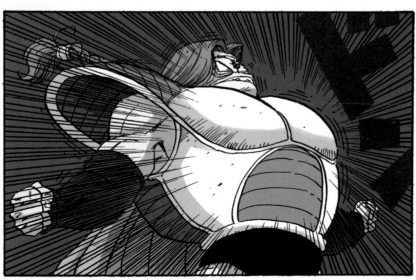

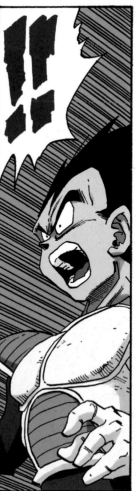

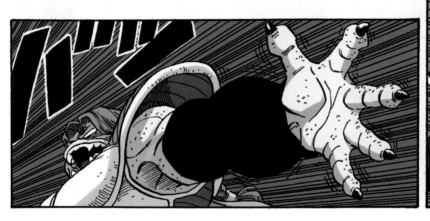

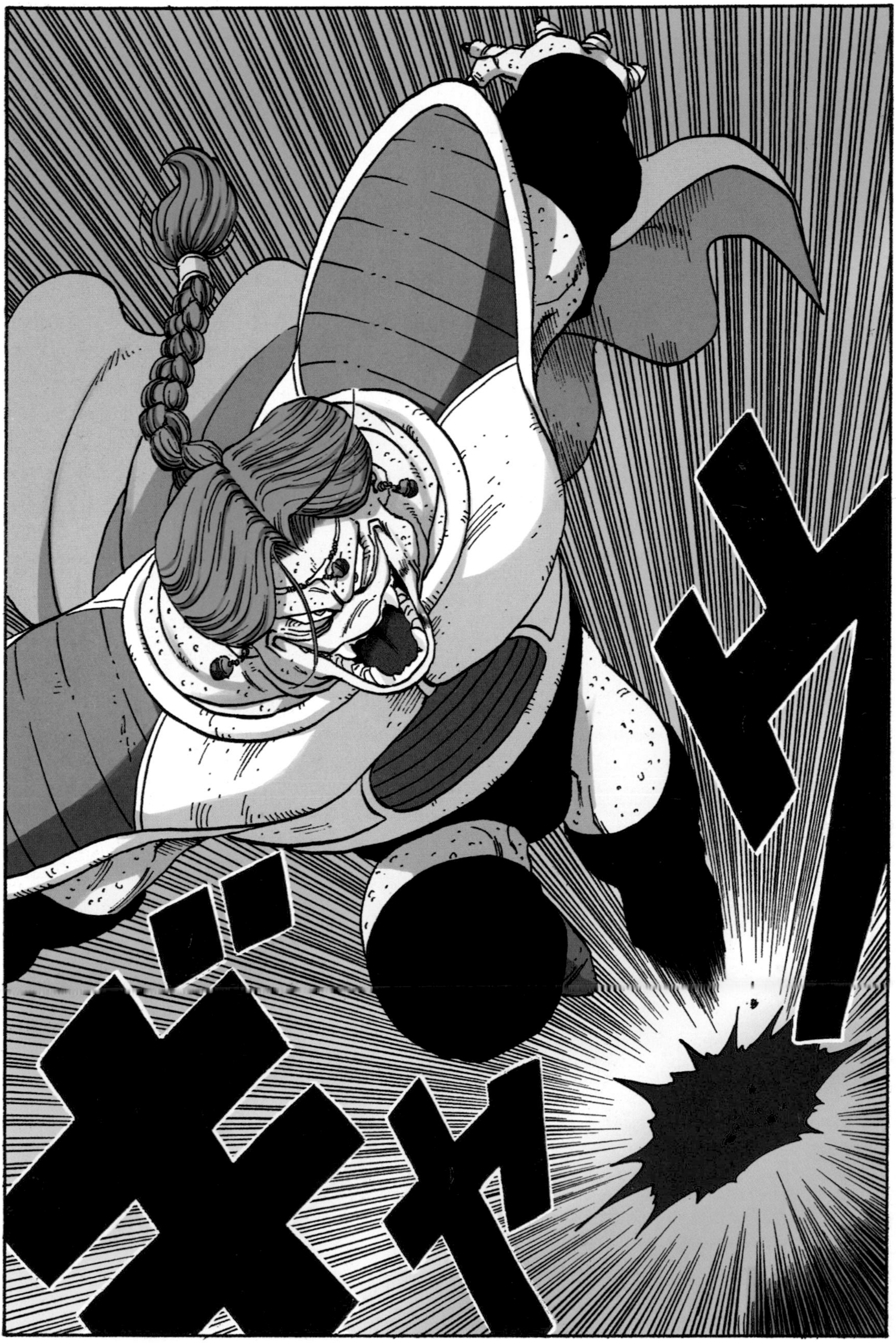

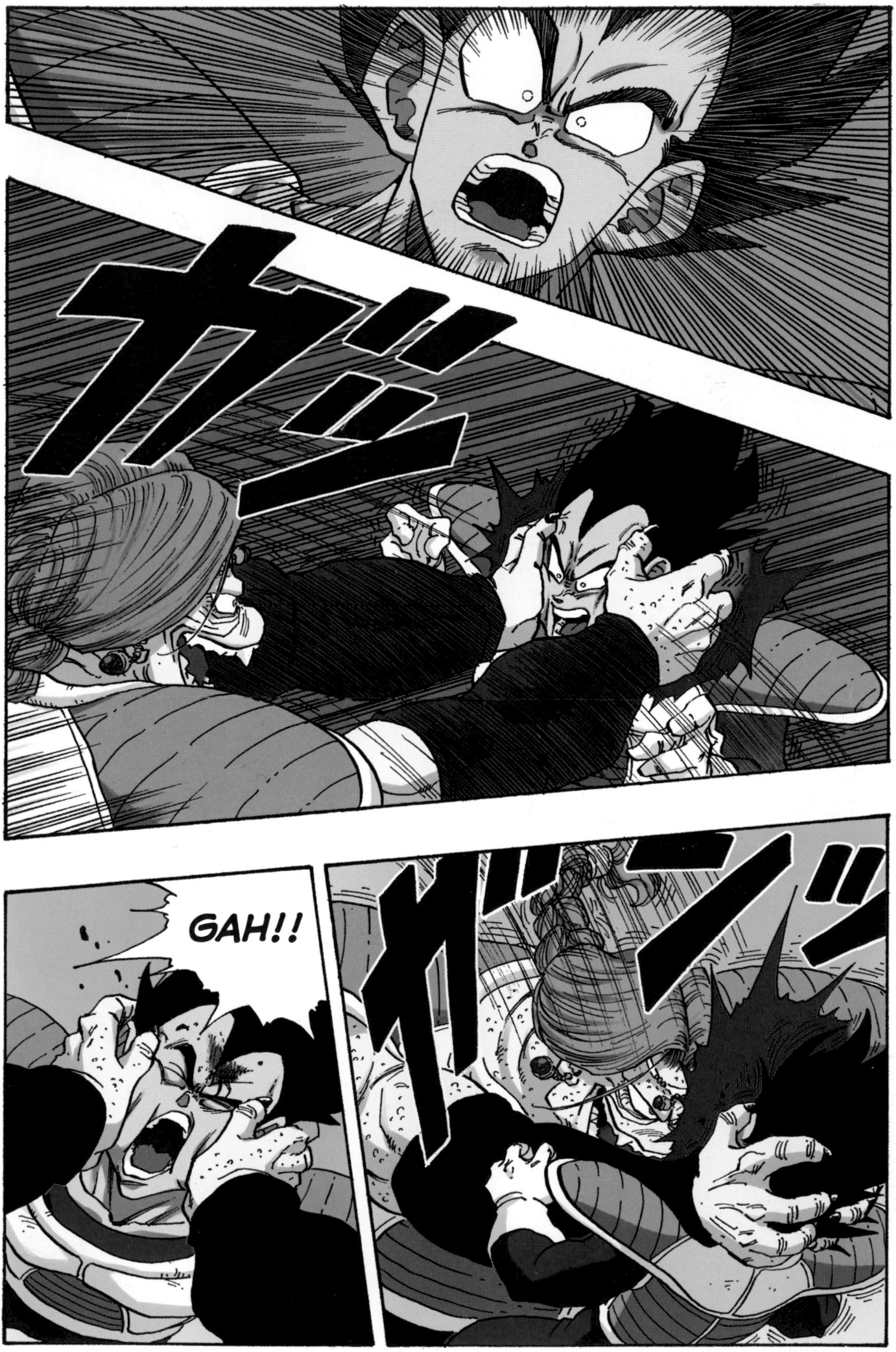
ガッ
GAH!!

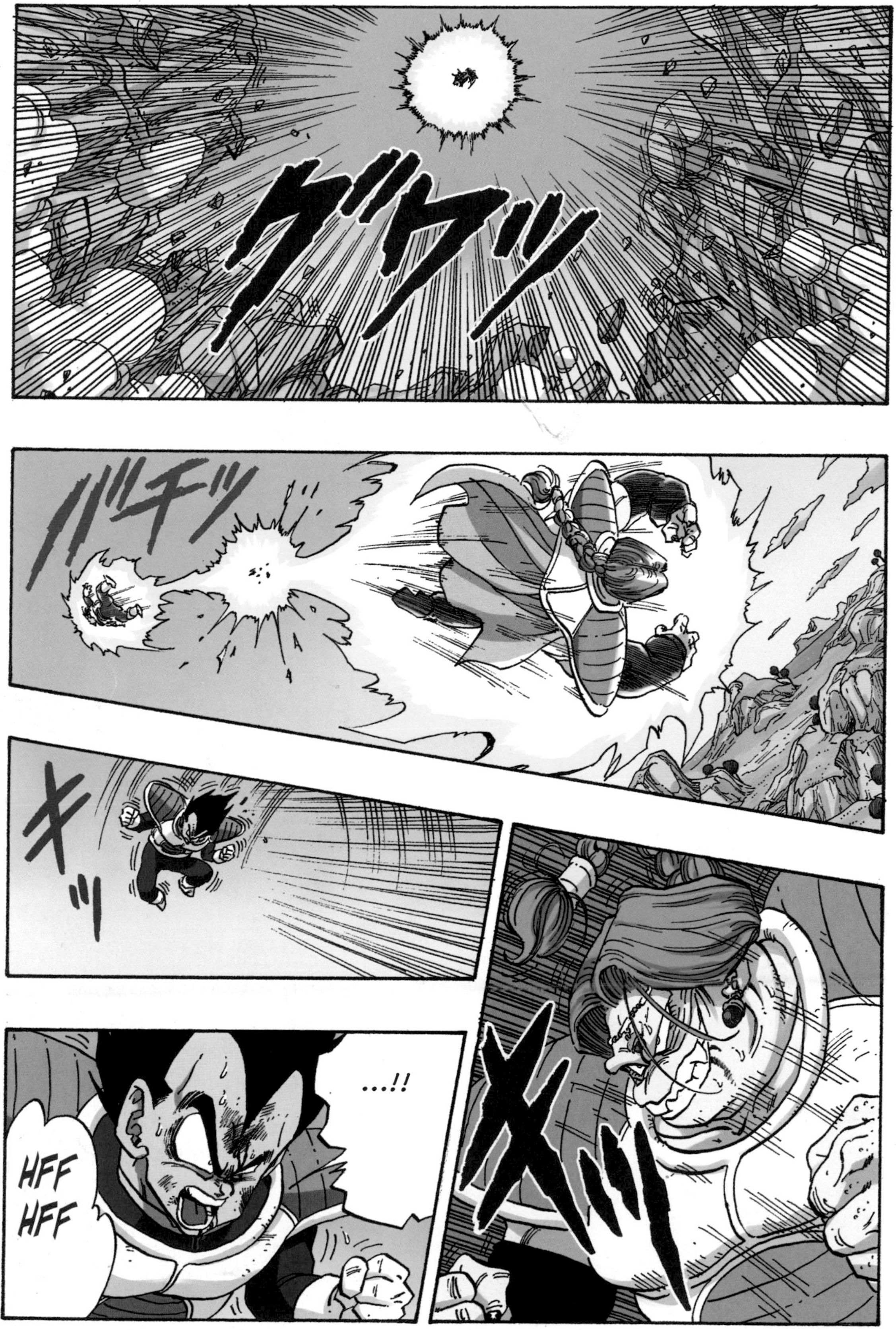
ググッ
バチッ
キッ
...!!
HFF HFF

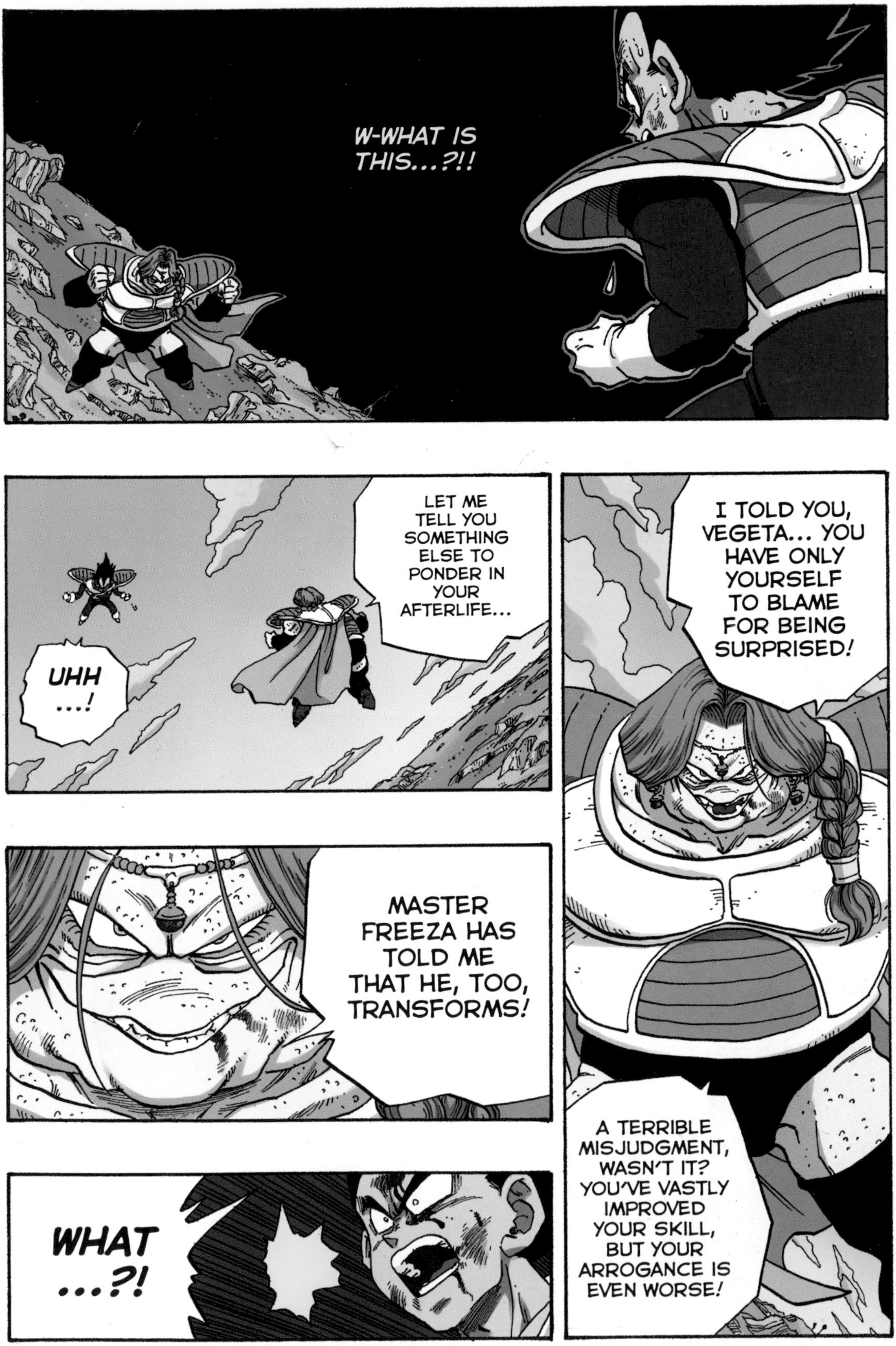
W-WHAT IS THIS...?!!
I TOLD YOU, VEGETA... YOU HAVE ONLY YOURSELF TO BLAME FOR BEING SURPRISED!
A TERRIBLE MISJUDGMENT, WASN'T IT? YOU'VE VASTLY IMPROVED YOUR SKILL, BUT YOUR ARROGANCE IS EVEN WORSE!
LET ME TELL YOU SOMETHING ELSE TO PONDER IN YOUR AFTERLIFE...
UHH...!
MASTER FREEZA HAS TOLD ME THAT HE, TOO, TRANSFORMS!
WHAT...?!

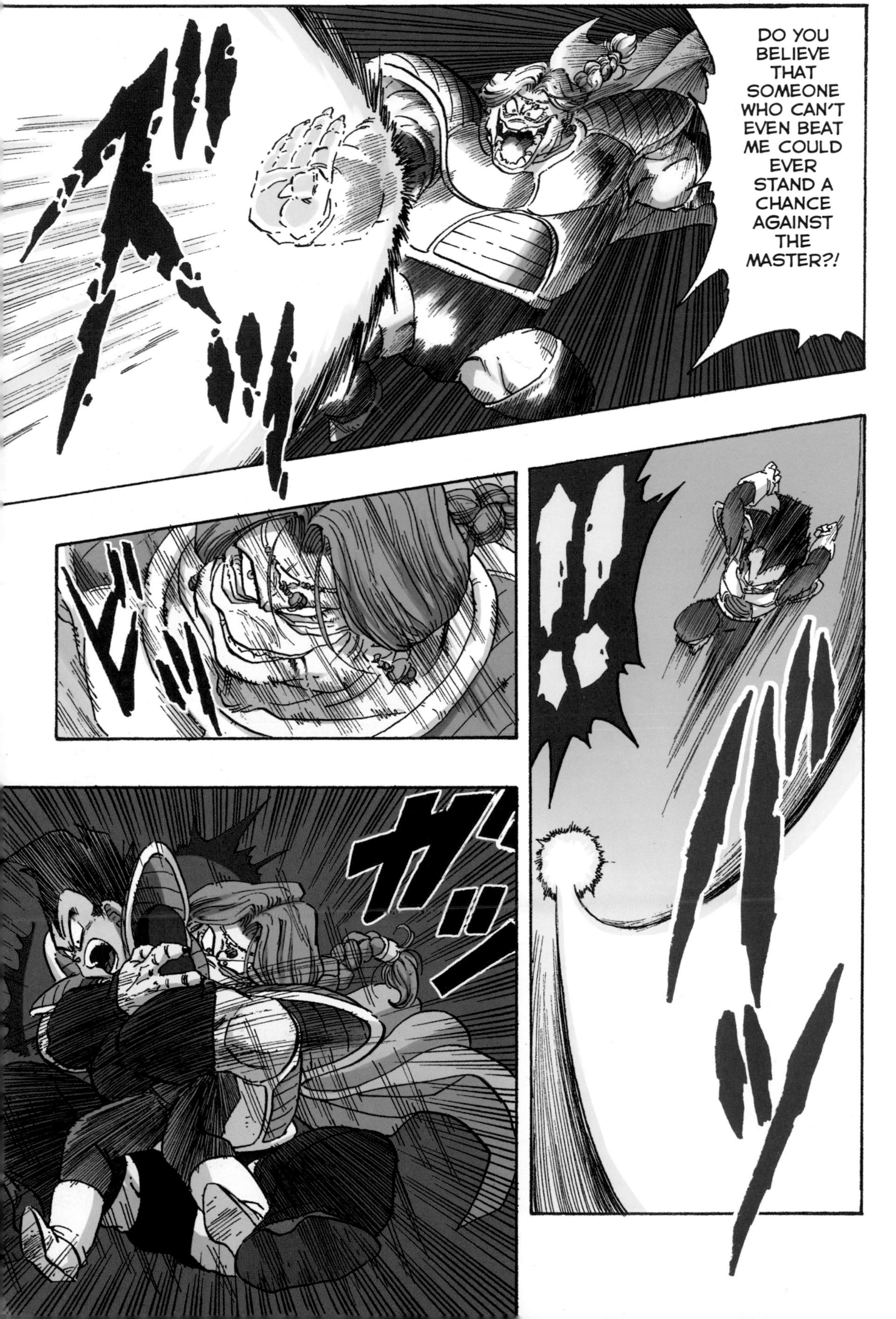
DO YOU BELIEVE THAT SOMEONE WHO CAN'T EVEN BEAT ME COULD EVER STAND A CHANCE AGAINST THE MASTER?!

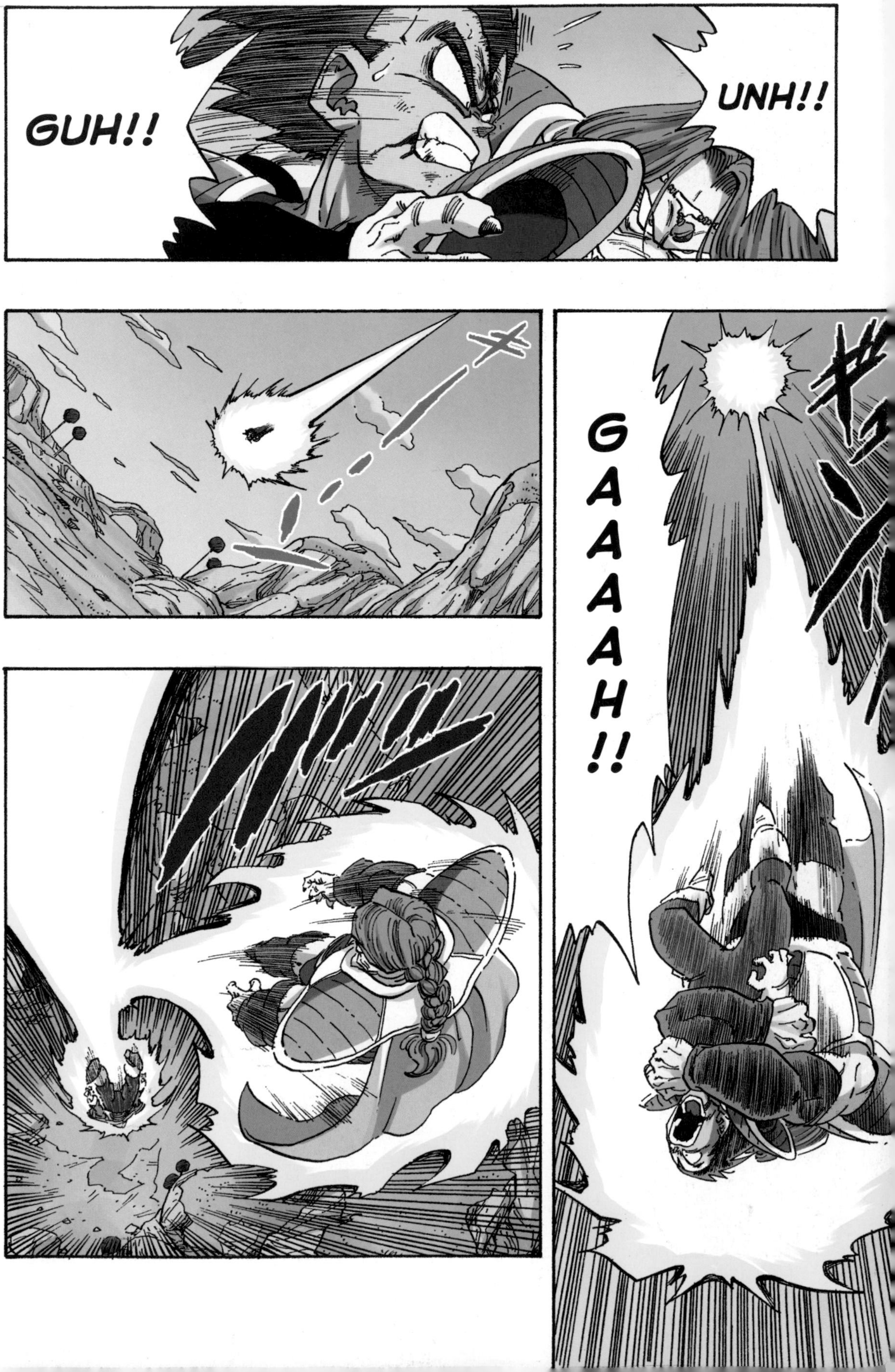
UNH!!
GUH!!
GAAAAAH!!

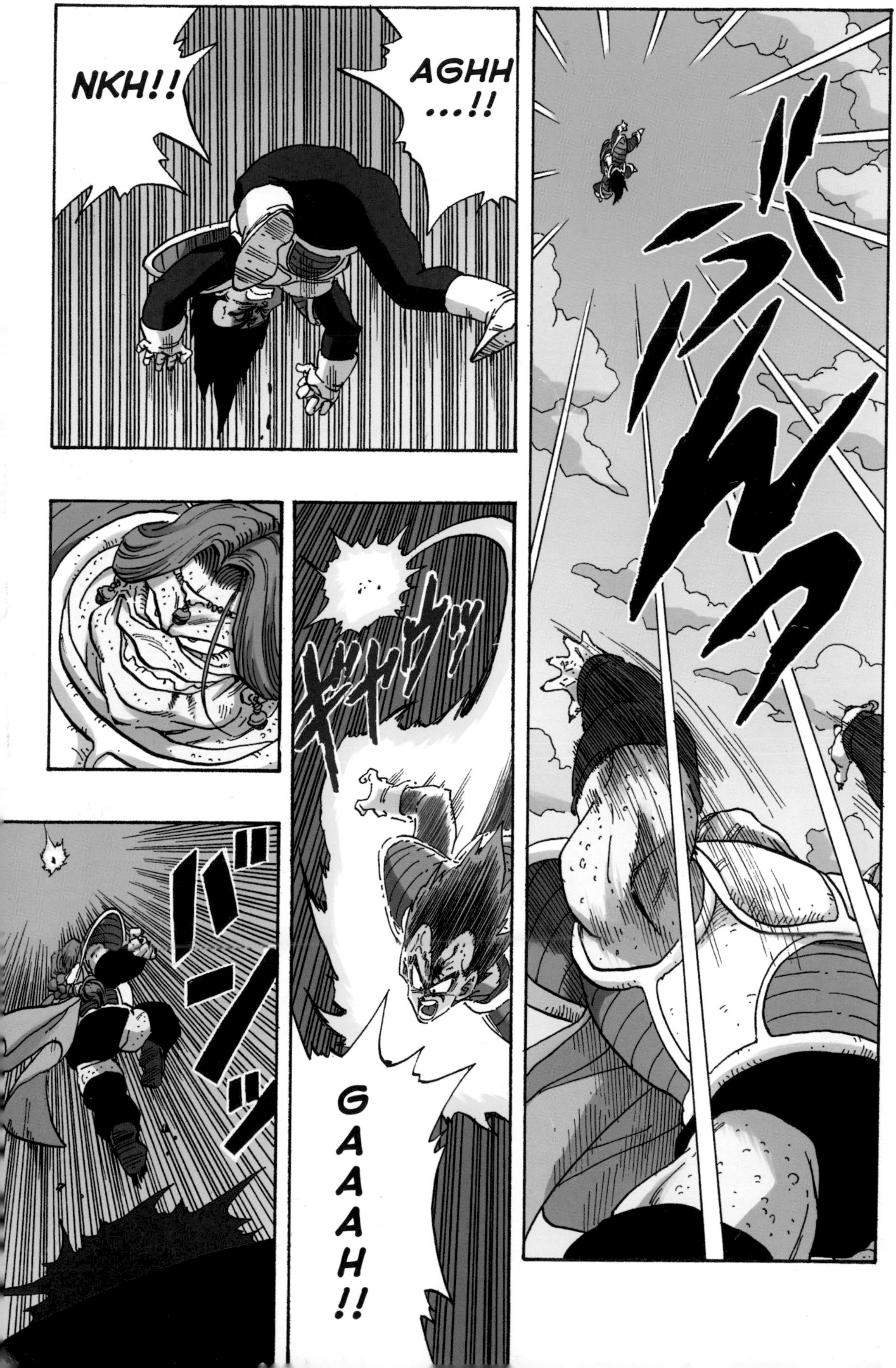
AGHH ...!!
NKH!!
GAAAAH!!

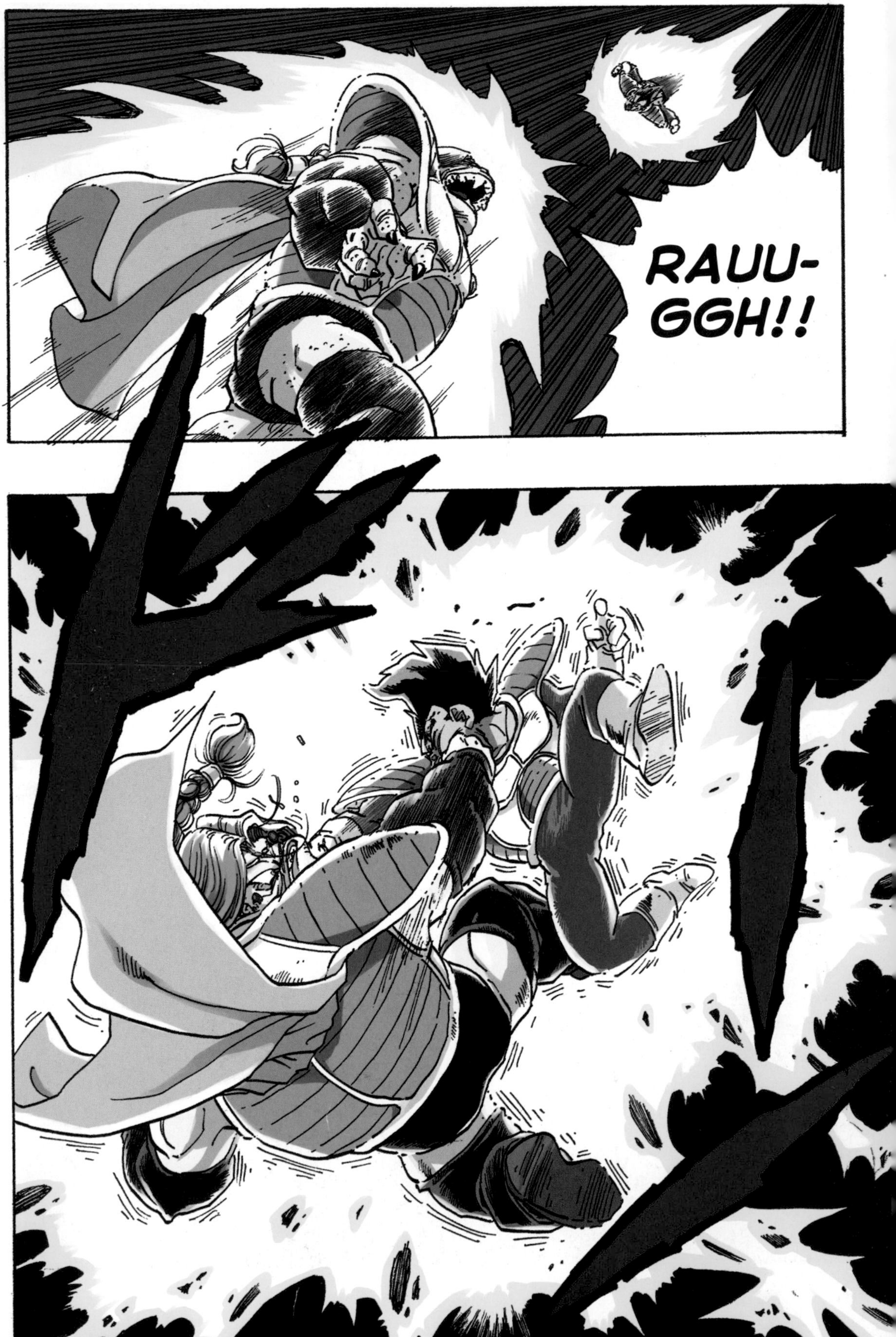
RAUU-
GGH!!

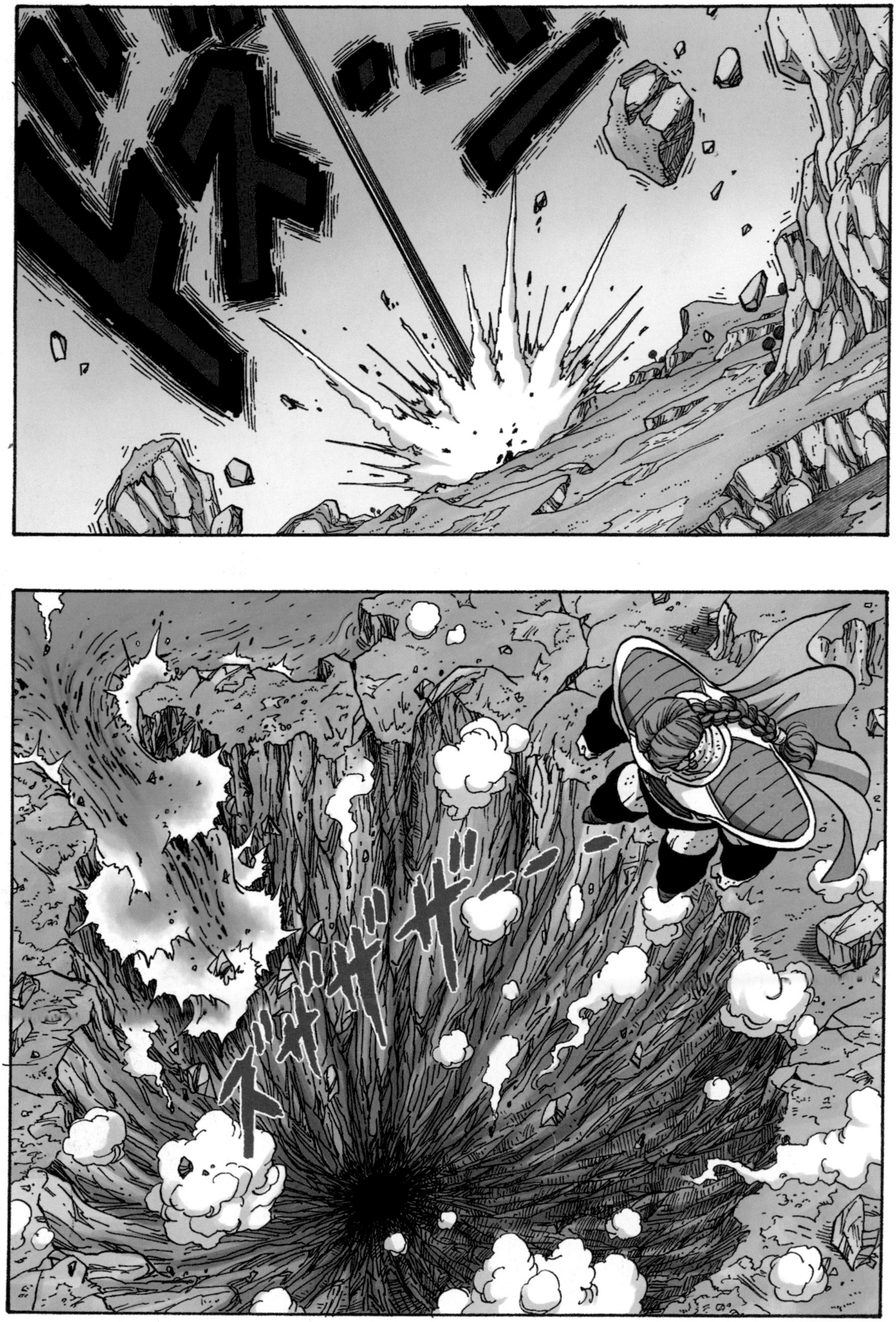
ズザザザーー

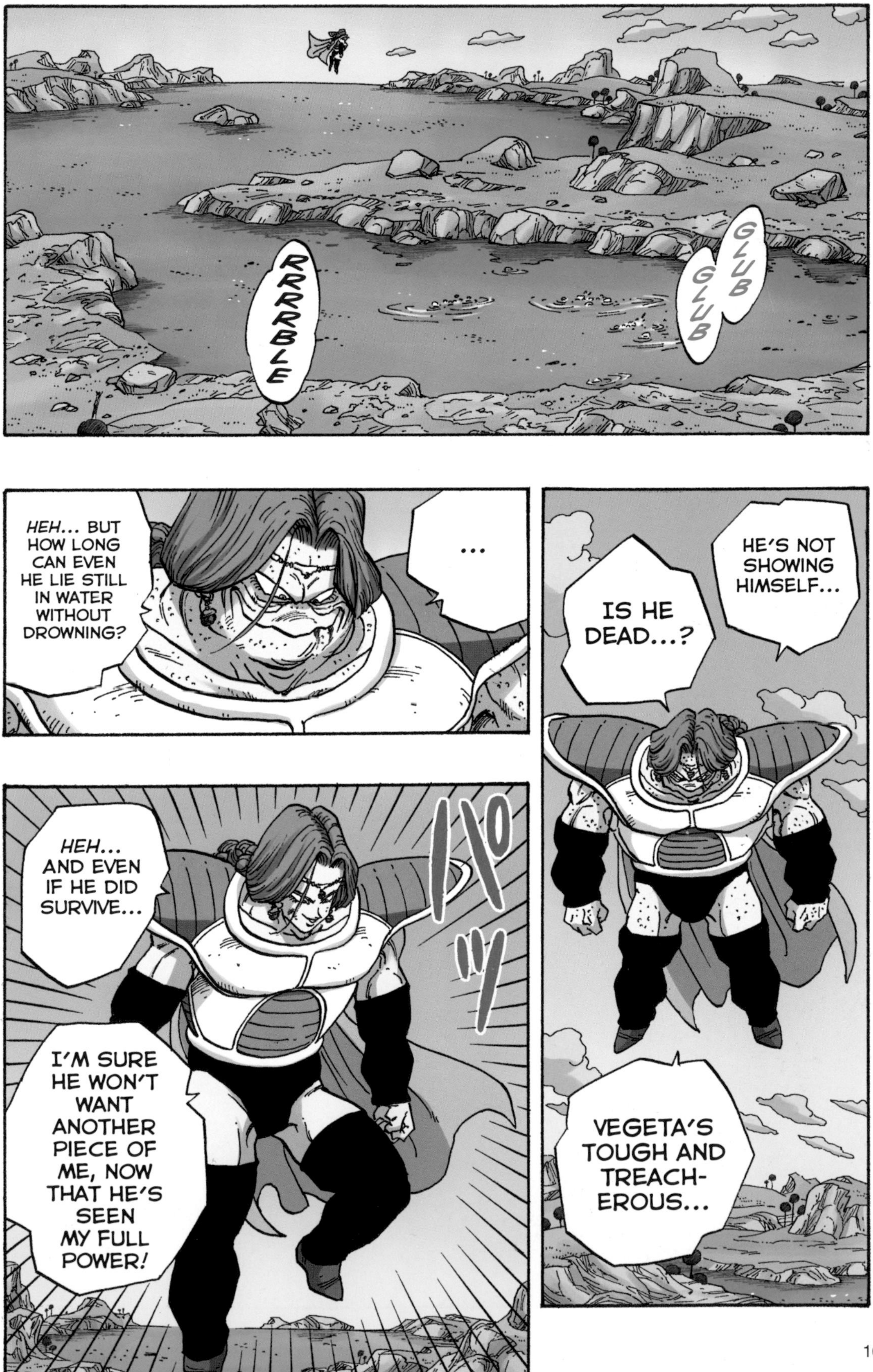
GLUB GLUB
RRRRBLE
HE'S NOT SHOWING HIMSELF...
IS HE DEAD...?
VEGETA'S TOUGH AND TREACH-EROUS...
...
HEH... BUT HOW LONG CAN EVEN HE LIE STILL IN WATER WITHOUT DROWNING?
バッ
HEH... AND EVEN IF HE DID SURVIVE...
I'M SURE HE WON'T WANT ANOTHER PIECE OF ME, NOW THAT HE'S SEEN MY FULL POWER!

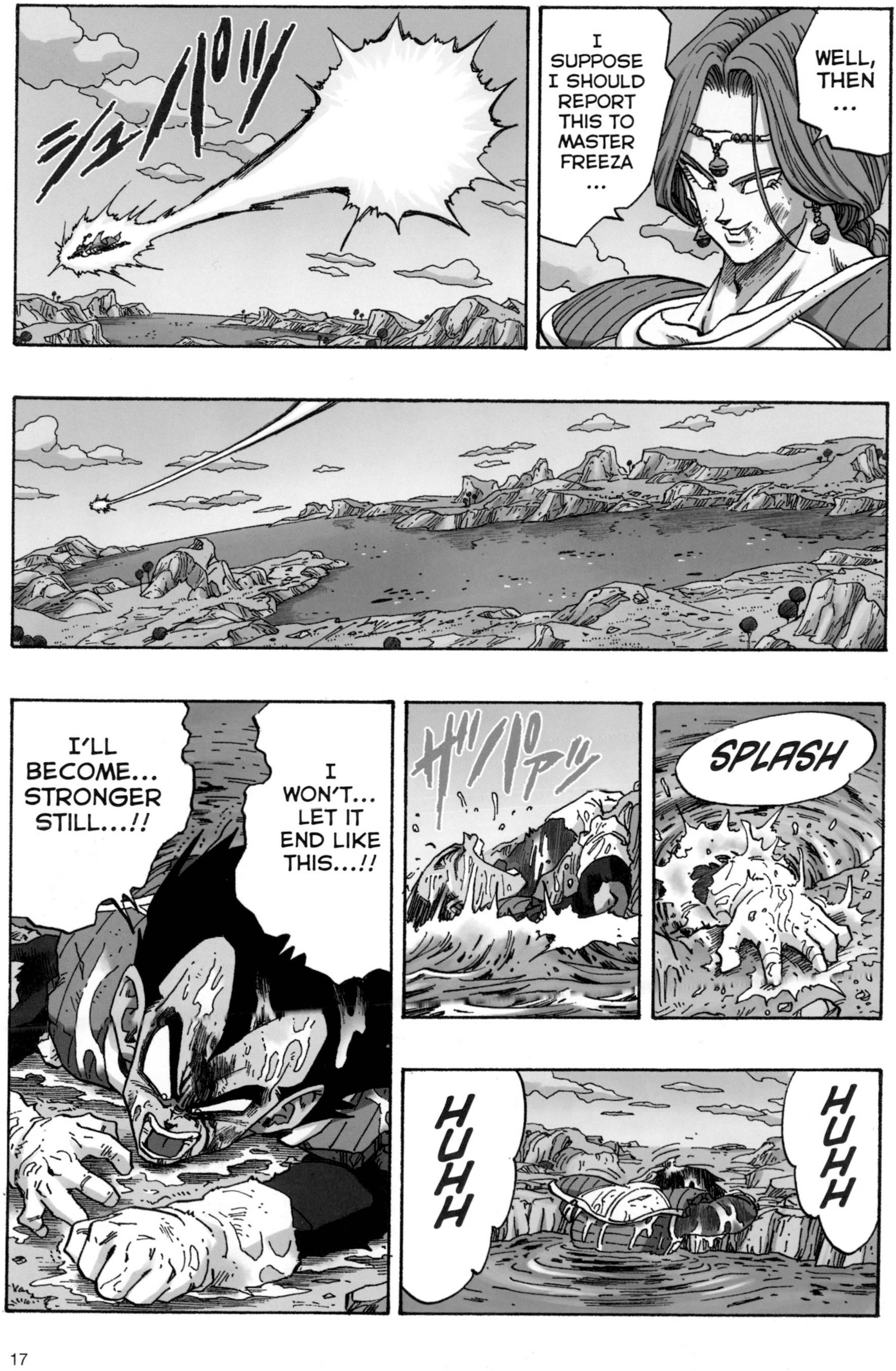
WELL, THEN ...
I SUPPOSE I SHOULD REPORT THIS TO MASTER FREEZA ...
SPLASH
I WON'T... LET IT END LIKE THIS...!!
I'LL BECOME... STRONGER STILL...!!
HUHH
HUHH

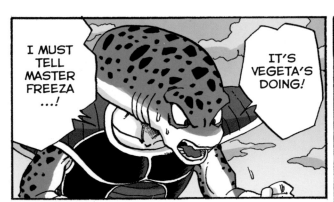

Chapter 19 • The Great Elder's House

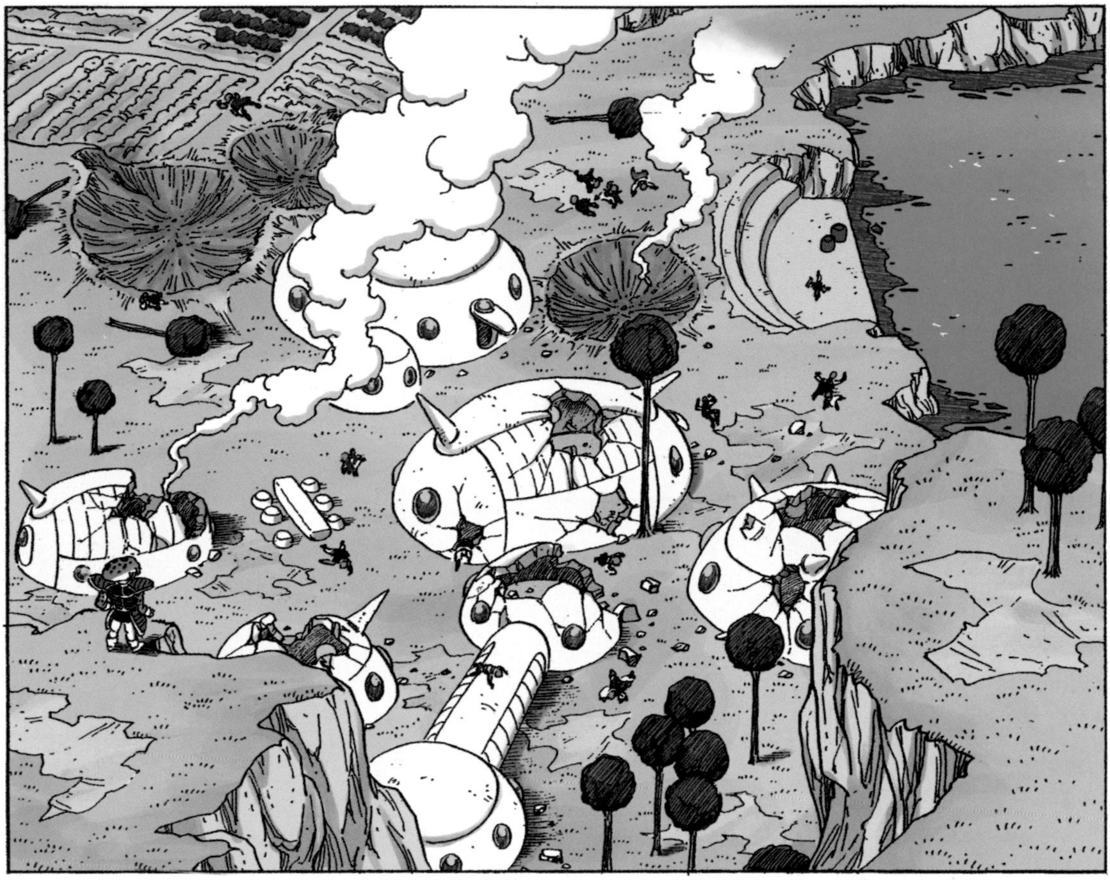

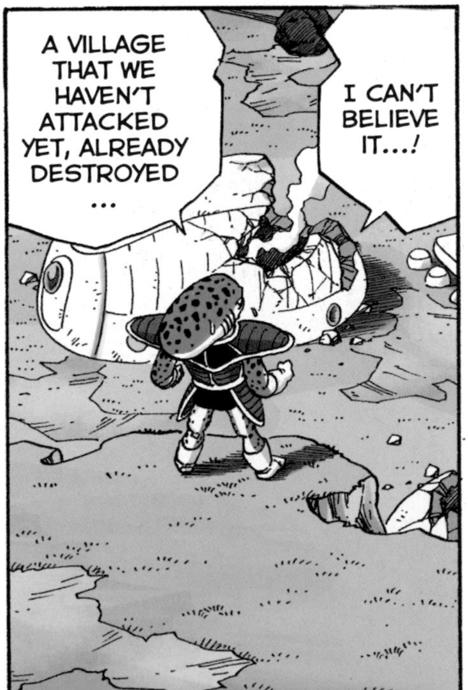
I CAN'T BELIEVE IT...!
A VILLAGE THAT WE HAVEN'T ATTACKED YET, ALREADY DESTROYED...

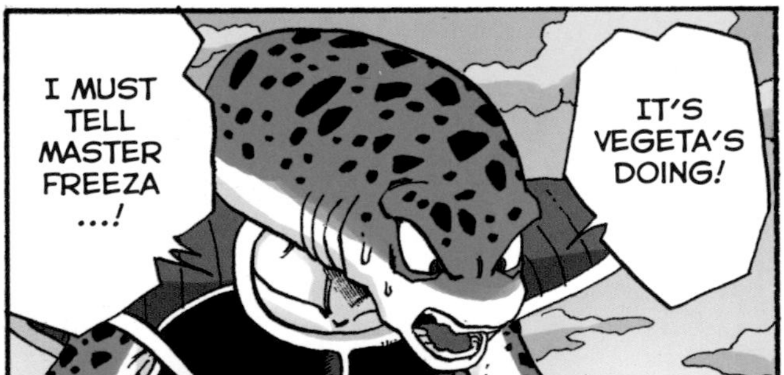
IT'S VEGETA'S DOING!
I MUST TELL MASTER FREEZA...!

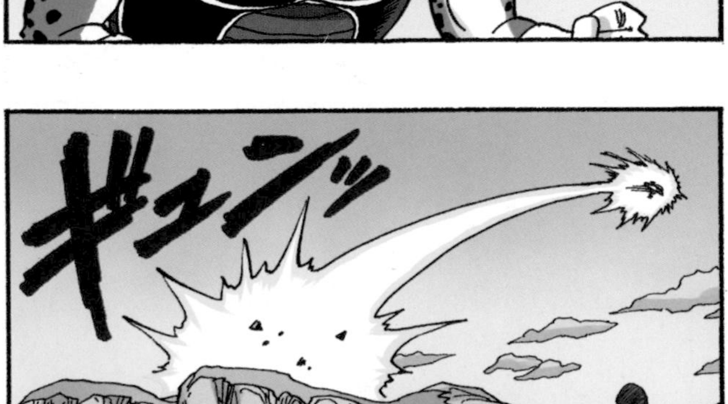
ギュンッ

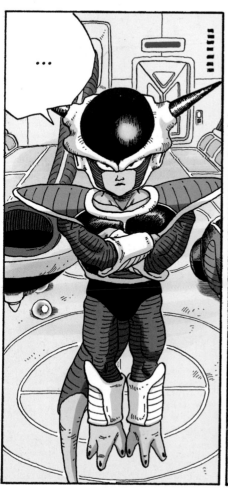

. . .

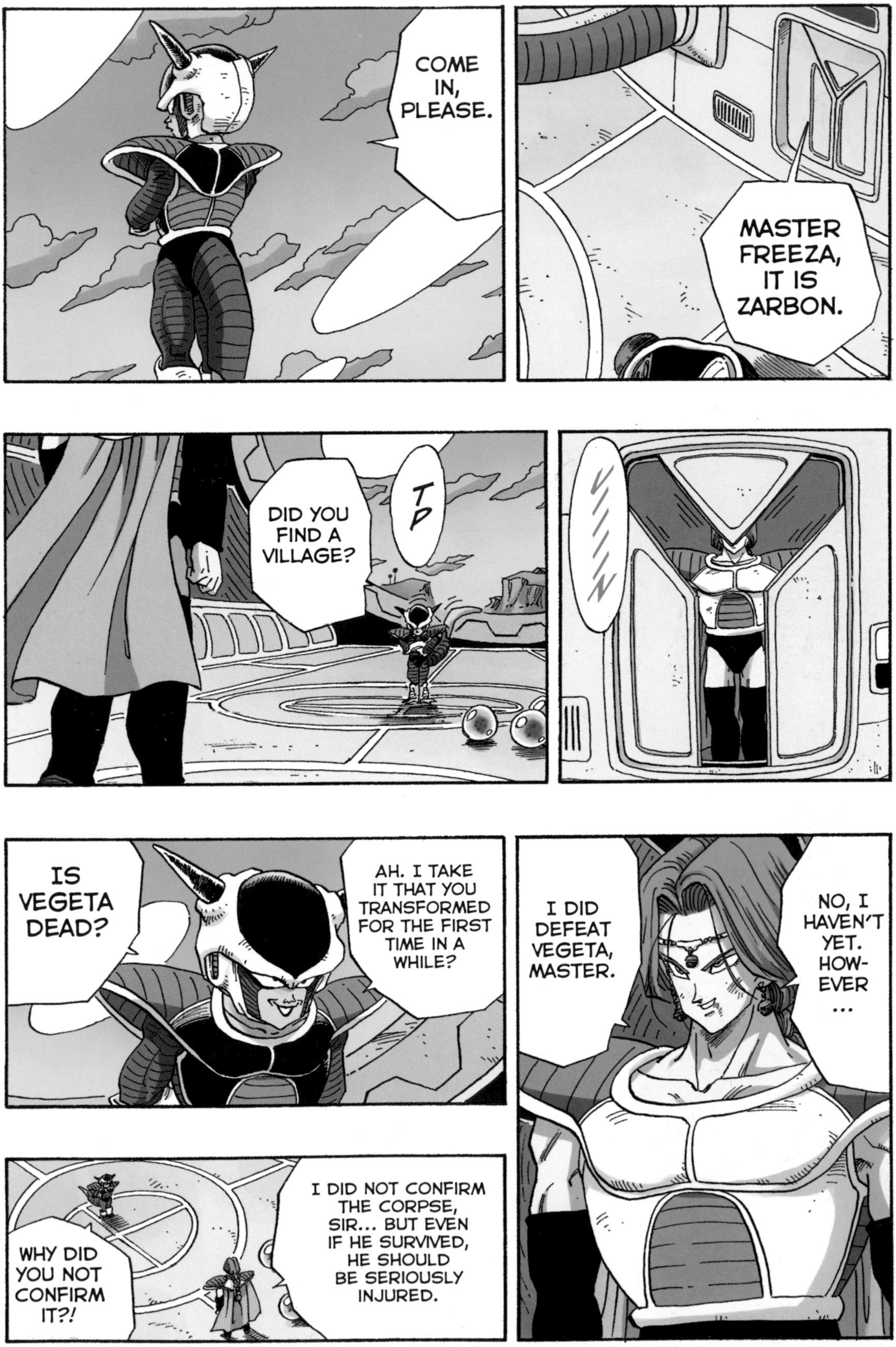
MASTER FREEZA, IT IS ZARBON.
COME IN, PLEASE.
DID YOU FIND A VILLAGE?
NO, I HAVEN'T YET. HOW-EVER...
I DID DEFEAT VEGETA, MASTER.
AH. I TAKE IT THAT YOU TRANSFORMED FOR THE FIRST TIME IN A WHILE?
IS VEGETA DEAD?
I DID NOT CONFIRM THE CORPSE, SIR... BUT EVEN IF HE SURVIVED, HE SHOULD BE SERIOUSLY INJURED.
WHY DID YOU NOT CONFIRM IT?!

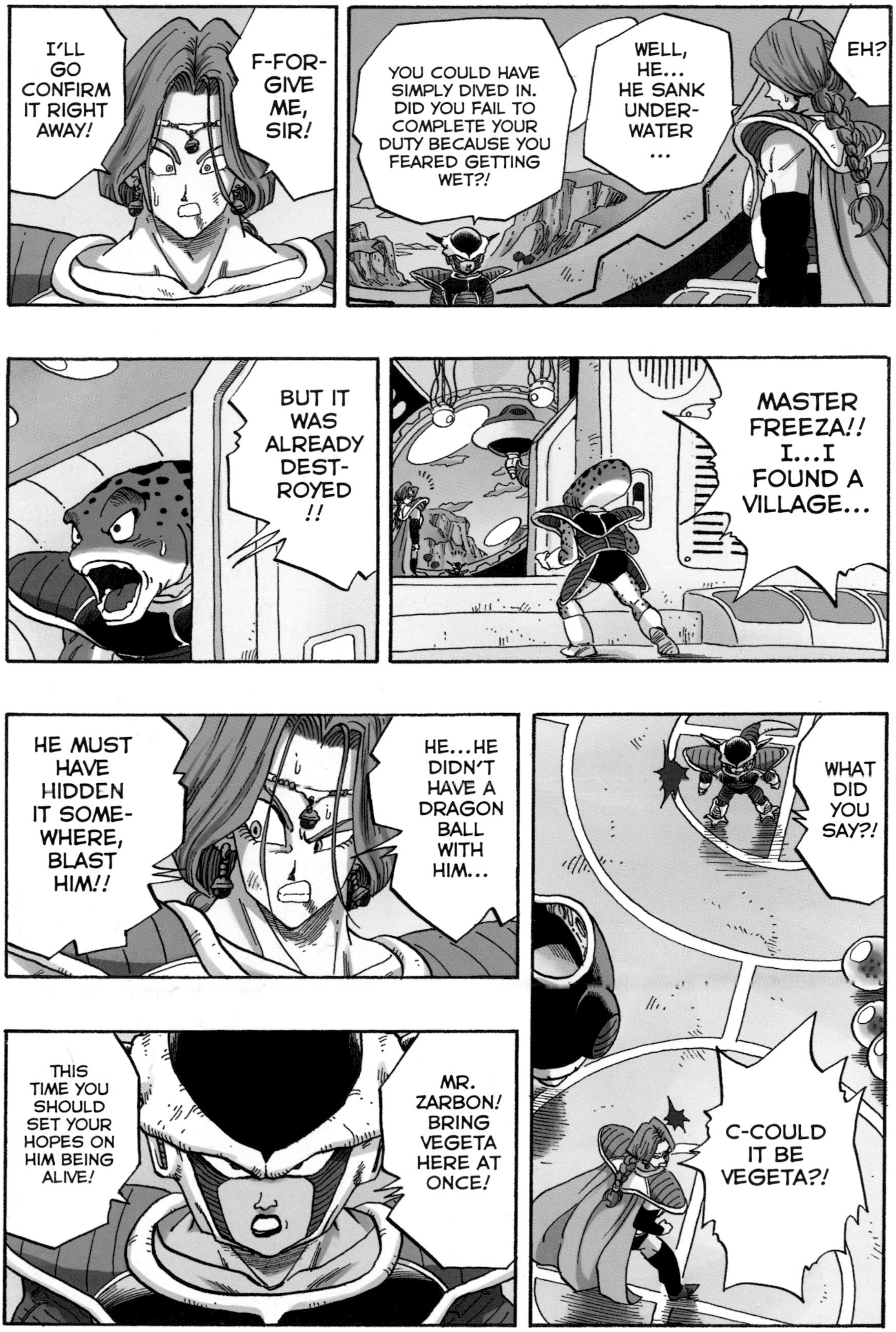
EH?
WELL, HE... HE SANK UNDERWATER...
YOU COULD HAVE SIMPLY DIVED IN. DID YOU FAIL TO COMPLETE YOUR DUTY BECAUSE YOU FEARED GETTING WET?!
F-FORGIVE ME, SIR!
I'LL GO CONFIRM IT RIGHT AWAY!
MASTER FREEZA!! I...I FOUND A VILLAGE...
BUT IT WAS ALREADY DESTROYED!!
WHAT DID YOU SAY?!
C-COULD IT BE VEGETA?!
HE...HE DIDN'T HAVE A DRAGON BALL WITH HIM...
HE MUST HAVE HIDDEN IT SOMEWHERE, BLAST HIM!!
MR. ZARBON! BRING VEGETA HERE AT ONCE!
THIS TIME YOU SHOULD SET YOUR HOPES ON HIM BEING ALIVE!

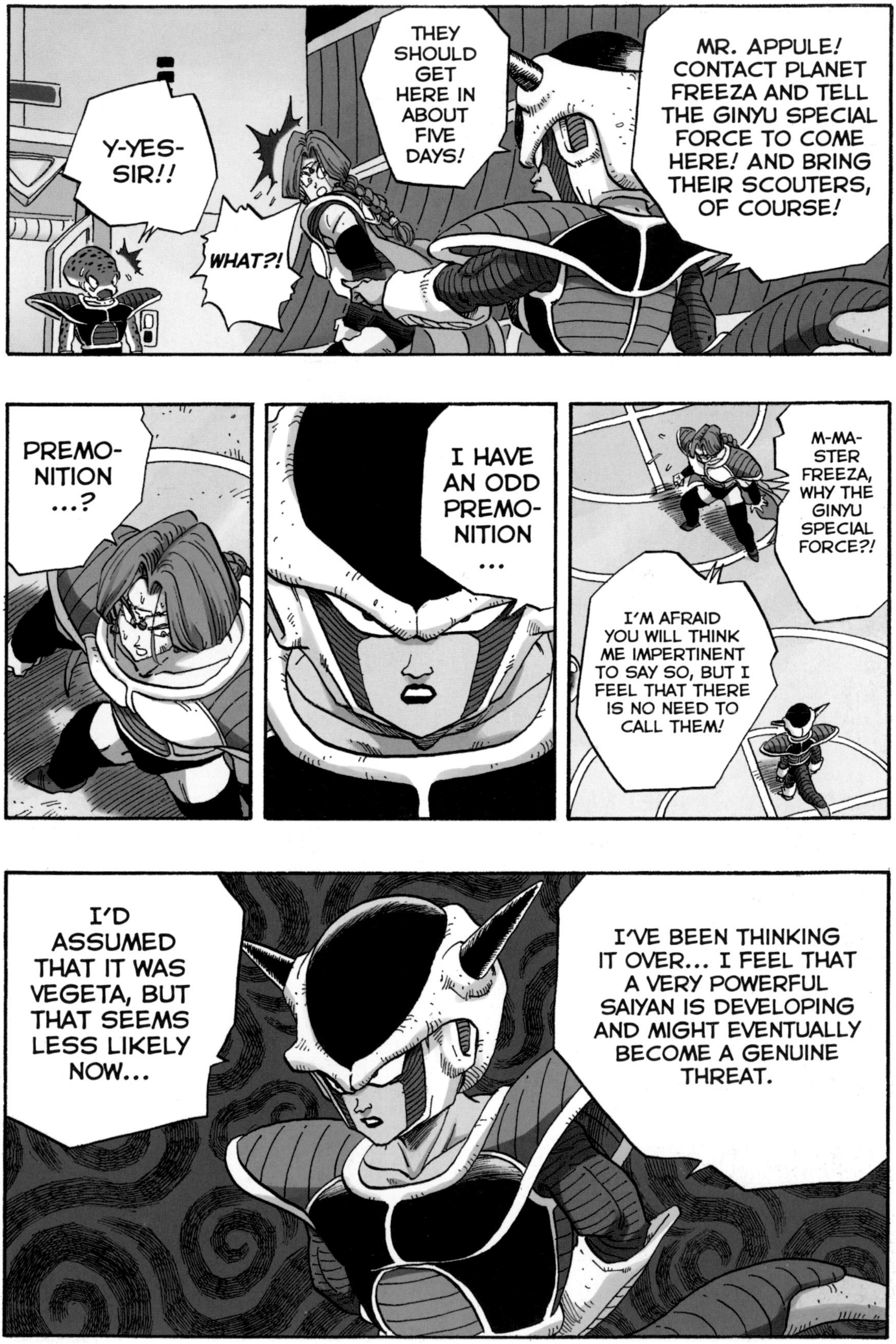
MR. APPULE! CONTACT PLANET FREEZA AND TELL THE GINYU SPECIAL FORCE TO COME HERE! AND BRING THEIR SCOUTERS, OF COURSE!
THEY SHOULD GET HERE IN ABOUT FIVE DAYS!
Y-YES-SIR!!
WHAT?!
M-MASTER FREEZA, WHY THE GINYU SPECIAL FORCE?!
I'M AFRAID YOU WILL THINK ME IMPERTINENT TO SAY SO, BUT I FEEL THAT THERE IS NO NEED TO CALL THEM!
I HAVE AN ODD PREMONITION...
PREMONITION...?
I'VE BEEN THINKING IT OVER... I FEEL THAT A VERY POWERFUL SAIYAN IS DEVELOPING AND MIGHT EVENTUALLY BECOME A GENUINE THREAT.
I'D ASSUMED THAT IT WAS VEGETA, BUT THAT SEEMS LESS LIKELY NOW...

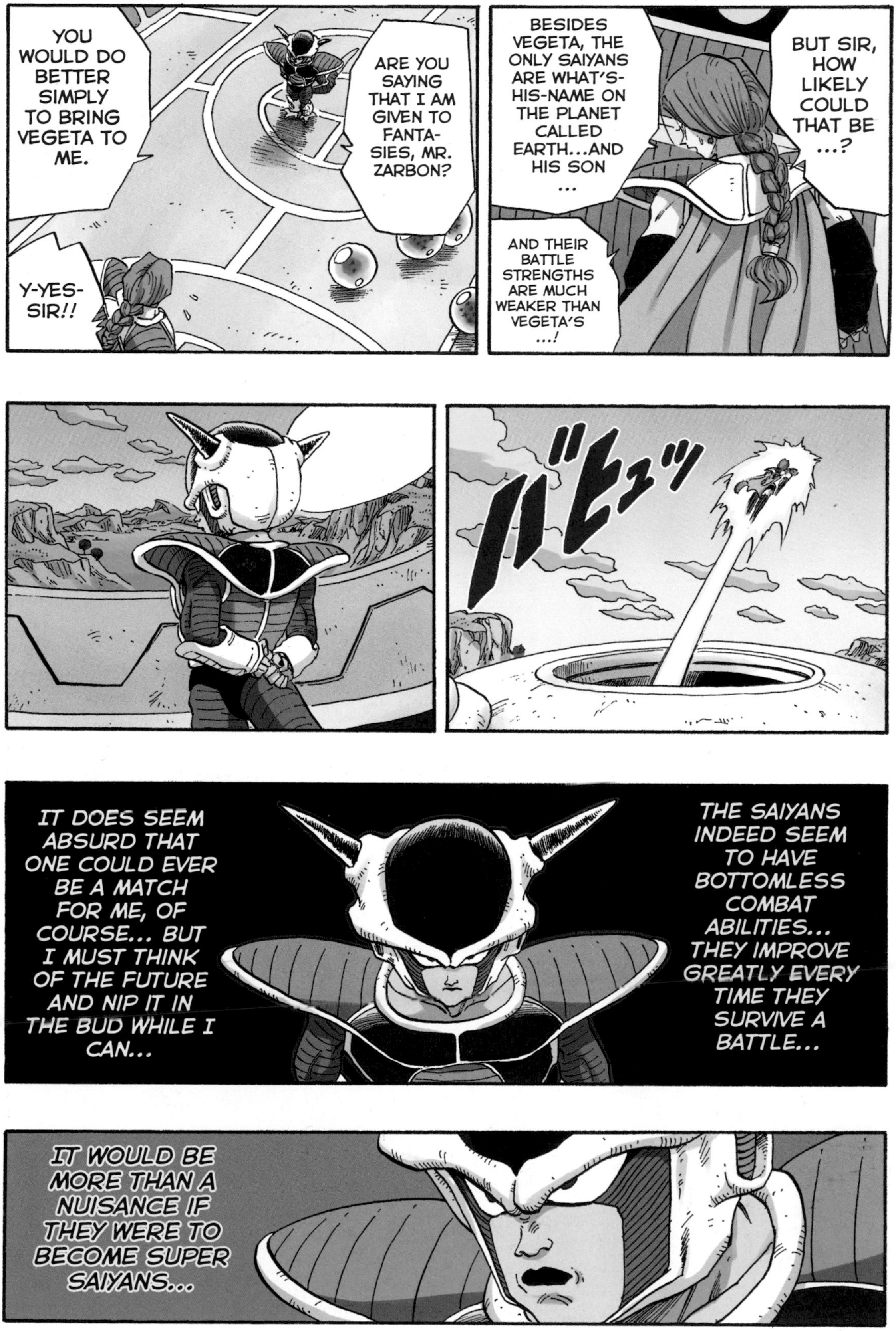
BUT SIR, HOW LIKELY COULD THAT BE ...?
BESIDES VEGETA, THE ONLY SAIYANS ARE WHAT'S-HIS-NAME ON THE PLANET CALLED EARTH...AND HIS SON ...
AND THEIR BATTLE STRENGTHS ARE MUCH WEAKER THAN VEGETA'S ...!
ARE YOU SAYING THAT I AM GIVEN TO FANTA-SIES, MR. ZARBON?
YOU WOULD DO BETTER SIMPLY TO BRING VEGETA TO ME.
Y-YES-SIR!!
バビュッ
THE SAIYANS INDEED SEEM TO HAVE BOTTOMLESS COMBAT ABILITIES... THEY IMPROVE GREATLY EVERY TIME THEY SURVIVE A BATTLE...
IT DOES SEEM ABSURD THAT ONE COULD EVER BE A MATCH FOR ME, OF COURSE... BUT I MUST THINK OF THE FUTURE AND NIP IT IN THE BUD WHILE I CAN...
IT WOULD BE MORE THAN A NUISANCE IF THEY WERE TO BECOME SUPER SAIYANS...

...DIE...

I... WILL... NOT...

TUNK

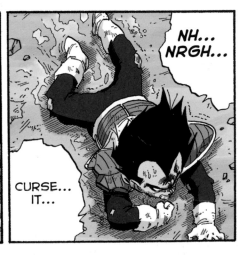

NH... NRGH...

CURSE... IT...

BY THE GODS...!

EH?!

THE GINYU SPECIAL FORCE...

24

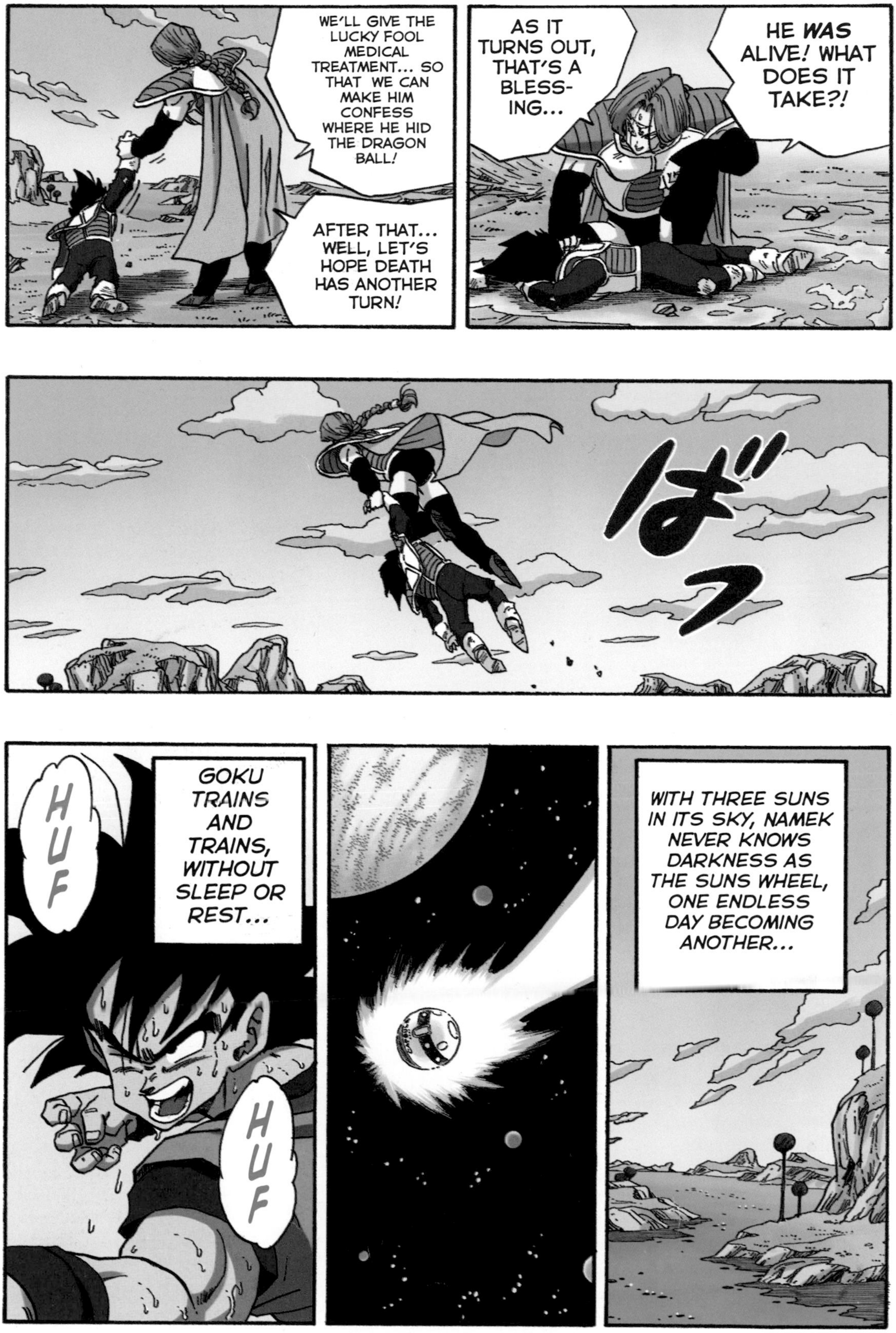
HE *WAS* ALIVE! WHAT DOES IT TAKE?!
AS IT TURNS OUT, THAT'S A BLESS-ING...
WE'LL GIVE THE LUCKY FOOL MEDICAL TREATMENT... SO THAT WE CAN MAKE HIM CONFESS WHERE HE HID THE DRAGON BALL!
AFTER THAT... WELL, LET'S HOPE DEATH HAS ANOTHER TURN!
ばっ
WITH THREE SUNS IN ITS SKY, NAMEK NEVER KNOWS DARKNESS AS THE SUNS WHEEL, ONE ENDLESS DAY BECOMING ANOTHER...
GOKU TRAINS AND TRAINS, WITHOUT SLEEP OR REST...
HUF
HUF

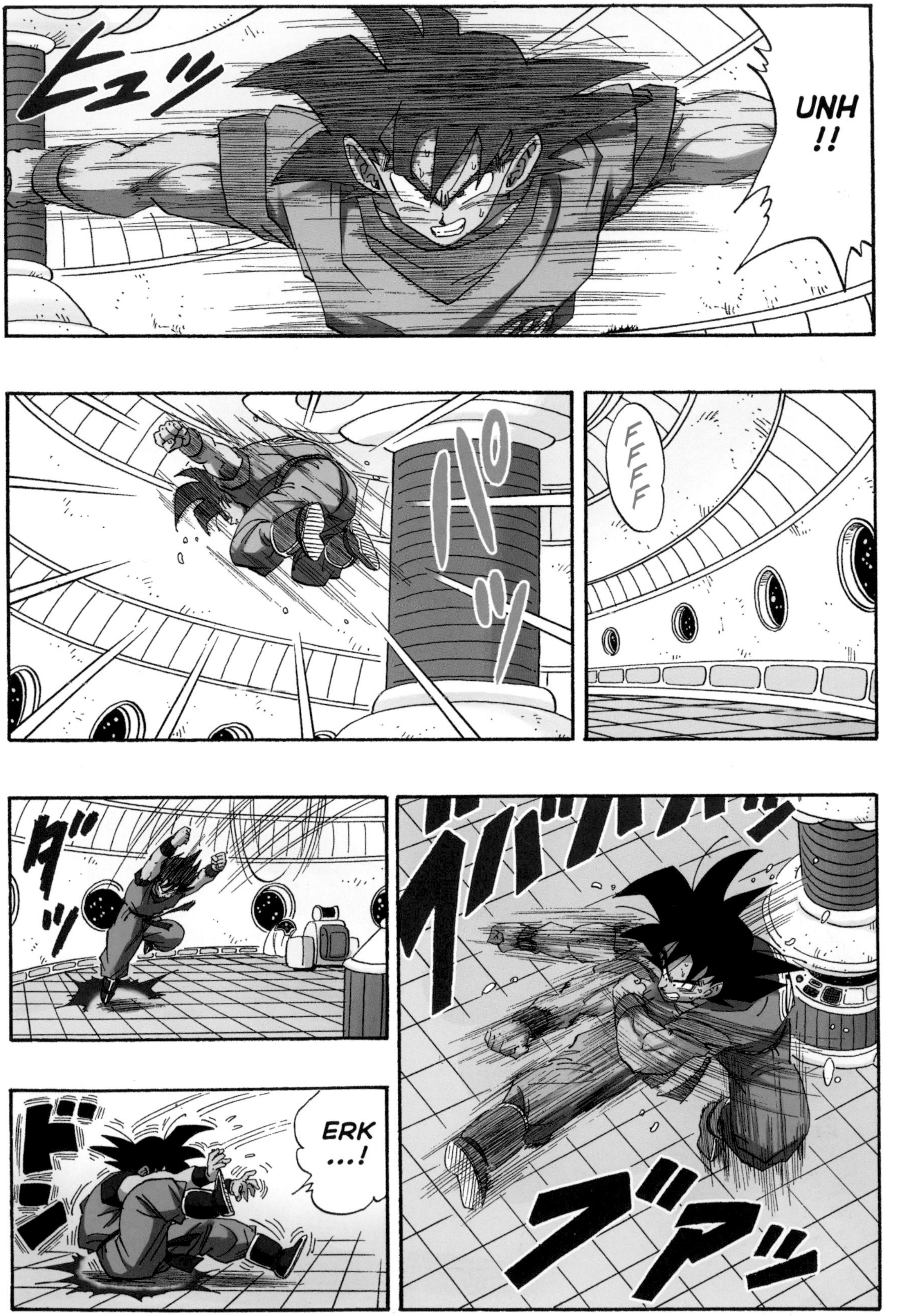
UNH !!
ヒュッ
FFFF
パッ
ブァッ
ダッ
ERK ...!
ドン

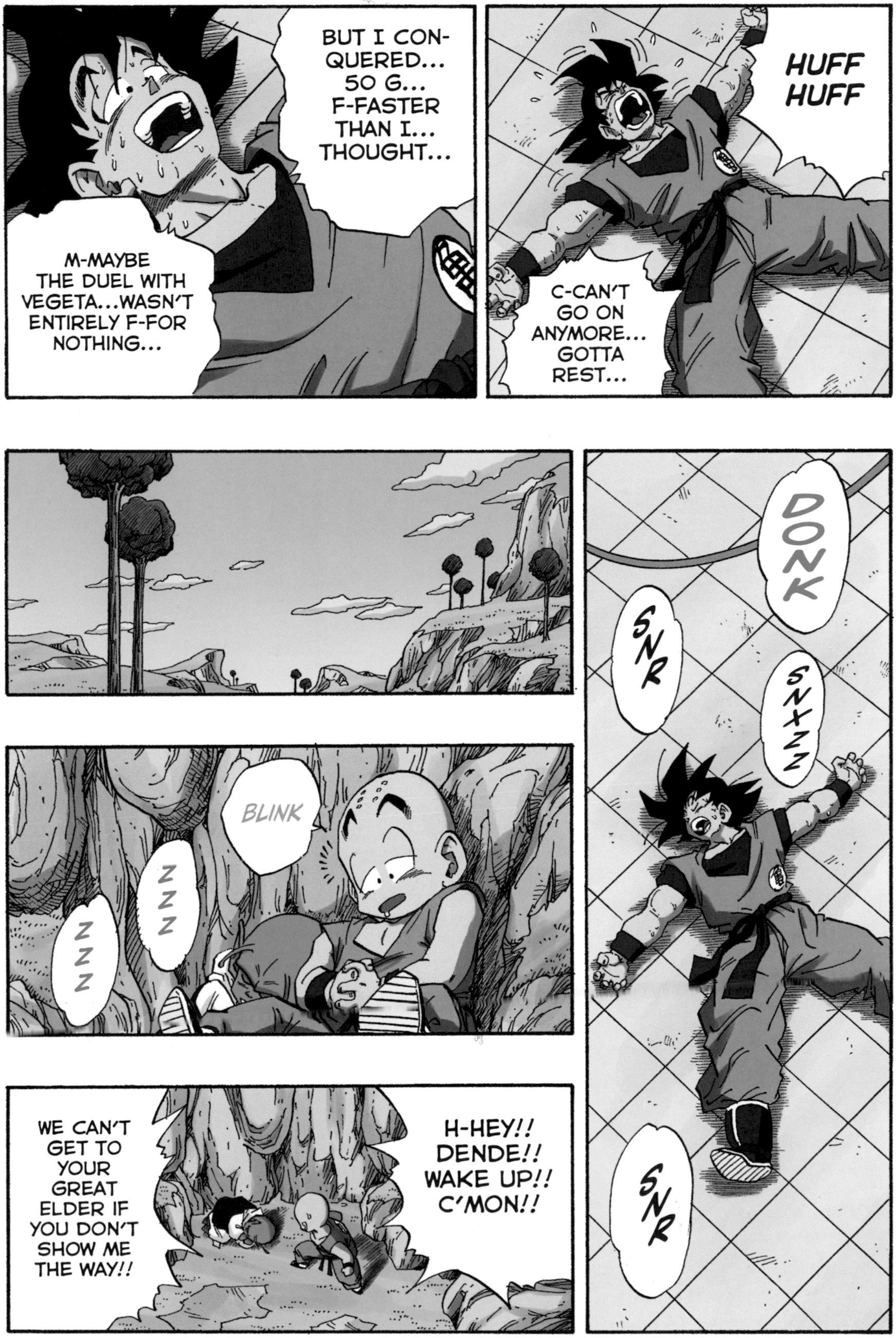
HUFF HUFF
C-CAN'T GO ON ANYMORE... GOTTA REST...
BUT I CONQUERED... 50 G... F-FASTER THAN I... THOUGHT...
M-MAYBE THE DUEL WITH VEGETA...WASN'T ENTIRELY F-FOR NOTHING...
DONK
SNR
SNXZZ
SNR
BLINK
ZZZ
ZZZ
H-HEY!! DENDE!! WAKE UP!! C'MON!!
WE CAN'T GET TO YOUR GREAT ELDER IF YOU DON'T SHOW ME THE WAY!!

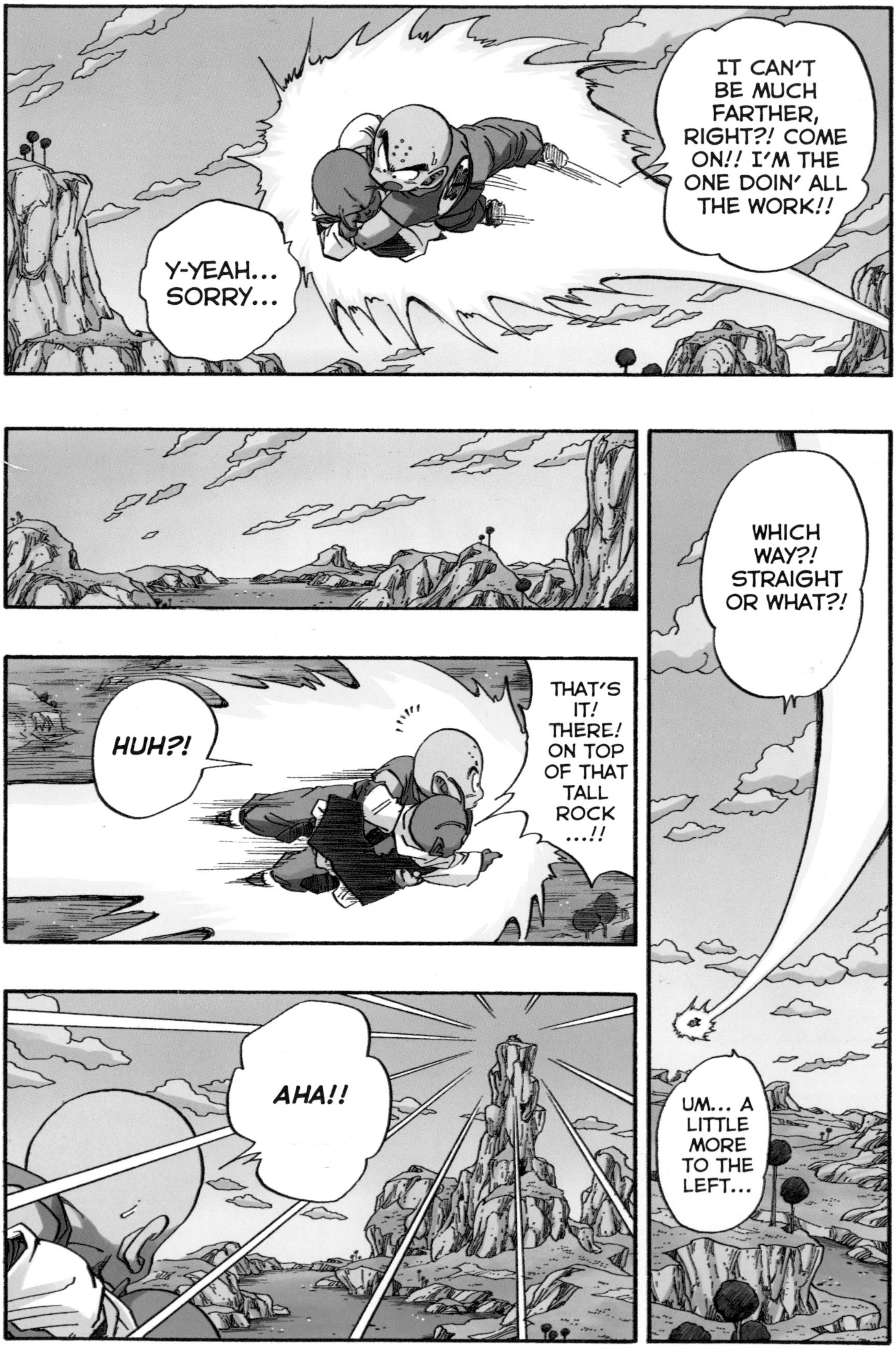
IT CAN'T BE MUCH FARTHER, RIGHT?! COME ON!! I'M THE ONE DOIN' ALL THE WORK!!
Y-YEAH... SORRY...
WHICH WAY?! STRAIGHT OR WHAT?!
UM... A LITTLE MORE TO THE LEFT...
THAT'S IT! THERE! ON TOP OF THAT TALL ROCK ...!!
HUH?!
AHA!!

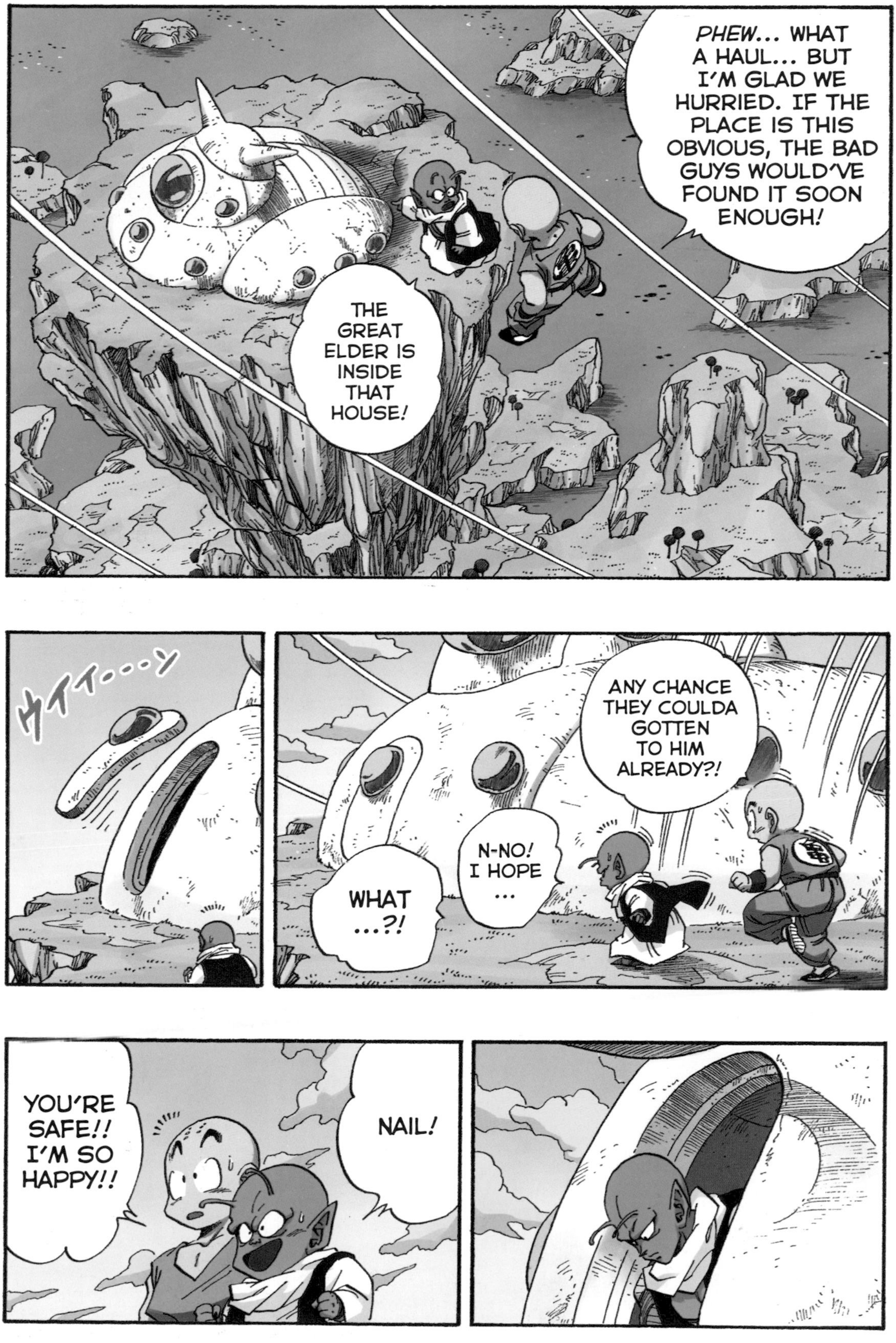
PHEW... WHAT A HAUL... BUT I'M GLAD WE HURRIED. IF THE PLACE IS THIS OBVIOUS, THE BAD GUYS WOULD'VE FOUND IT SOON ENOUGH!
THE GREAT ELDER IS INSIDE THAT HOUSE!
ANY CHANCE THEY COULDA GOTTEN TO HIM ALREADY?!
N-NO! I HOPE ...
WHAT ...?!
ウイイ・・・ン
NAIL!
YOU'RE SAFE!! I'M SO HAPPY!!

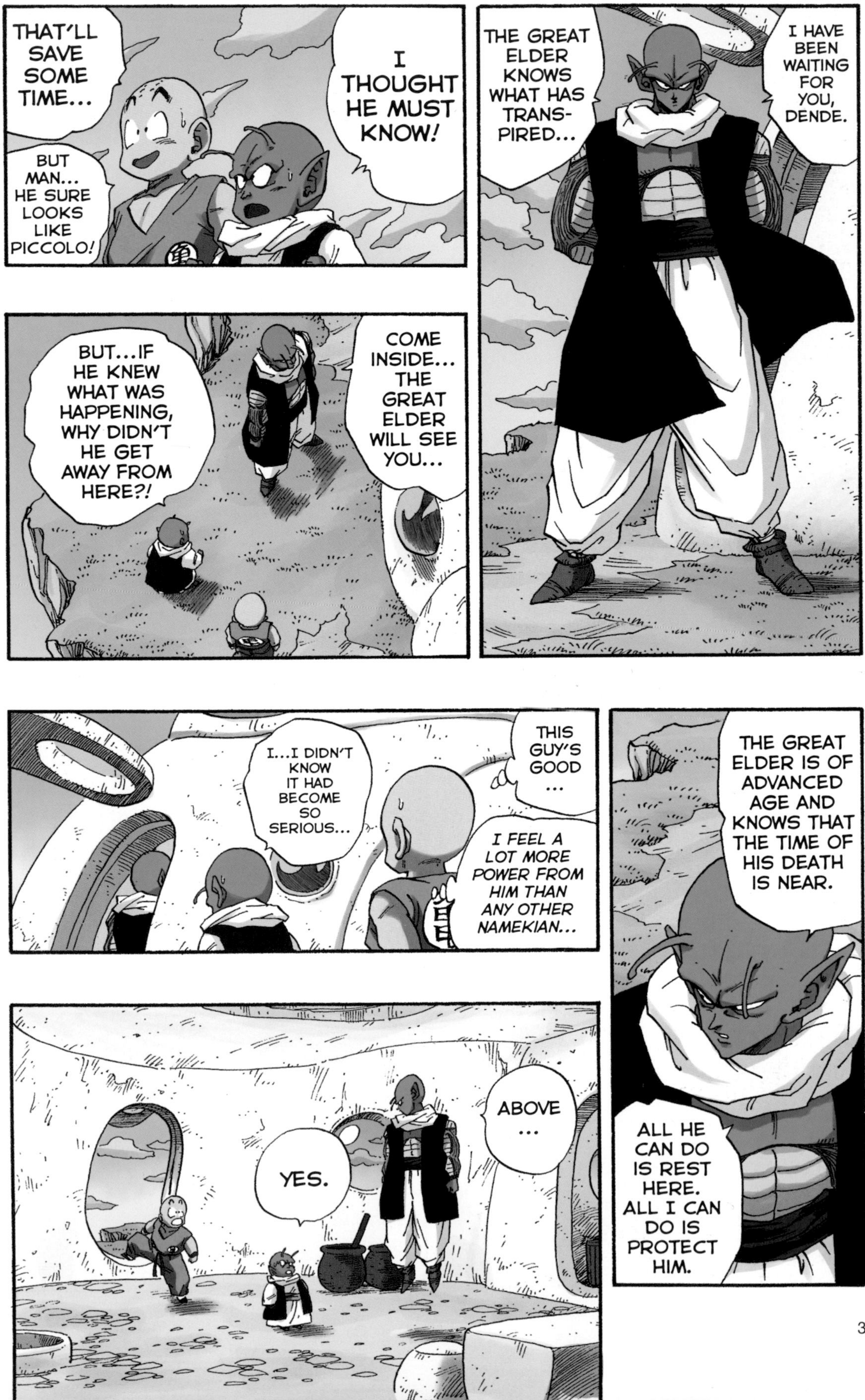
I HAVE BEEN WAITING FOR YOU, DENDE.
THE GREAT ELDER KNOWS WHAT HAS TRANS-PIRED...
I THOUGHT HE MUST KNOW!
THAT'LL SAVE SOME TIME...
BUT MAN... HE SURE LOOKS LIKE PICCOLO!
COME INSIDE... THE GREAT ELDER WILL SEE YOU...
BUT...IF HE KNEW WHAT WAS HAPPENING, WHY DIDN'T HE GET AWAY FROM HERE?!
THE GREAT ELDER IS OF ADVANCED AGE AND KNOWS THAT THE TIME OF HIS DEATH IS NEAR.
ALL HE CAN DO IS REST HERE. ALL I CAN DO IS PROTECT HIM.
THIS GUY'S GOOD ...
I FEEL A LOT MORE POWER FROM HIM THAN ANY OTHER NAMEKIAN...
I...I DIDN'T KNOW IT HAD BECOME SO SERIOUS...
ABOVE ...
YES.

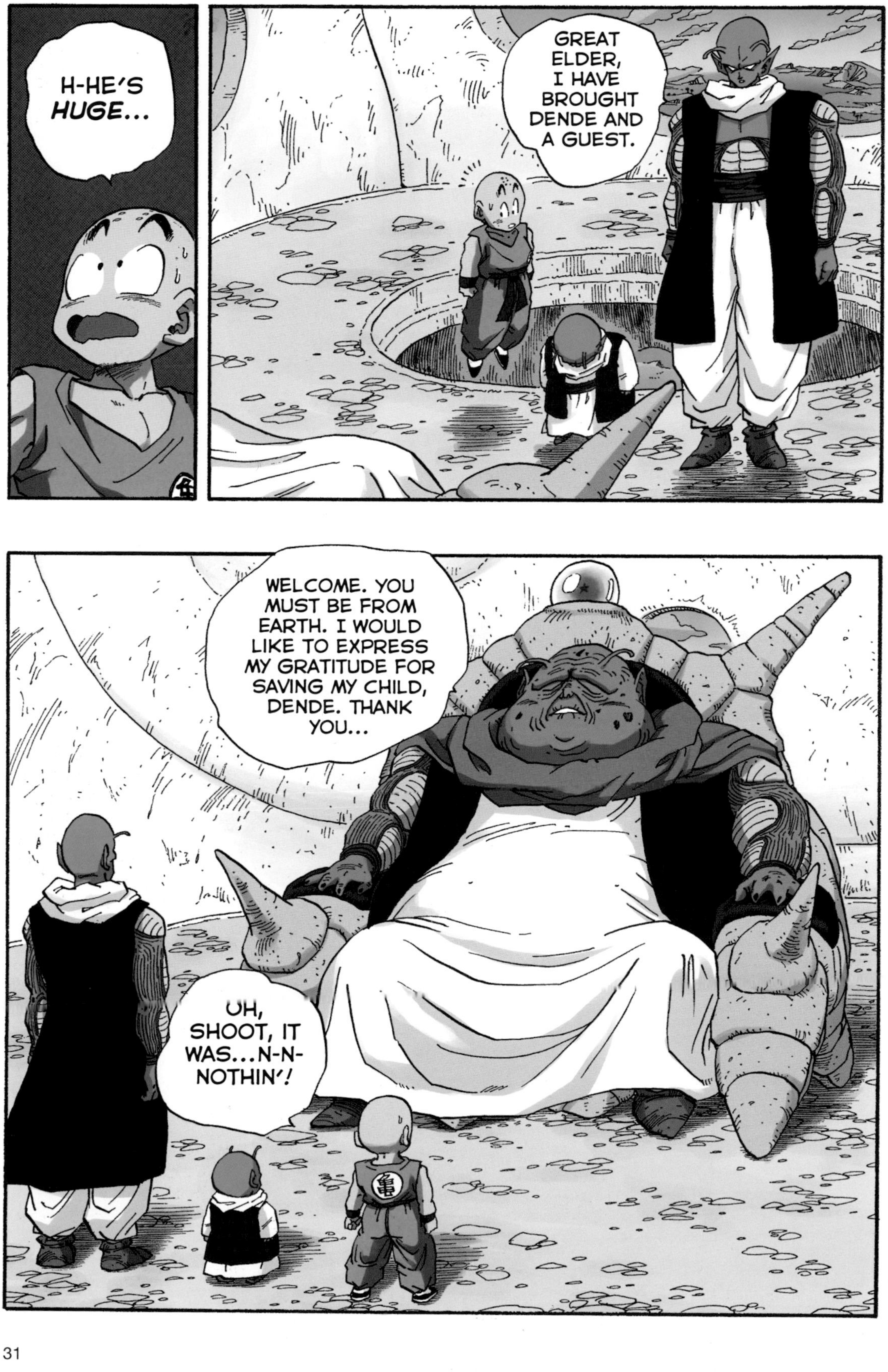
GREAT ELDER, I HAVE BROUGHT DENDE AND A GUEST.
H-HE'S *HUGE...*
WELCOME. YOU MUST BE FROM EARTH. I WOULD LIKE TO EXPRESS MY GRATITUDE FOR SAVING MY CHILD, DENDE. THANK YOU...
OH, SHOOT, IT WAS...N-N-NOTHIN'!

Tale 20 • The Dragon Balls Change Hands

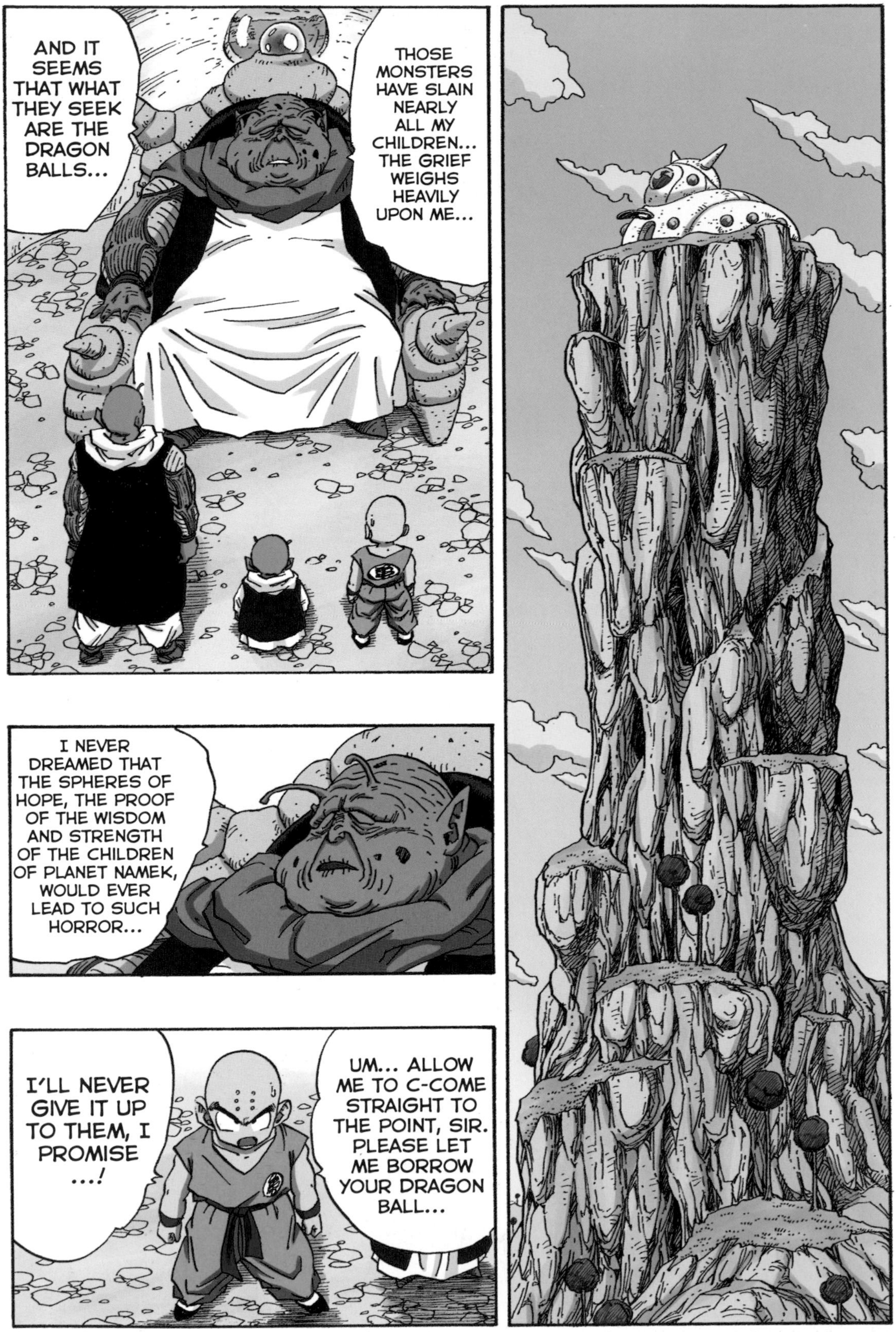
THOSE MONSTERS HAVE SLAIN NEARLY ALL MY CHILDREN... THE GRIEF WEIGHS HEAVILY UPON ME...
AND IT SEEMS THAT WHAT THEY SEEK ARE THE DRAGON BALLS...
I NEVER DREAMED THAT THE SPHERES OF HOPE, THE PROOF OF THE WISDOM AND STRENGTH OF THE CHILDREN OF PLANET NAMEK, WOULD EVER LEAD TO SUCH HORROR...
UM... ALLOW ME TO C-COME STRAIGHT TO THE POINT, SIR. PLEASE LET ME BORROW YOUR DRAGON BALL...
I'LL NEVER GIVE IT UP TO THEM, I PROMISE ...!

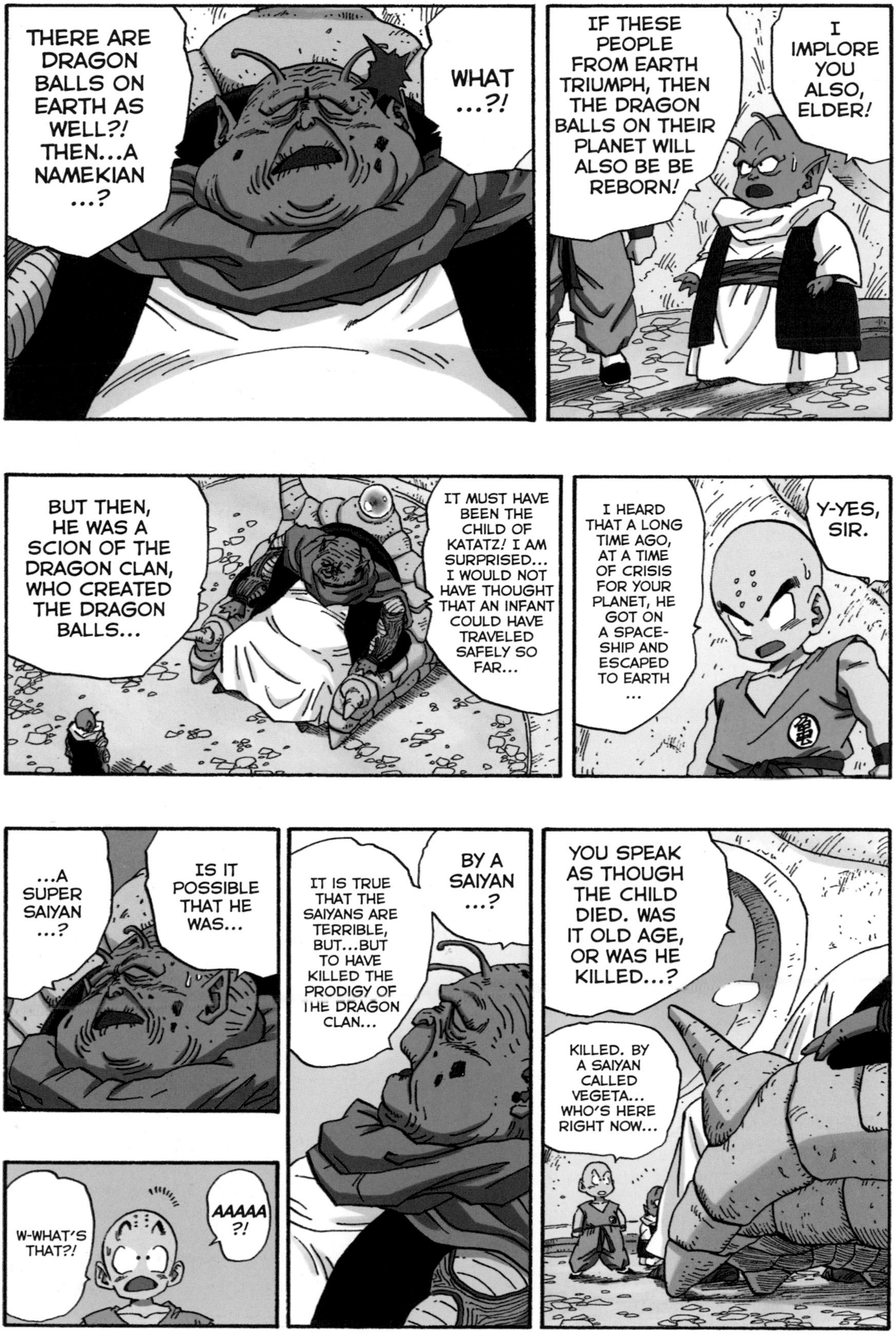
I IMPLORE YOU ALSO, ELDER!
IF THESE PEOPLE FROM EARTH TRIUMPH, THEN THE DRAGON BALLS ON THEIR PLANET WILL ALSO BE BE REBORN!
WHAT ...?!
THERE ARE DRAGON BALLS ON EARTH AS WELL?! THEN...A NAMEKIAN ...?
Y-YES, SIR.
I HEARD THAT A LONG TIME AGO, AT A TIME OF CRISIS FOR YOUR PLANET, HE GOT ON A SPACE-SHIP AND ESCAPED TO EARTH ...
IT MUST HAVE BEEN THE CHILD OF KATATZ! I AM SURPRISED... I WOULD NOT HAVE THOUGHT THAT AN INFANT COULD HAVE TRAVELED SAFELY SO FAR...
BUT THEN, HE WAS A SCION OF THE DRAGON CLAN, WHO CREATED THE DRAGON BALLS...
YOU SPEAK AS THOUGH THE CHILD DIED. WAS IT OLD AGE, OR WAS HE KILLED...?
KILLED. BY A SAIYAN CALLED VEGETA... WHO'S HERE RIGHT NOW...
BY A SAIYAN ...?
IT IS TRUE THAT THE SAIYANS ARE TERRIBLE, BUT...BUT TO HAVE KILLED THE PRODIGY OF THE DRAGON CLAN...
IS IT POSSIBLE THAT HE WAS...
...A SUPER SAIYAN ...?
AAAAA ?!
W-WHAT'S THAT?!

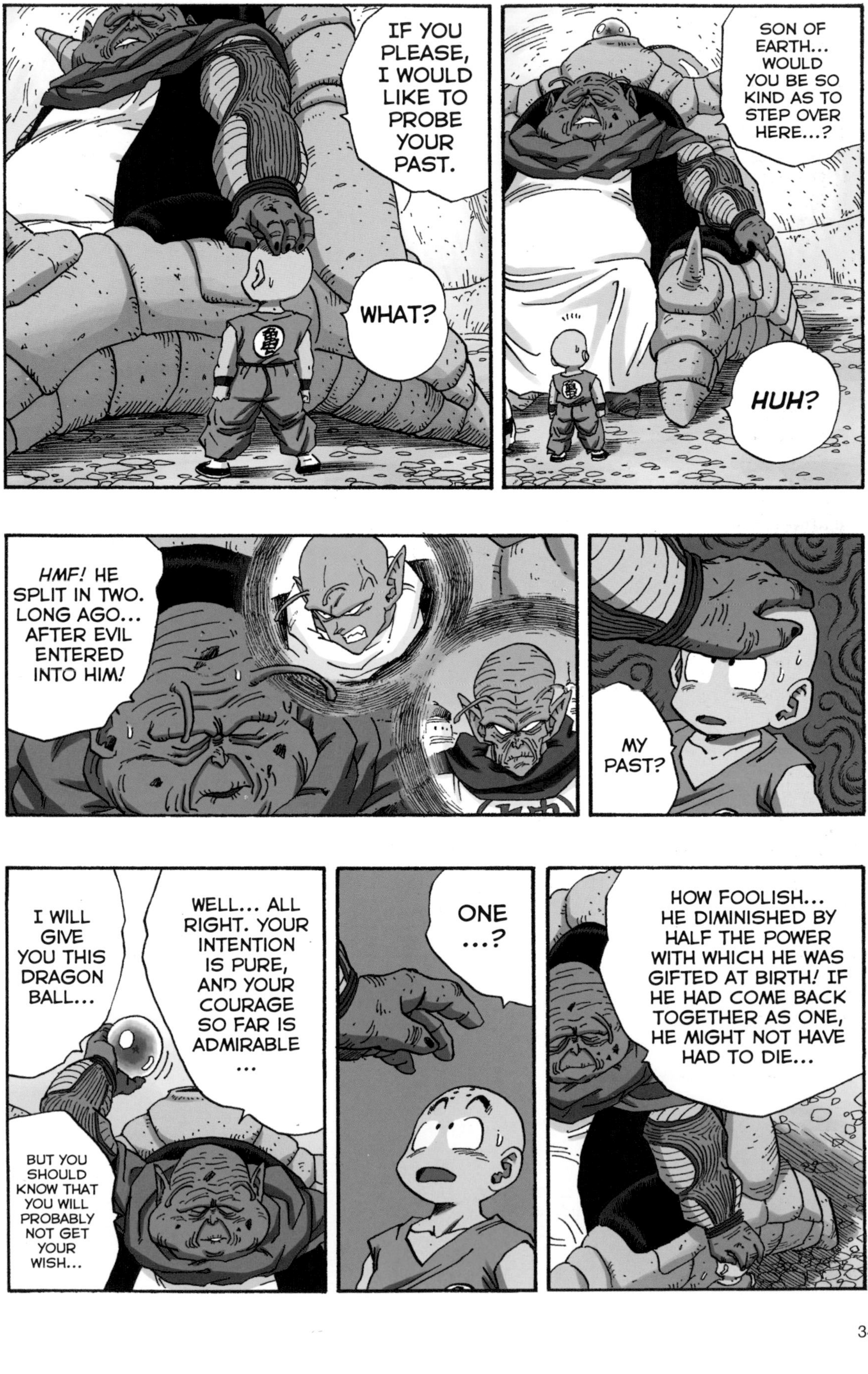
SON OF EARTH... WOULD YOU BE SO KIND AS TO STEP OVER HERE...?
HUH?
IF YOU PLEASE, I WOULD LIKE TO PROBE YOUR PAST.
WHAT?
MY PAST?
HMF! HE SPLIT IN TWO. LONG AGO... AFTER EVIL ENTERED INTO HIM!
HOW FOOLISH... HE DIMINISHED BY HALF THE POWER WITH WHICH HE WAS GIFTED AT BIRTH! IF HE HAD COME BACK TOGETHER AS ONE, HE MIGHT NOT HAVE HAD TO DIE...
ONE ...?
WELL... ALL RIGHT. YOUR INTENTION IS PURE, AND YOUR COURAGE SO FAR IS ADMIRABLE ...
I WILL GIVE YOU THIS DRAGON BALL...
BUT YOU SHOULD KNOW THAT YOU WILL PROBABLY NOT GET YOUR WISH...

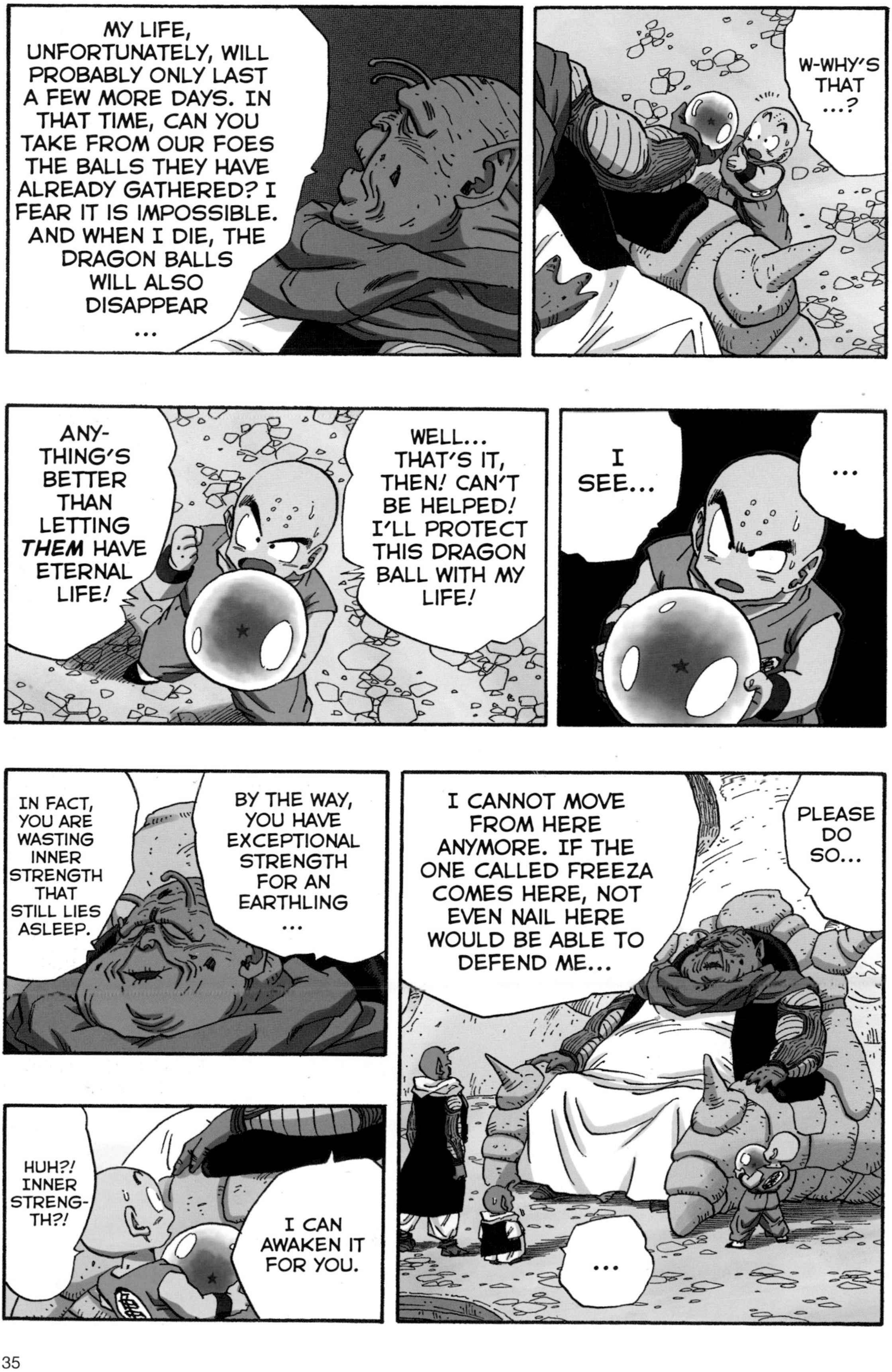
W-WHY'S THAT ...?
MY LIFE, UNFORTUNATELY, WILL PROBABLY ONLY LAST A FEW MORE DAYS. IN THAT TIME, CAN YOU TAKE FROM OUR FOES THE BALLS THEY HAVE ALREADY GATHERED? I FEAR IT IS IMPOSSIBLE. AND WHEN I DIE, THE DRAGON BALLS WILL ALSO DISAPPEAR ...
...
I SEE...
WELL... THAT'S IT, THEN! CAN'T BE HELPED! I'LL PROTECT THIS DRAGON BALL WITH MY LIFE!
ANY-THING'S BETTER THAN LETTING *THEM* HAVE ETERNAL LIFE!
PLEASE DO SO...
I CANNOT MOVE FROM HERE ANYMORE. IF THE ONE CALLED FREEZA COMES HERE, NOT EVEN NAIL HERE WOULD BE ABLE TO DEFEND ME...
...
BY THE WAY, YOU HAVE EXCEPTIONAL STRENGTH FOR AN EARTHLING ...
IN FACT, YOU ARE WASTING INNER STRENGTH THAT STILL LIES ASLEEP.
HUH?! INNER STRENG-TH?!
I CAN AWAKEN IT FOR YOU.

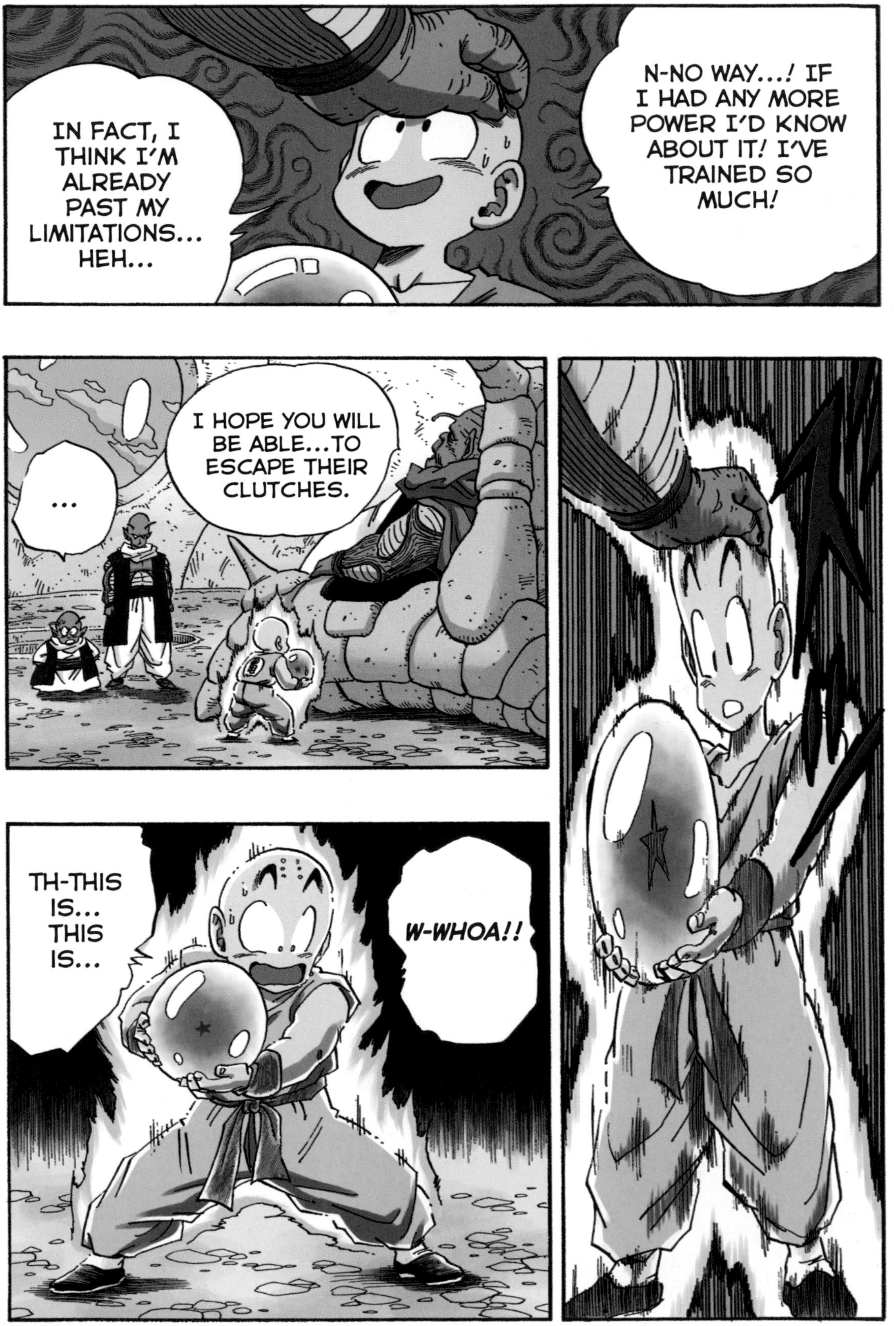

N-NO WAY...! IF I HAD ANY MORE POWER I'D KNOW ABOUT IT! I'VE TRAINED SO MUCH!
IN FACT, I THINK I'M ALREADY PAST MY LIMITATIONS... HEH...
I HOPE YOU WILL BE ABLE...TO ESCAPE THEIR CLUTCHES.
...
W-WHOA!!
TH-THIS IS... THIS IS...

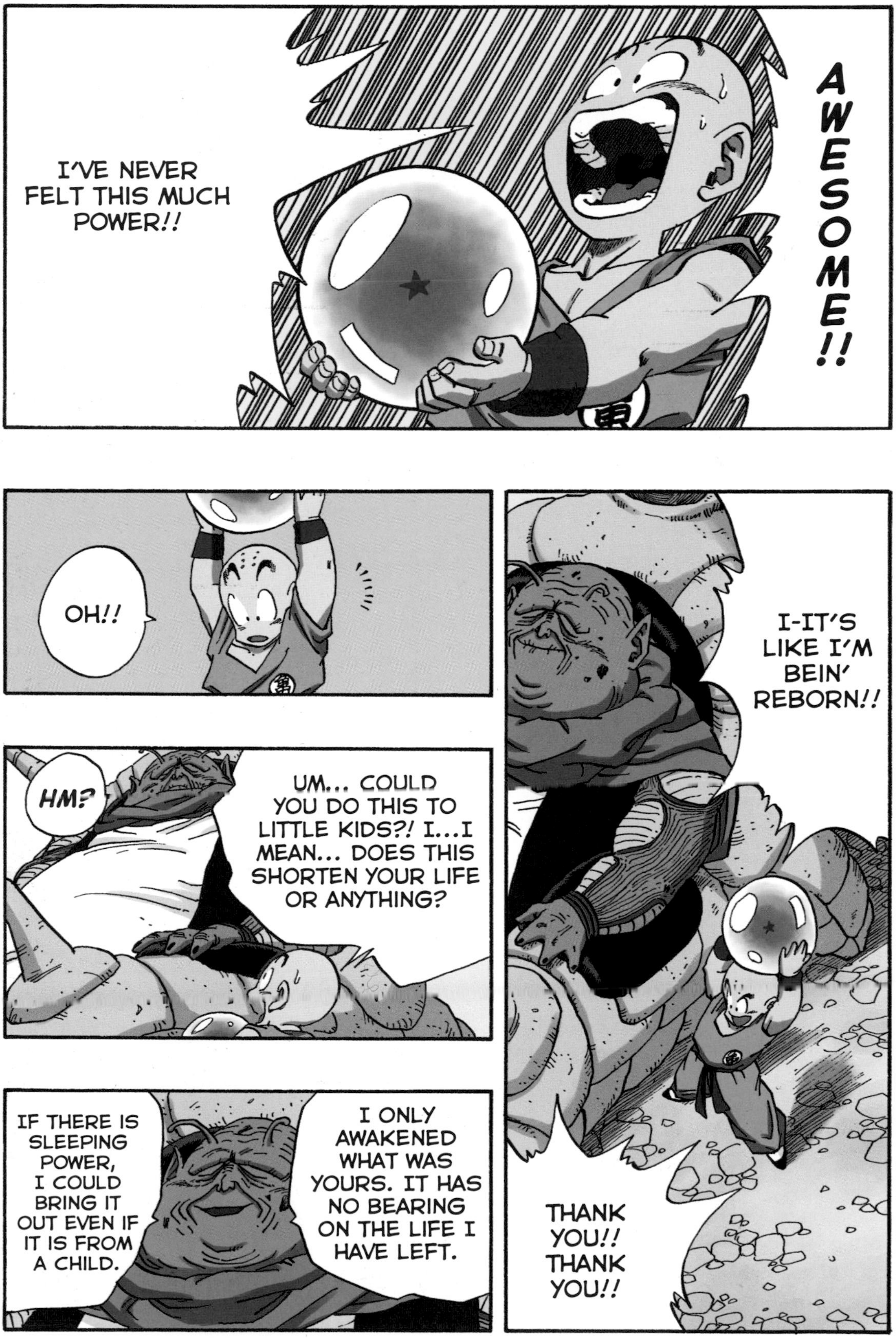
AWESOME!!
I'VE NEVER FELT THIS MUCH POWER!!
I-IT'S LIKE I'M BEIN' REBORN!!
THANK YOU!! THANK YOU!!
OH!!
UM... COULD YOU DO THIS TO LITTLE KIDS?! I...I MEAN... DOES THIS SHORTEN YOUR LIFE OR ANYTHING?
HM?
I ONLY AWAKENED WHAT WAS YOURS. IT HAS NO BEARING ON THE LIFE I HAVE LEFT.
IF THERE IS SLEEPING POWER, I COULD BRING IT OUT EVEN IF IT IS FROM A CHILD.

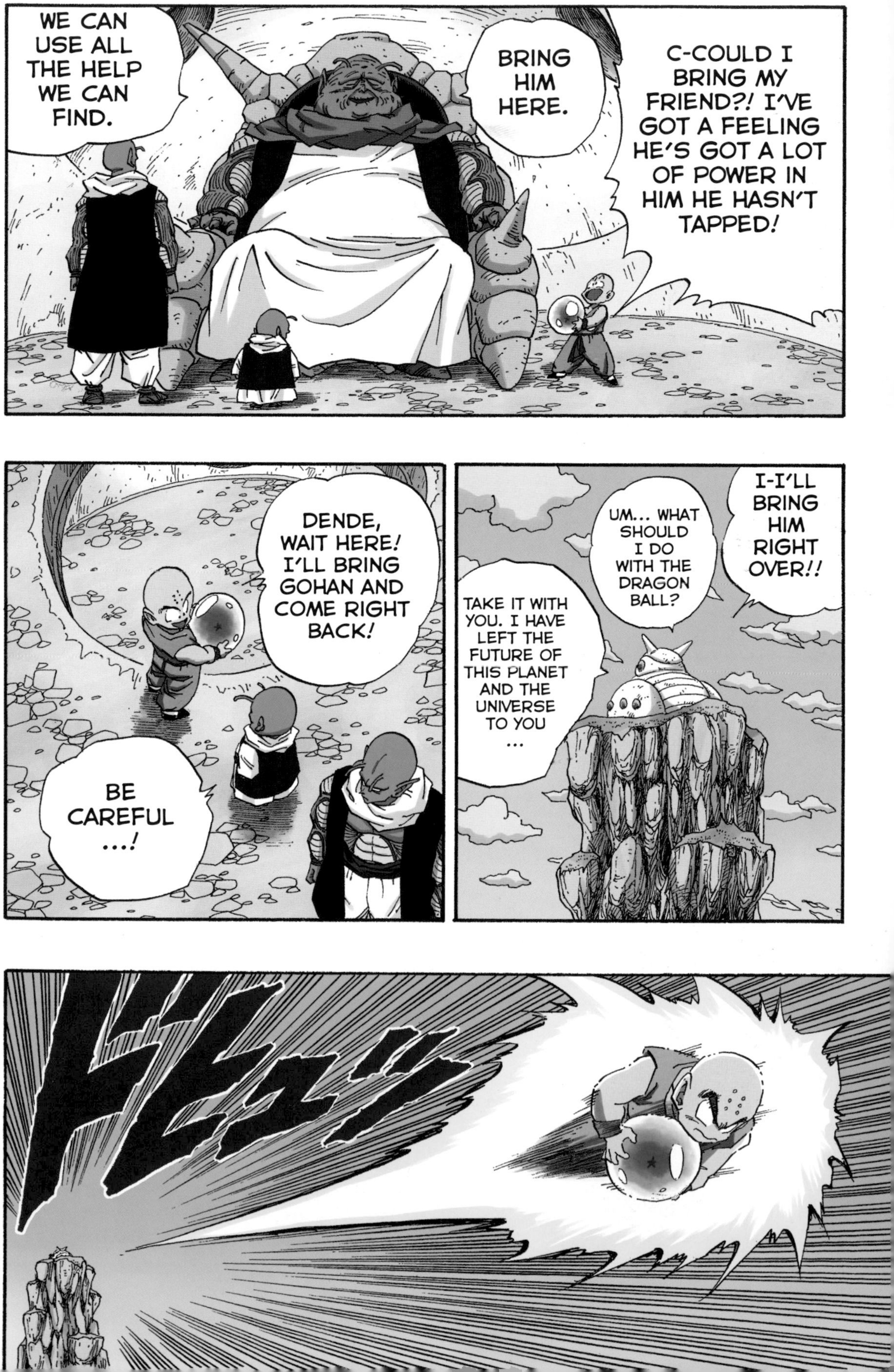
C-COULD I BRING MY FRIEND?! I'VE GOT A FEELING HE'S GOT A LOT OF POWER IN HIM HE HASN'T TAPPED!
BRING HIM HERE.
WE CAN USE ALL THE HELP WE CAN FIND.
I-I'LL BRING HIM RIGHT OVER!!
UM... WHAT SHOULD I DO WITH THE DRAGON BALL?
TAKE IT WITH YOU. I HAVE LEFT THE FUTURE OF THIS PLANET AND THE UNIVERSE TO YOU ...
DENDE, WAIT HERE! I'LL BRING GOHAN AND COME RIGHT BACK!
BE CAREFUL ...!

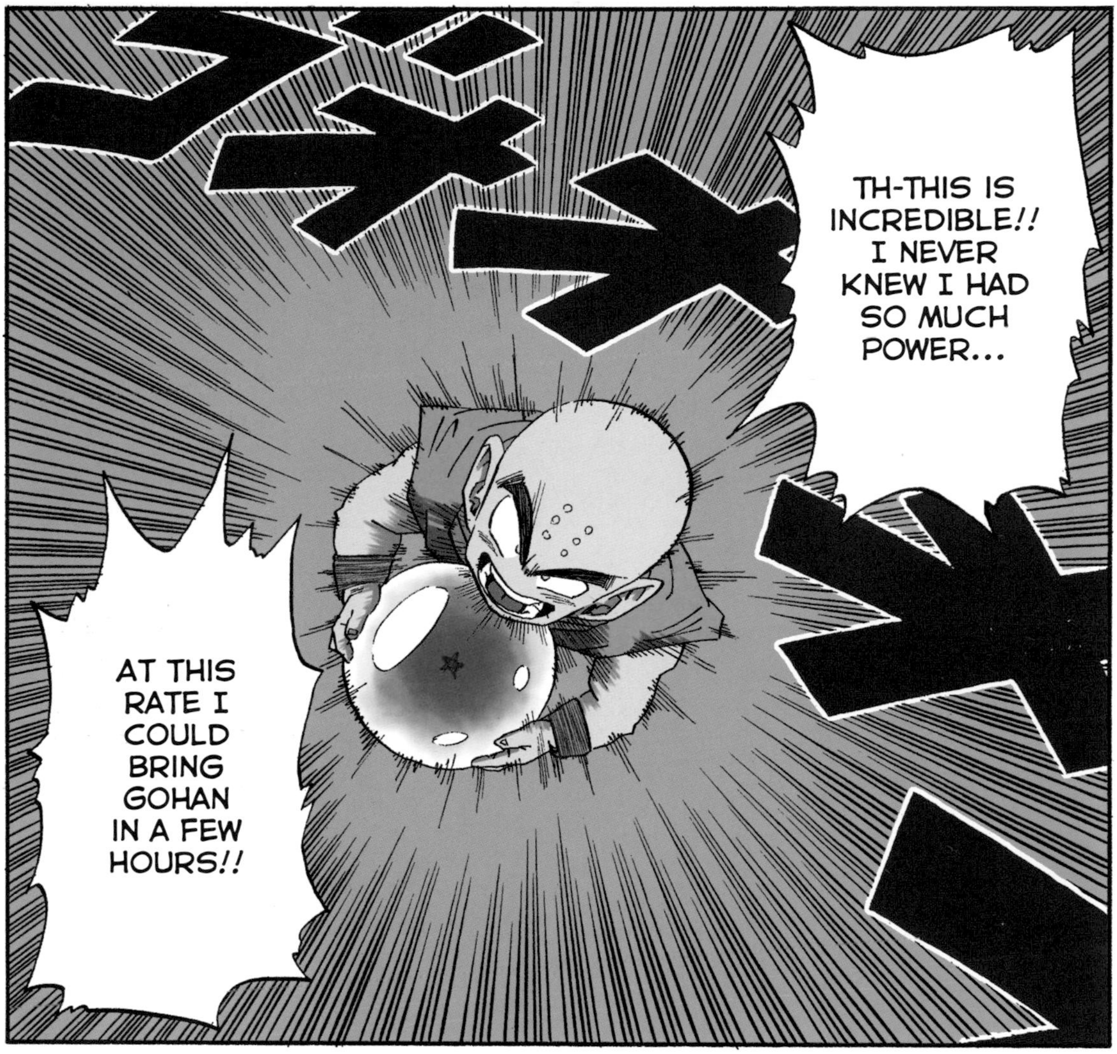
TH-THIS IS INCREDIBLE!! I NEVER KNEW I HAD SO MUCH POWER...
AT THIS RATE I COULD BRING GOHAN IN A FEW HOURS!!
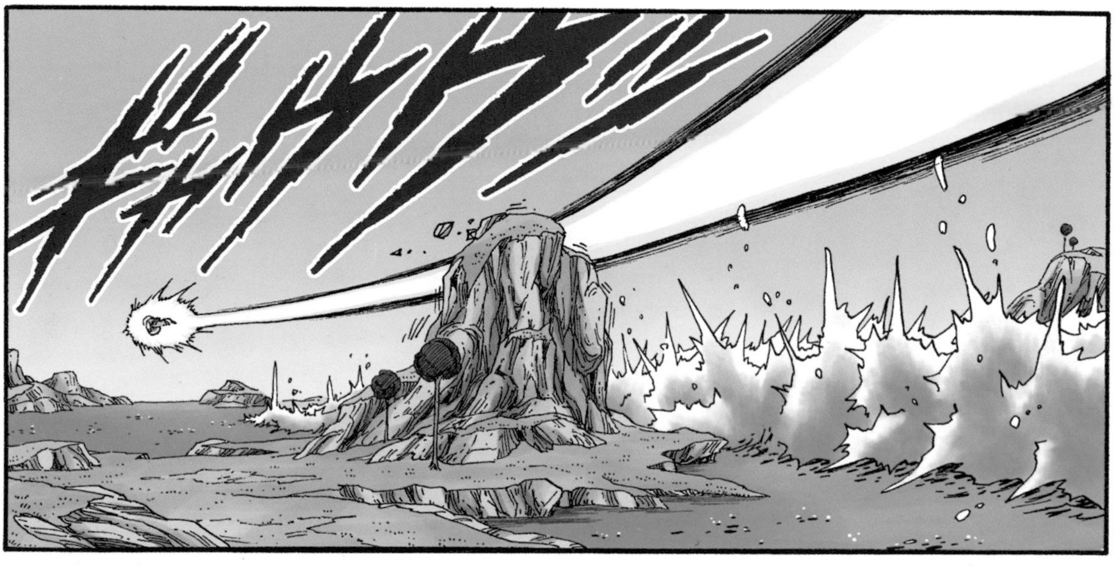

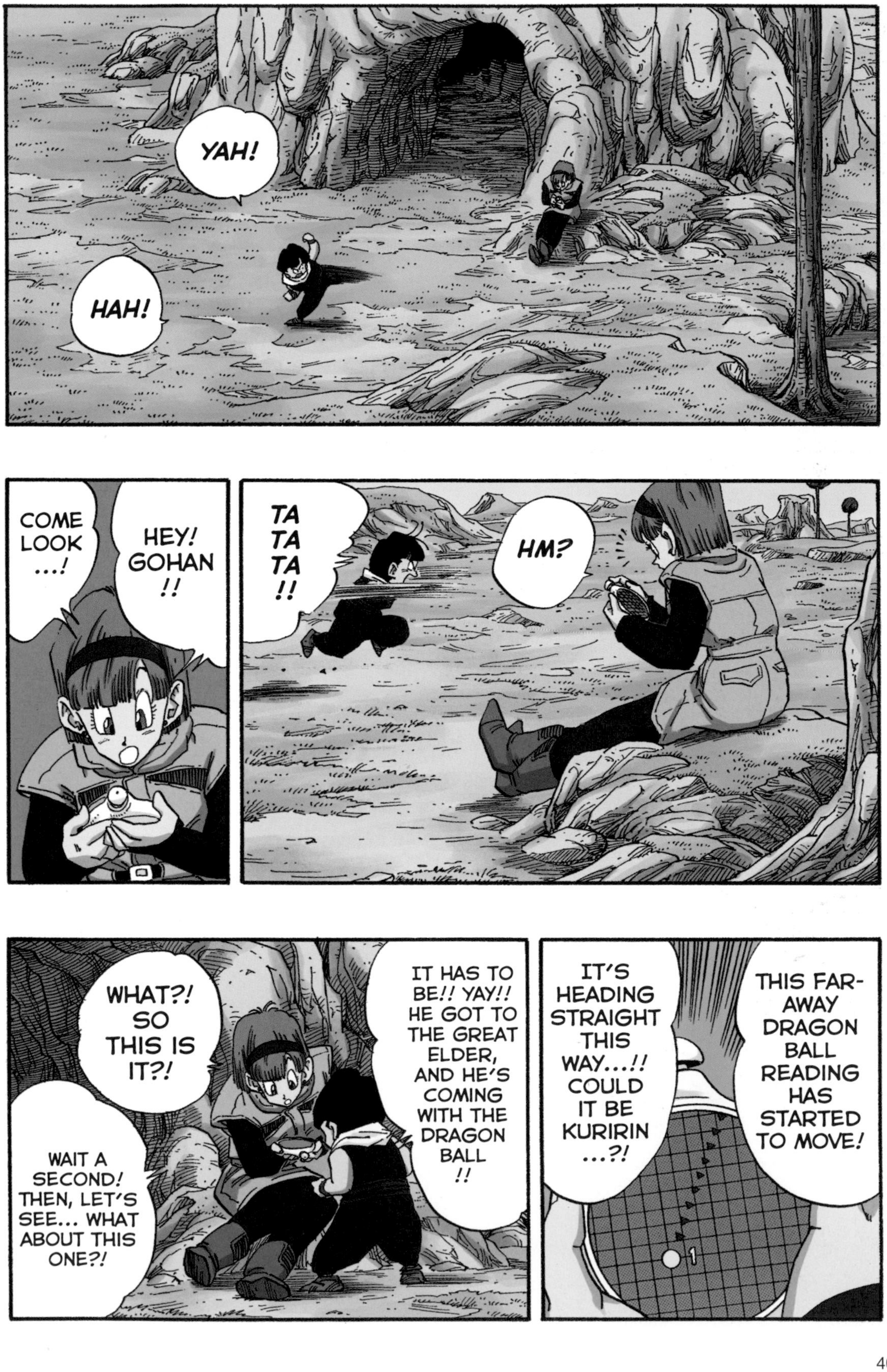

YAH!
HAH!
HM?
TA TA TA!!
HEY! GOHAN!!
COME LOOK...!
THIS FAR-AWAY DRAGON BALL READING HAS STARTED TO MOVE!
IT'S HEADING STRAIGHT THIS WAY...!! COULD IT BE KURIRIN...?!
IT HAS TO BE!! YAY!! HE GOT TO THE GREAT ELDER, AND HE'S COMING WITH THE DRAGON BALL!!
WHAT?! SO THIS IS IT?!
WAIT A SECOND! THEN, LET'S SEE... WHAT ABOUT THIS ONE?!

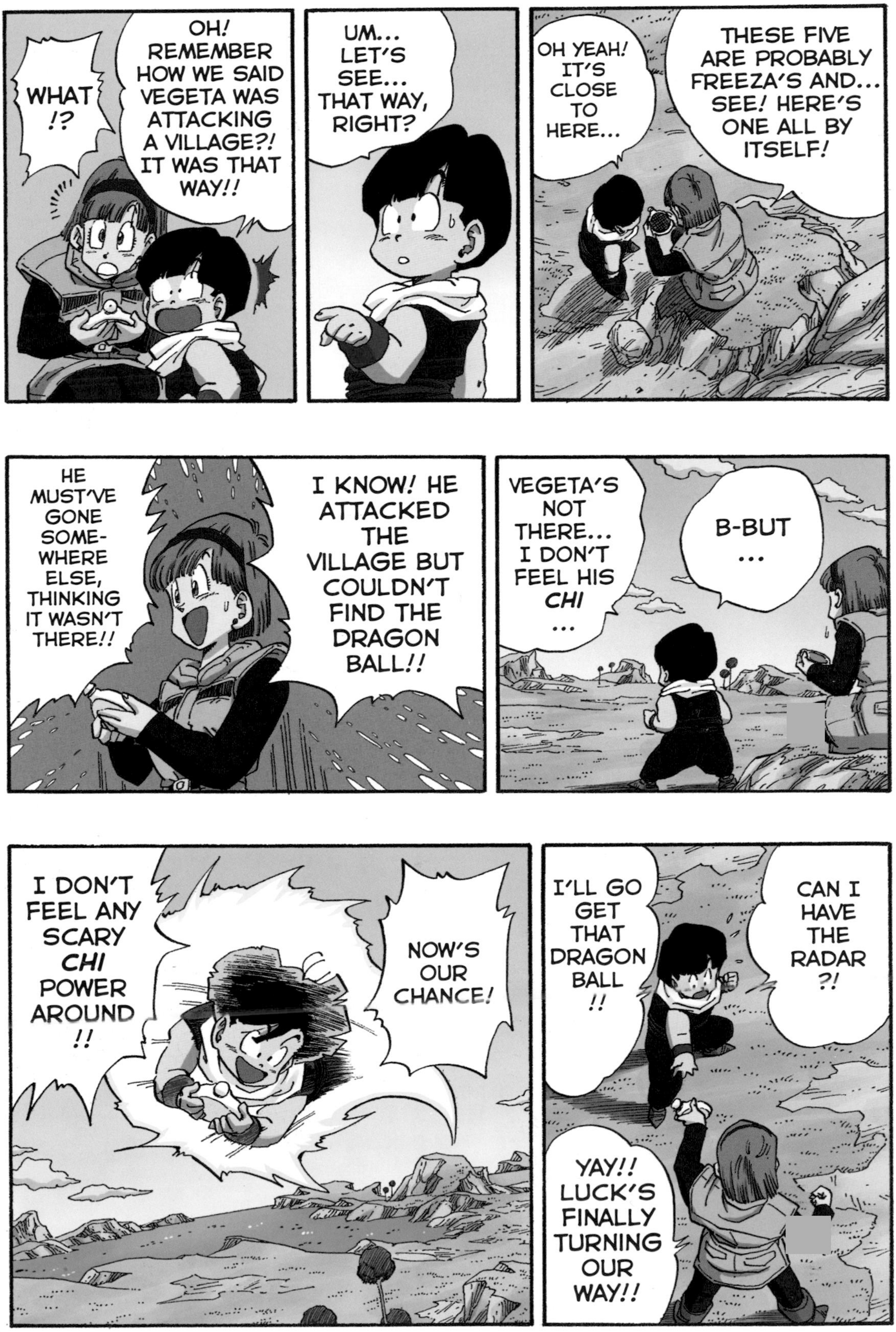
THESE FIVE ARE PROBABLY FREEZA'S AND... SEE! HERE'S ONE ALL BY ITSELF!
OH YEAH! IT'S CLOSE TO HERE...
UM... LET'S SEE... THAT WAY, RIGHT?
OH! REMEMBER HOW WE SAID VEGETA WAS ATTACKING A VILLAGE?! IT WAS THAT WAY!!
WHAT!?
B-BUT...
VEGETA'S NOT THERE... I DON'T FEEL HIS CHI...
I KNOW! HE ATTACKED THE VILLAGE BUT COULDN'T FIND THE DRAGON BALL!!
HE MUST'VE GONE SOMEWHERE ELSE, THINKING IT WASN'T THERE!!
CAN I HAVE THE RADAR?!
I'LL GO GET THAT DRAGON BALL!!
YAY!! LUCK'S FINALLY TURNING OUR WAY!!
NOW'S OUR CHANCE!
I DON'T FEEL ANY SCARY CHI POWER AROUND!!

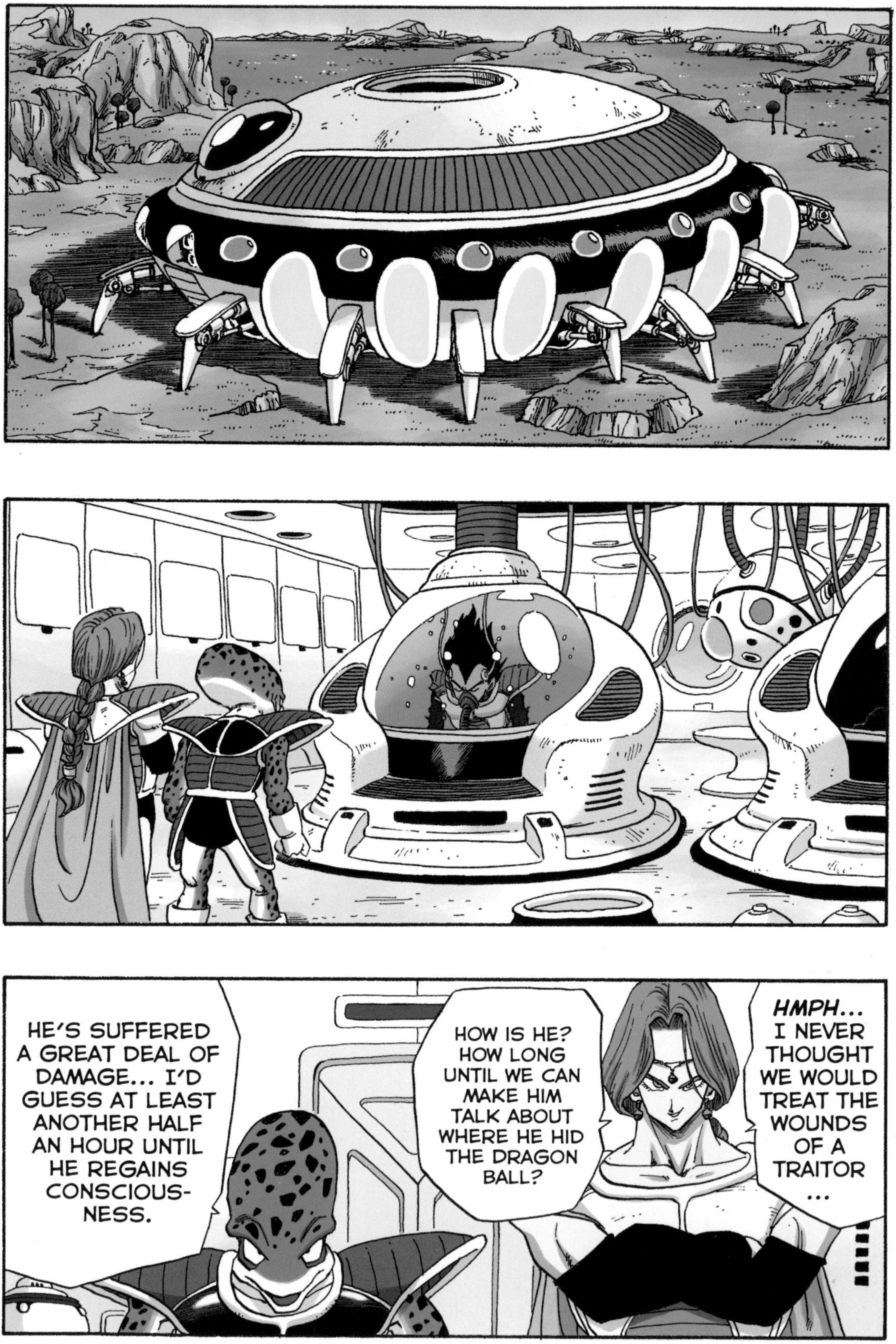
HMPH... I NEVER THOUGHT WE WOULD TREAT THE WOUNDS OF A TRAITOR ...
HOW IS HE? HOW LONG UNTIL WE CAN MAKE HIM TALK ABOUT WHERE HE HID THE DRAGON BALL?
HE'S SUFFERED A GREAT DEAL OF DAMAGE... I'D GUESS AT LEAST ANOTHER HALF AN HOUR UNTIL HE REGAINS CONSCIOUS-NESS.

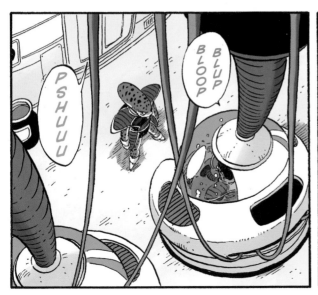

PSHUUU

BLOOP BLUP

WIIIIIN

I'LL REPORT THAT TO MASTER FREEZA...

EVEN VEGETA WILL TELL WHERE HE HID THE DRAGON BALL... AFTER A LITTLE "INTERRO-GATION" BY MASTER FREEZA...

HEH...

BLOOP BLUB

BLUP

EH?!

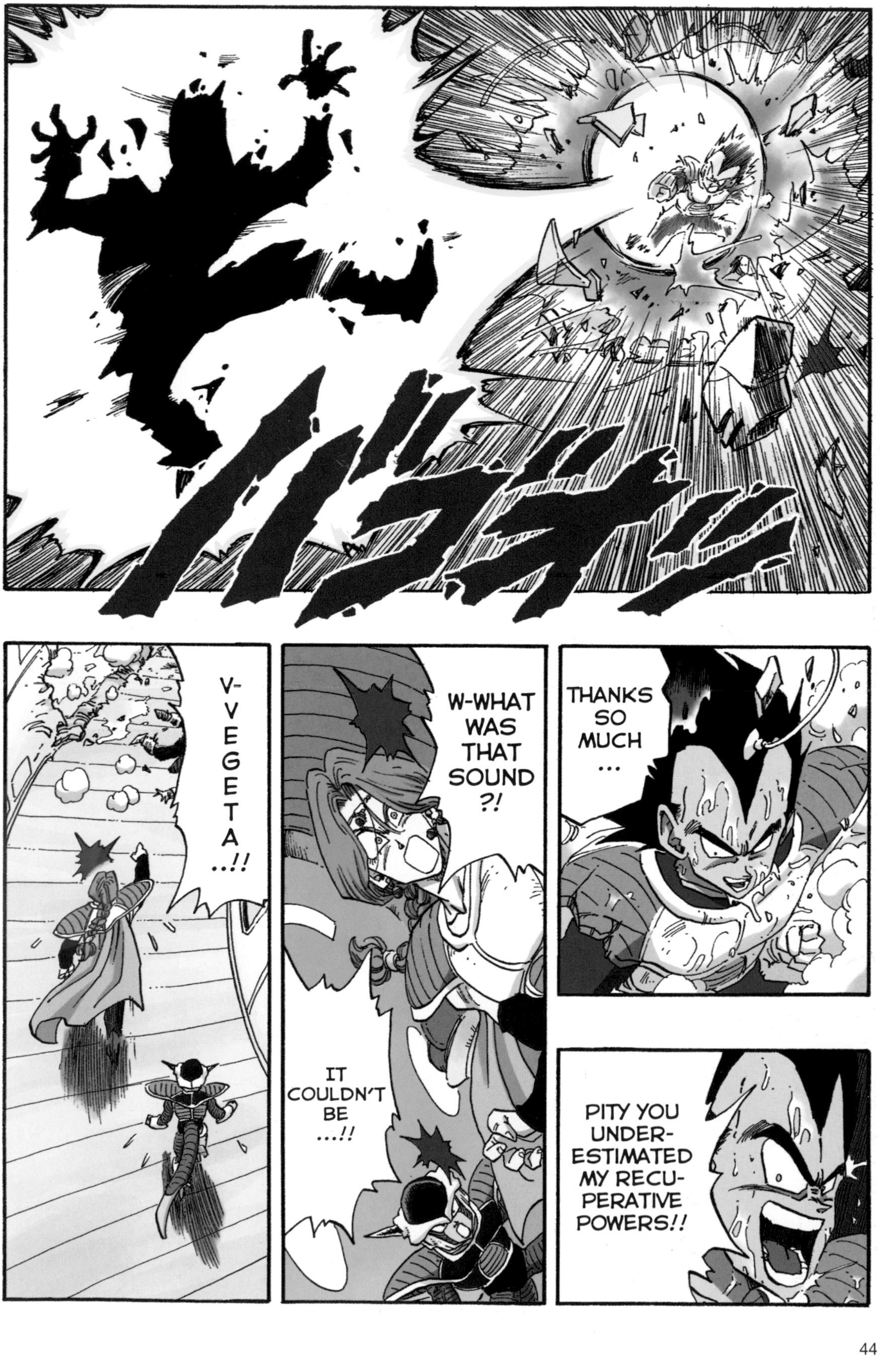
THANKS SO MUCH ...
PITY YOU UNDER-ESTIMATED MY RECU-PERATIVE POWERS!!
W-WHAT WAS THAT SOUND ?!
IT COULDN'T BE ...!!
V-VEGETA ...!!

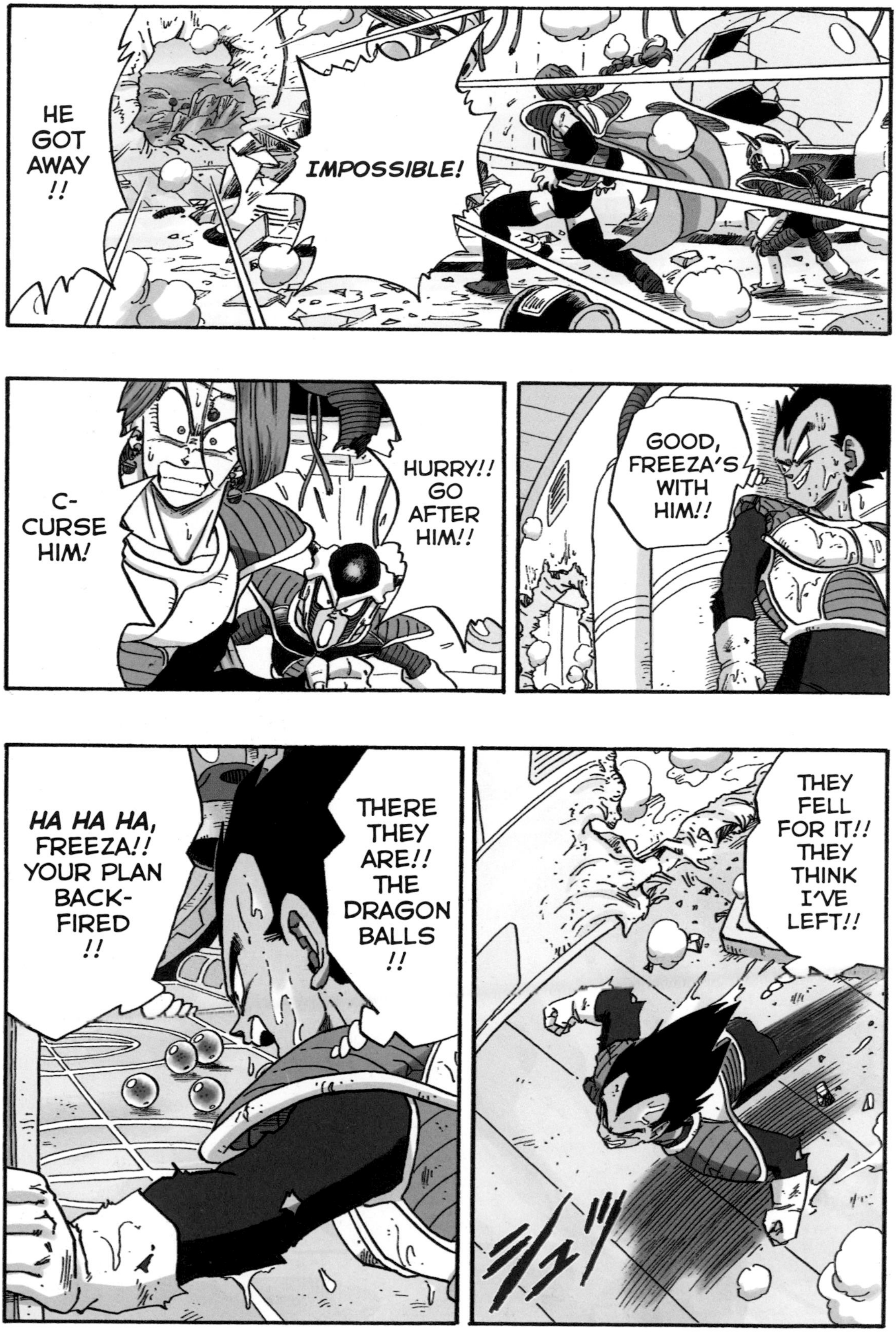
IMPOSSIBLE!
HE GOT AWAY!!
GOOD, FREEZA'S WITH HIM!!
HURRY!! GO AFTER HIM!!
C-CURSE HIM!
THEY FELL FOR IT!! THEY THINK I'VE LEFT!!
THERE THEY ARE!! THE DRAGON BALLS!!
HA HA HA, FREEZA!! YOUR PLAN BACKFIRED!!

Chapter 21 • Vegeta's Laughter, Freeza's Rage

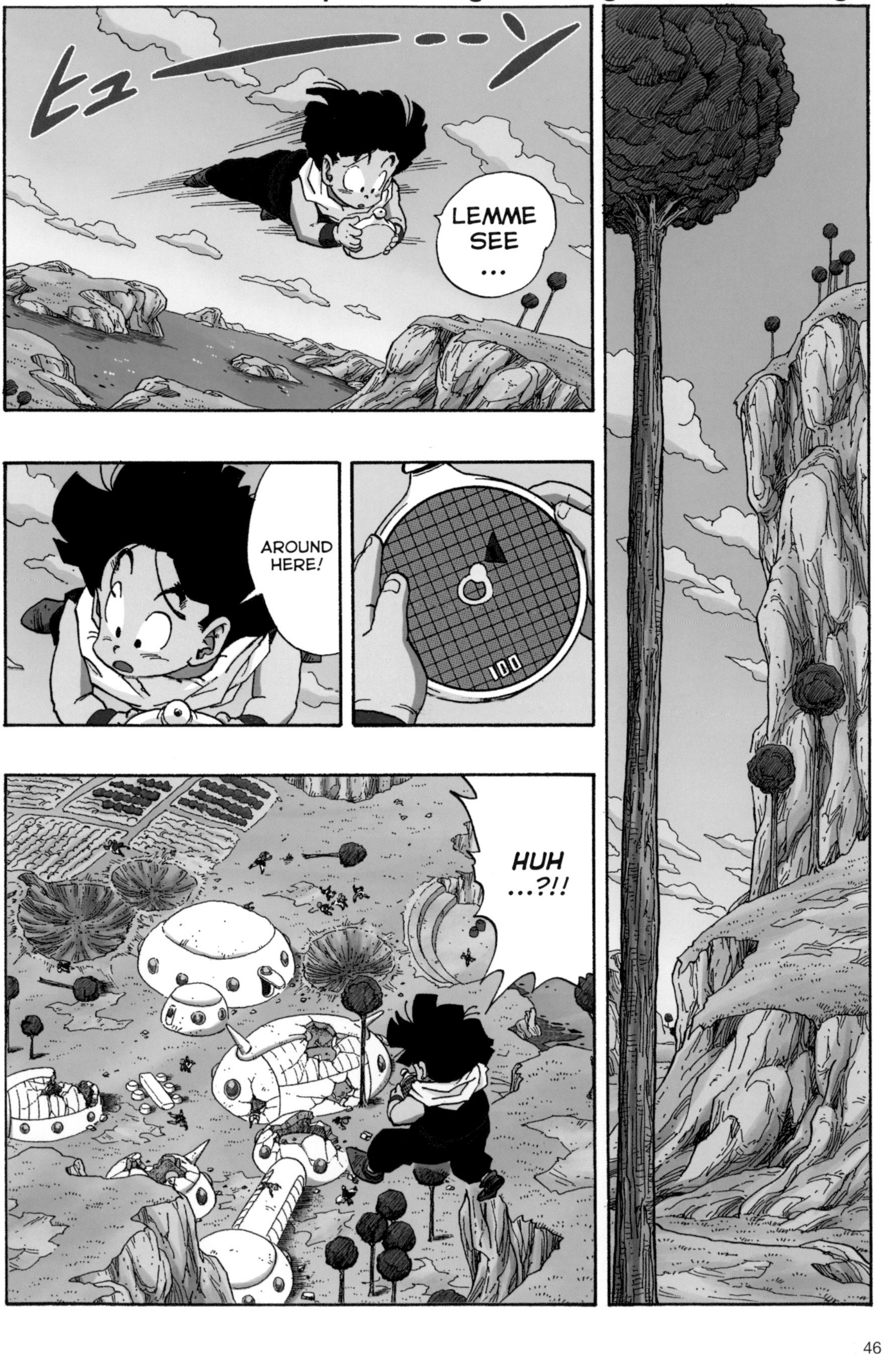
LEMME SEE ...
100
AROUND HERE!
HUH ...?!!

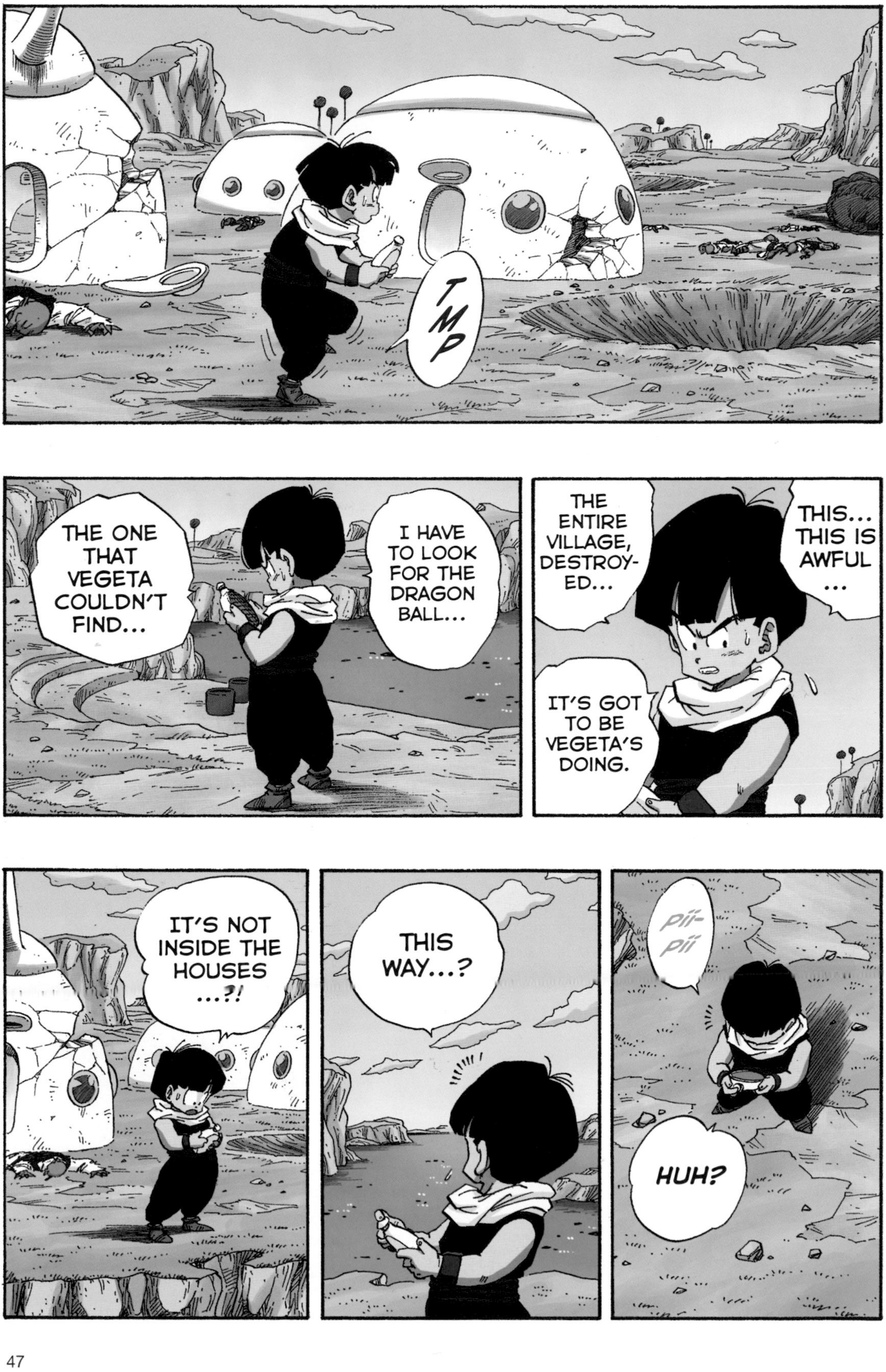
TMP
THIS... THIS IS AWFUL ...
THE ENTIRE VILLAGE, DESTROYED...
IT'S GOT TO BE VEGETA'S DOING.
I HAVE TO LOOK FOR THE DRAGON BALL...
THE ONE THAT VEGETA COULDN'T FIND...
PII-PII
HUH?
THIS WAY...?
IT'S NOT INSIDE THE HOUSES ...?!

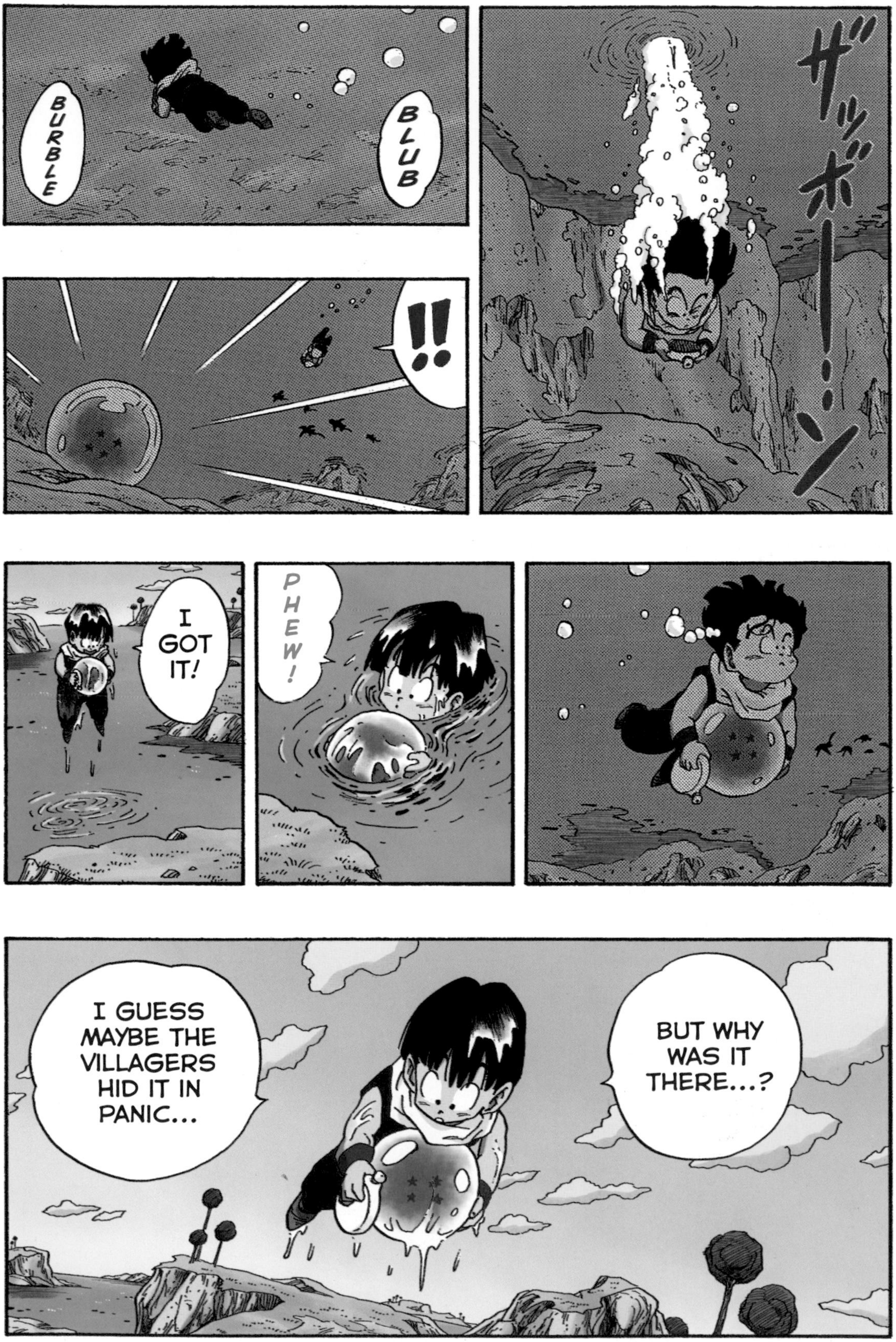
ザッボー!!ン
BLUB
BURBLE
!!
PHEW!
I GOT IT!
BUT WHY WAS IT THERE...?
I GUESS MAYBE THE VILLAGERS HID IT IN PANIC...

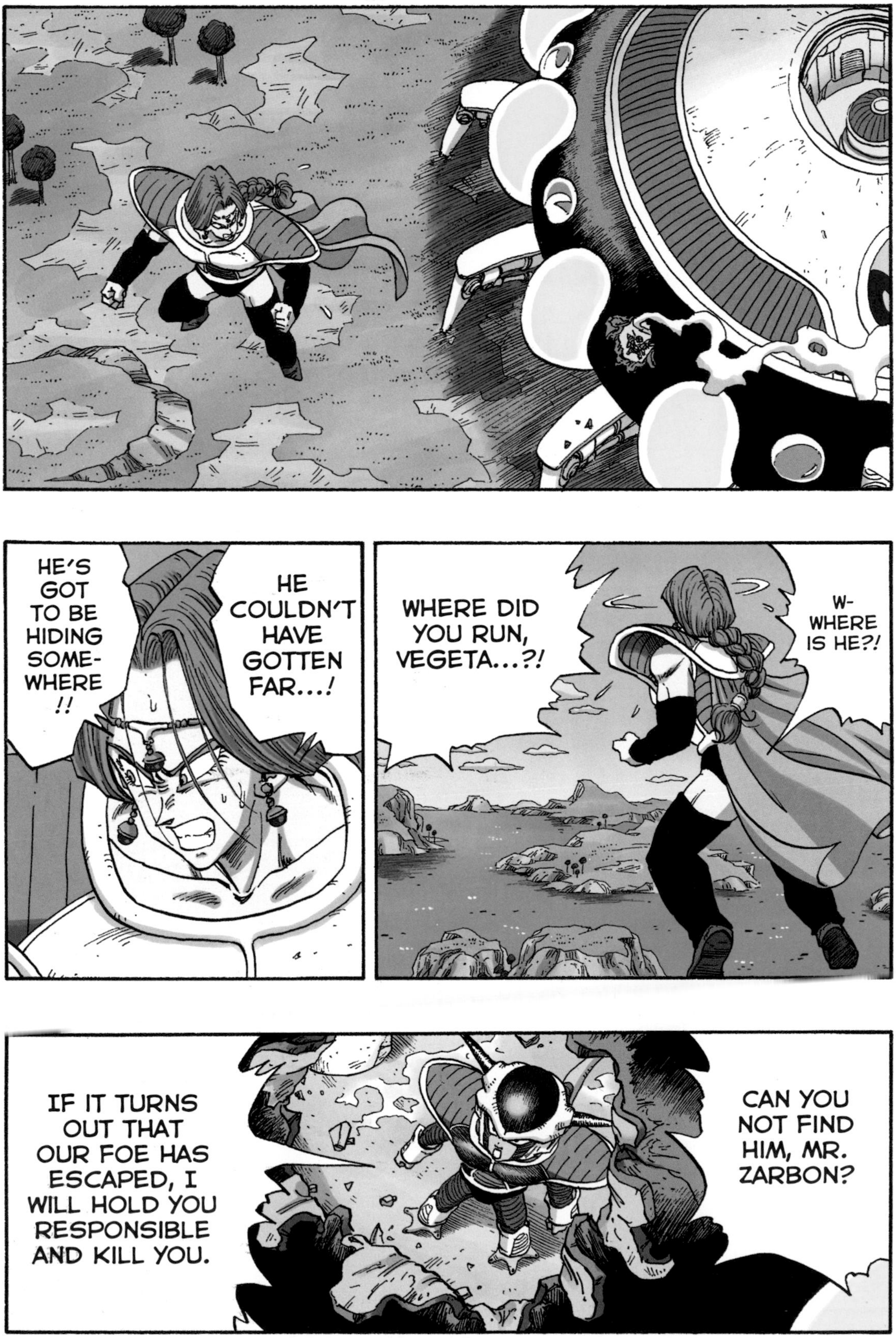
W-WHERE IS HE?!
WHERE DID YOU RUN, VEGETA...?!
HE COULDN'T HAVE GOTTEN FAR...!
HE'S GOT TO BE HIDING SOMEWHERE!!
CAN YOU NOT FIND HIM, MR. ZARBON?
IF IT TURNS OUT THAT OUR FOE HAS ESCAPED, I WILL HOLD YOU RESPONSIBLE AND KILL YOU.

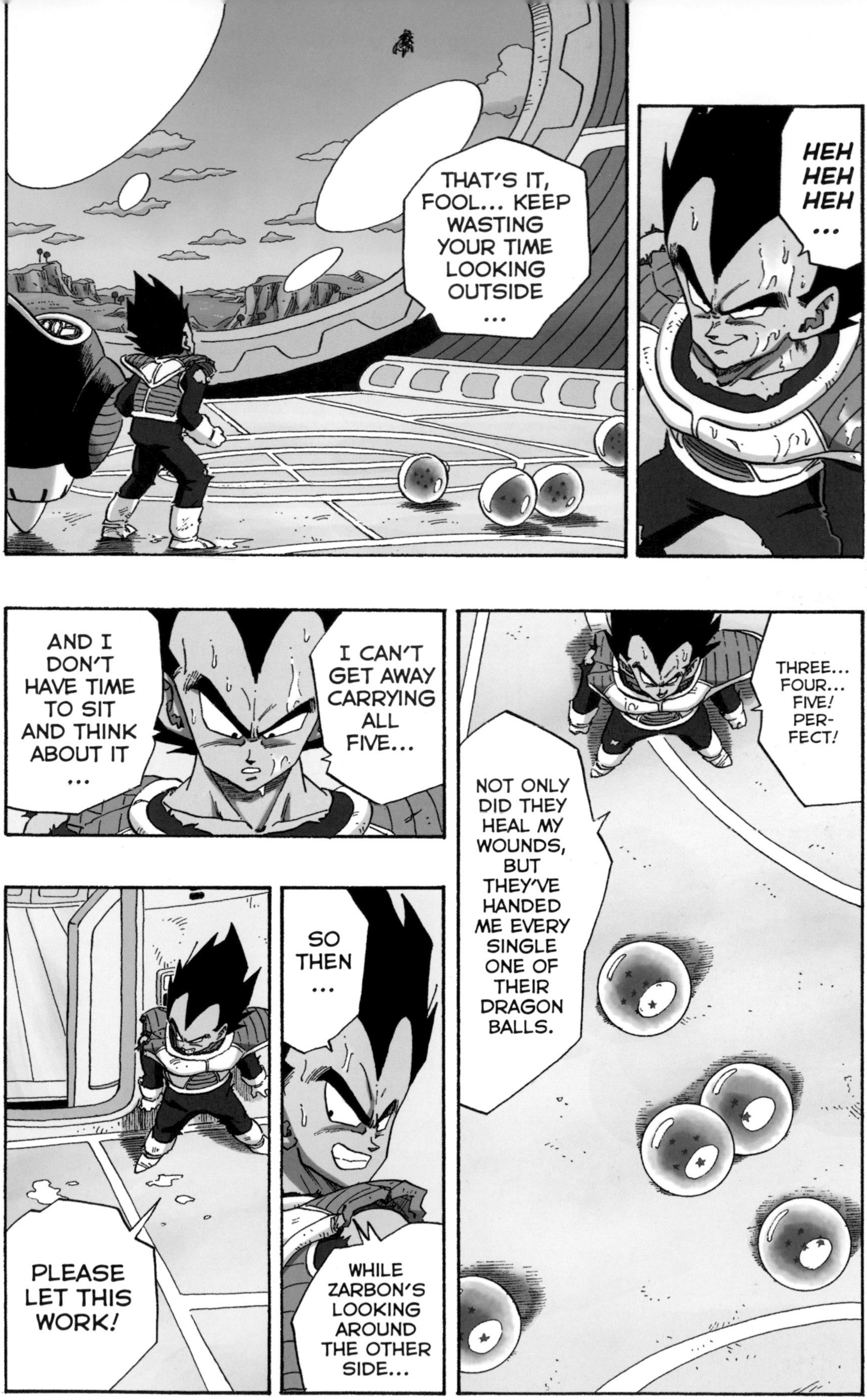
HEH HEH HEH...
THAT'S IT, FOOL... KEEP WASTING YOUR TIME LOOKING OUTSIDE...
THREE... FOUR... FIVE! PERFECT!
NOT ONLY DID THEY HEAL MY WOUNDS, BUT THEY'VE HANDED ME EVERY SINGLE ONE OF THEIR DRAGON BALLS.
I CAN'T GET AWAY CARRYING ALL FIVE...
AND I DON'T HAVE TIME TO SIT AND THINK ABOUT IT...
SO THEN...
WHILE ZARBON'S LOOKING AROUND THE OTHER SIDE...
PLEASE LET THIS WORK!

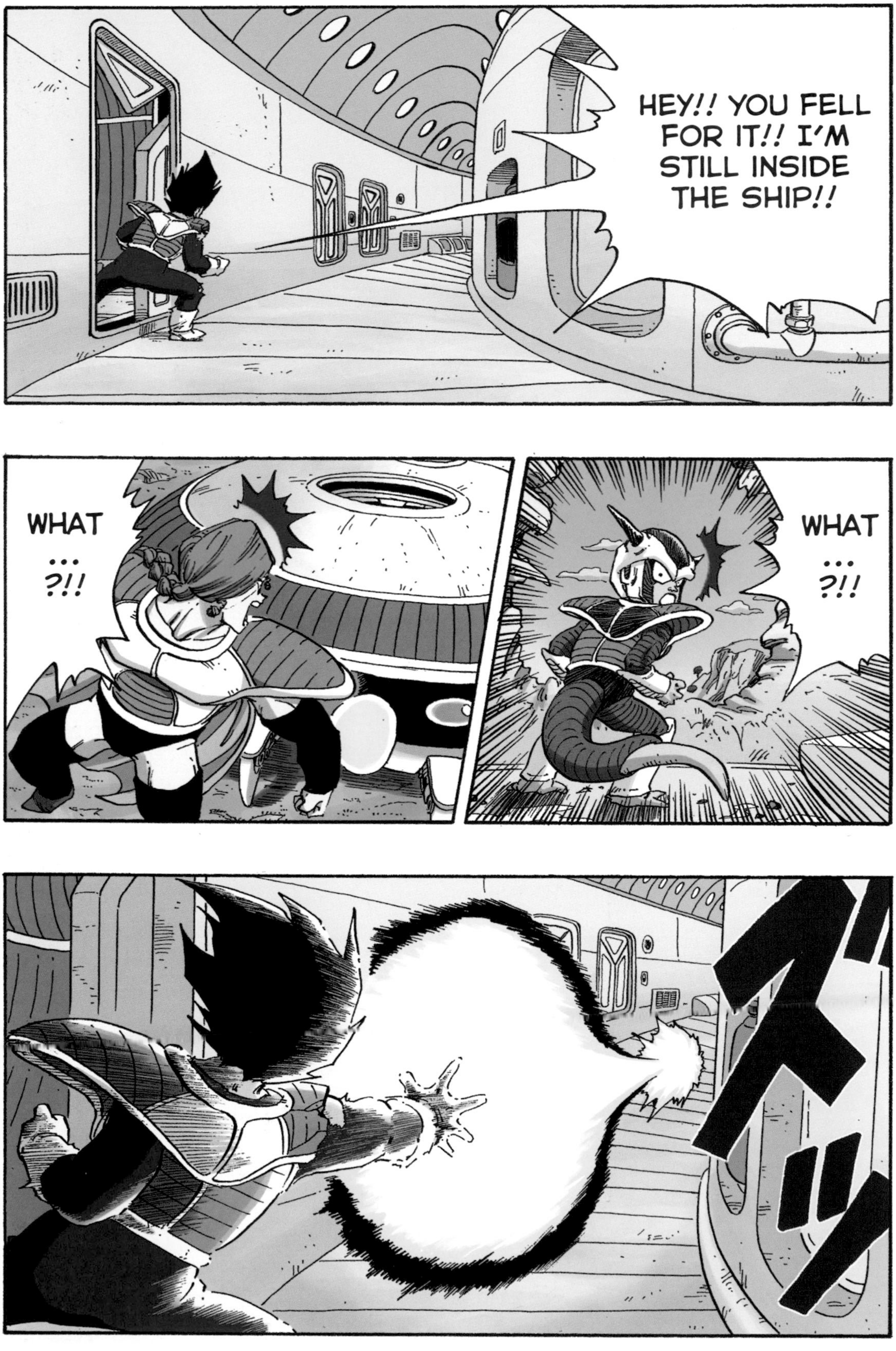
HEY!! YOU FELL FOR IT!! I'M STILL INSIDE THE SHIP!!
WHAT ...?!!
WHAT ...?!!

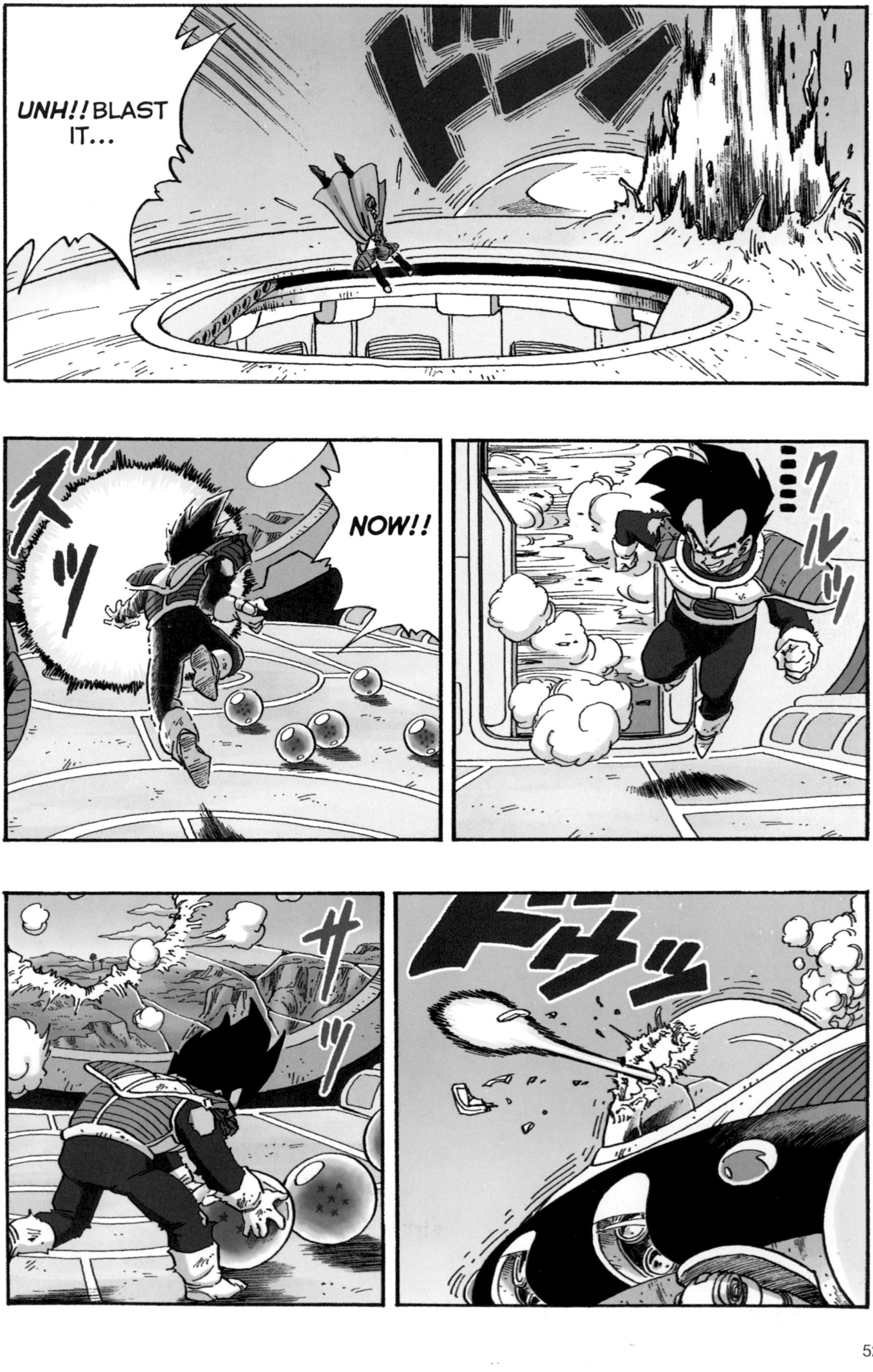
ドーン
UNH!! BLAST IT...
クルッ
NOW!!
ズッ
ドウッ
サッ

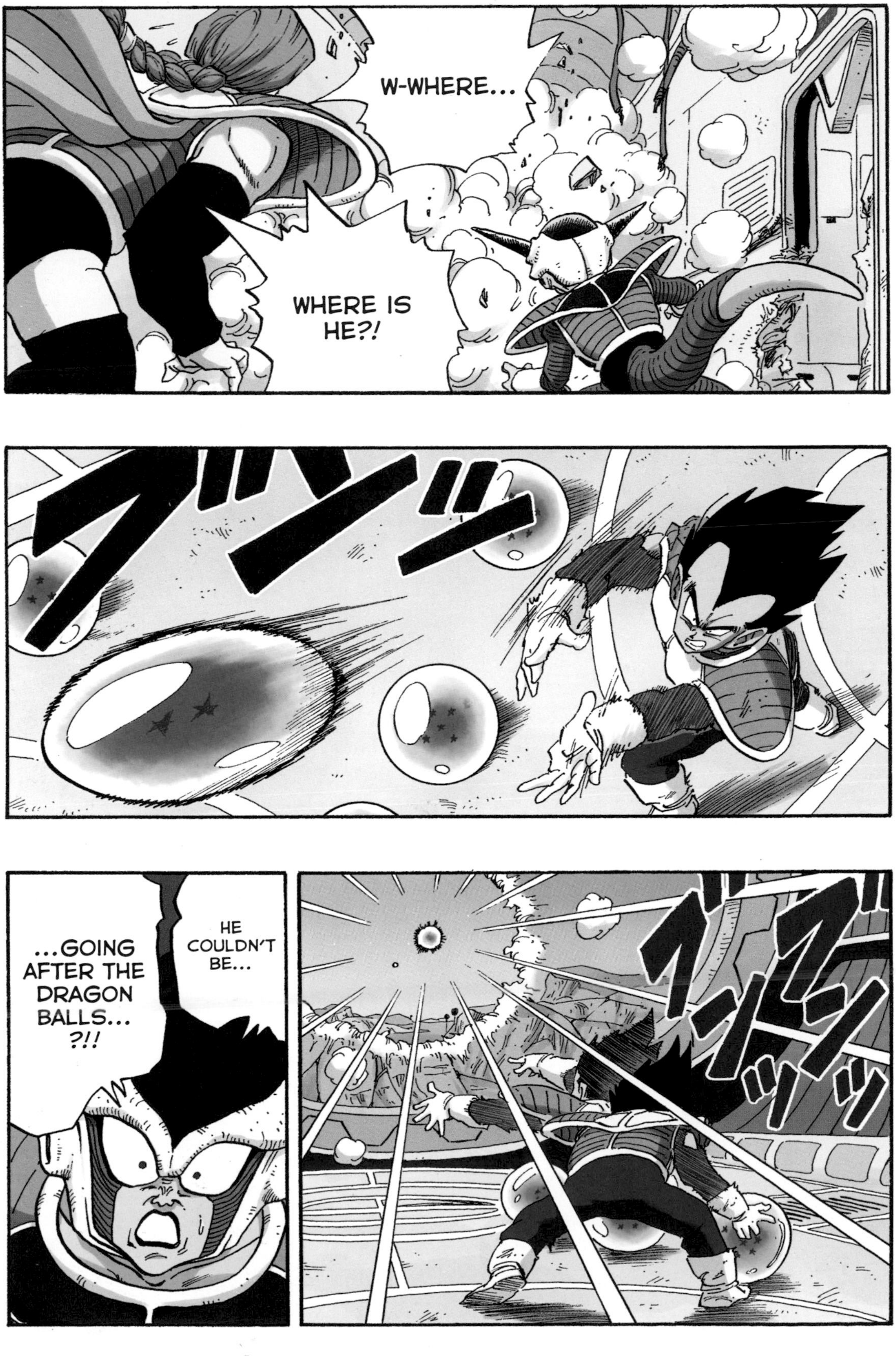
W-WHERE...
WHERE IS HE?!
HE COULDN'T BE...
...GOING AFTER THE DRAGON BALLS... ?!!

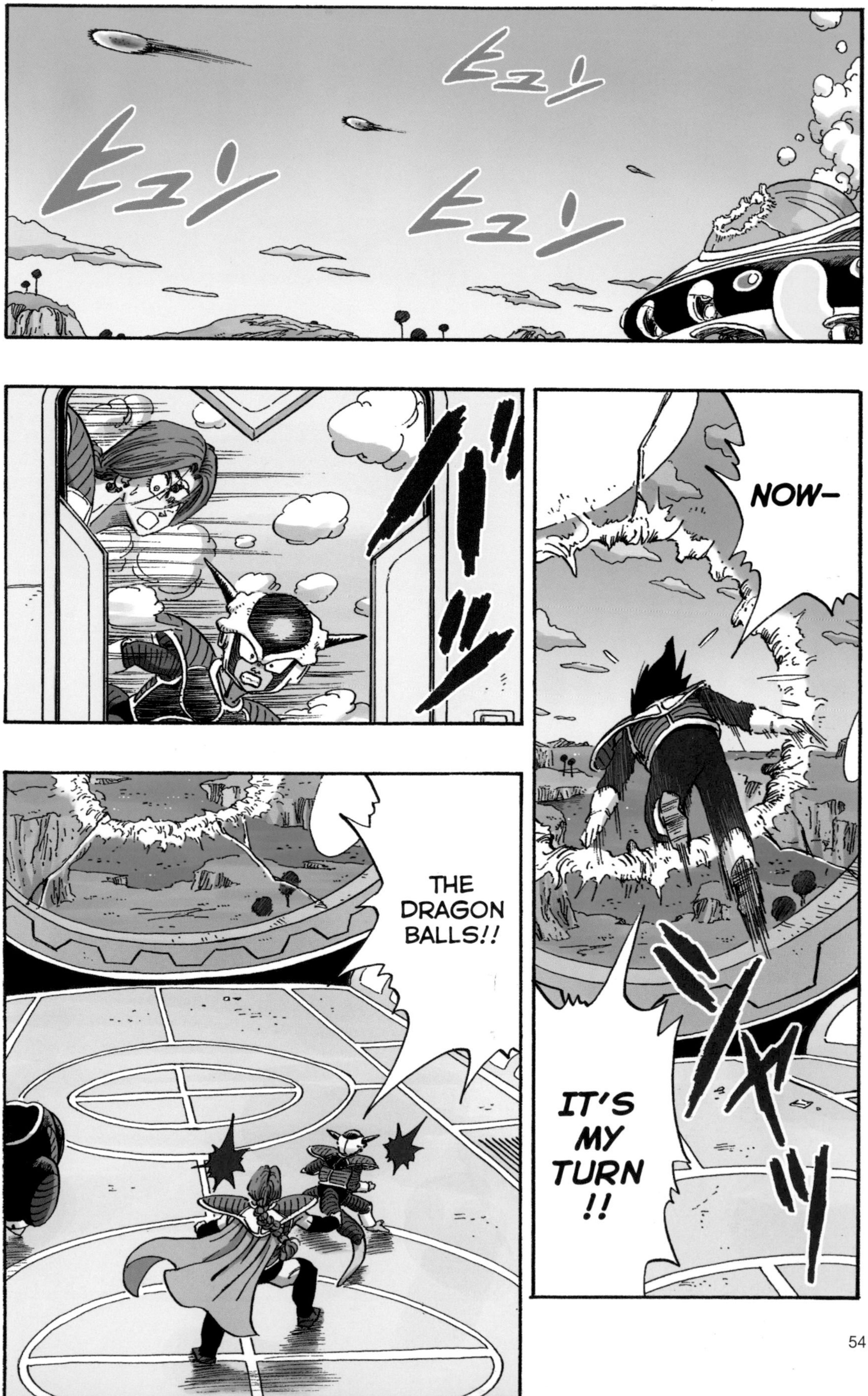
ヒュン
ヒュン
ヒュン
NOW–
IT'S MY TURN!!
THE DRAGON BALLS!!

Y-Y-

YOU LITTLE −!!

M-MASTER FREEZA!! IS HE IN THE SHIP AGAIN...?!

LOOK FOR HIM!!

W...

WHERE IS HE?!!

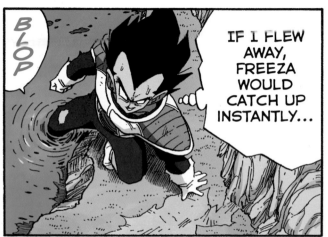

BLOP

IF I FLEW AWAY, FREEZA WOULD CATCH UP INSTANTLY...

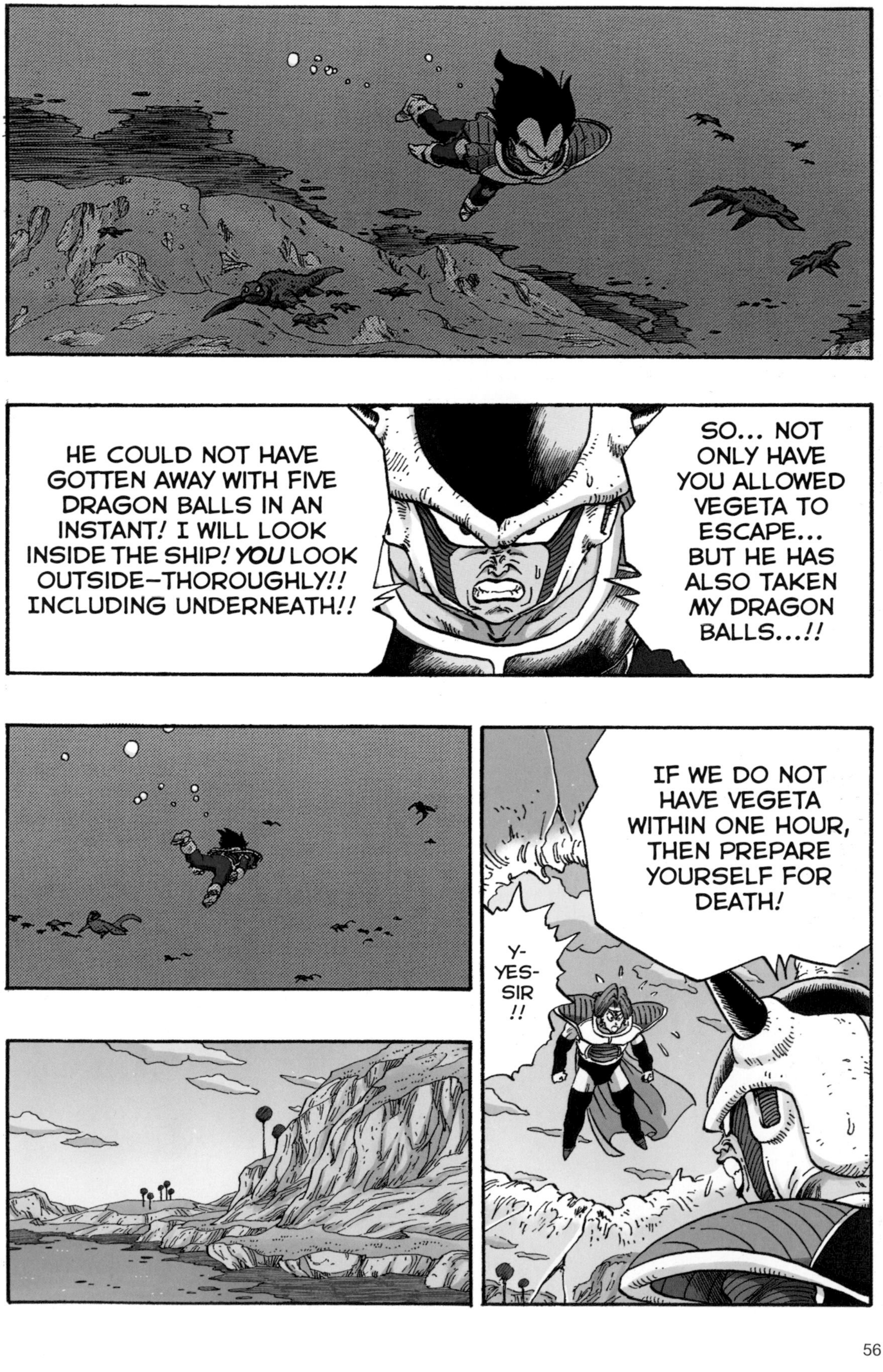
SO... NOT ONLY HAVE YOU ALLOWED VEGETA TO ESCAPE... BUT HE HAS ALSO TAKEN MY DRAGON BALLS...!!
HE COULD NOT HAVE GOTTEN AWAY WITH FIVE DRAGON BALLS IN AN INSTANT! I WILL LOOK INSIDE THE SHIP! *YOU* LOOK OUTSIDE—THOROUGHLY!! INCLUDING UNDERNEATH!!
IF WE DO NOT HAVE VEGETA WITHIN ONE HOUR, THEN PREPARE YOURSELF FOR DEATH!
Y-YES-SIR!!

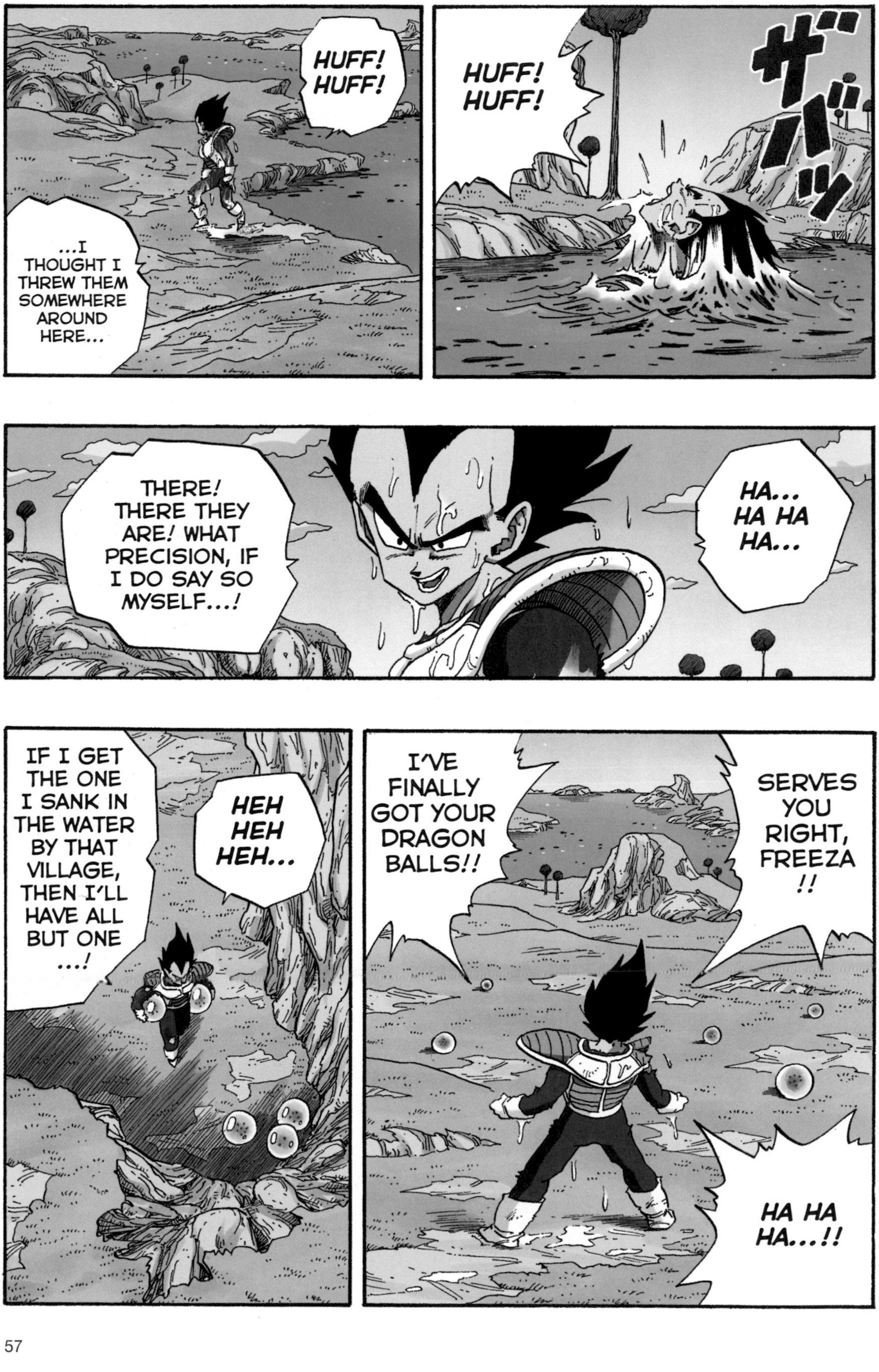
ザバッ
HUFF! HUFF!
HUFF! HUFF!
...I THOUGHT I THREW THEM SOMEWHERE AROUND HERE...
HA... HA HA HA...
THERE! THERE THEY ARE! WHAT PRECISION, IF I DO SAY SO MYSELF...!
SERVES YOU RIGHT, FREEZA!!
I'VE FINALLY GOT YOUR DRAGON BALLS!!
HA HA HA...!!
HEH HEH HEH...
IF I GET THE ONE I SANK IN THE WATER BY THAT VILLAGE, THEN I'LL HAVE ALL BUT ONE...!

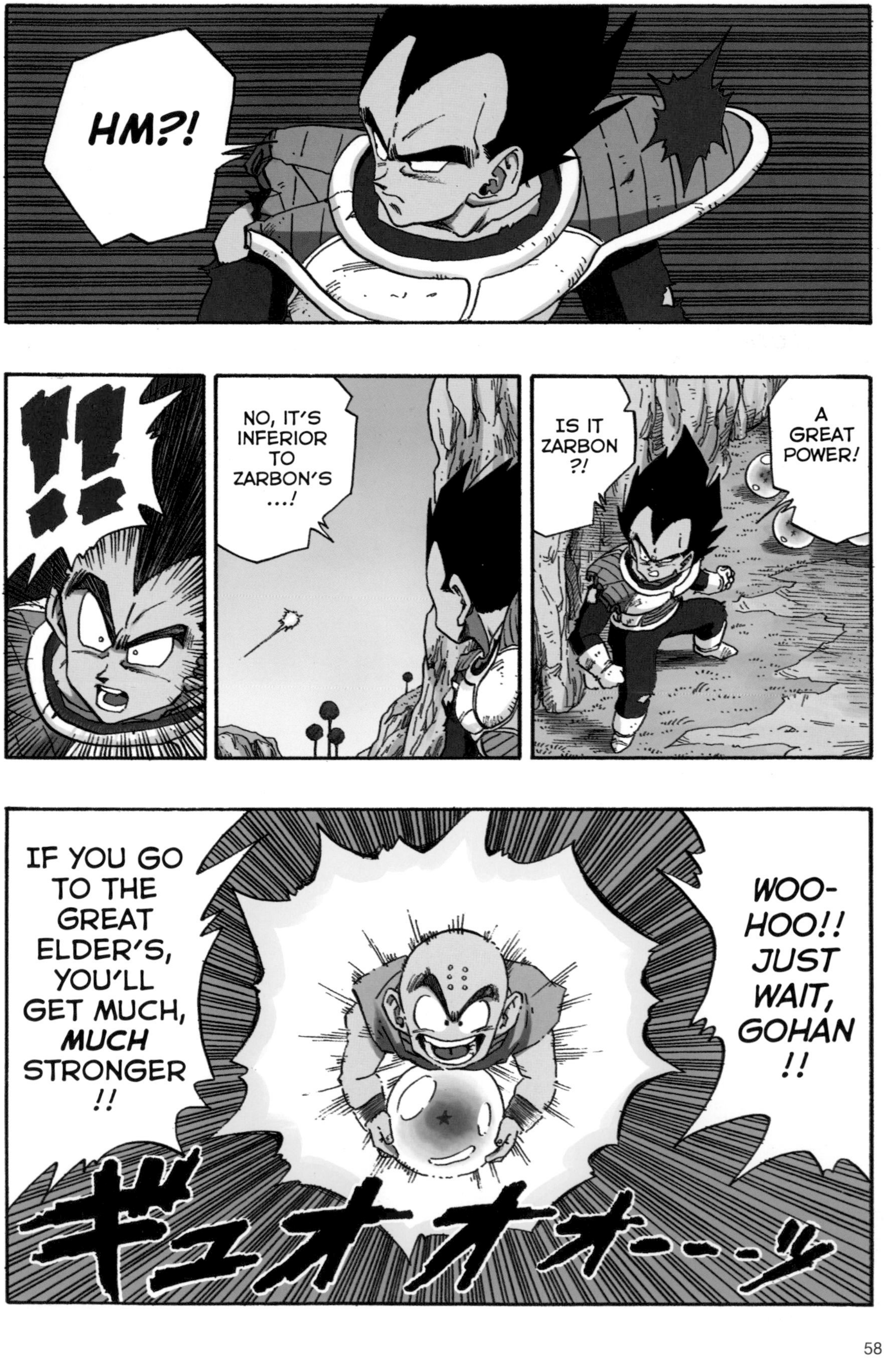
HM?!
A GREAT POWER!
IS IT ZARBON?!
NO, IT'S INFERIOR TO ZARBON'S...!
!!
WOO-HOO!! JUST WAIT, GOHAN!!
IF YOU GO TO THE GREAT ELDER'S, YOU'LL GET MUCH, MUCH STRONGER!!
ギュオオオーーッ

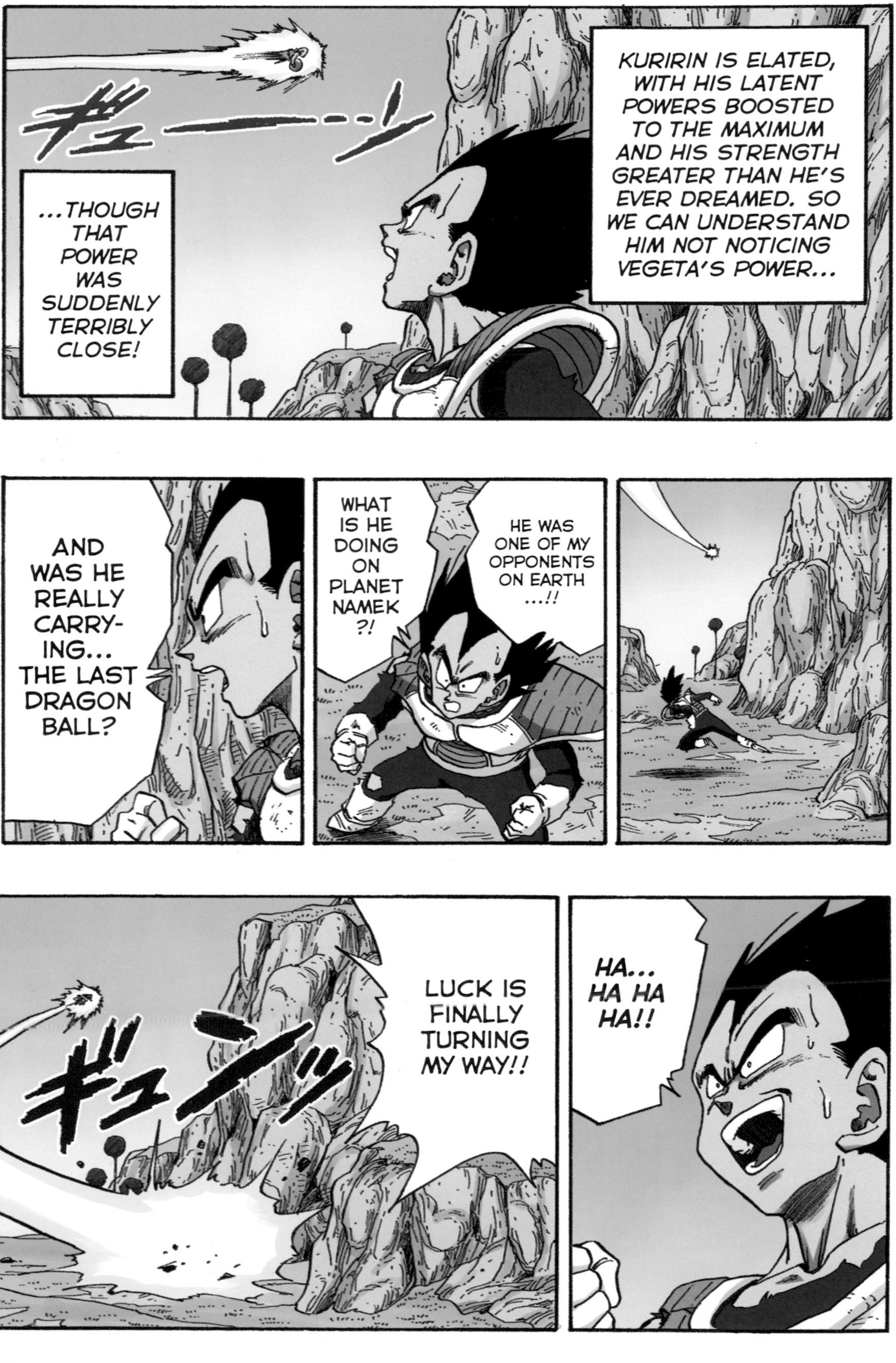
KURIRIN IS ELATED, WITH HIS LATENT POWERS BOOSTED TO THE MAXIMUM AND HIS STRENGTH GREATER THAN HE'S EVER DREAMED. SO WE CAN UNDERSTAND HIM NOT NOTICING VEGETA'S POWER...
ギューーーン
...THOUGH THAT POWER WAS SUDDENLY TERRIBLY CLOSE!
HE WAS ONE OF MY OPPONENTS ON EARTH...!!
WHAT IS HE DOING ON PLANET NAMEK?!
AND WAS HE REALLY CARRYING... THE LAST DRAGON BALL?
HA... HA HA HA!!
LUCK IS FINALLY TURNING MY WAY!!
ギュンッ

Chapter 22 • Reunion of Terror!

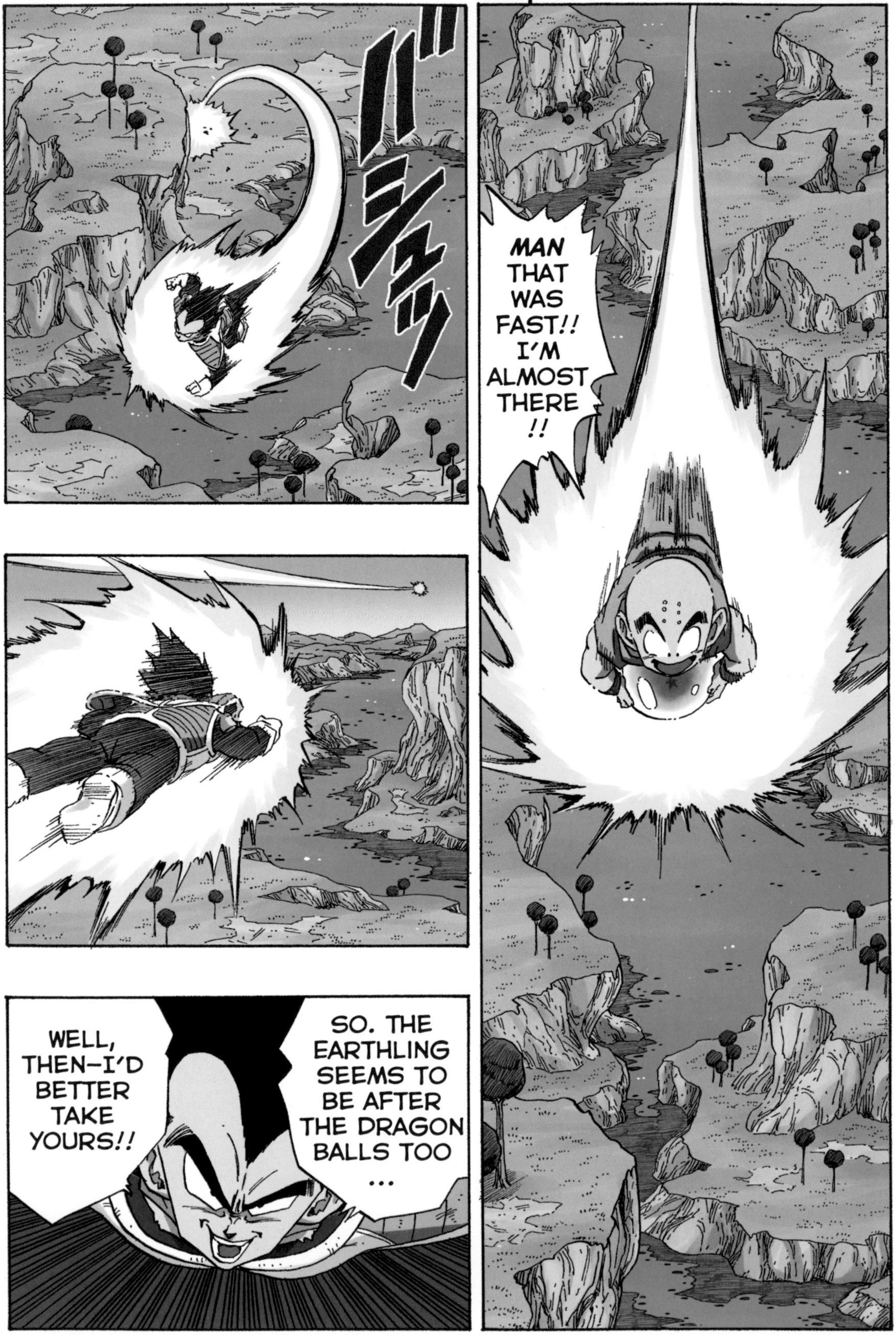
MAN THAT WAS FAST!! I'M ALMOST THERE !!
バシュッ
SO. THE EARTHLING SEEMS TO BE AFTER THE DRAGON BALLS TOO ...
WELL, THEN—I'D BETTER TAKE YOURS!!

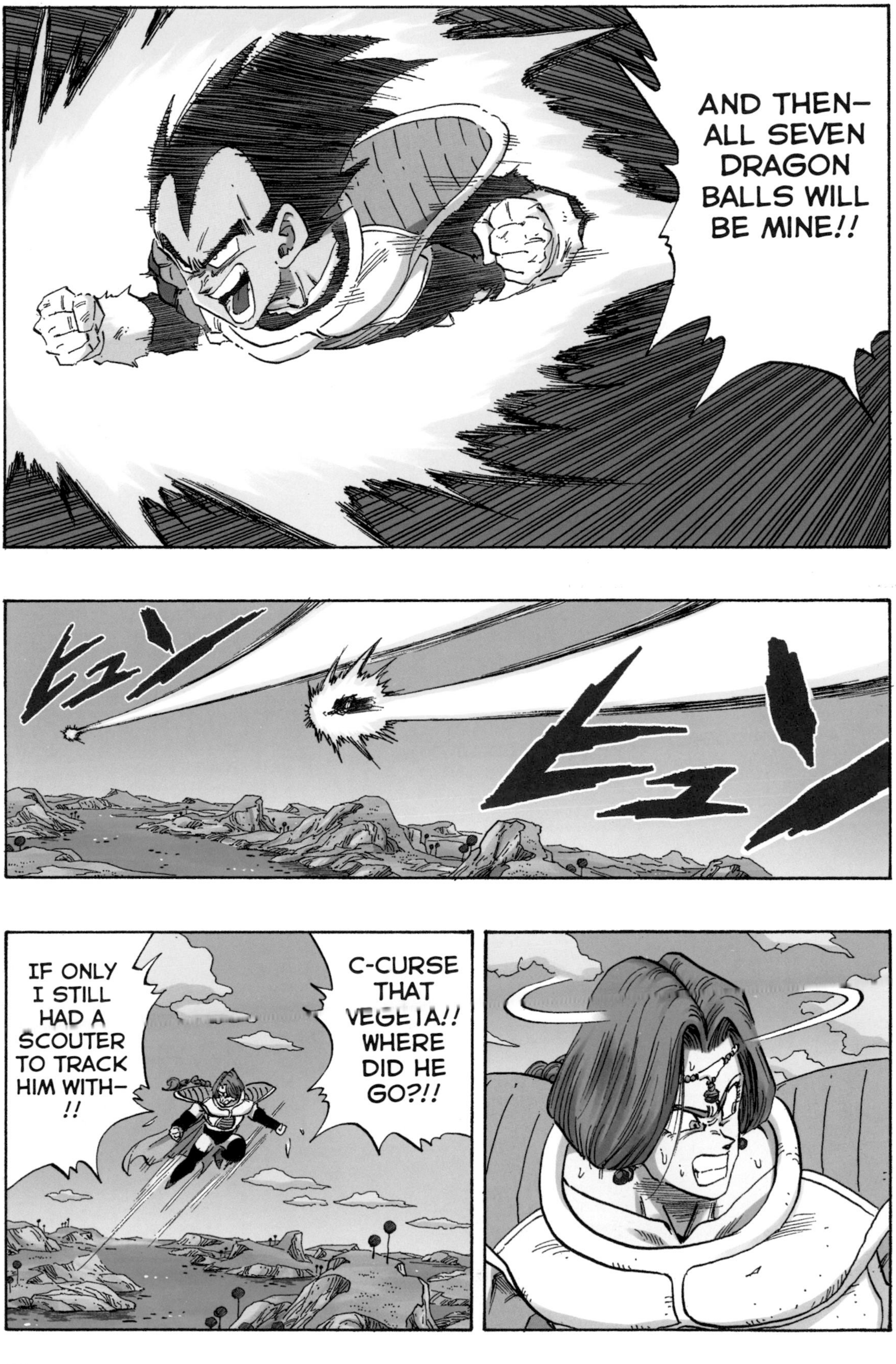
AND THEN—ALL SEVEN DRAGON BALLS WILL BE MINE!!
ヒュン
ヒュン
C-CURSE THAT VEGETA!! WHERE DID HE GO?!!
IF ONLY I STILL HAD A SCOUTER TO TRACK HIM WITH—
!!

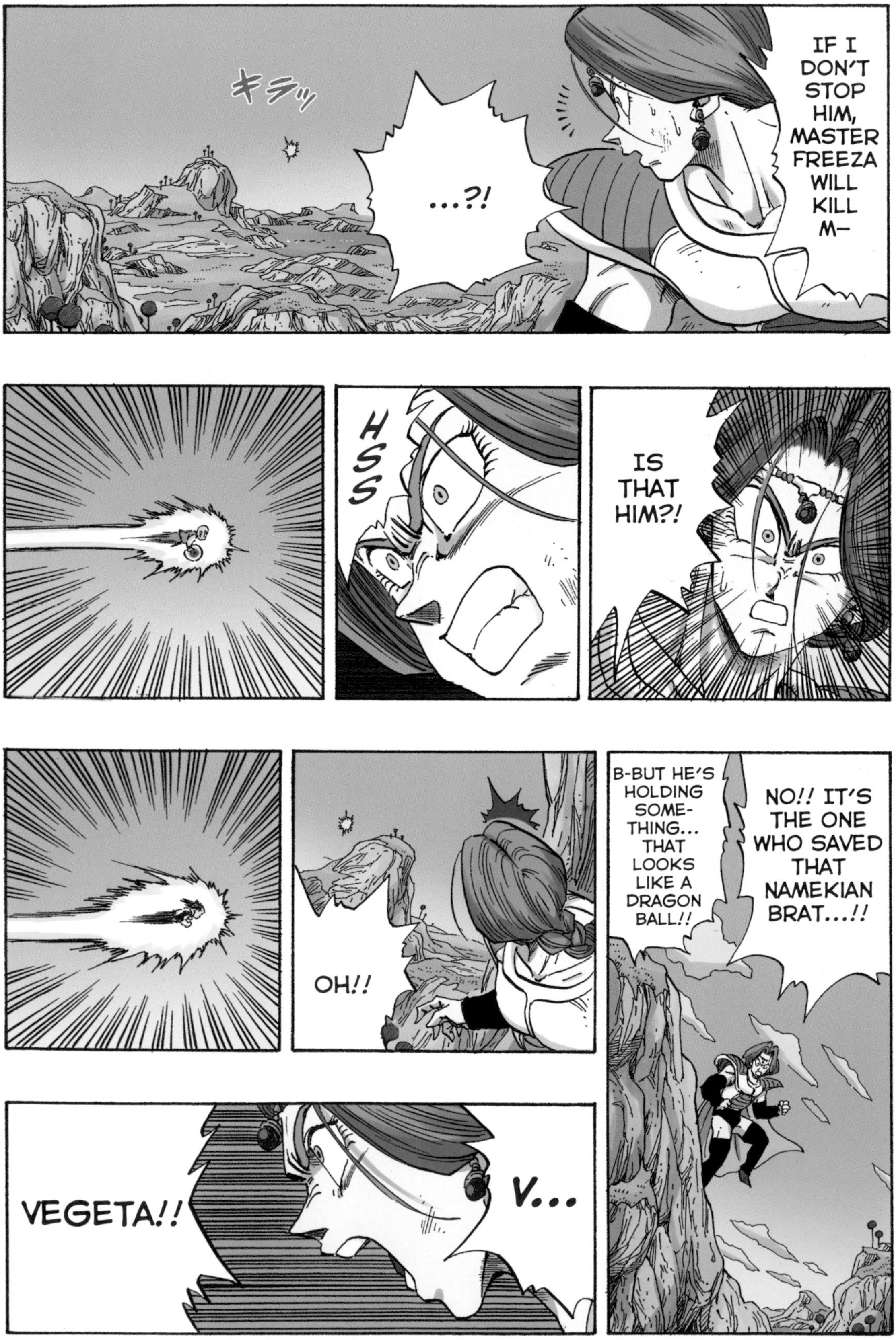
IF I DON'T STOP HIM, MASTER FREEZA WILL KILL M—
...?!
キラッ
IS THAT HIM?!
HSS
NO!! IT'S THE ONE WHO SAVED THAT NAMEKIAN BRAT...!!
B-BUT HE'S HOLDING SOME-THING... THAT LOOKS LIKE A DRAGON BALL!!
OH!!
V...
VEGETA!!

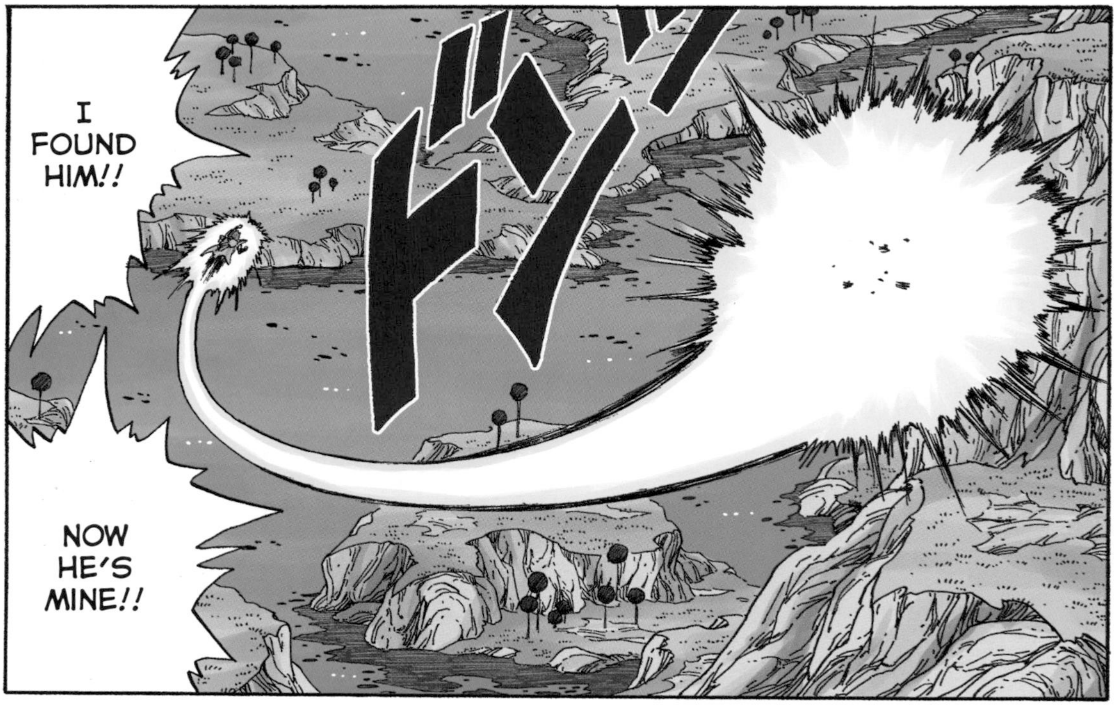
I FOUND HIM!!
NOW HE'S MINE!!
ドン
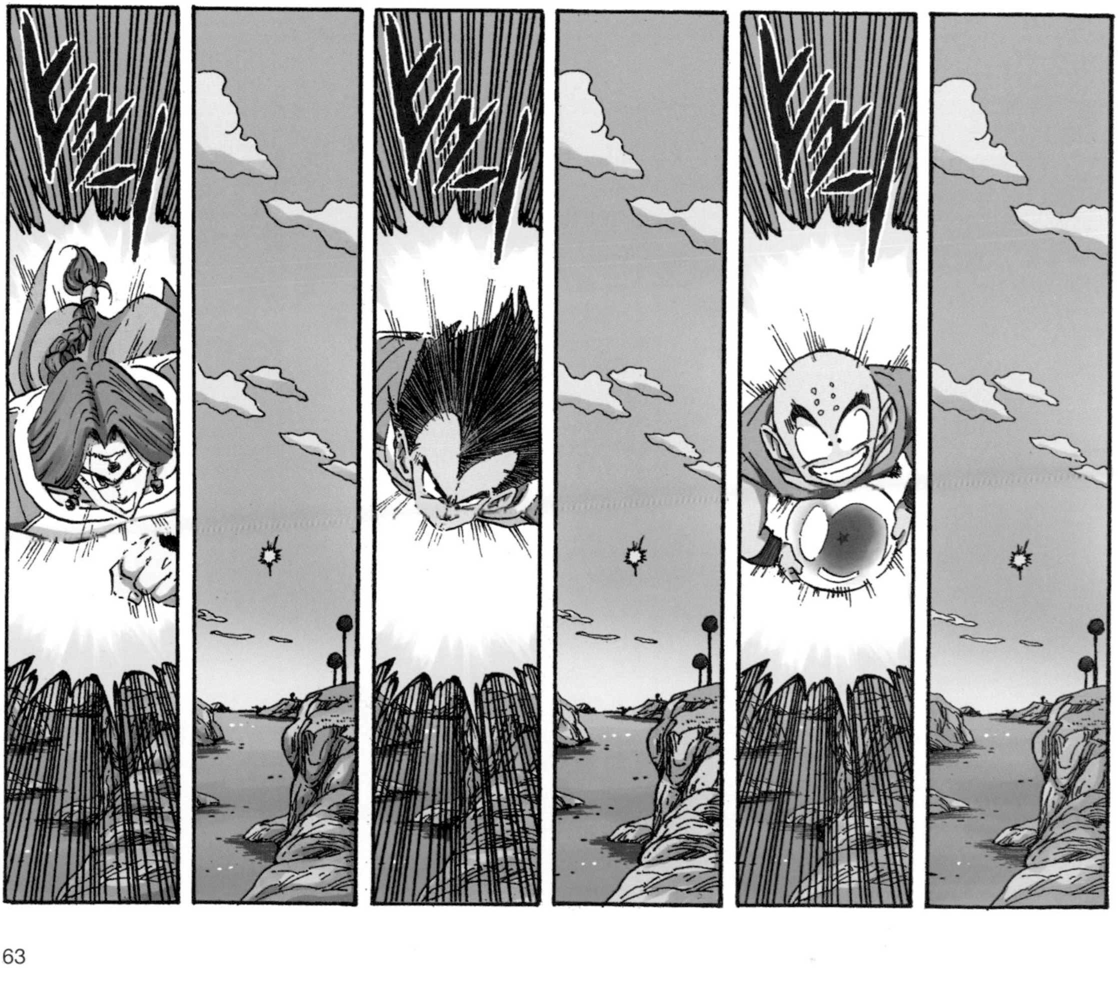

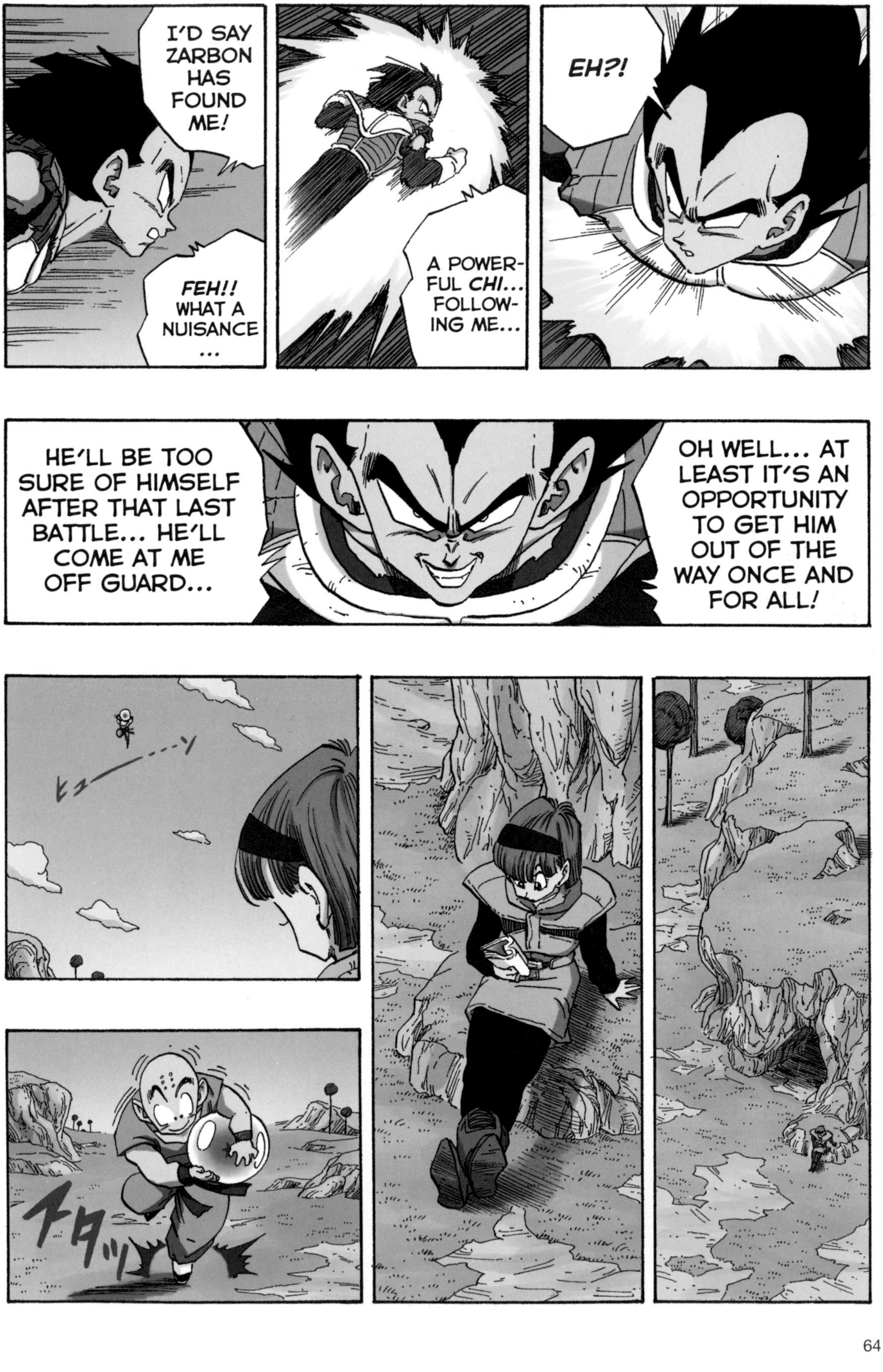
EH?!
A POWER-
FUL *CHI*...
FOLLOW-
ING ME...
I'D SAY ZARBON HAS FOUND ME!
FEH!! WHAT A NUISANCE...
OH WELL... AT LEAST IT'S AN OPPORTUNITY TO GET HIM OUT OF THE WAY ONCE AND FOR ALL!
HE'LL BE TOO SURE OF HIMSELF AFTER THAT LAST BATTLE... HE'LL COME AT ME OFF GUARD...
ヒュー…ン
タタッ

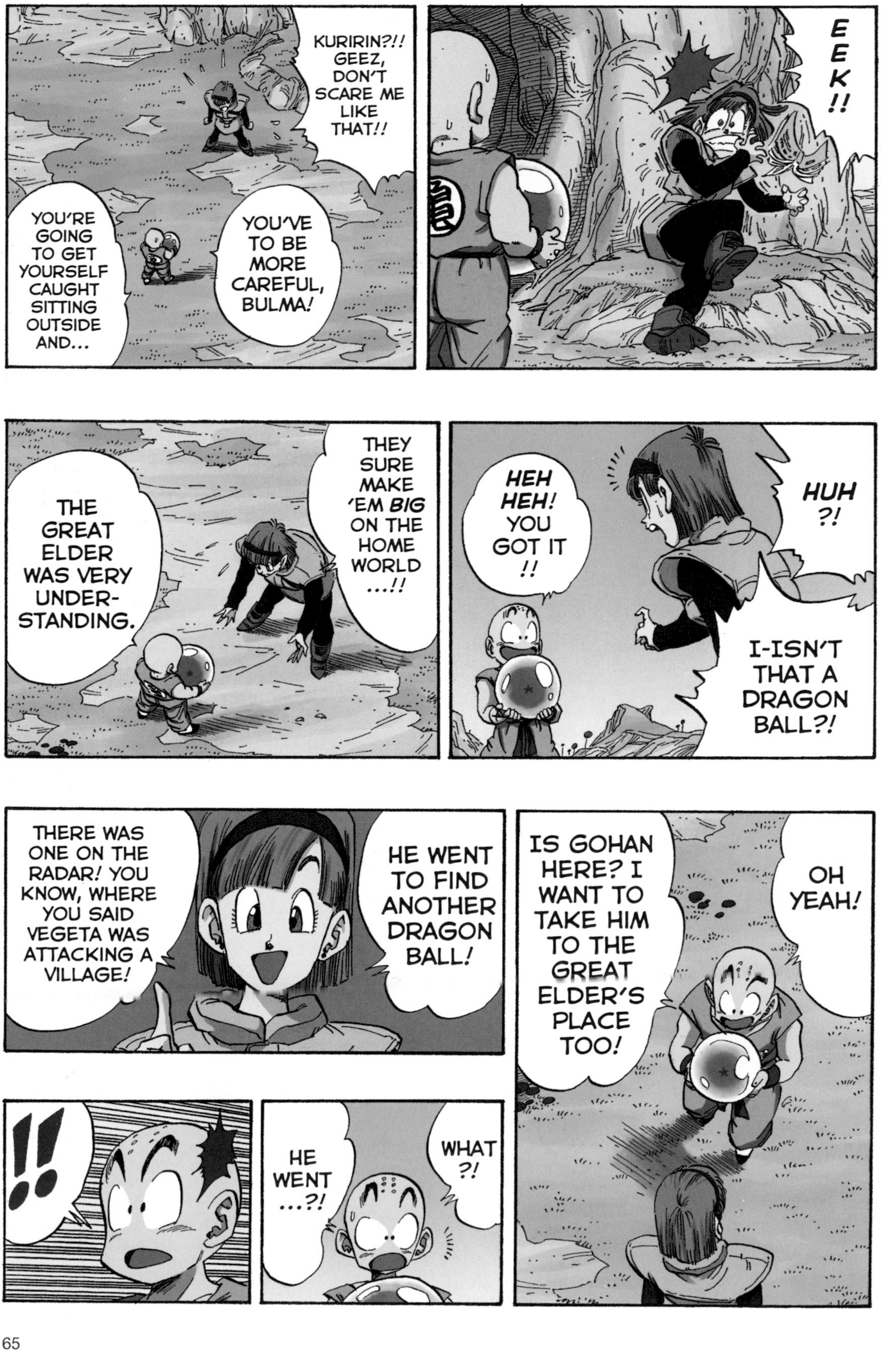

EEK!!
KURIRIN?!! GEEZ, DON'T SCARE ME LIKE THAT!!
YOU'VE TO BE MORE CAREFUL, BULMA!
YOU'RE GOING TO GET YOURSELF CAUGHT SITTING OUTSIDE AND...
HUH ?!
I-ISN'T THAT A DRAGON BALL?!
HEH HEH! YOU GOT IT !!
THEY SURE MAKE 'EM BIG ON THE HOME WORLD ...!!
THE GREAT ELDER WAS VERY UNDER-STANDING.
OH YEAH!
IS GOHAN HERE? I WANT TO TAKE HIM TO THE GREAT ELDER'S PLACE TOO!
HE WENT TO FIND ANOTHER DRAGON BALL!
THERE WAS ONE ON THE RADAR! YOU KNOW, WHERE YOU SAID VEGETA WAS ATTACKING A VILLAGE!
WHAT ?!
HE WENT ...?!
!!

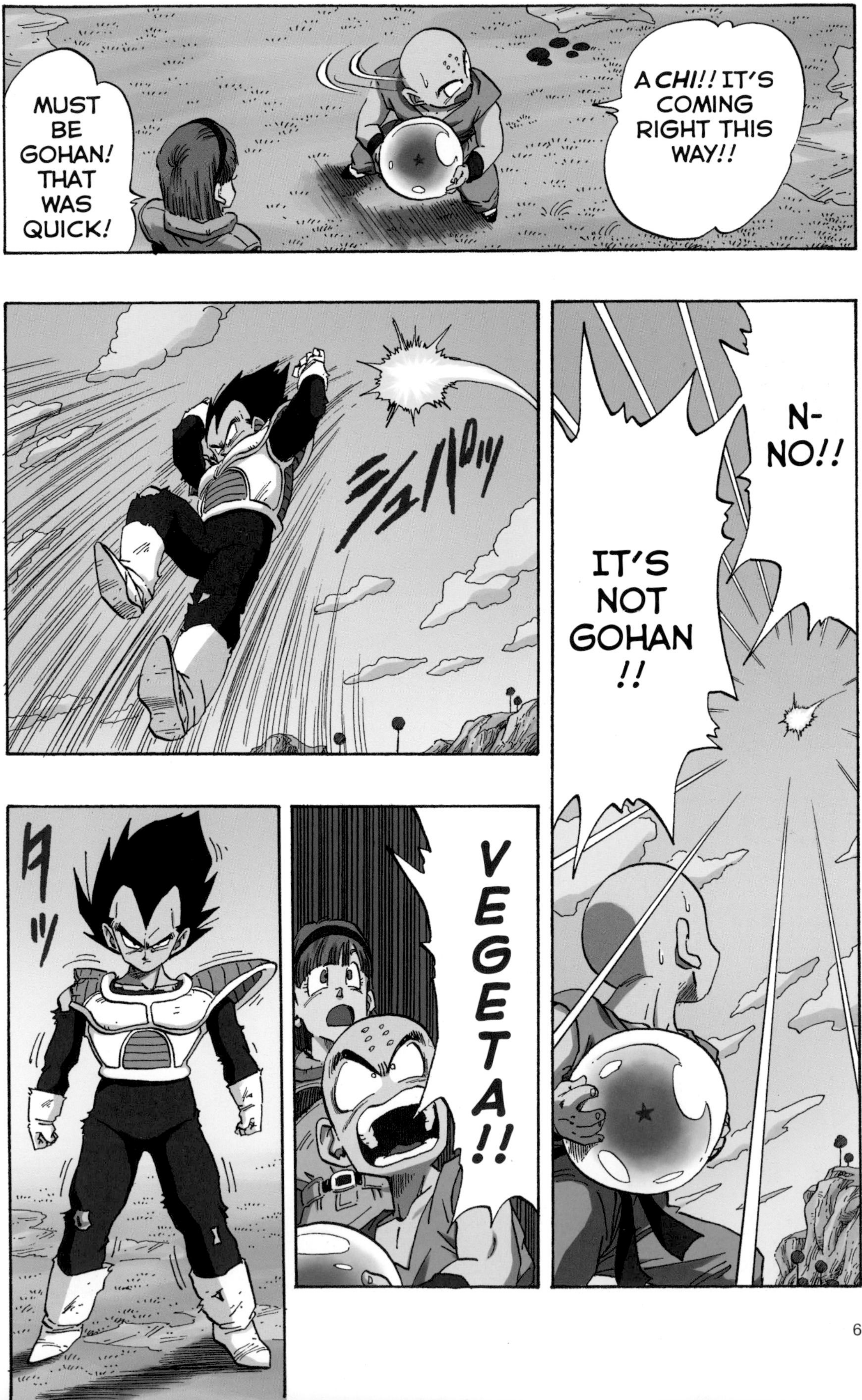
A CHI!! IT'S COMING RIGHT THIS WAY!!
MUST BE GOHAN! THAT WAS QUICK!
N- NO!!
IT'S NOT GOHAN!!
シュバッ
VEGETA!!
タッ

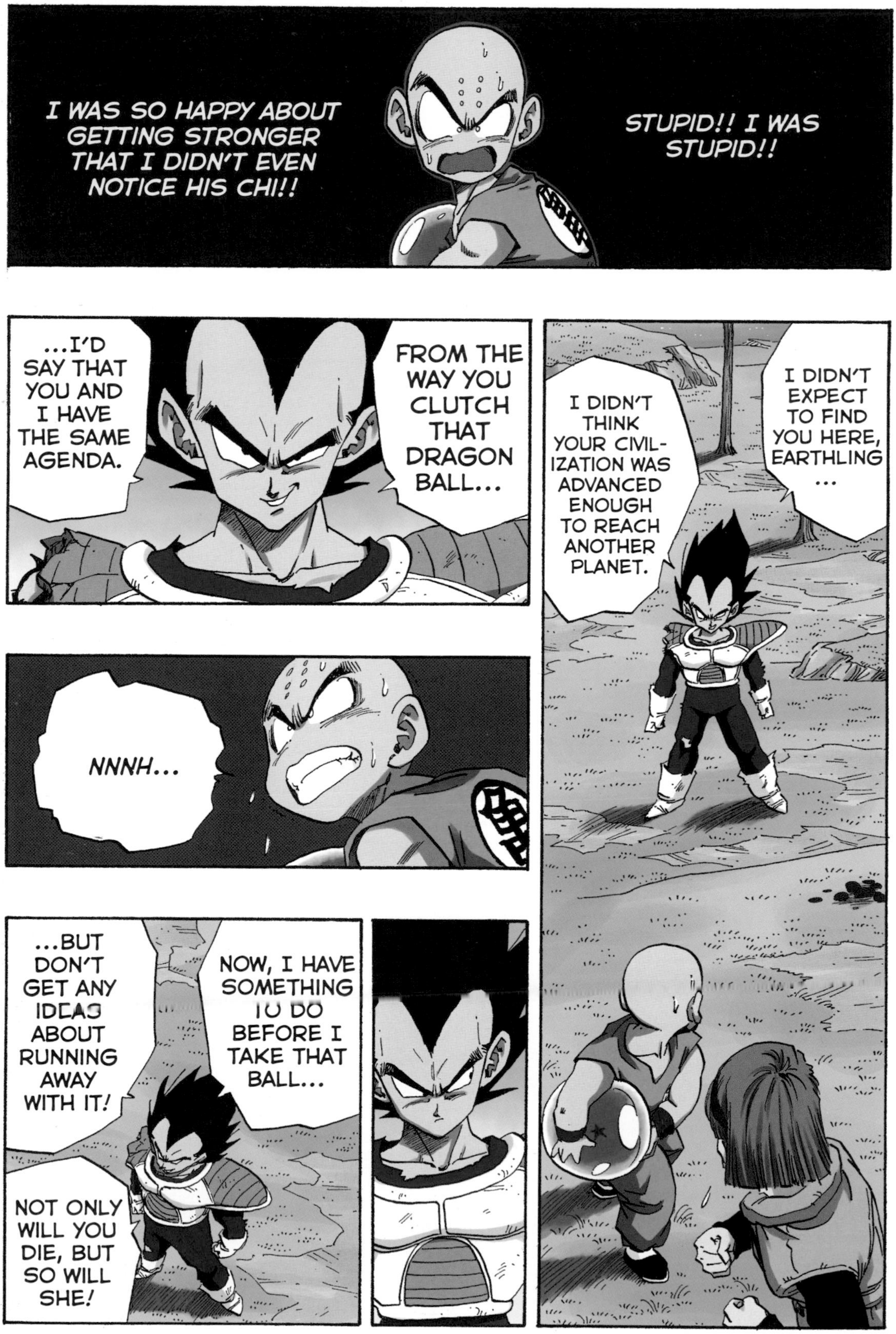
STUPID!! I WAS STUPID!!
I WAS SO HAPPY ABOUT GETTING STRONGER THAT I DIDN'T EVEN NOTICE HIS CHI!!
I DIDN'T EXPECT TO FIND YOU HERE, EARTHLING...
I DIDN'T THINK YOUR CIVILIZATION WAS ADVANCED ENOUGH TO REACH ANOTHER PLANET.
FROM THE WAY YOU CLUTCH THAT DRAGON BALL...
...I'D SAY THAT YOU AND I HAVE THE SAME AGENDA.
NNNH...
NOW, I HAVE SOMETHING TO DO BEFORE I TAKE THAT BALL...
...BUT DON'T GET ANY IDEAS ABOUT RUNNING AWAY WITH IT!
NOT ONLY WILL YOU DIE, BUT SO WILL SHE!

OH!!

HE'S HERE ...

HUH?!

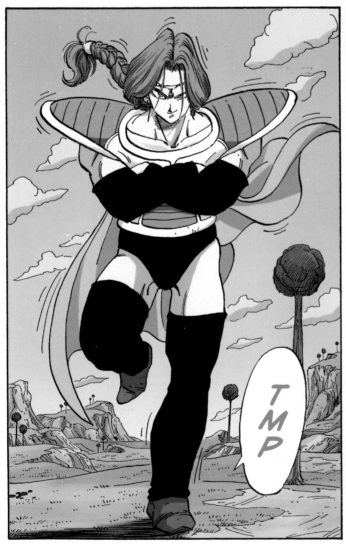

TMP

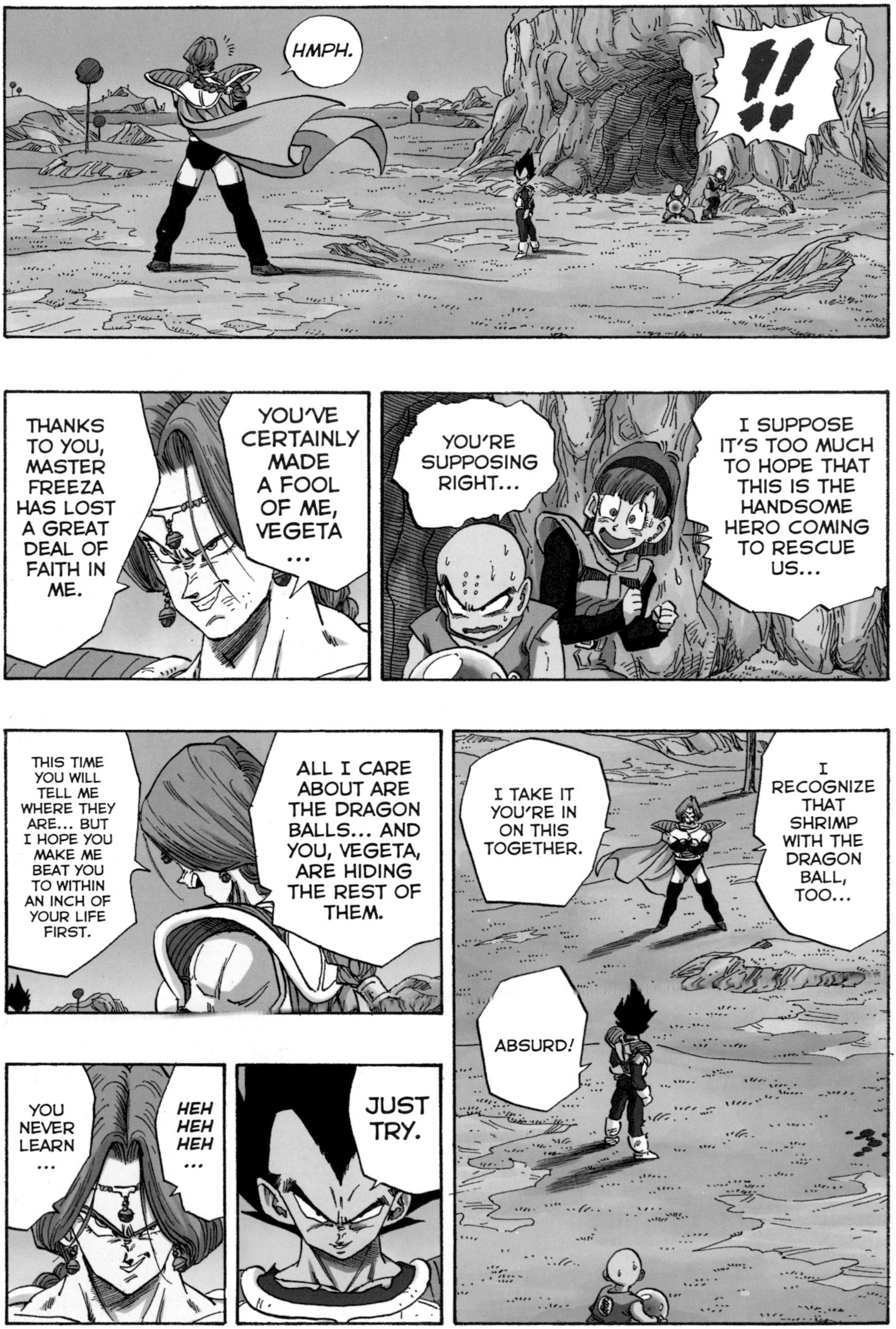
!!
HMPH.
I SUPPOSE IT'S TOO MUCH TO HOPE THAT THIS IS THE HANDSOME HERO COMING TO RESCUE US...
YOU'RE SUPPOSING RIGHT...
YOU'VE CERTAINLY MADE A FOOL OF ME, VEGETA ...
THANKS TO YOU, MASTER FREEZA HAS LOST A GREAT DEAL OF FAITH IN ME.
I RECOGNIZE THAT SHRIMP WITH THE DRAGON BALL, TOO...
I TAKE IT YOU'RE IN ON THIS TOGETHER.
ABSURD!
ALL I CARE ABOUT ARE THE DRAGON BALLS... AND YOU, VEGETA, ARE HIDING THE REST OF THEM.
THIS TIME YOU WILL TELL ME WHERE THEY ARE... BUT I HOPE YOU MAKE ME BEAT YOU TO WITHIN AN INCH OF YOUR LIFE FIRST.
JUST TRY.
HEH HEH HEH ...
YOU NEVER LEARN ...

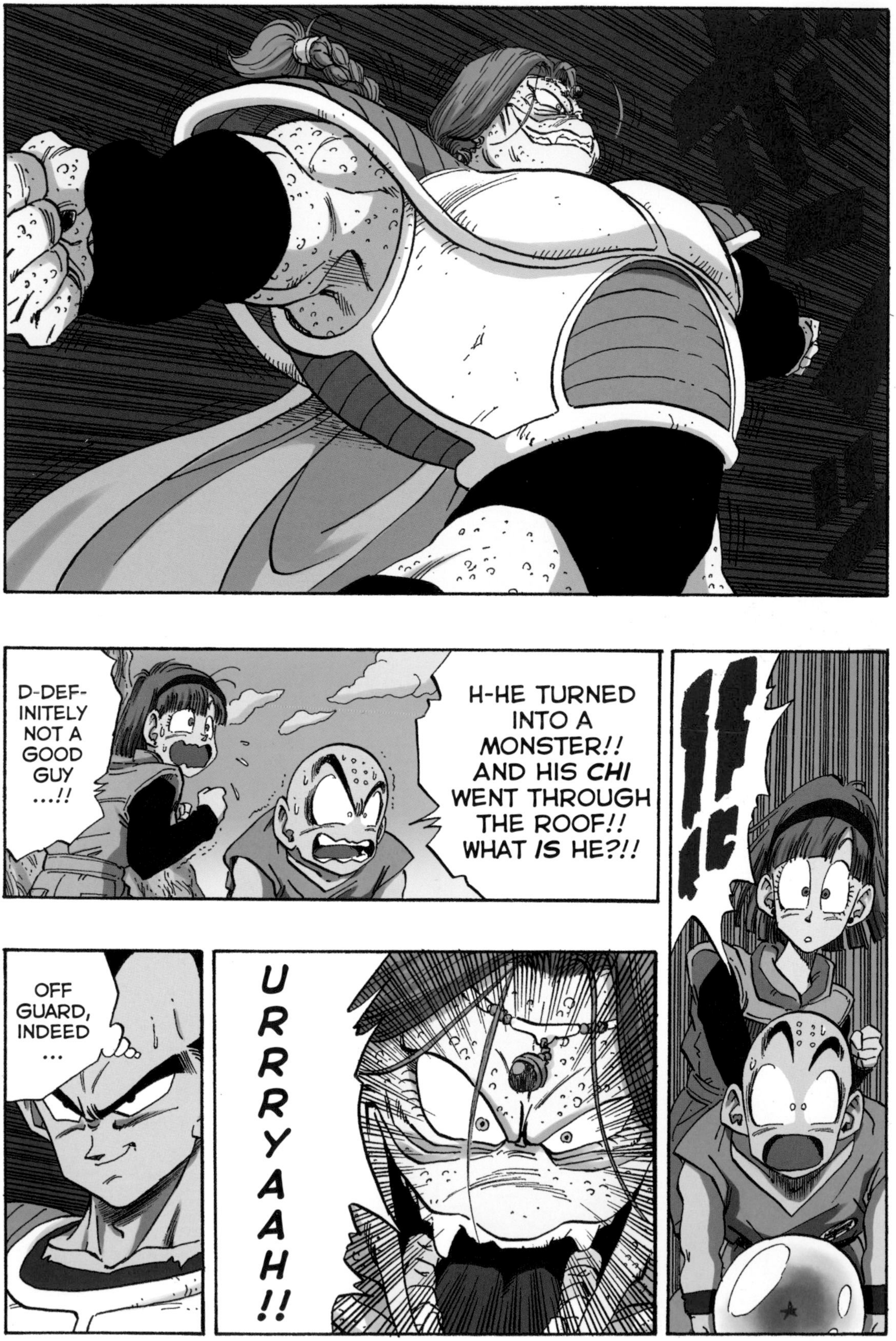
H-HE TURNED INTO A MONSTER!! AND HIS *CHI* WENT THROUGH THE ROOF!! WHAT *IS* HE?!!
D-DEF-INITELY NOT A GOOD GUY ...!!
URRRYAAAH!!
OFF GUARD, INDEED ...

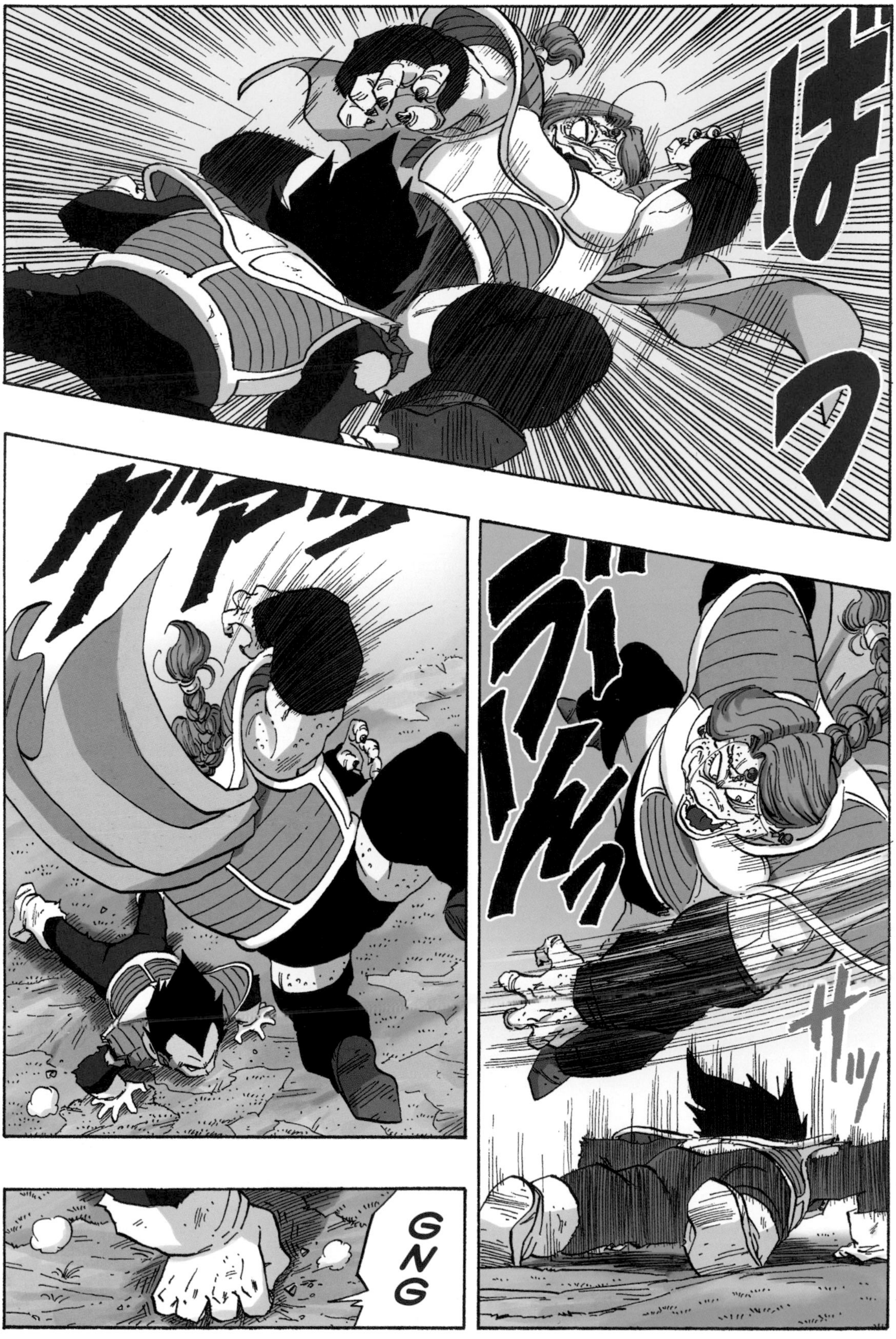
ばっ
ザッ
GNG

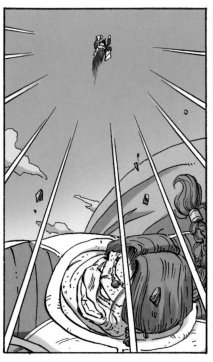

PFF

HA HA HA! DID YOU THINK YOU COULD GET AWAY?!!

UH?!

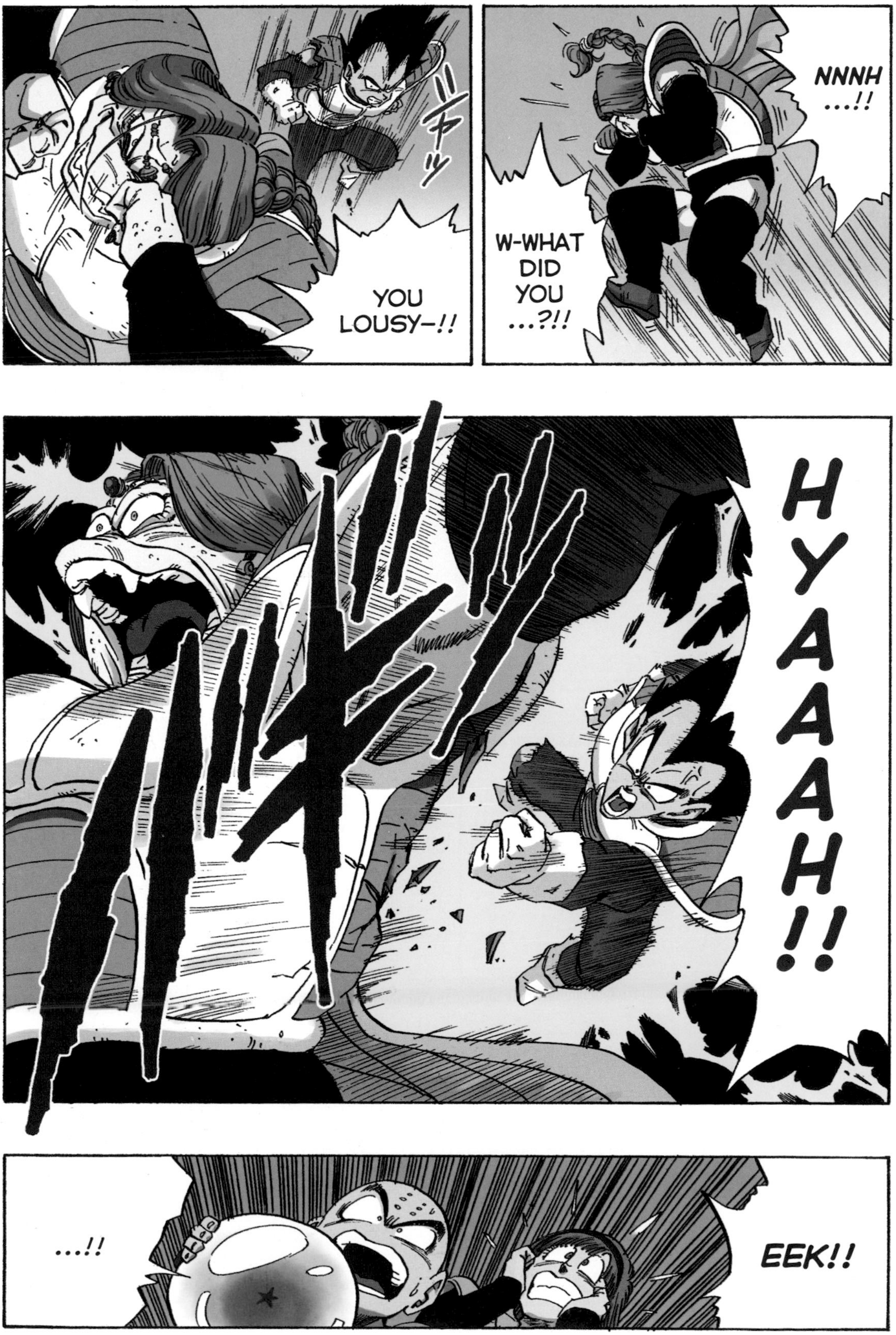
NNNH ...!!
W-WHAT DID YOU ...?!!
YOU LOUSY-!!
HYAAAAH!!
EEK!!
...!!

Chapter 23 • Vegeta in Overdrive!

HYAH!!

RAAUGH!!

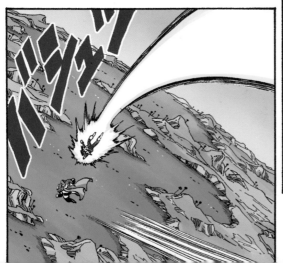

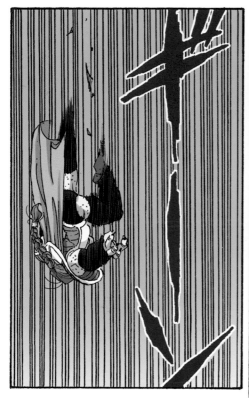

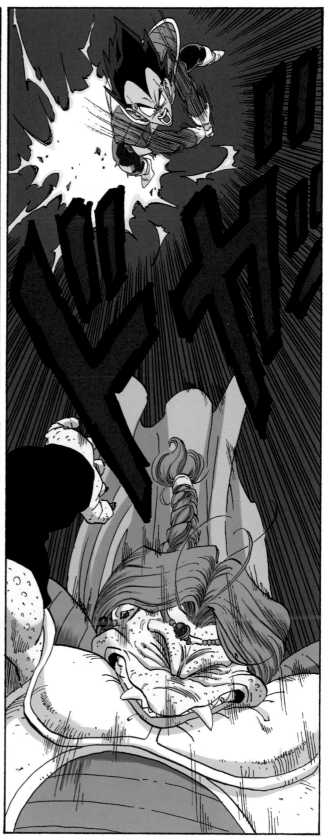

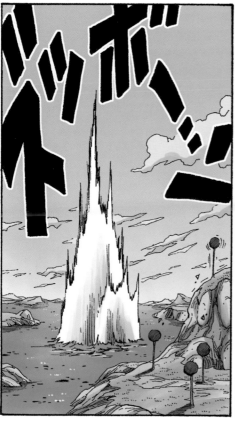

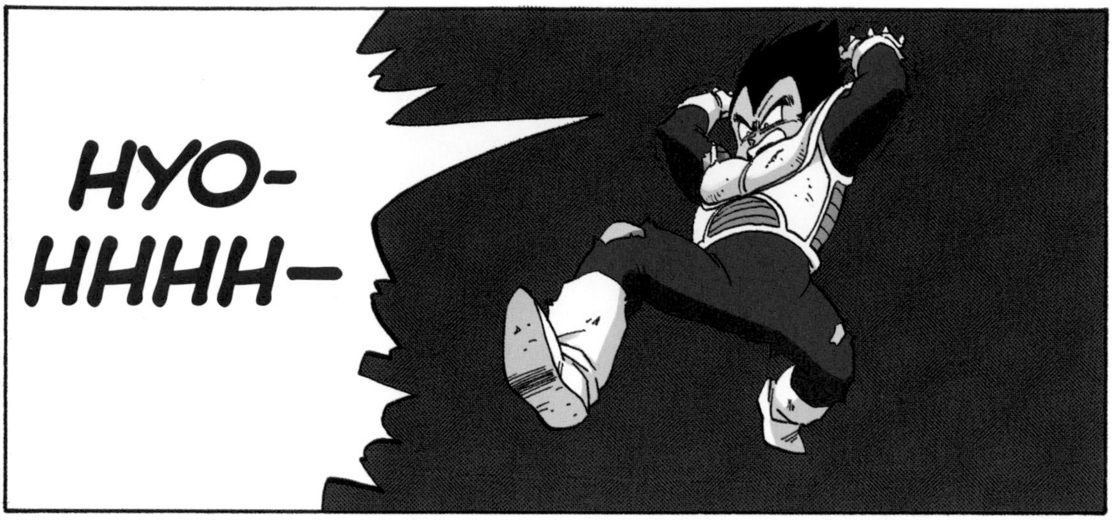
HYO-
HHHH–

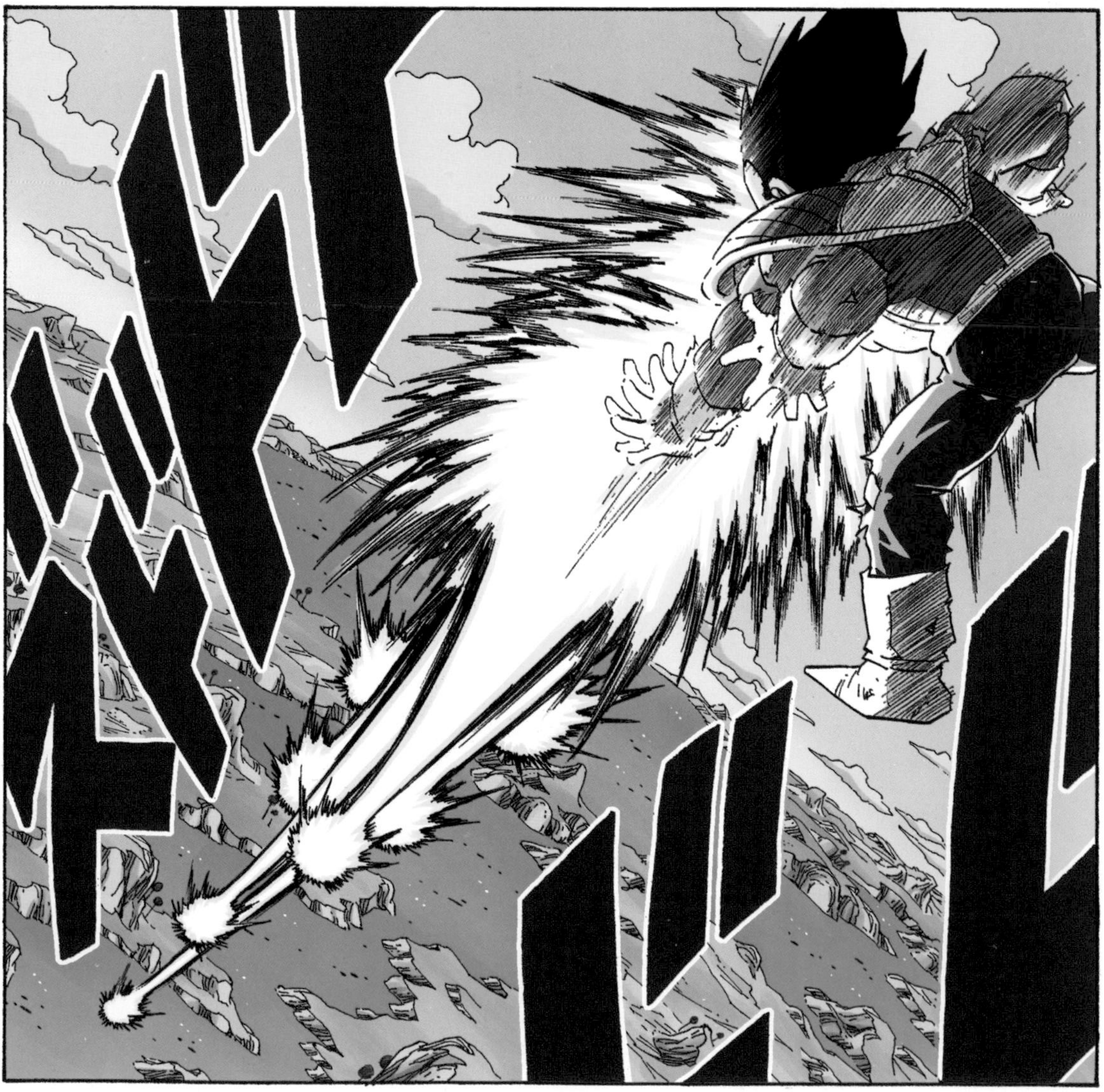

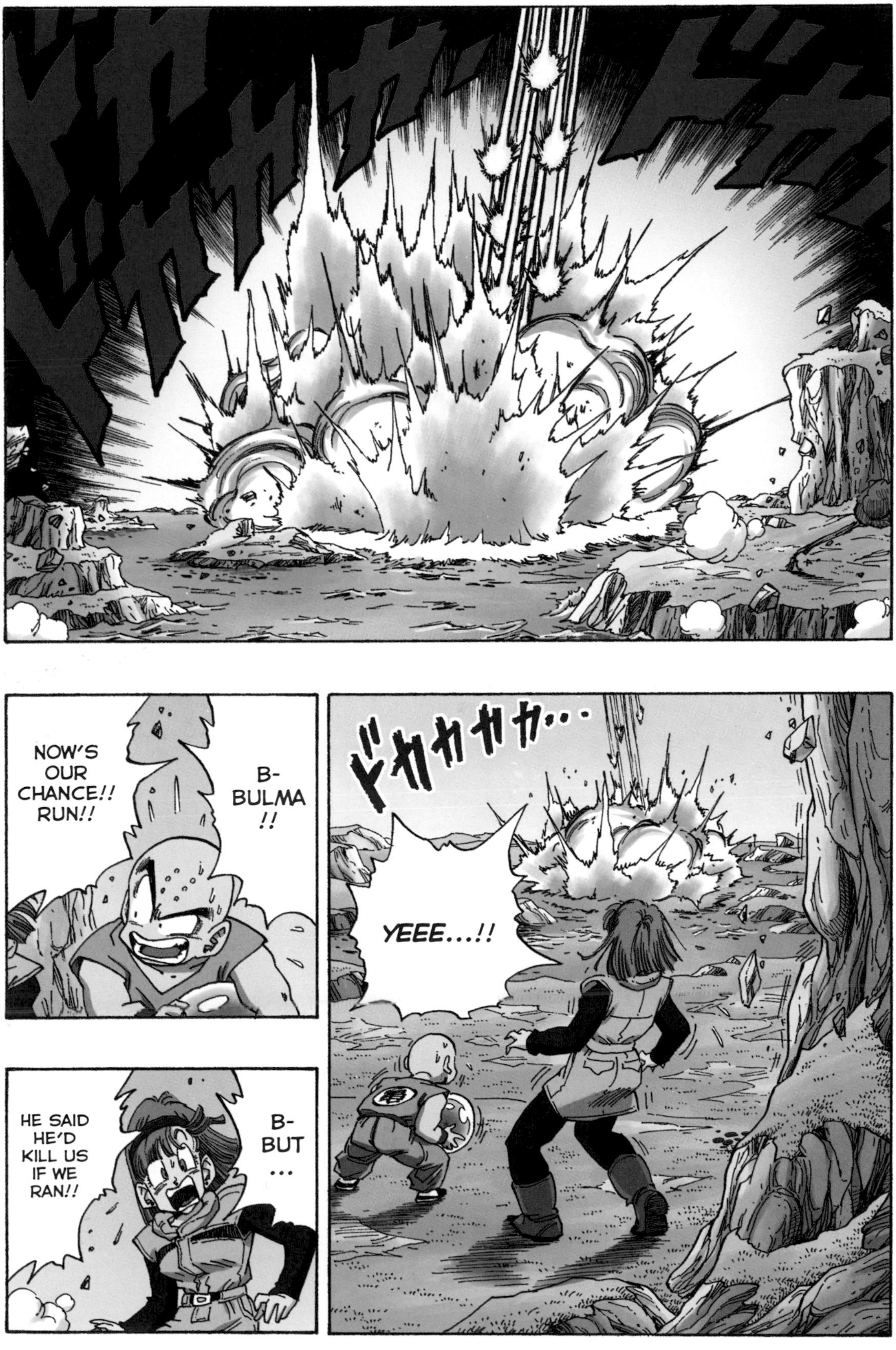
ドカカカカ…
YEEE...!!
B-BULMA!!
NOW'S OUR CHANCE!! RUN!!
B-BUT...
HE SAID HE'D KILL US IF WE RAN!!

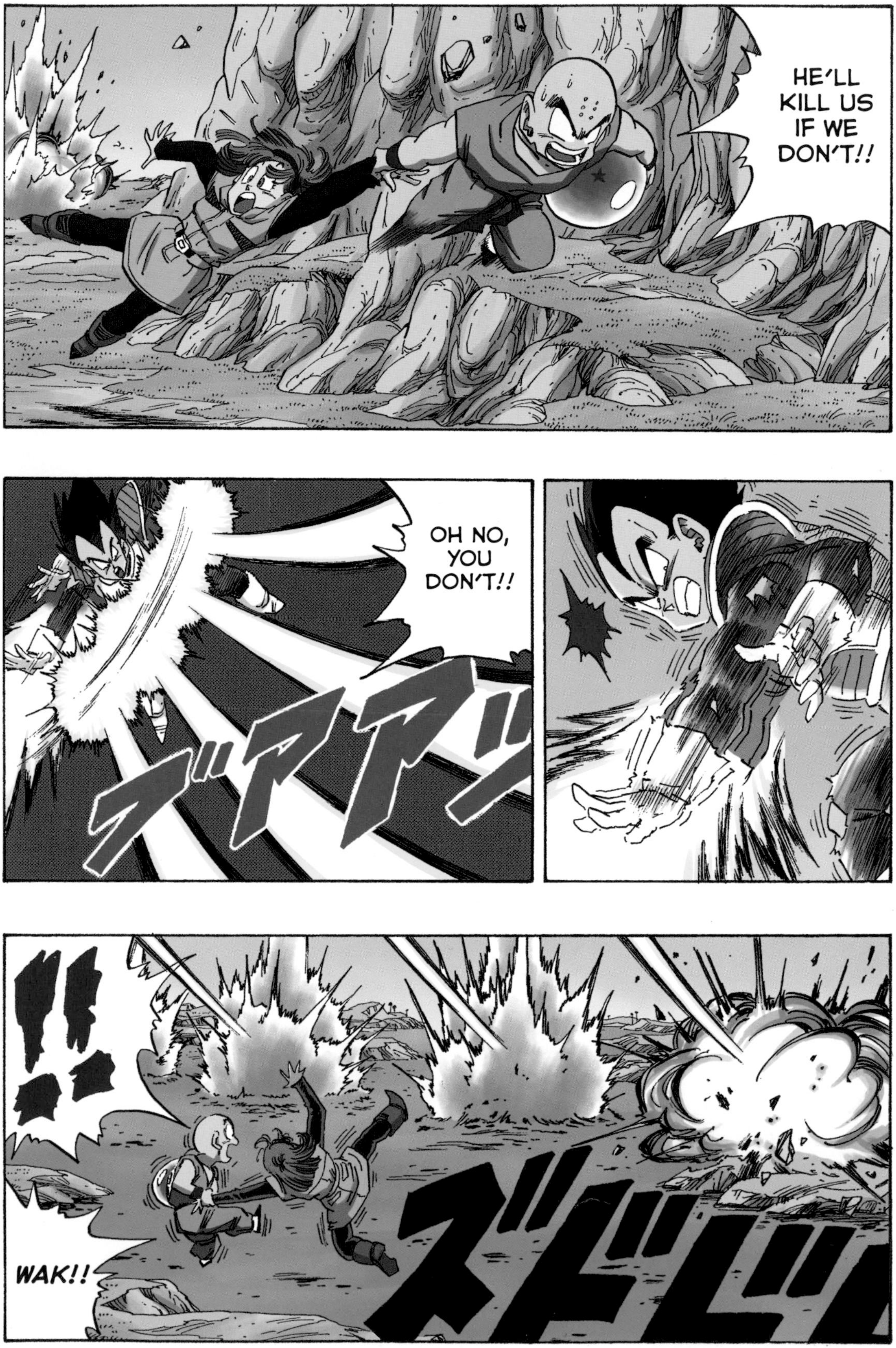
HE'LL KILL US IF WE DON'T!!
OH NO, YOU DON'T!!
!!
WAK!!

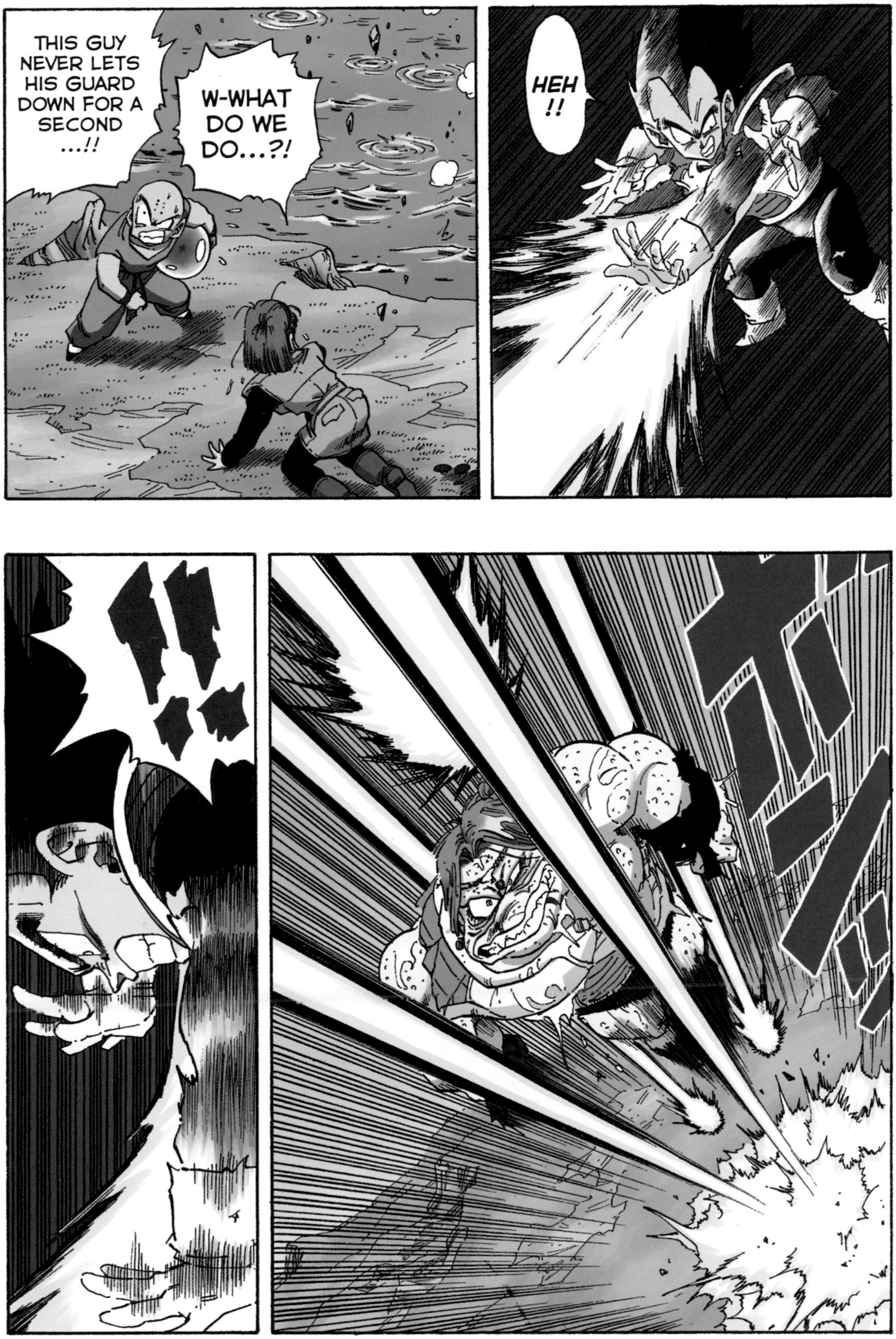
HEH !!
W-WHAT DO WE DO...?!
THIS GUY NEVER LETS HIS GUARD DOWN FOR A SECOND ...!!

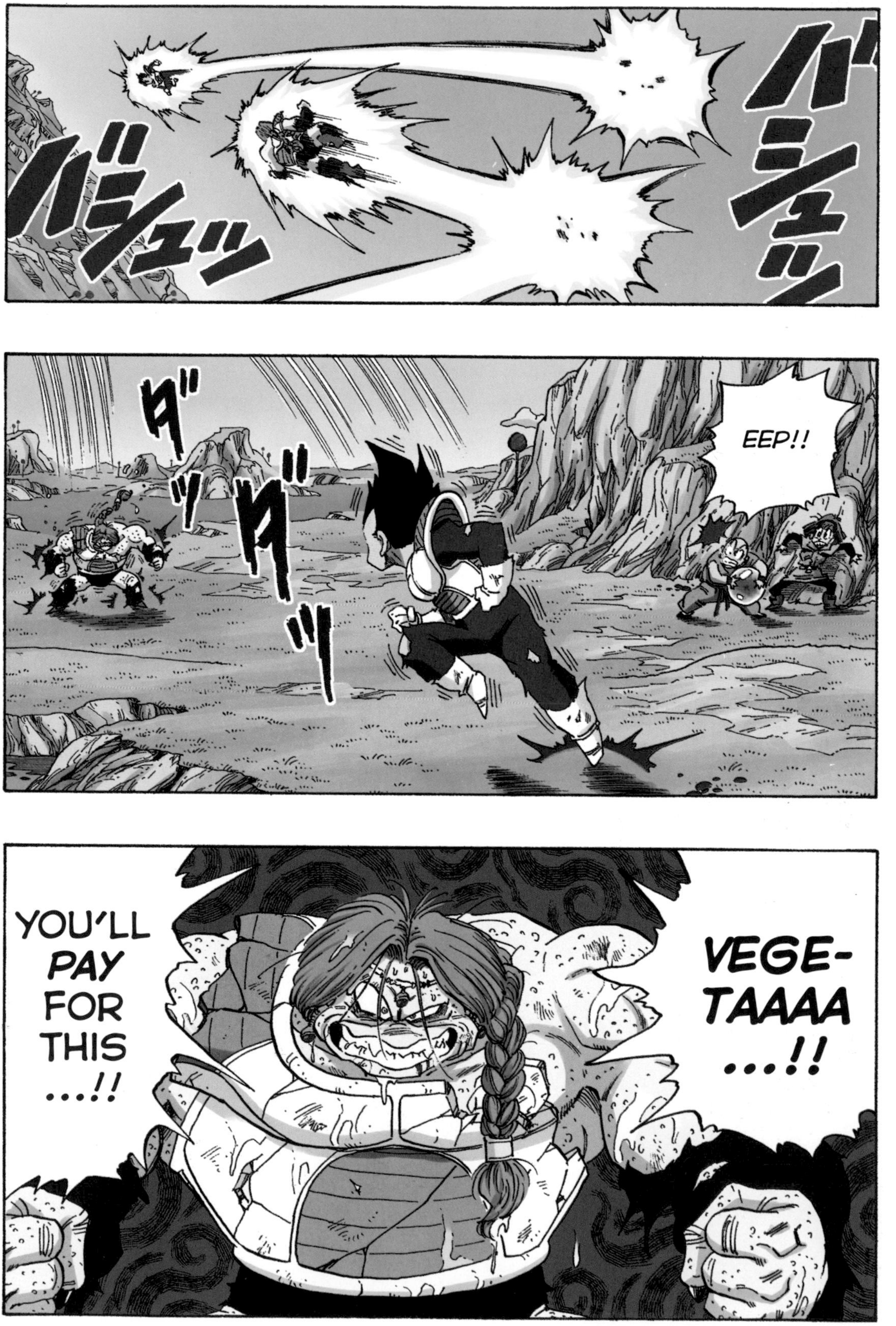
バシュッ
バシュッ
EEP!!
ダッ
ダッ
VEGE-TAAAA...!!
YOU'LL PAY FOR THIS...!!

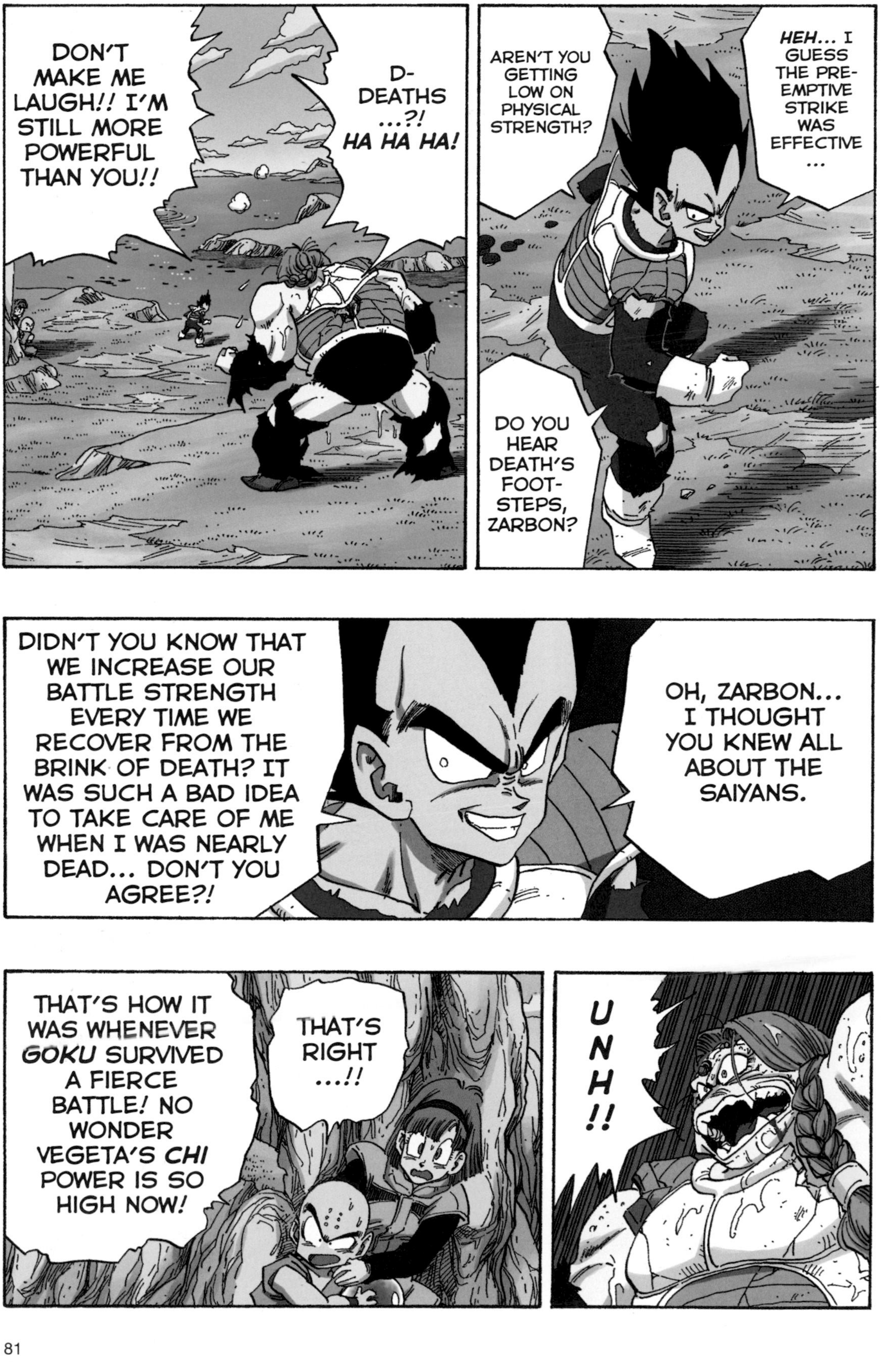
HEH... I GUESS THE PRE-EMPTIVE STRIKE WAS EFFECTIVE...
AREN'T YOU GETTING LOW ON PHYSICAL STRENGTH?
DO YOU HEAR DEATH'S FOOT-STEPS, ZARBON?
D-DEATHS...?! HA HA HA!
DON'T MAKE ME LAUGH!! I'M STILL MORE POWERFUL THAN YOU!!
OH, ZARBON... I THOUGHT YOU KNEW ALL ABOUT THE SAIYANS.
DIDN'T YOU KNOW THAT WE INCREASE OUR BATTLE STRENGTH EVERY TIME WE RECOVER FROM THE BRINK OF DEATH? IT WAS SUCH A BAD IDEA TO TAKE CARE OF ME WHEN I WAS NEARLY DEAD... DON'T YOU AGREE?!
UNH!!
THAT'S RIGHT...!!
THAT'S HOW IT WAS WHENEVER GOKU SURVIVED A FIERCE BATTLE! NO WONDER VEGETA'S CHI POWER IS SO HIGH NOW!

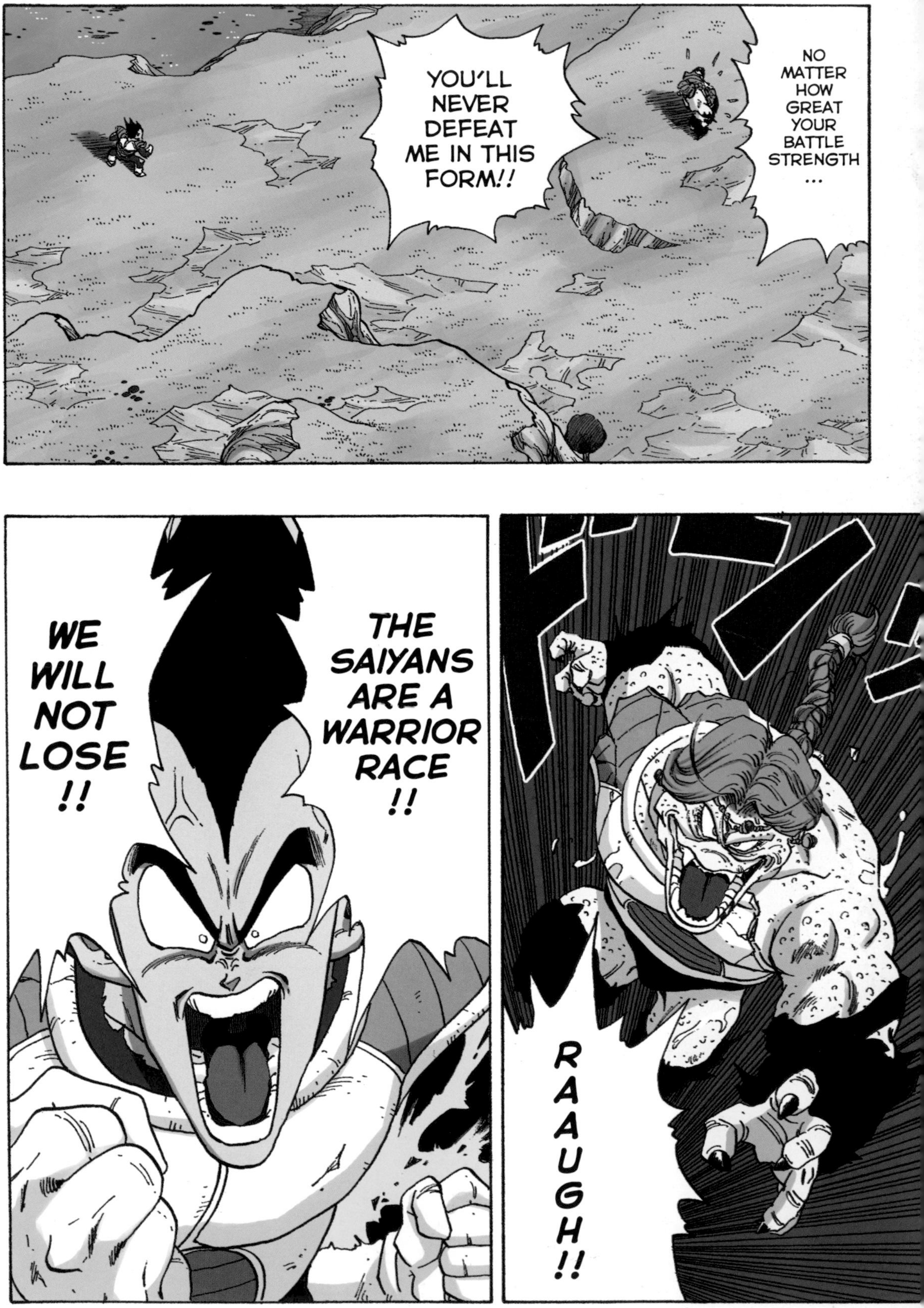
NO MATTER HOW GREAT YOUR BATTLE STRENGTH ...
YOU'LL NEVER DEFEAT ME IN THIS FORM!!
RAAAUGH!!
THE SAIYANS ARE A WARRIOR RACE!!
WE WILL NOT LOSE!!

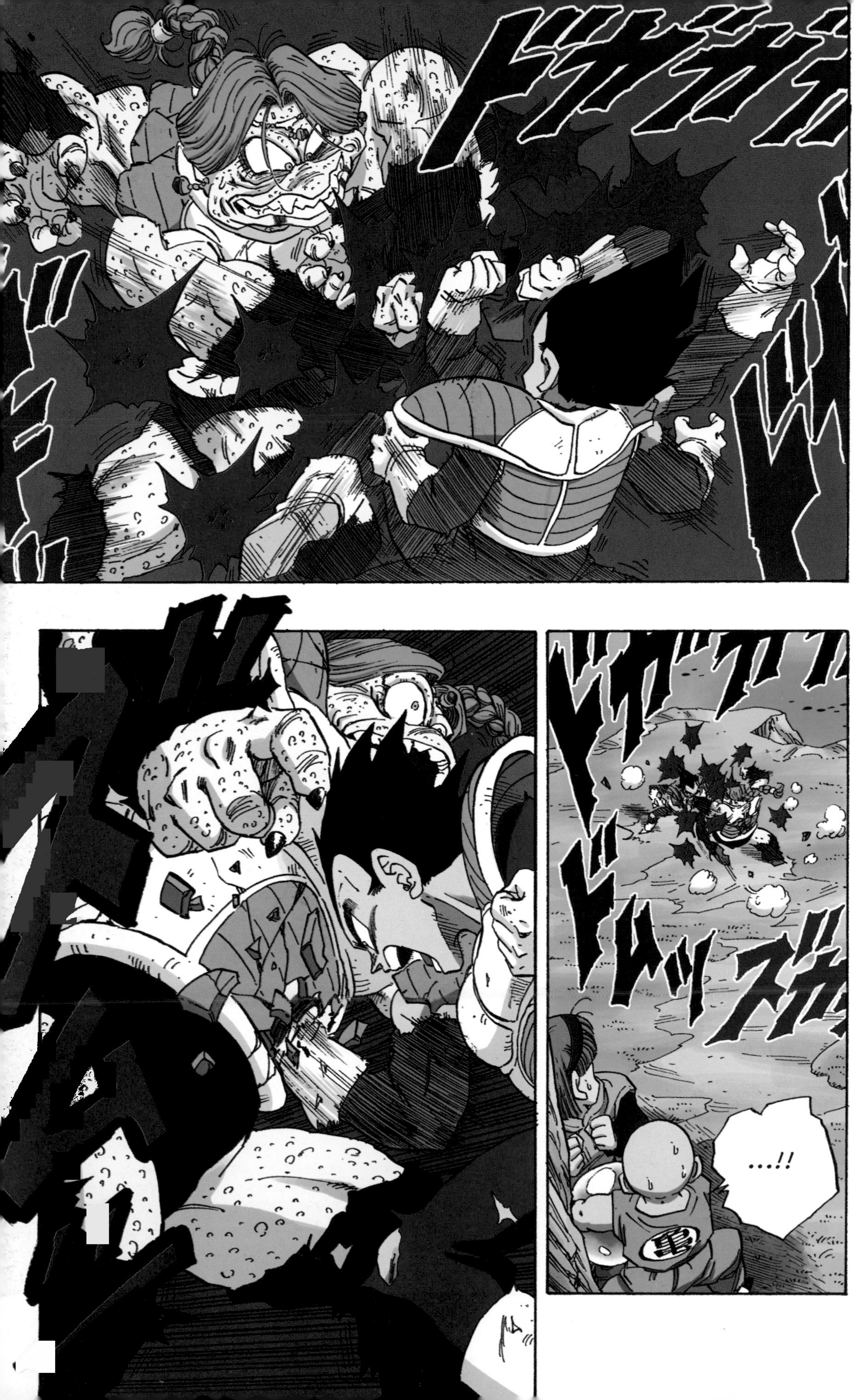
...!!

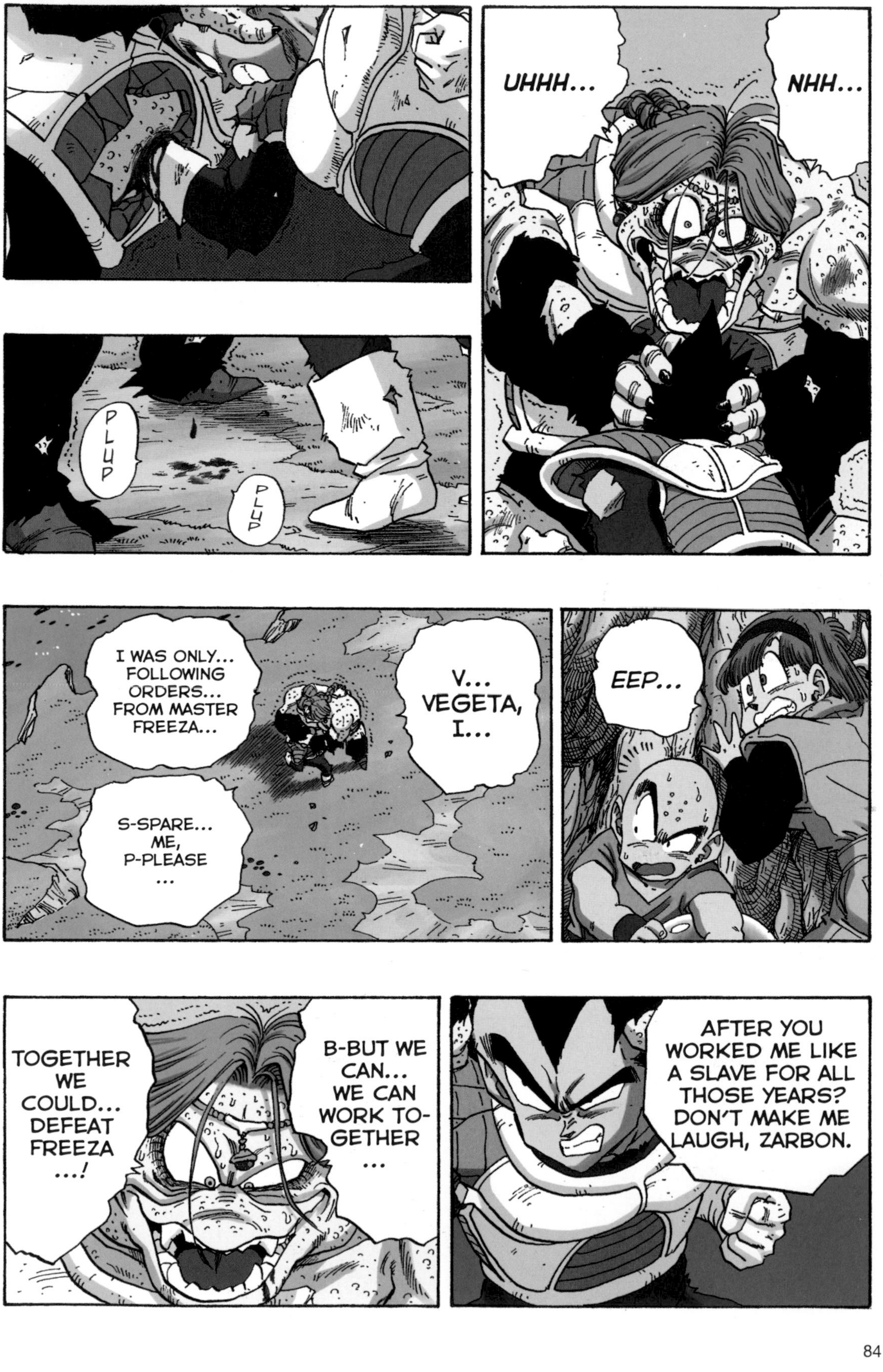
PLUP
PLUP
UHHH...
NHH...
V... VEGETA, I...
I WAS ONLY... FOLLOWING ORDERS... FROM MASTER FREEZA...
S-SPARE... ME, P-PLEASE ...
EEP...
B-BUT WE CAN... WE CAN WORK TO-GETHER ...
TOGETHER WE COULD... DEFEAT FREEZA ...!
AFTER YOU WORKED ME LIKE A SLAVE FOR ALL THOSE YEARS? DON'T MAKE ME LAUGH, ZARBON.

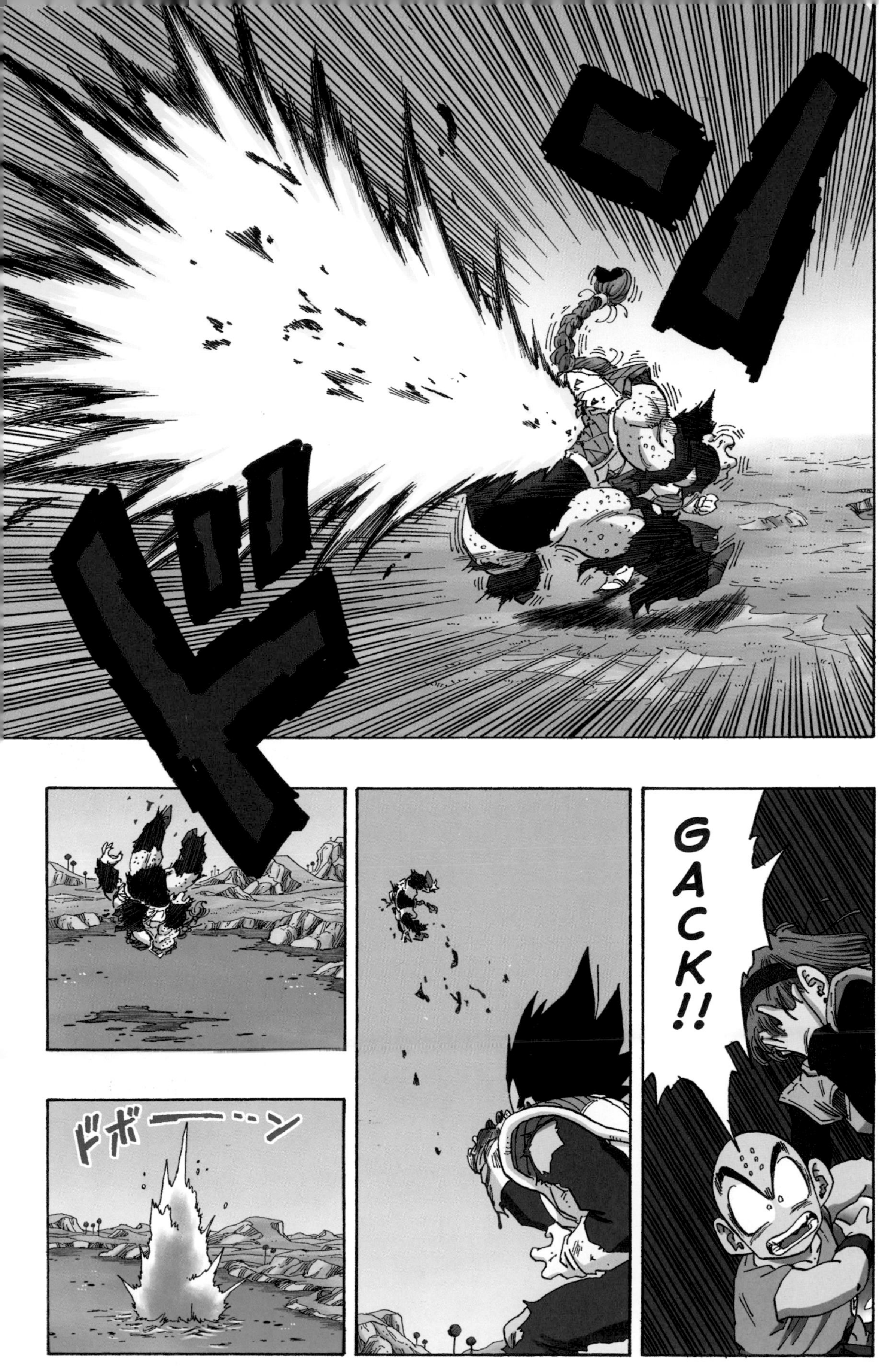
ドン
GACK!!
ドボーー‥ン

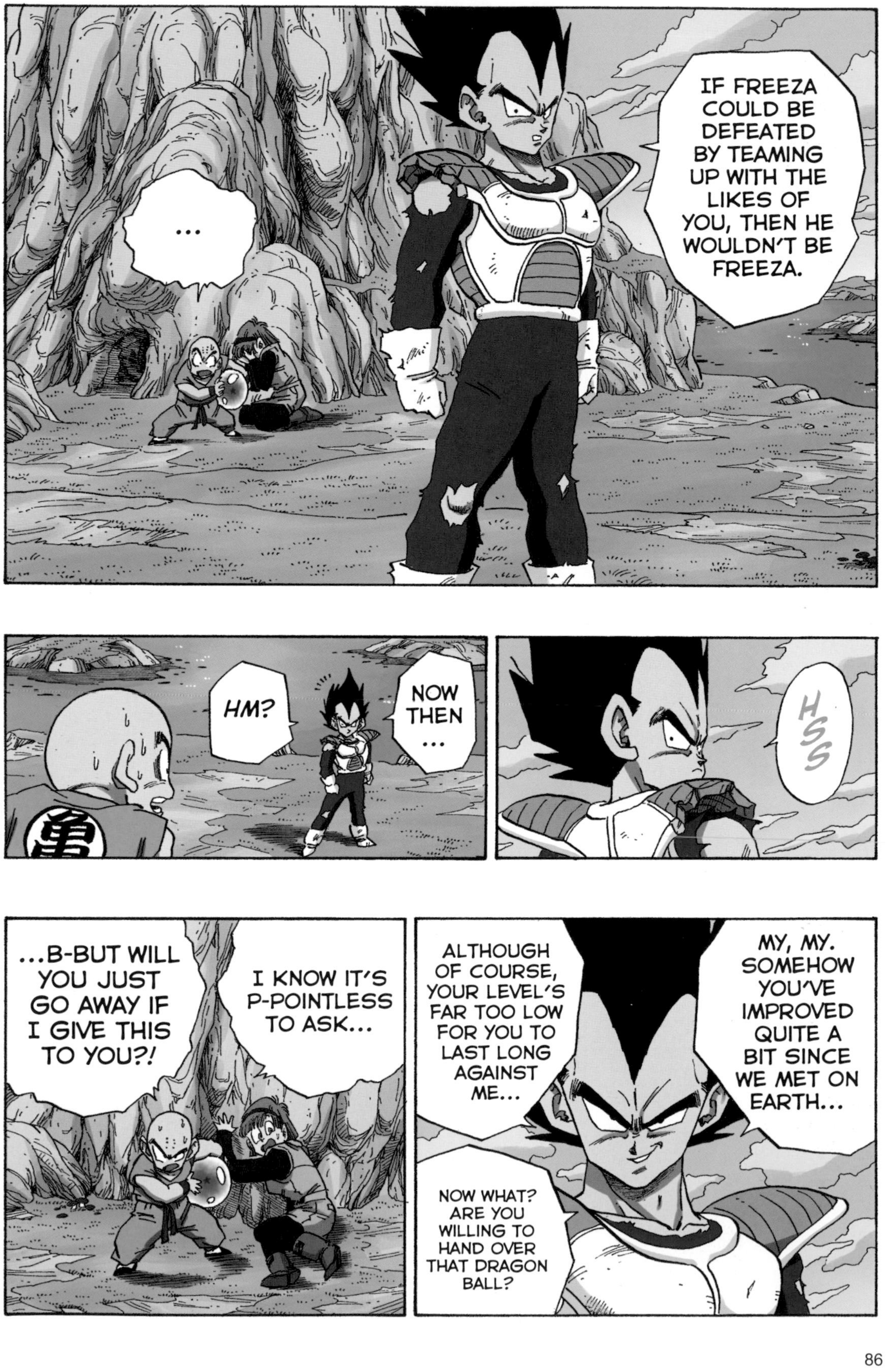
IF FREEZA COULD BE DEFEATED BY TEAMING UP WITH THE LIKES OF YOU, THEN HE WOULDN'T BE FREEZA.
...
HSS
NOW THEN ...
HM?
MY, MY. SOMEHOW YOU'VE IMPROVED QUITE A BIT SINCE WE MET ON EARTH...
ALTHOUGH OF COURSE, YOUR LEVEL'S FAR TOO LOW FOR YOU TO LAST LONG AGAINST ME...
NOW WHAT? ARE YOU WILLING TO HAND OVER THAT DRAGON BALL?
I KNOW IT'S P-POINTLESS TO ASK...
...B-BUT WILL YOU JUST GO AWAY IF I GIVE THIS TO YOU?!

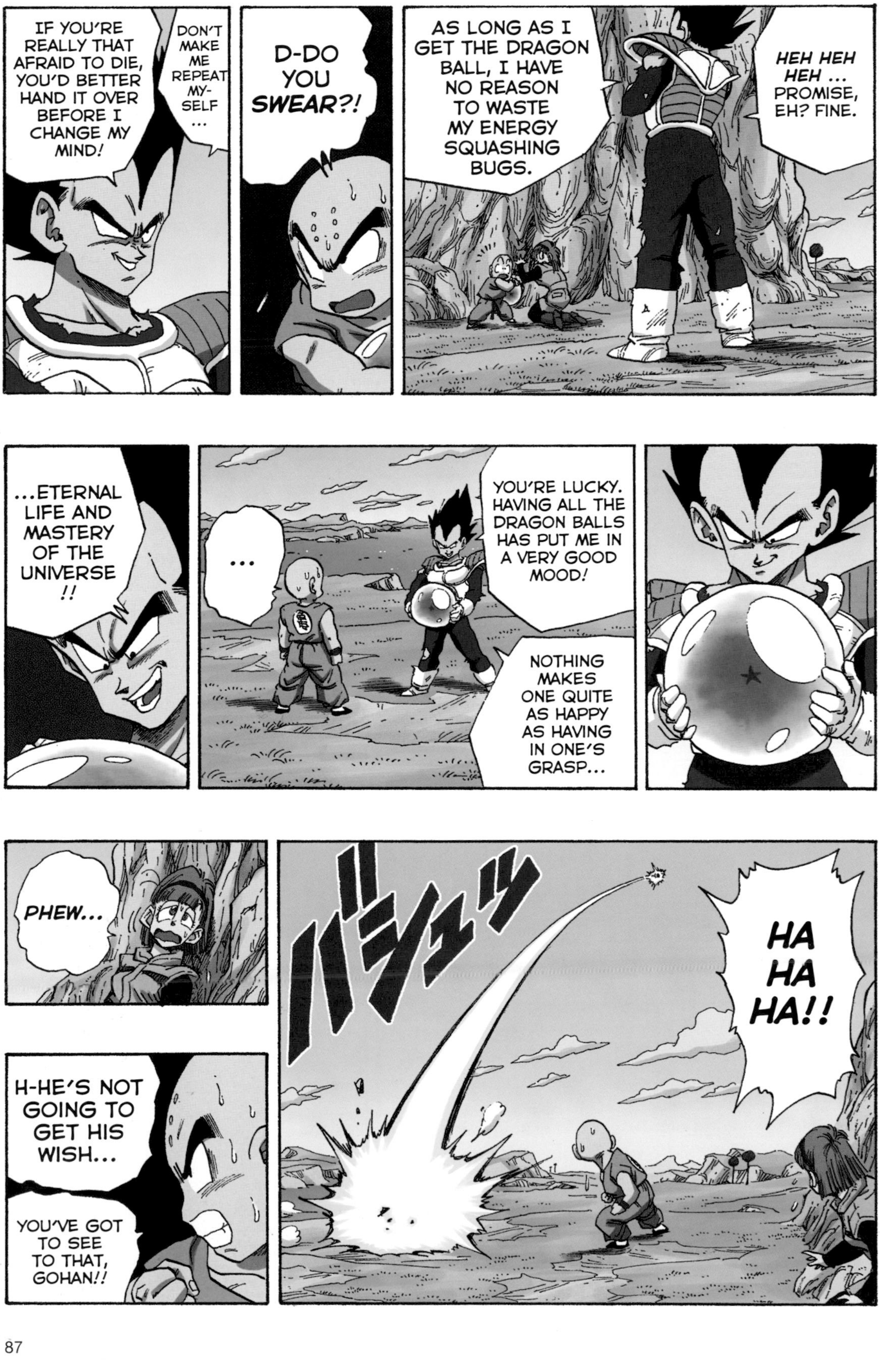
HEH HEH HEH ... PROMISE, EH? FINE.
AS LONG AS I GET THE DRAGON BALL, I HAVE NO REASON TO WASTE MY ENERGY SQUASHING BUGS.
D-DO YOU SWEAR?!
DON'T MAKE ME REPEAT MY-SELF ...
IF YOU'RE REALLY THAT AFRAID TO DIE, YOU'D BETTER HAND IT OVER BEFORE I CHANGE MY MIND!
YOU'RE LUCKY. HAVING ALL THE DRAGON BALLS HAS PUT ME IN A VERY GOOD MOOD!
...
NOTHING MAKES ONE QUITE AS HAPPY AS HAVING IN ONE'S GRASP...
...ETERNAL LIFE AND MASTERY OF THE UNIVERSE!!
HA HA HA!!
バシュッ
PHEW...
H-HE'S NOT GOING TO GET HIS WISH...
YOU'VE GOT TO SEE TO THAT, GOHAN!!

Chapter 24 • Brains and Brawn

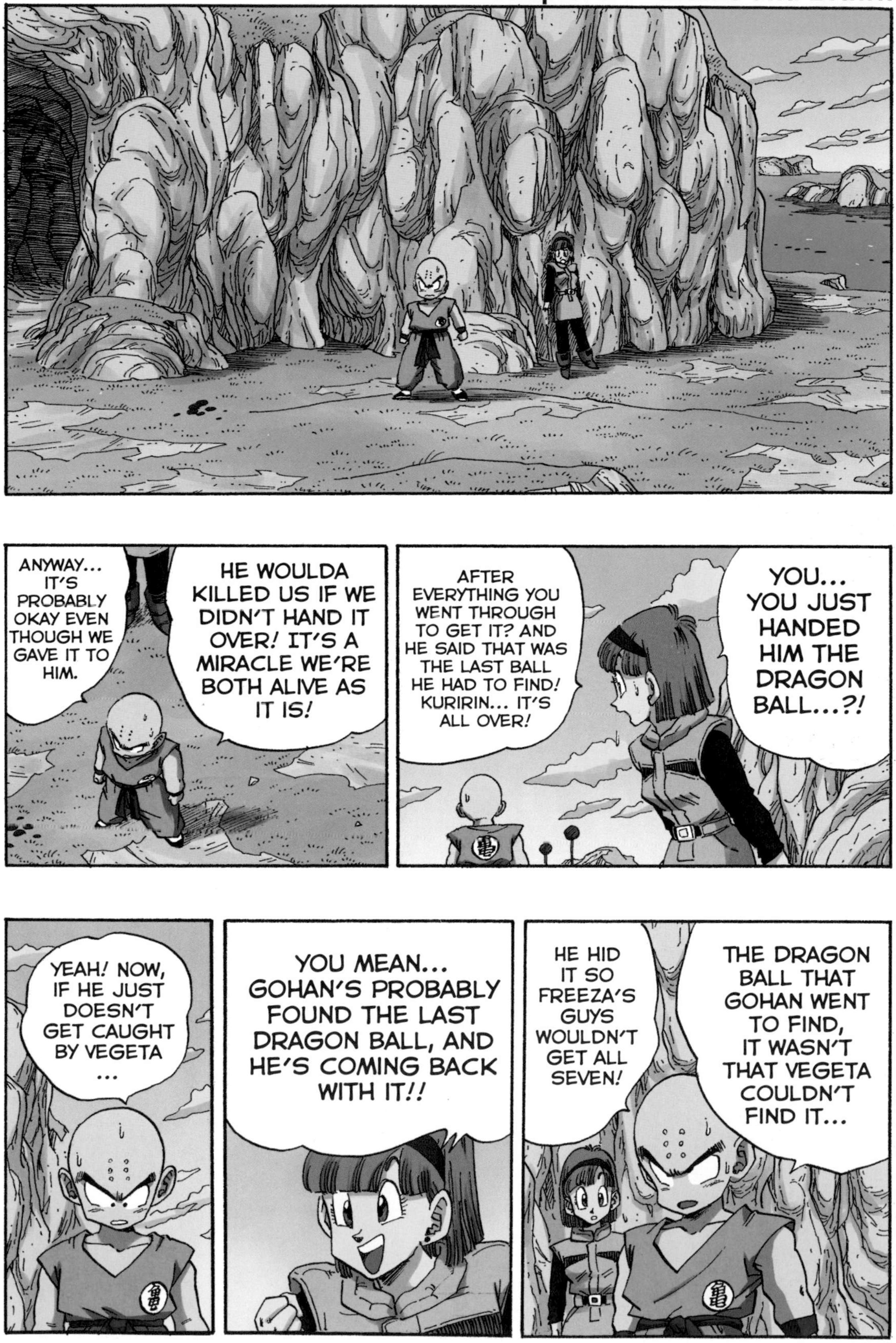
YOU... YOU JUST HANDED HIM THE DRAGON BALL...?!
AFTER EVERYTHING YOU WENT THROUGH TO GET IT? AND HE SAID THAT WAS THE LAST BALL HE HAD TO FIND! KURIRIN... IT'S ALL OVER!
HE WOULDA KILLED US IF WE DIDN'T HAND IT OVER! IT'S A MIRACLE WE'RE BOTH ALIVE AS IT IS!
ANYWAY... IT'S PROBABLY OKAY EVEN THOUGH WE GAVE IT TO HIM.
THE DRAGON BALL THAT GOHAN WENT TO FIND, IT WASN'T THAT VEGETA COULDN'T FIND IT...
HE HID IT SO FREEZA'S GUYS WOULDN'T GET ALL SEVEN!
YOU MEAN... GOHAN'S PROBABLY FOUND THE LAST DRAGON BALL, AND HE'S COMING BACK WITH IT!!
YEAH! NOW, IF HE JUST DOESN'T GET CAUGHT BY VEGETA ...

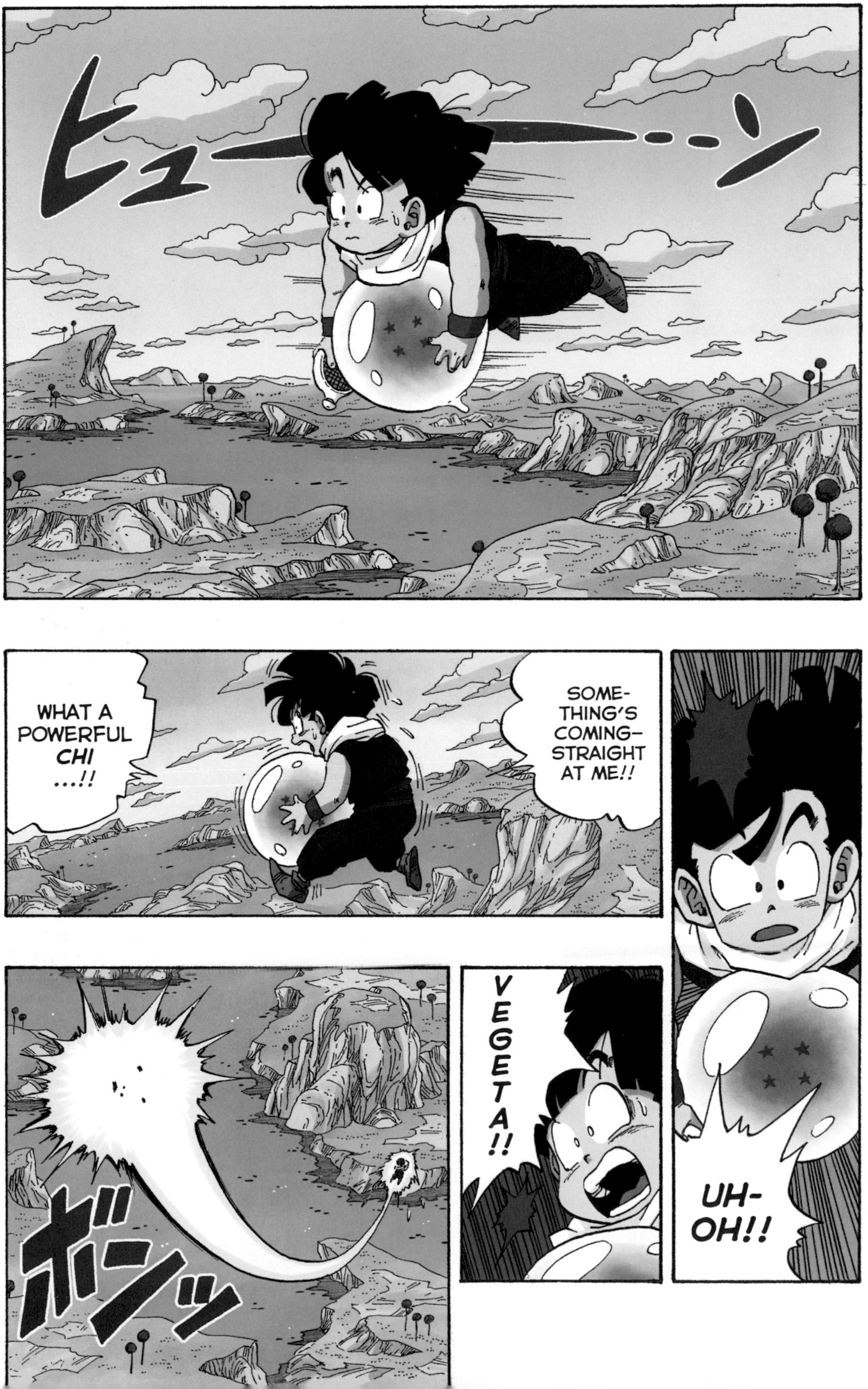
ヒューーン
UH-OH!!
SOME-THING'S COMING–STRAIGHT AT ME!!
WHAT A POWERFUL *CHI* ...!!
VEGETA!!
ボンッ

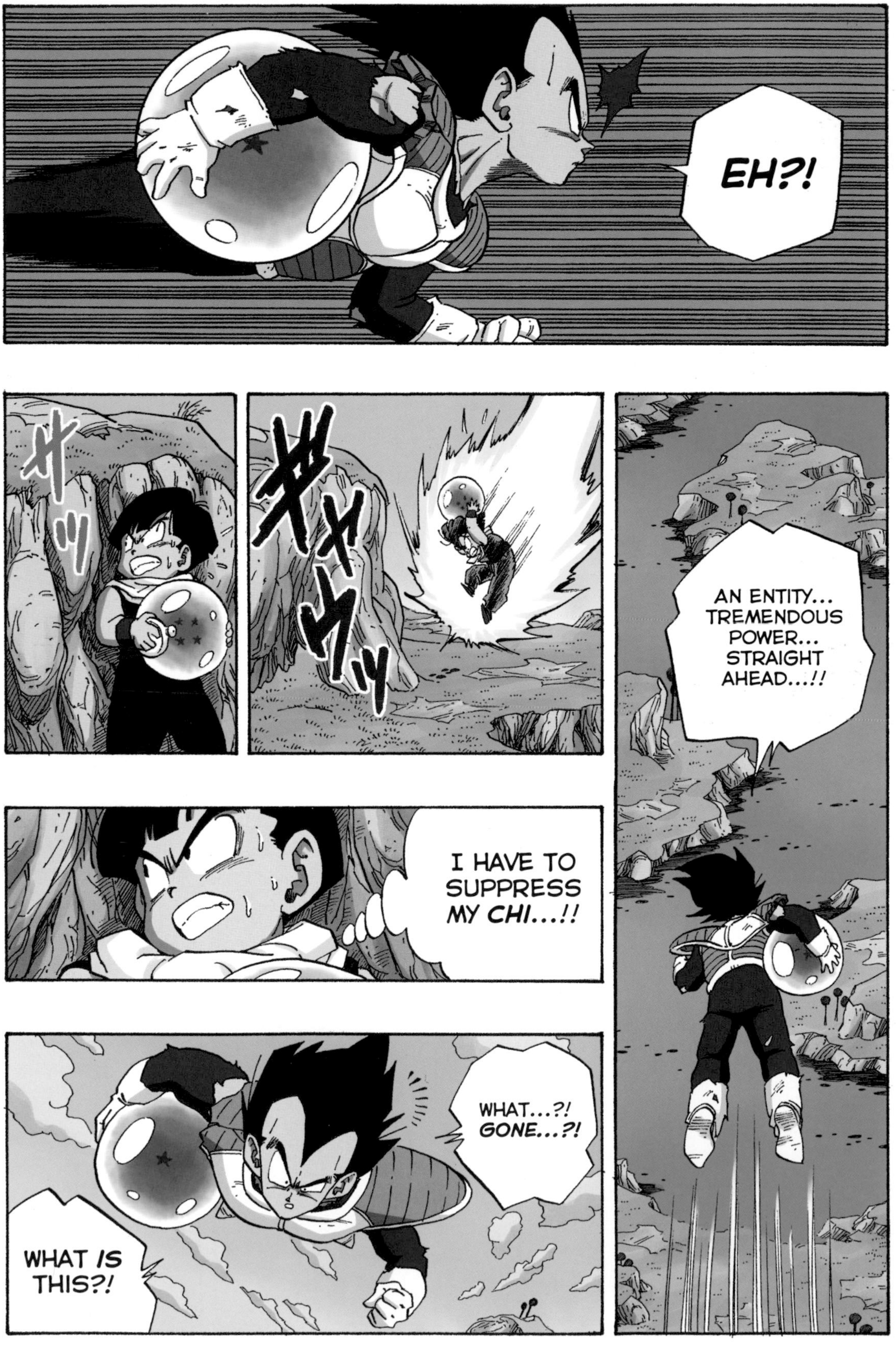
EH?!
AN ENTITY... TREMENDOUS POWER... STRAIGHT AHEAD...!!
I HAVE TO SUPPRESS MY *CHI*...!!
WHAT...?! *GONE*...?!
WHAT *IS* THIS?!

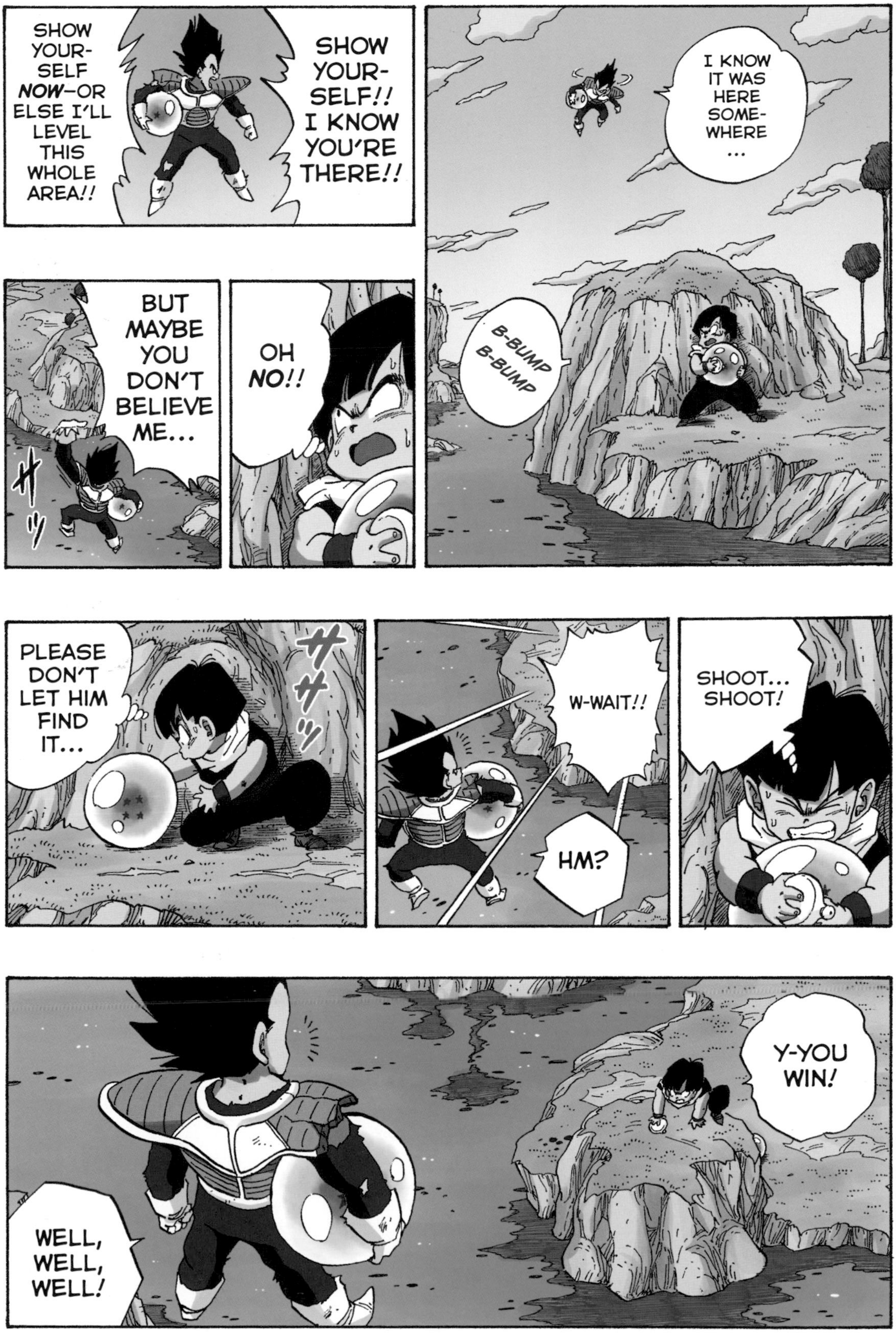
I KNOW IT WAS HERE SOMEWHERE ...
B-BUMP B-BUMP
SHOW YOURSELF!! I KNOW YOU'RE THERE!!
SHOW YOURSELF NOW—OR ELSE I'LL LEVEL THIS WHOLE AREA!!
OH NO!!
BUT MAYBE YOU DON'T BELIEVE ME...
ハッ
SHOOT... SHOOT!
W-WAIT!!
HM?
ササッ
PLEASE DON'T LET HIM FIND IT...
Y-YOU WIN!
WELL, WELL, WELL!

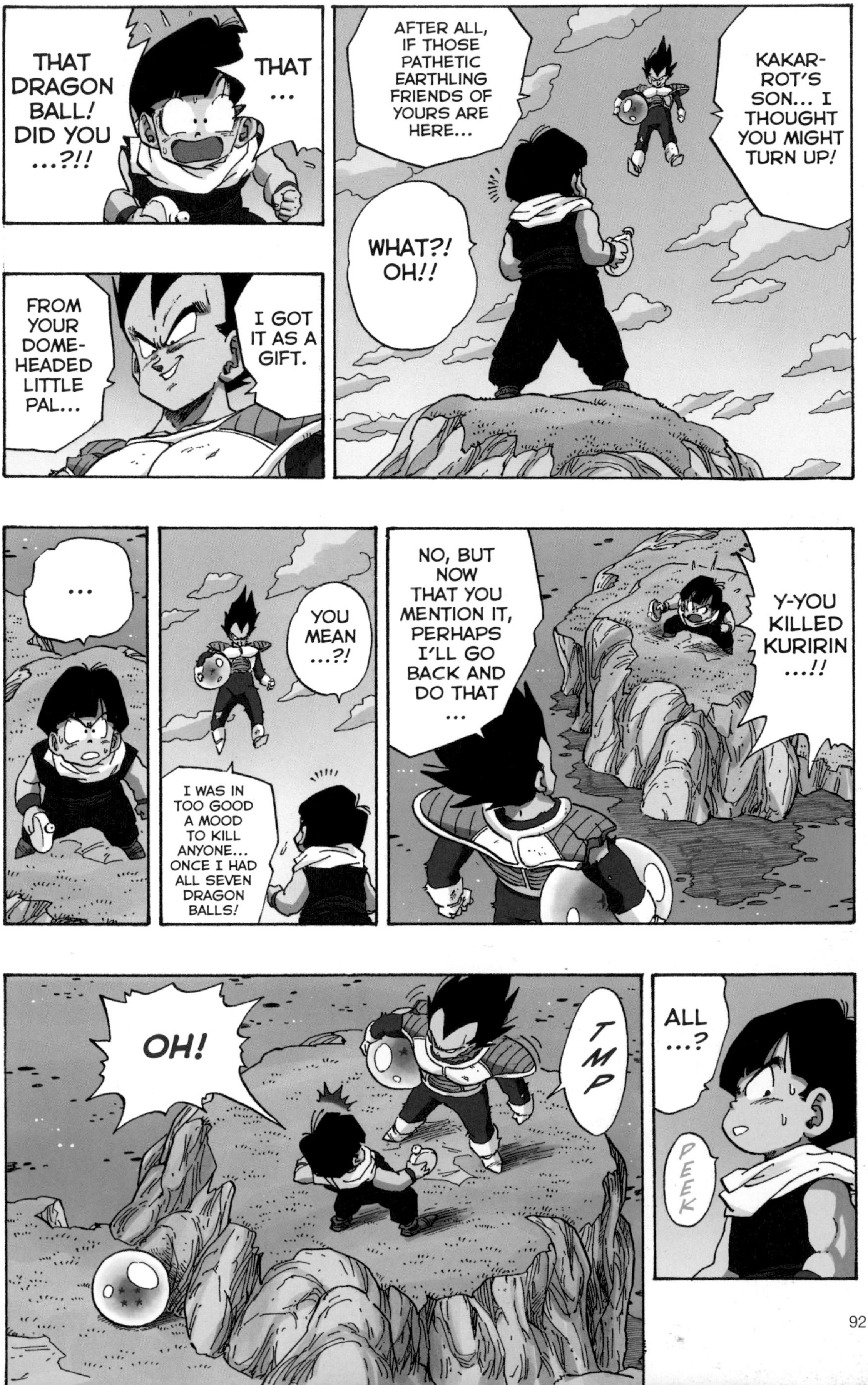
KAKAROT'S SON... I THOUGHT YOU MIGHT TURN UP!
AFTER ALL, IF THOSE PATHETIC EARTHLING FRIENDS OF YOURS ARE HERE...
WHAT?! OH!!
THAT ...
THAT DRAGON BALL! DID YOU ...?!!
I GOT IT AS A GIFT.
FROM YOUR DOME-HEADED LITTLE PAL...
Y-YOU KILLED KURIRIN ...!!
NO, BUT NOW THAT YOU MENTION IT, PERHAPS I'LL GO BACK AND DO THAT ...
YOU MEAN ...?!
I WAS IN TOO GOOD A MOOD TO KILL ANYONE... ONCE I HAD ALL SEVEN DRAGON BALLS!
...
ALL ...?
PEEK
TMP
OH!

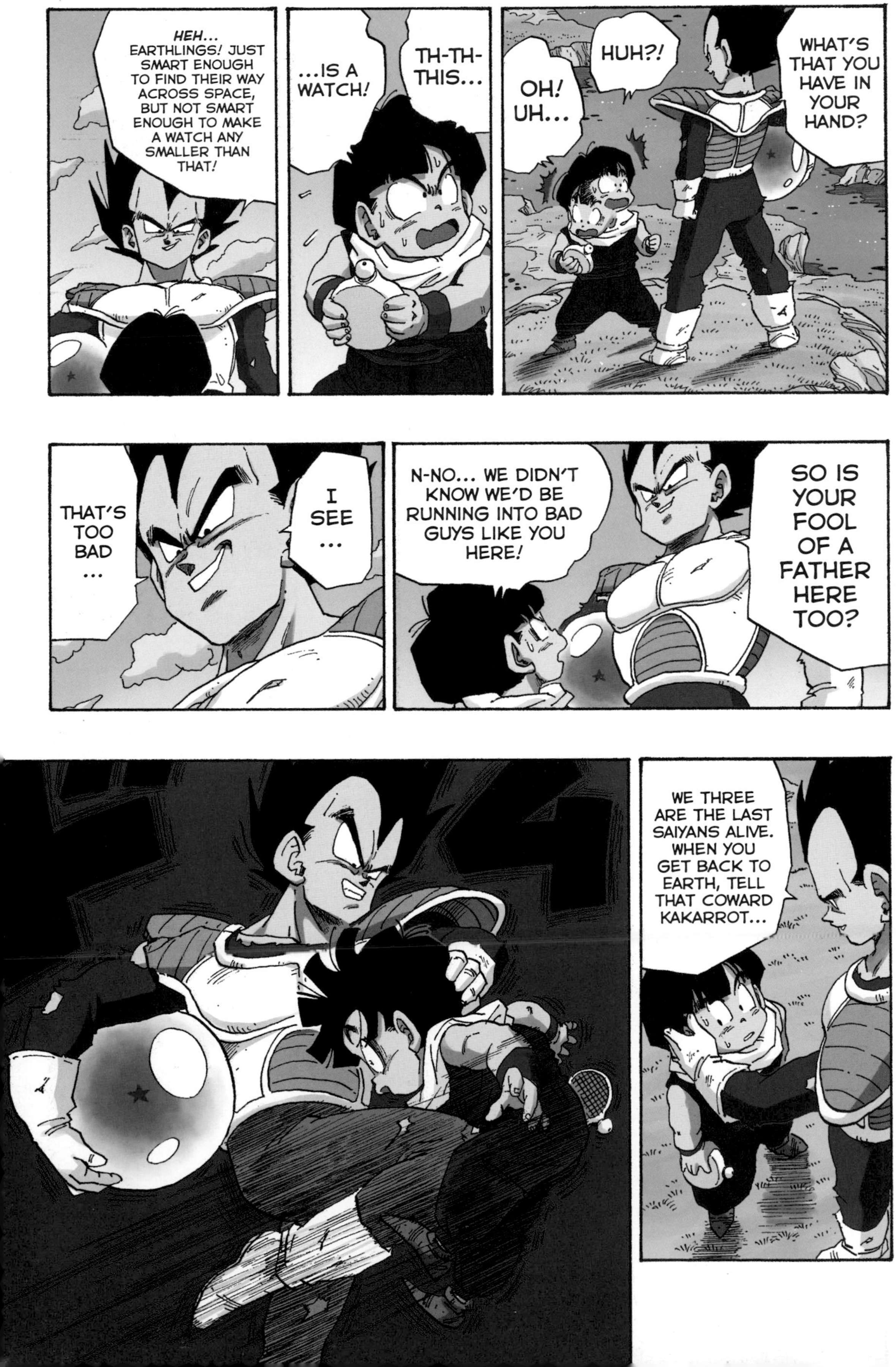
WHAT'S THAT YOU HAVE IN YOUR HAND?
HUH?!
OH! UH...
TH-TH-THIS...
...IS A WATCH!
HEH... EARTHLINGS! JUST SMART ENOUGH TO FIND THEIR WAY ACROSS SPACE, BUT NOT SMART ENOUGH TO MAKE A WATCH ANY SMALLER THAN THAT!
SO IS YOUR FOOL OF A FATHER HERE TOO?
N-NO... WE DIDN'T KNOW WE'D BE RUNNING INTO BAD GUYS LIKE YOU HERE!
I SEE...
THAT'S TOO BAD...
WE THREE ARE THE LAST SAIYANS ALIVE. WHEN YOU GET BACK TO EARTH, TELL THAT COWARD KAKARROT...

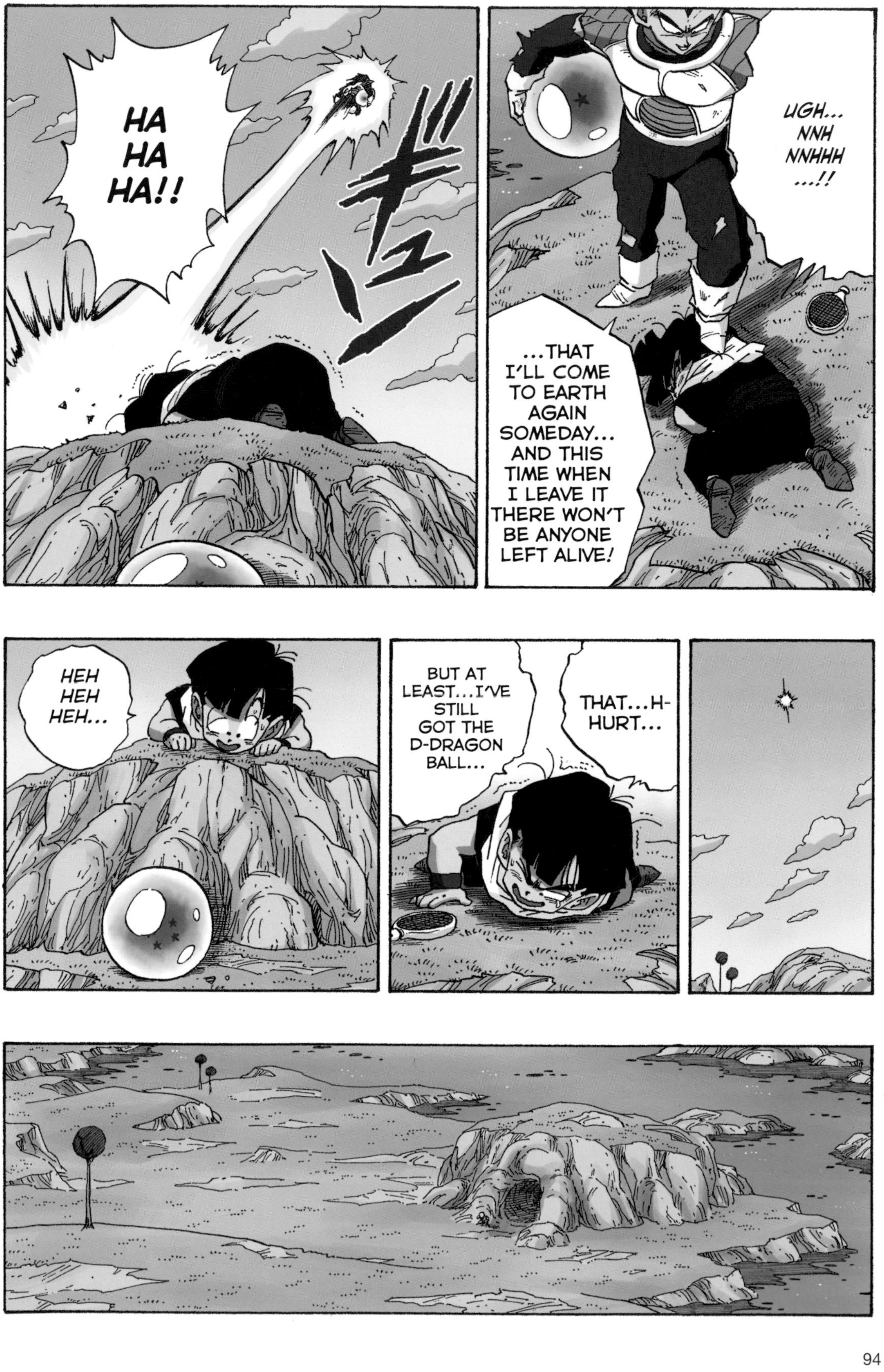
UGH... NNH NNHHH ...!!
...THAT I'LL COME TO EARTH AGAIN SOMEDAY... AND THIS TIME WHEN I LEAVE IT THERE WON'T BE ANYONE LEFT ALIVE!
HA HA HA!!
THAT...H-HURT...
BUT AT LEAST...I'VE STILL GOT THE D-DRAGON BALL...
HEH HEH HEH...

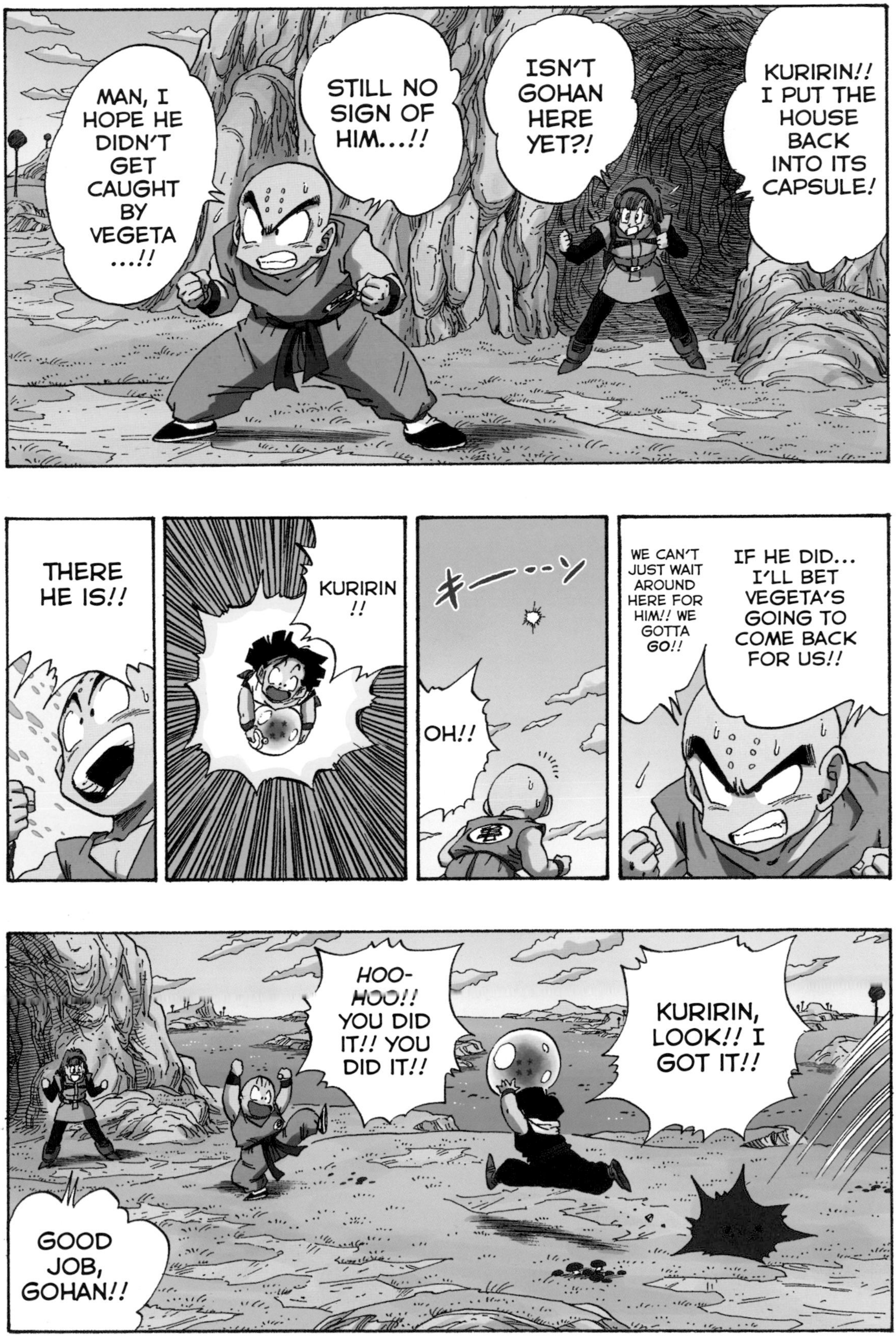
KURIRIN!! I PUT THE HOUSE BACK INTO ITS CAPSULE!
ISN'T GOHAN HERE YET?!
STILL NO SIGN OF HIM...!!
MAN, I HOPE HE DIDN'T GET CAUGHT BY VEGETA ...!!
IF HE DID... I'LL BET VEGETA'S GOING TO COME BACK FOR US!!
WE CAN'T JUST WAIT AROUND HERE FOR HIM!! WE GOTTA GO!!
キー・・ン
OH!!
KURIRIN!!
THERE HE IS!!
KURIRIN, LOOK!! I GOT IT!!
HOO-HOO!! YOU DID IT!! YOU DID IT!!
GOOD JOB, GOHAN!!

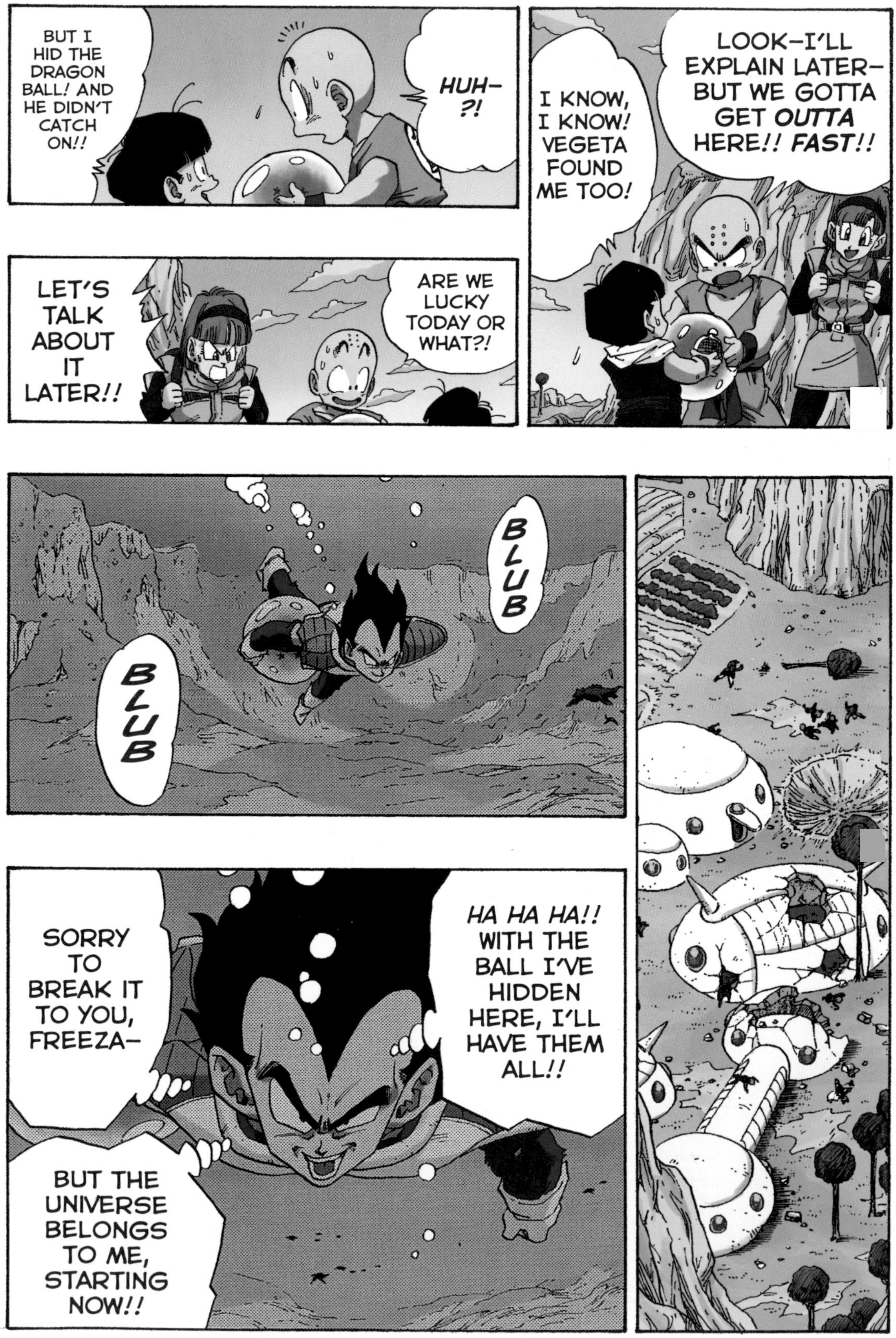
LOOK—I'LL EXPLAIN LATER—BUT WE GOTTA GET OUTTA HERE!! FAST!!
I KNOW, I KNOW! VEGETA FOUND ME TOO!
BUT I HID THE DRAGON BALL! AND HE DIDN'T CATCH ON!!
HUH—?!
ARE WE LUCKY TODAY OR WHAT?!
LET'S TALK ABOUT IT LATER!!
BLUB
BLUB
HA HA HA!! WITH THE BALL I'VE HIDDEN HERE, I'LL HAVE THEM ALL!!
SORRY TO BREAK IT TO YOU, FREEZA—
BUT THE UNIVERSE BELONGS TO ME, STARTING NOW!!

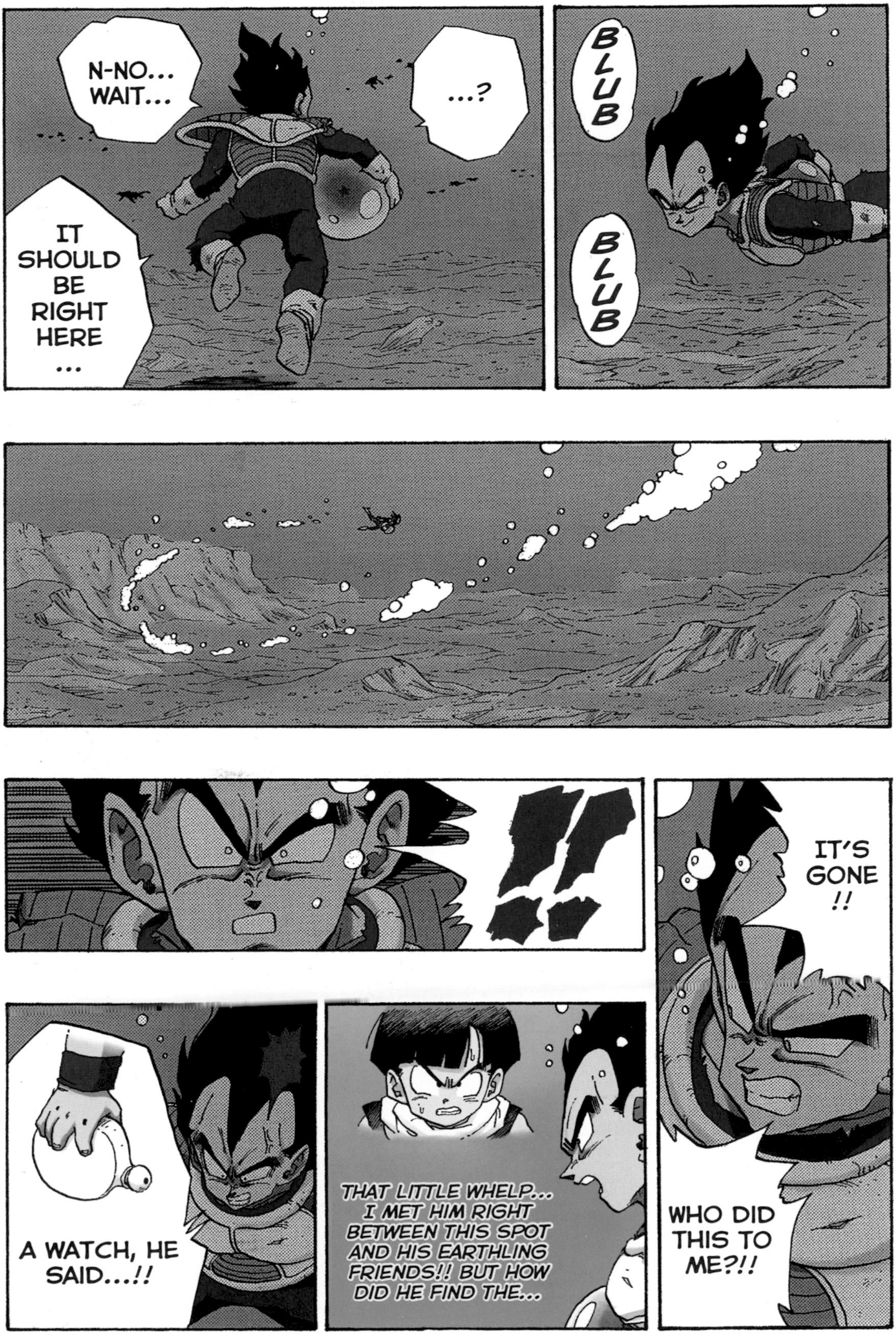
BLUB
BLUB
...?
N-NO... WAIT...
IT SHOULD BE RIGHT HERE ...
IT'S GONE !!
WHO DID THIS TO ME?!!
THAT LITTLE WHELP... I MET HIM RIGHT BETWEEN THIS SPOT AND HIS EARTHLING FRIENDS!! BUT HOW DID HE FIND THE...
A WATCH, HE SAID...!!

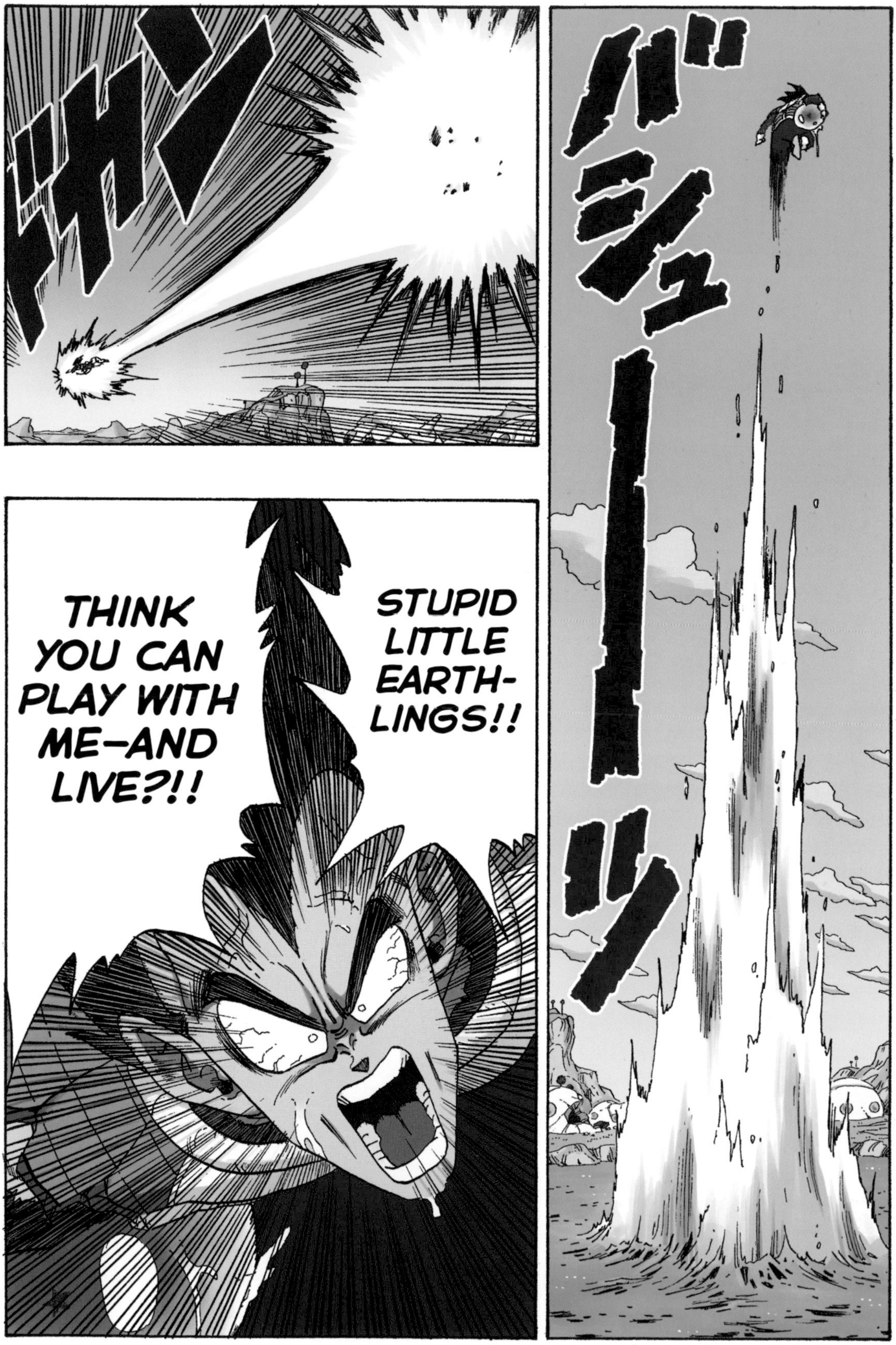
バシューッ
ドガン
STUPID LITTLE EARTH-LINGS!!
THINK YOU CAN PLAY WITH ME—AND LIVE?!!

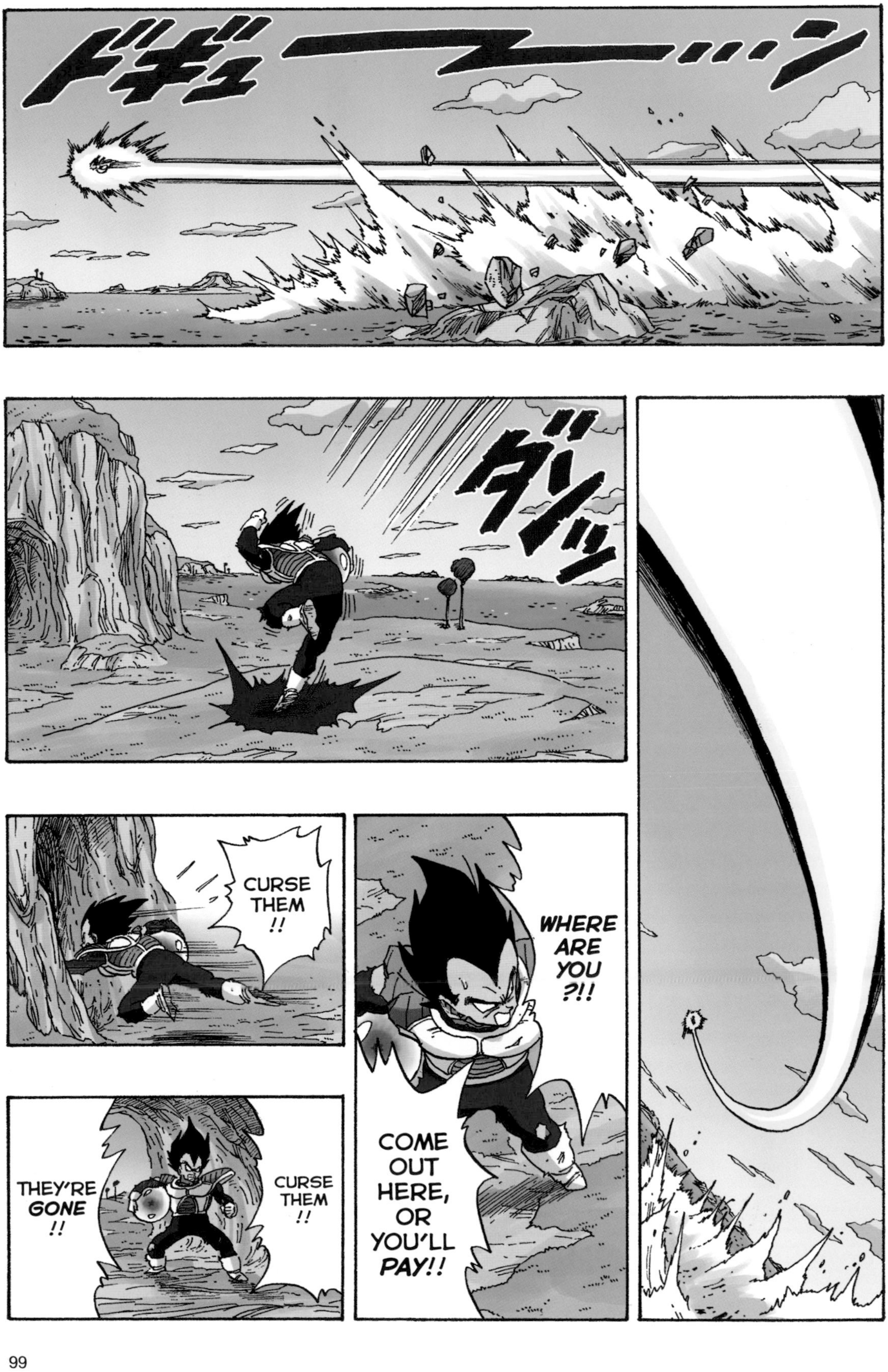
ドギューー…ン
ダンッ
WHERE ARE YOU ?!!
COME OUT HERE, OR YOU'LL PAY!!
CURSE THEM !!
CURSE THEM !!
THEY'RE GONE !!

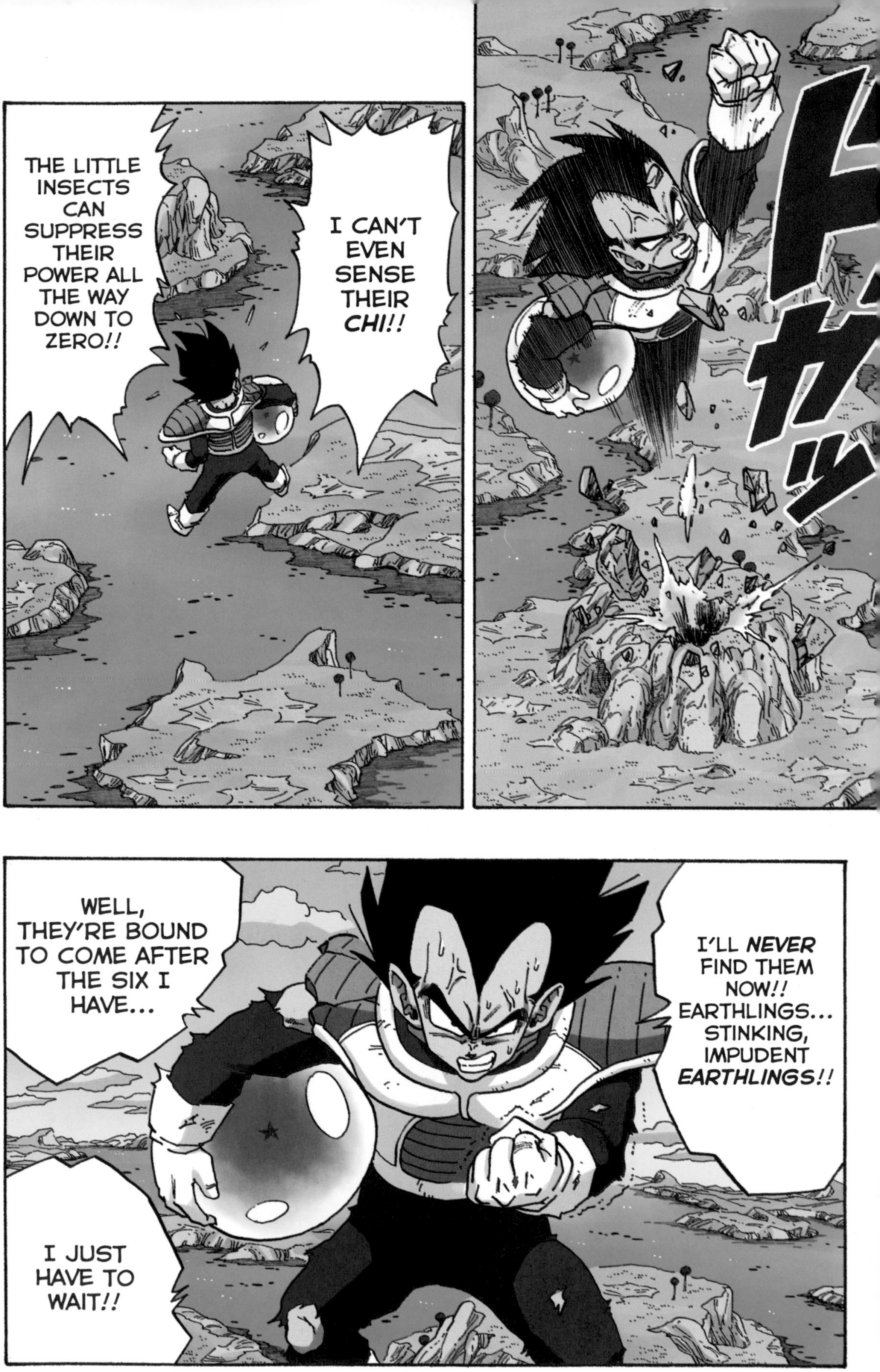
ドカッ
I CAN'T EVEN SENSE THEIR *CHI!!*
THE LITTLE INSECTS CAN SUPPRESS THEIR POWER ALL THE WAY DOWN TO ZERO!!
I'LL ***NEVER*** FIND THEM NOW!! EARTHLINGS... STINKING, IMPUDENT ***EARTHLINGS!!***
WELL, THEY'RE BOUND TO COME AFTER THE SIX I HAVE...
I JUST HAVE TO WAIT!!

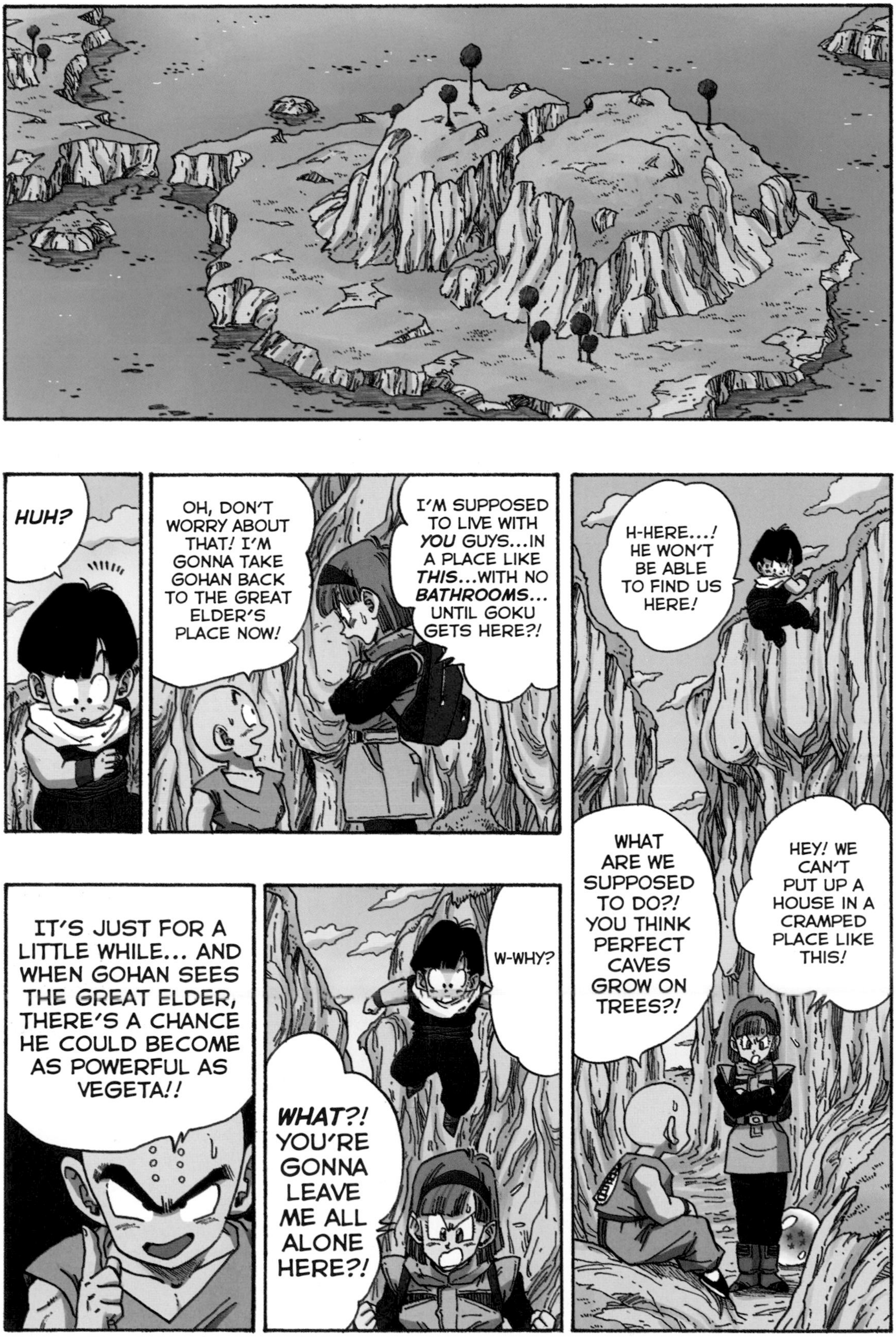
H-HERE...! HE WON'T BE ABLE TO FIND US HERE!
HEY! WE CAN'T PUT UP A HOUSE IN A CRAMPED PLACE LIKE THIS!
WHAT ARE WE SUPPOSED TO DO?! YOU THINK PERFECT CAVES GROW ON TREES?!
I'M SUPPOSED TO LIVE WITH *YOU* GUYS...IN A PLACE LIKE *THIS*...WITH NO *BATHROOMS*... UNTIL GOKU GETS HERE?!
OH, DON'T WORRY ABOUT THAT! I'M GONNA TAKE GOHAN BACK TO THE GREAT ELDER'S PLACE NOW!
HUH?
W-WHY?
WHAT?! YOU'RE GONNA LEAVE ME ALL ALONE HERE?!
IT'S JUST FOR A LITTLE WHILE... AND WHEN GOHAN SEES THE GREAT ELDER, THERE'S A CHANCE HE COULD BECOME AS POWERFUL AS VEGETA!!

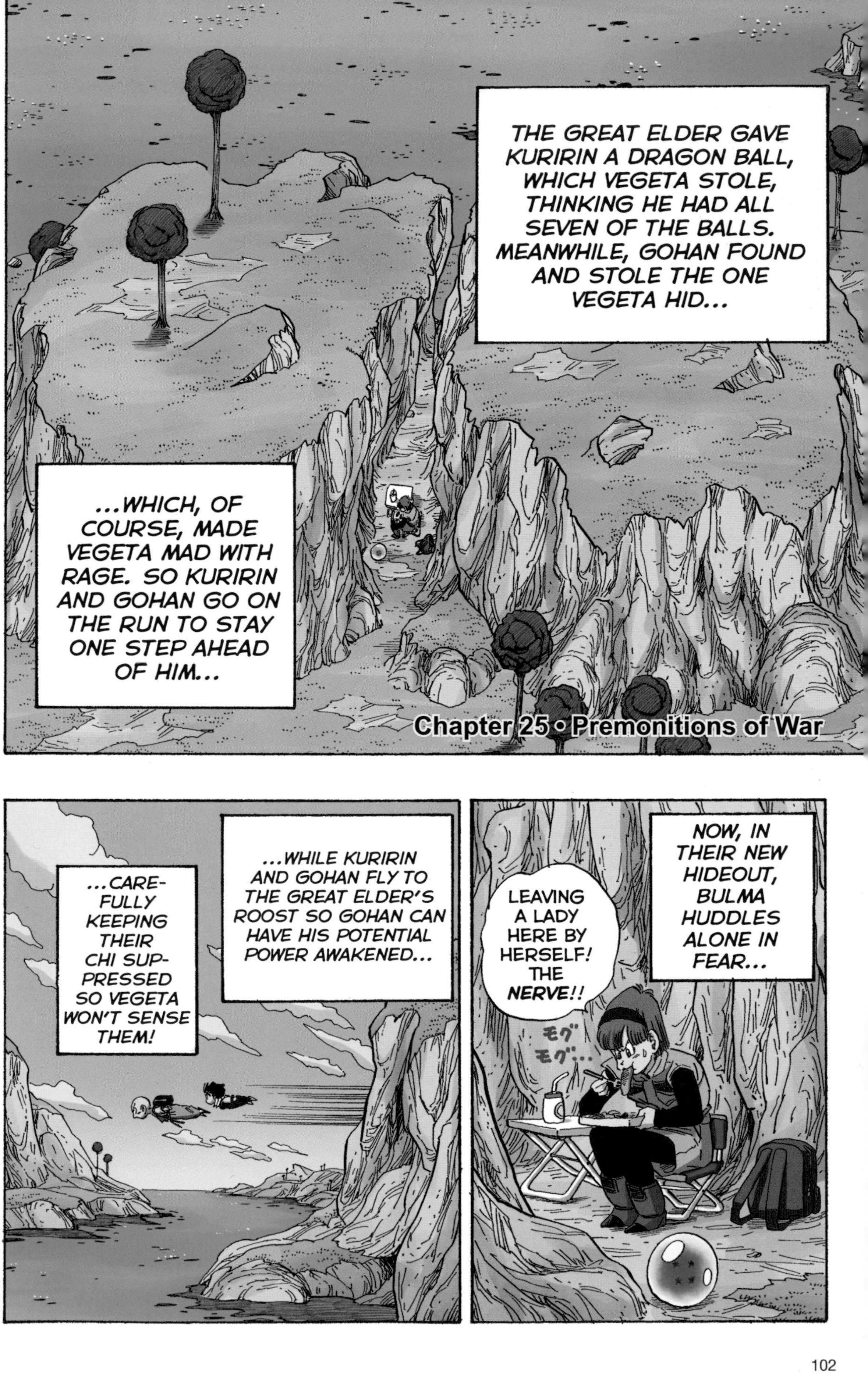
THE GREAT ELDER GAVE KURIRIN A DRAGON BALL, WHICH VEGETA STOLE, THINKING HE HAD ALL SEVEN OF THE BALLS. MEANWHILE, GOHAN FOUND AND STOLE THE ONE VEGETA HID...
...WHICH, OF COURSE, MADE VEGETA MAD WITH RAGE. SO KURIRIN AND GOHAN GO ON THE RUN TO STAY ONE STEP AHEAD OF HIM...
Chapter 25 • Premonitions of War
NOW, IN THEIR NEW HIDEOUT, BULMA HUDDLES ALONE IN FEAR...
LEAVING A LADY HERE BY HERSELF! THE NERVE!!
モグ モグ...
...WHILE KURIRIN AND GOHAN FLY TO THE GREAT ELDER'S ROOST SO GOHAN CAN HAVE HIS POTENTIAL POWER AWAKENED...
...CAREFULLY KEEPING THEIR CHI SUPPRESSED SO VEGETA WON'T SENSE THEM!

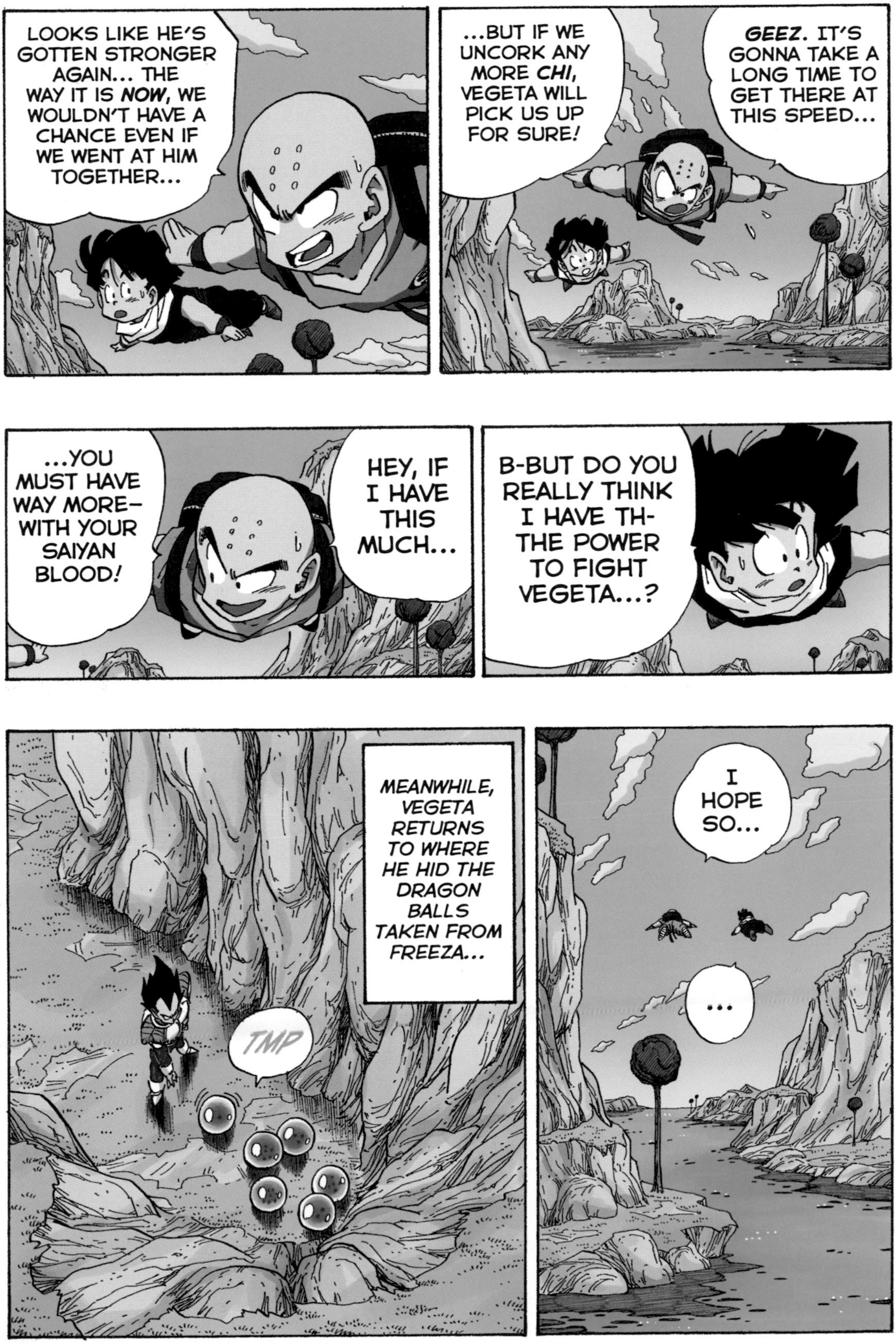
GEEZ. IT'S GONNA TAKE A LONG TIME TO GET THERE AT THIS SPEED...
...BUT IF WE UNCORK ANY MORE CHI, VEGETA WILL PICK US UP FOR SURE!
LOOKS LIKE HE'S GOTTEN STRONGER AGAIN... THE WAY IT IS NOW, WE WOULDN'T HAVE A CHANCE EVEN IF WE WENT AT HIM TOGETHER...
B-BUT DO YOU REALLY THINK I HAVE TH- THE POWER TO FIGHT VEGETA...?
HEY, IF I HAVE THIS MUCH...
...YOU MUST HAVE WAY MORE— WITH YOUR SAIYAN BLOOD!
I HOPE SO...
...
MEANWHILE, VEGETA RETURNS TO WHERE HE HID THE DRAGON BALLS TAKEN FROM FREEZA...
TMP

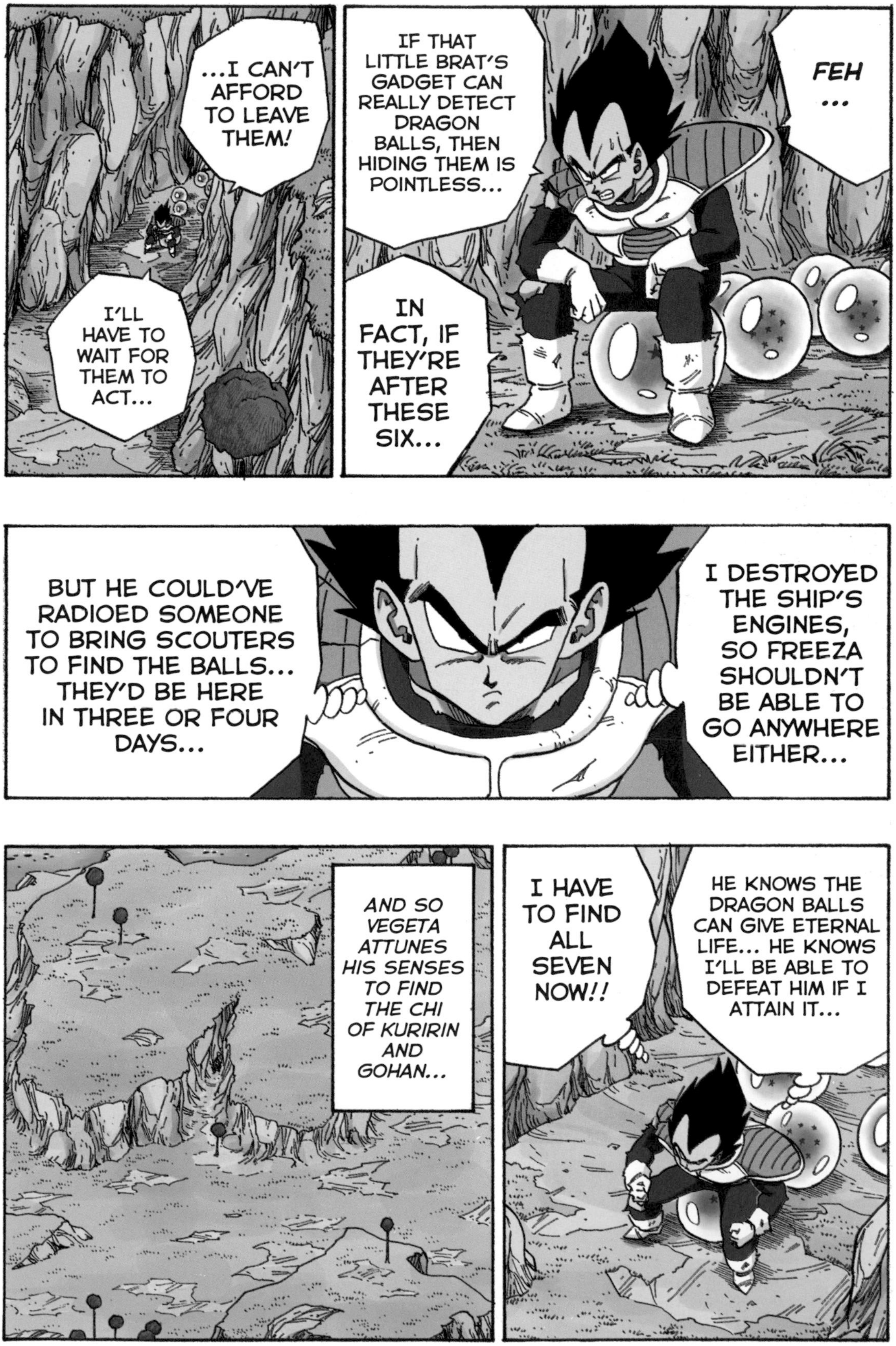
FEH ...
IF THAT LITTLE BRAT'S GADGET CAN REALLY DETECT DRAGON BALLS, THEN HIDING THEM IS POINTLESS...
IN FACT, IF THEY'RE AFTER THESE SIX...
...I CAN'T AFFORD TO LEAVE THEM!
I'LL HAVE TO WAIT FOR THEM TO ACT...
I DESTROYED THE SHIP'S ENGINES, SO FREEZA SHOULDN'T BE ABLE TO GO ANYWHERE EITHER...
BUT HE COULD'VE RADIOED SOMEONE TO BRING SCOUTERS TO FIND THE BALLS... THEY'D BE HERE IN THREE OR FOUR DAYS...
HE KNOWS THE DRAGON BALLS CAN GIVE ETERNAL LIFE... HE KNOWS I'LL BE ABLE TO DEFEAT HIM IF I ATTAIN IT...
I HAVE TO FIND ALL SEVEN NOW!!
AND SO VEGETA ATTUNES HIS SENSES TO FIND THE CHI OF KURIRIN AND GOHAN...

...WHILE IN THE DEPTHS OF SPACE...

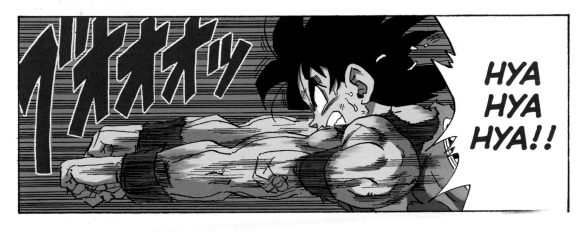

HYA HYA HYA!!

...GOKU CONTINUES HIS GRUELING TRAINING... NOW AT A GRAVITATION OF 100 G!

UNH!! UNH!!

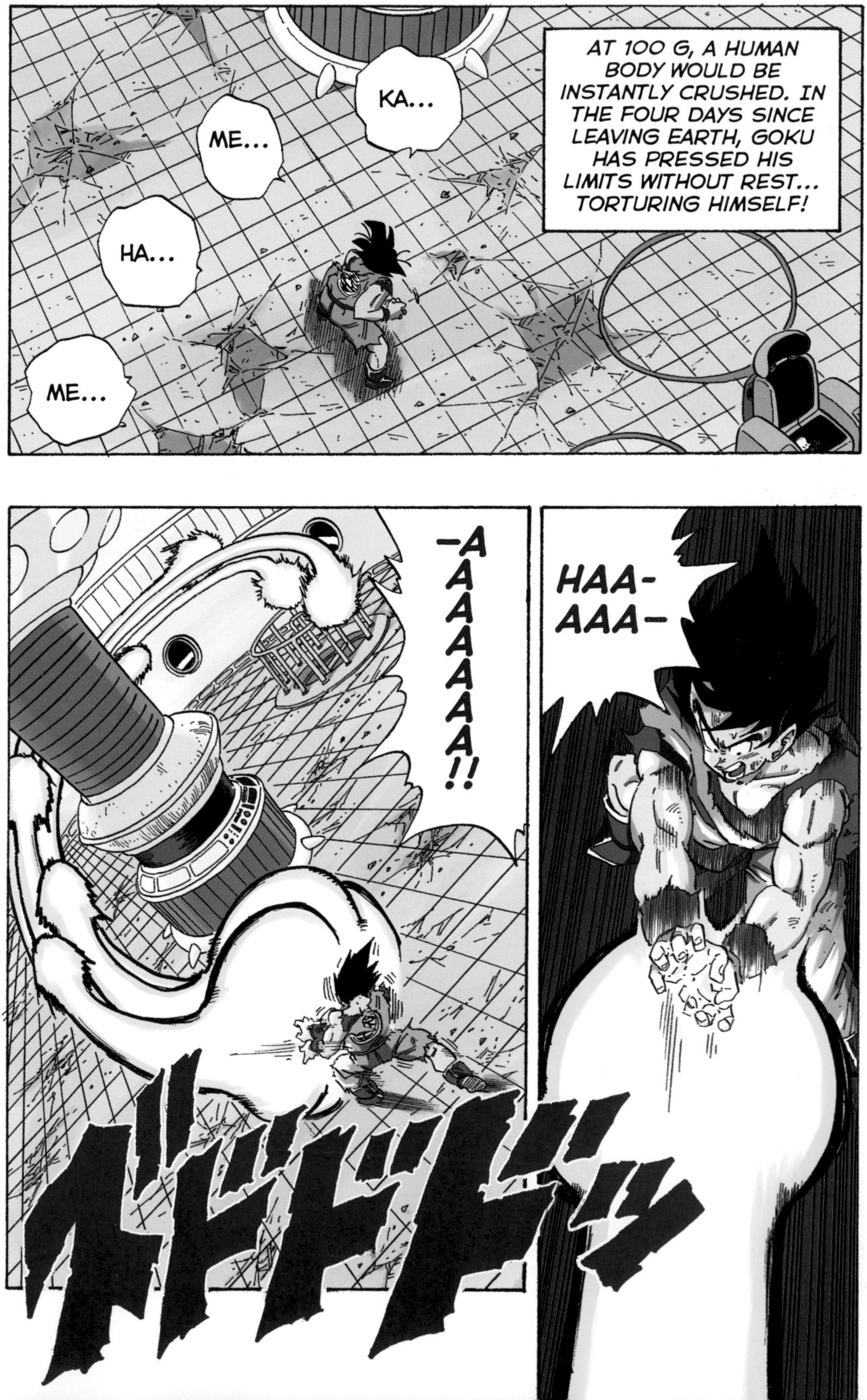
AT 100 G, A HUMAN BODY WOULD BE INSTANTLY CRUSHED. IN THE FOUR DAYS SINCE LEAVING EARTH, GOKU HAS PRESSED HIS LIMITS WITHOUT REST... TORTURING HIMSELF!
KA...
ME...
HA...
ME...
HAA-AAA-
-AAAAAAA!!

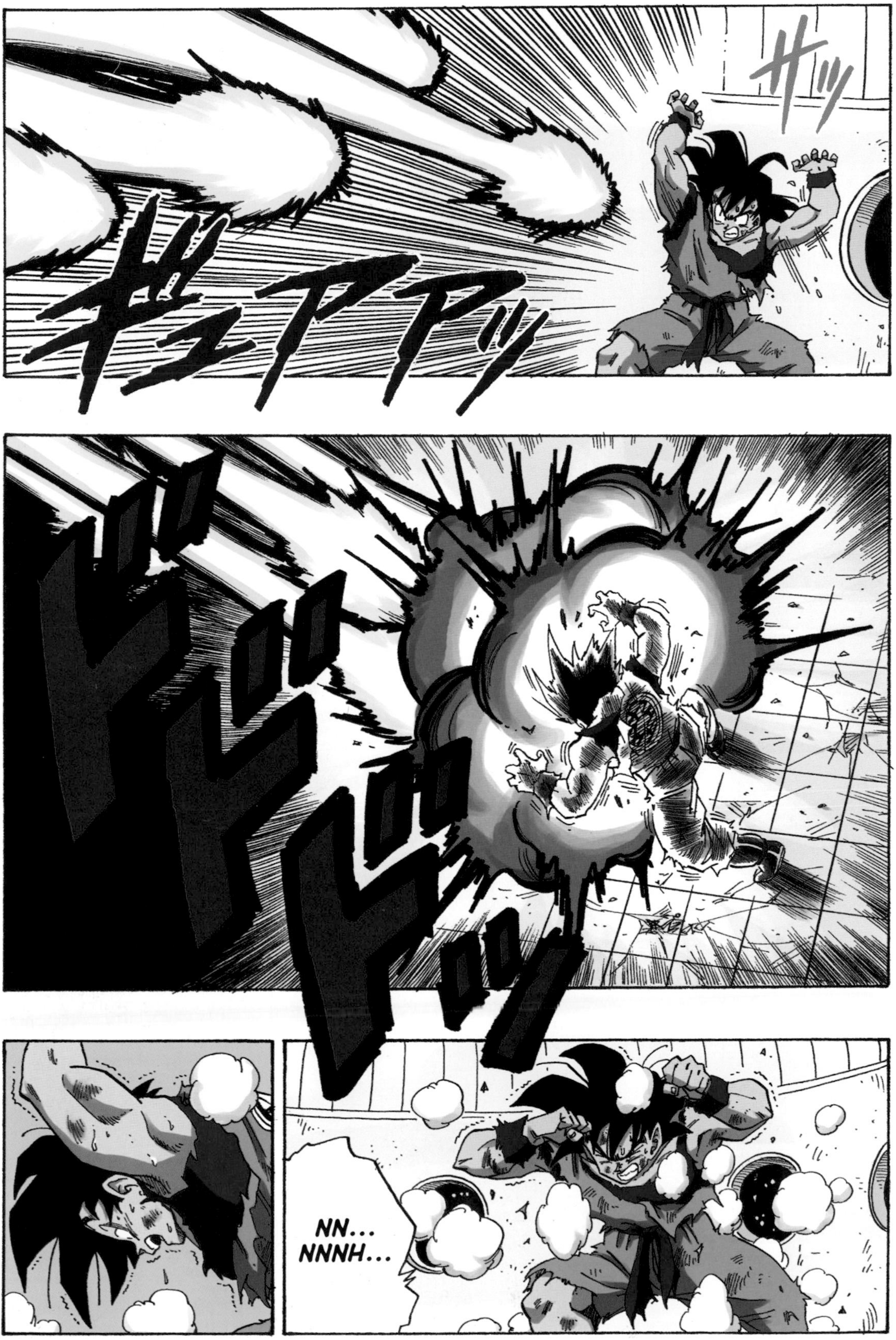
ザッ
ギュアアッ
NN... NNNH...

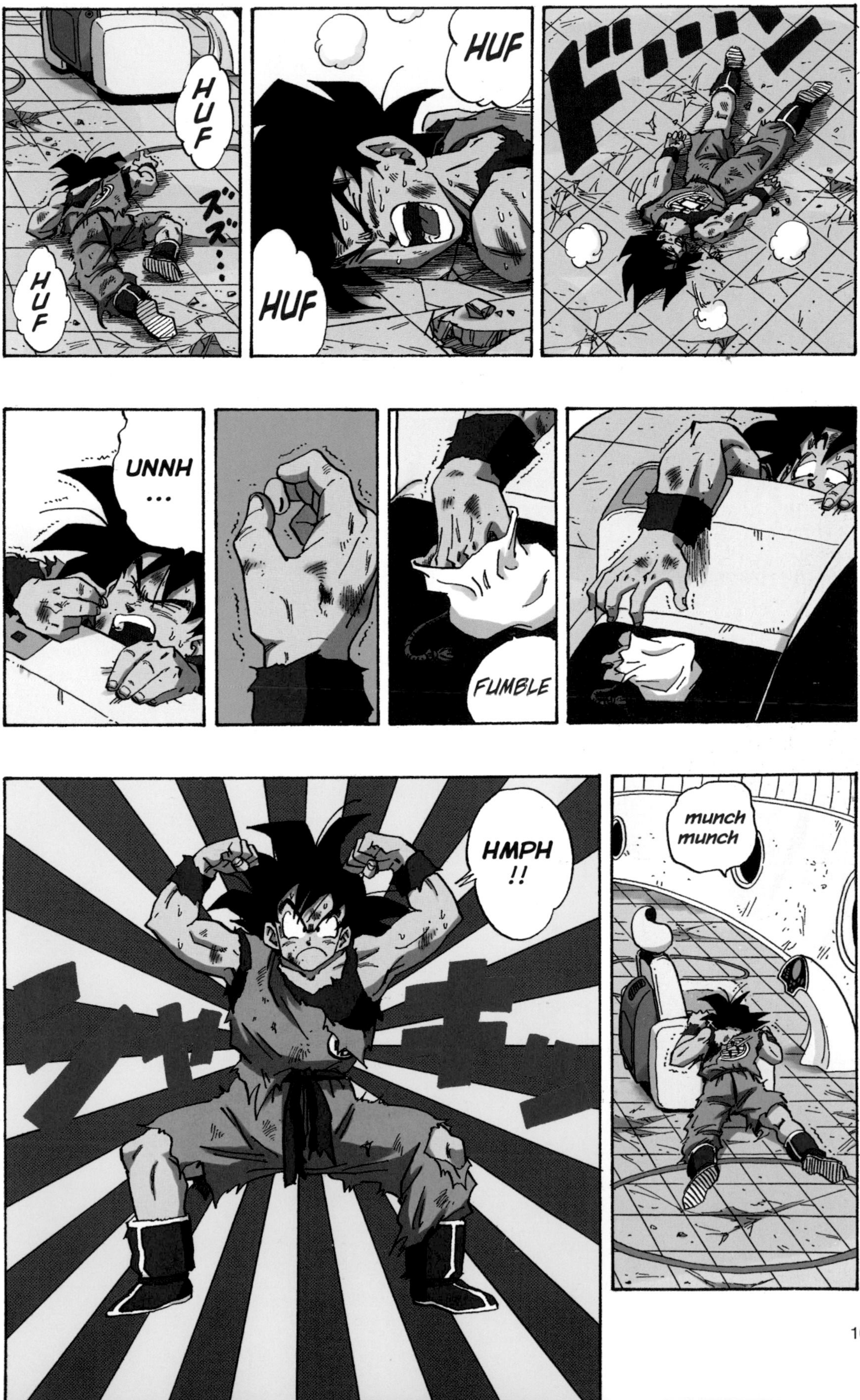
HUF
HUF
HUF
ズズ・・・
HUF
FUMBLE
UNNH ...
munch munch
HMPH !!

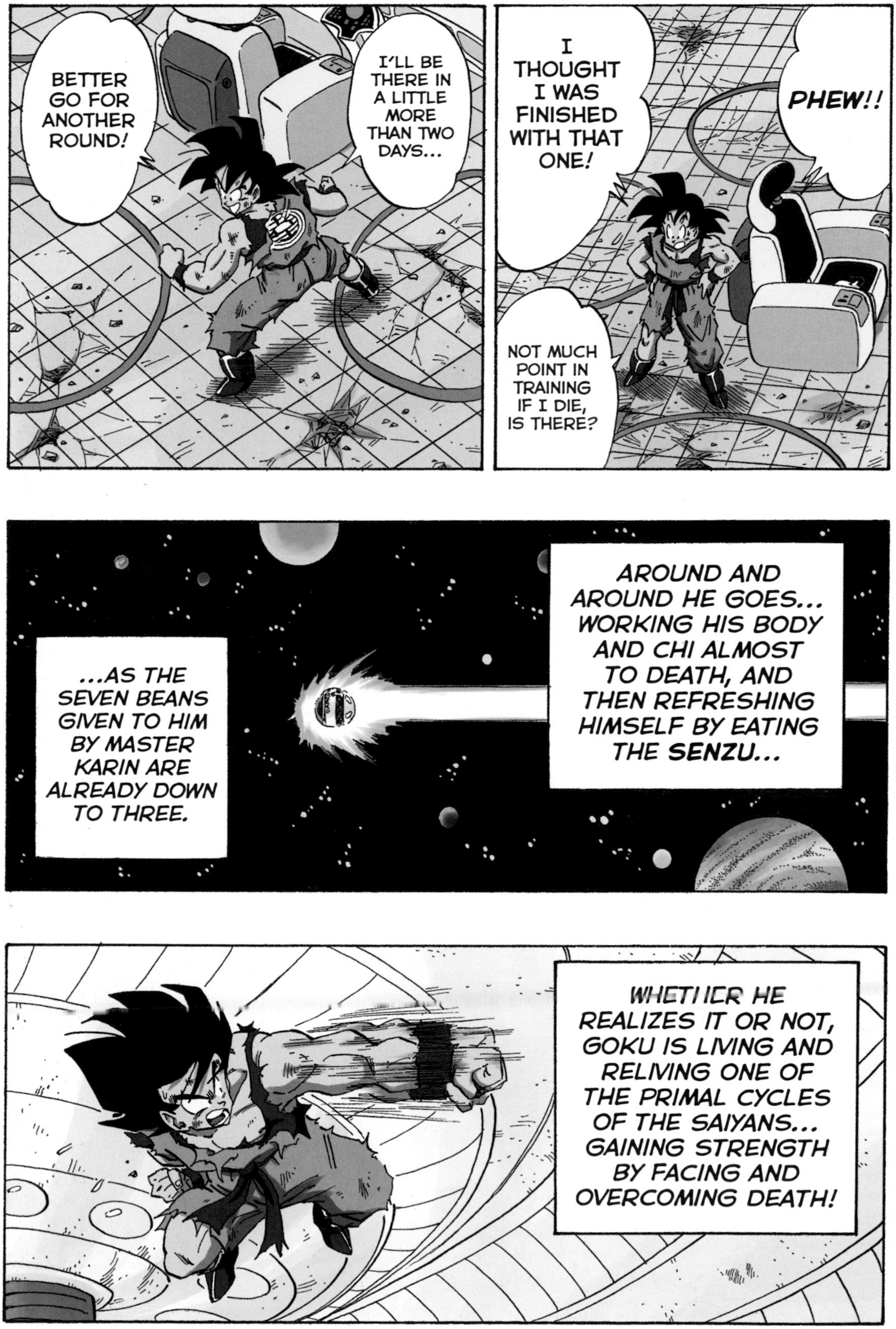
PHEW!!
I THOUGHT I WAS FINISHED WITH THAT ONE!
NOT MUCH POINT IN TRAINING IF I DIE, IS THERE?
I'LL BE THERE IN A LITTLE MORE THAN TWO DAYS...
BETTER GO FOR ANOTHER ROUND!
AROUND AND AROUND HE GOES... WORKING HIS BODY AND CHI ALMOST TO DEATH, AND THEN REFRESHING HIMSELF BY EATING THE **SENZU**...
...AS THE SEVEN BEANS GIVEN TO HIM BY MASTER KARIN ARE ALREADY DOWN TO THREE.
WHETHER HE REALIZES IT OR NOT, GOKU IS LIVING AND RELIVING ONE OF THE PRIMAL CYCLES OF THE SAIYANS... GAINING STRENGTH BY FACING AND OVERCOMING DEATH!

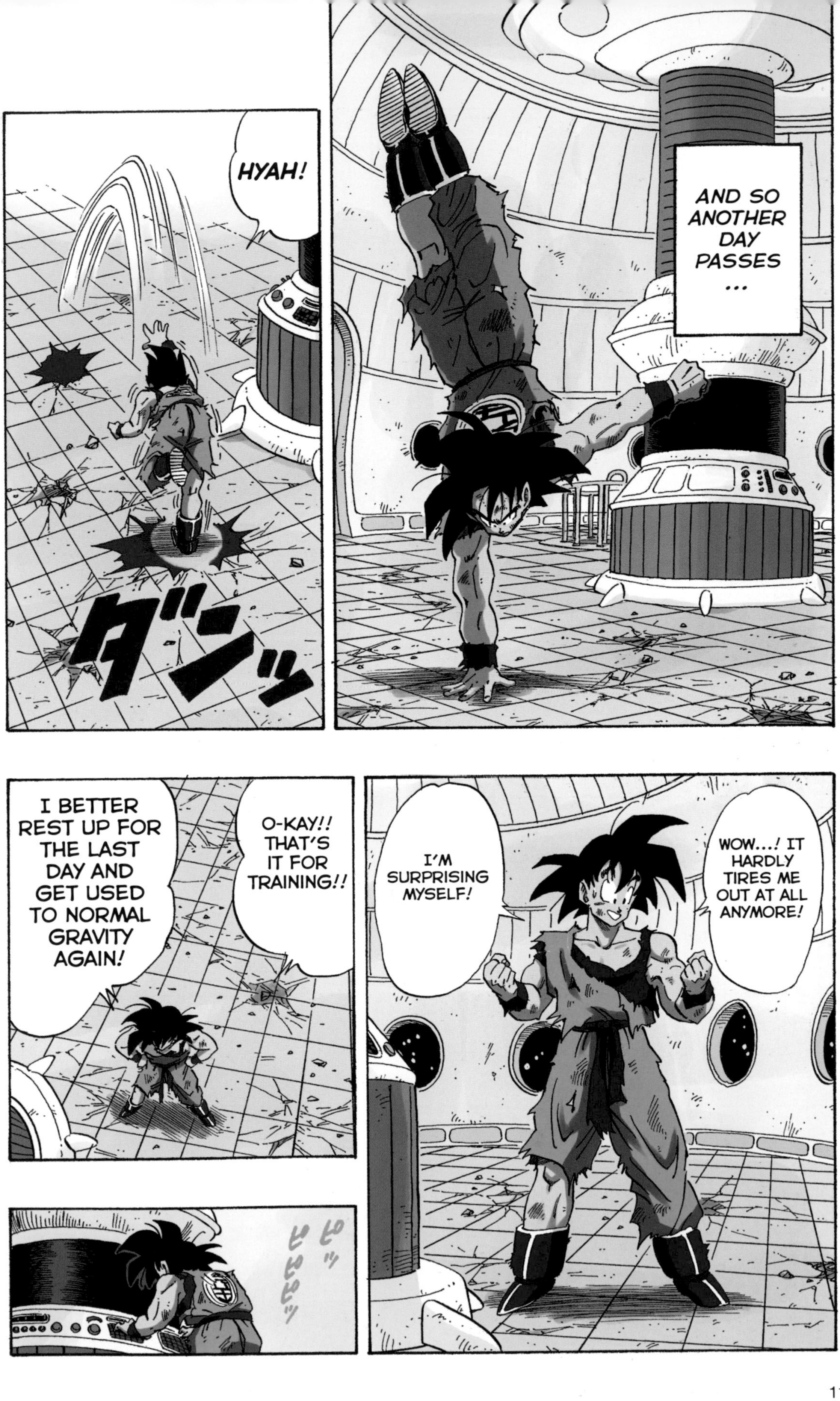

AND SO ANOTHER DAY PASSES ...
HYAH!
ダンッ
WOW...! IT HARDLY TIRES ME OUT AT ALL ANYMORE!
I'M SURPRISING MYSELF!
O-KAY!! THAT'S IT FOR TRAINING!!
I BETTER REST UP FOR THE LAST DAY AND GET USED TO NORMAL GRAVITY AGAIN!
ピッ
ピピピッ

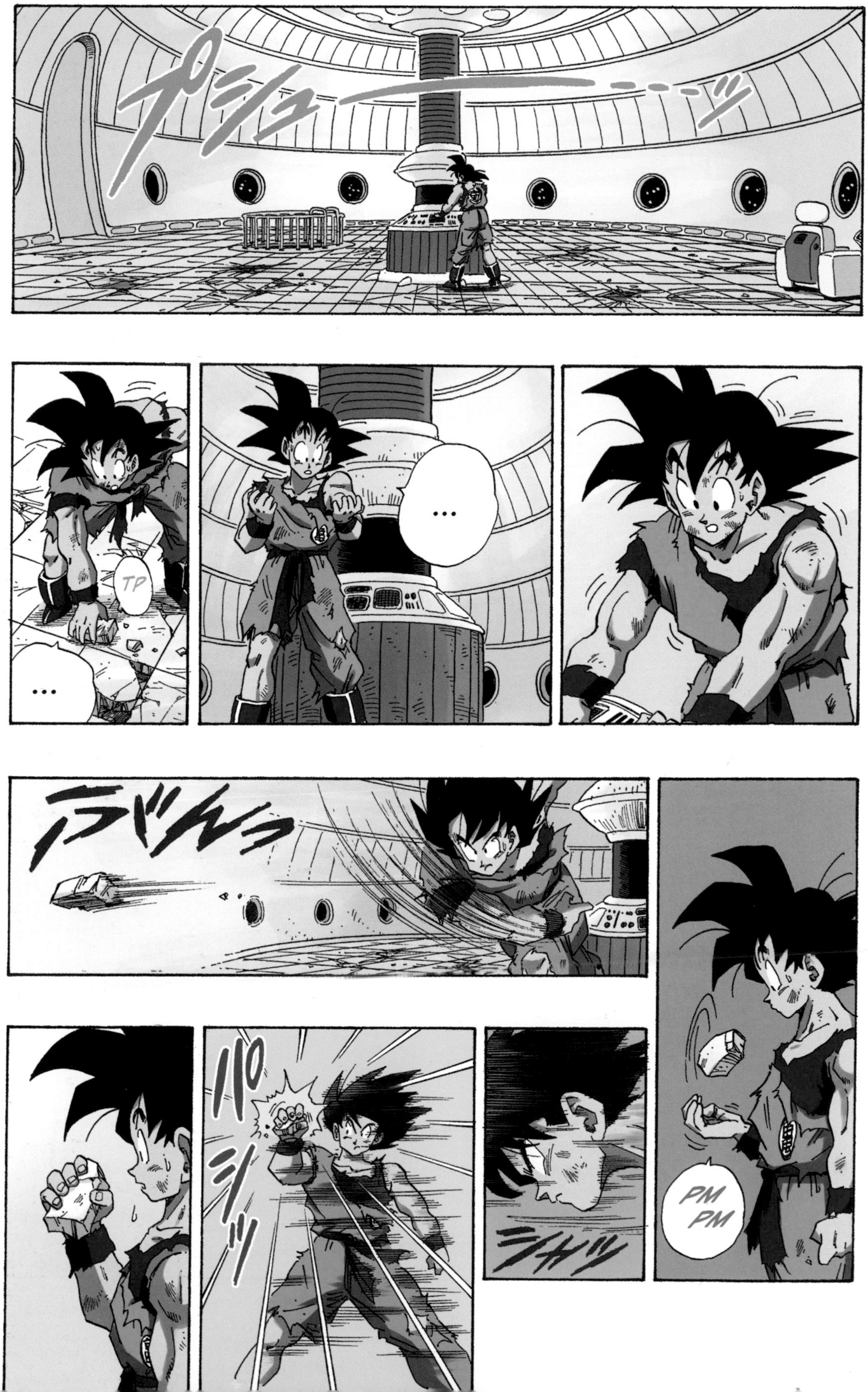

プシューーーーッ
...
TP
...
PM PM
ブンッ
シュッ
パシッ

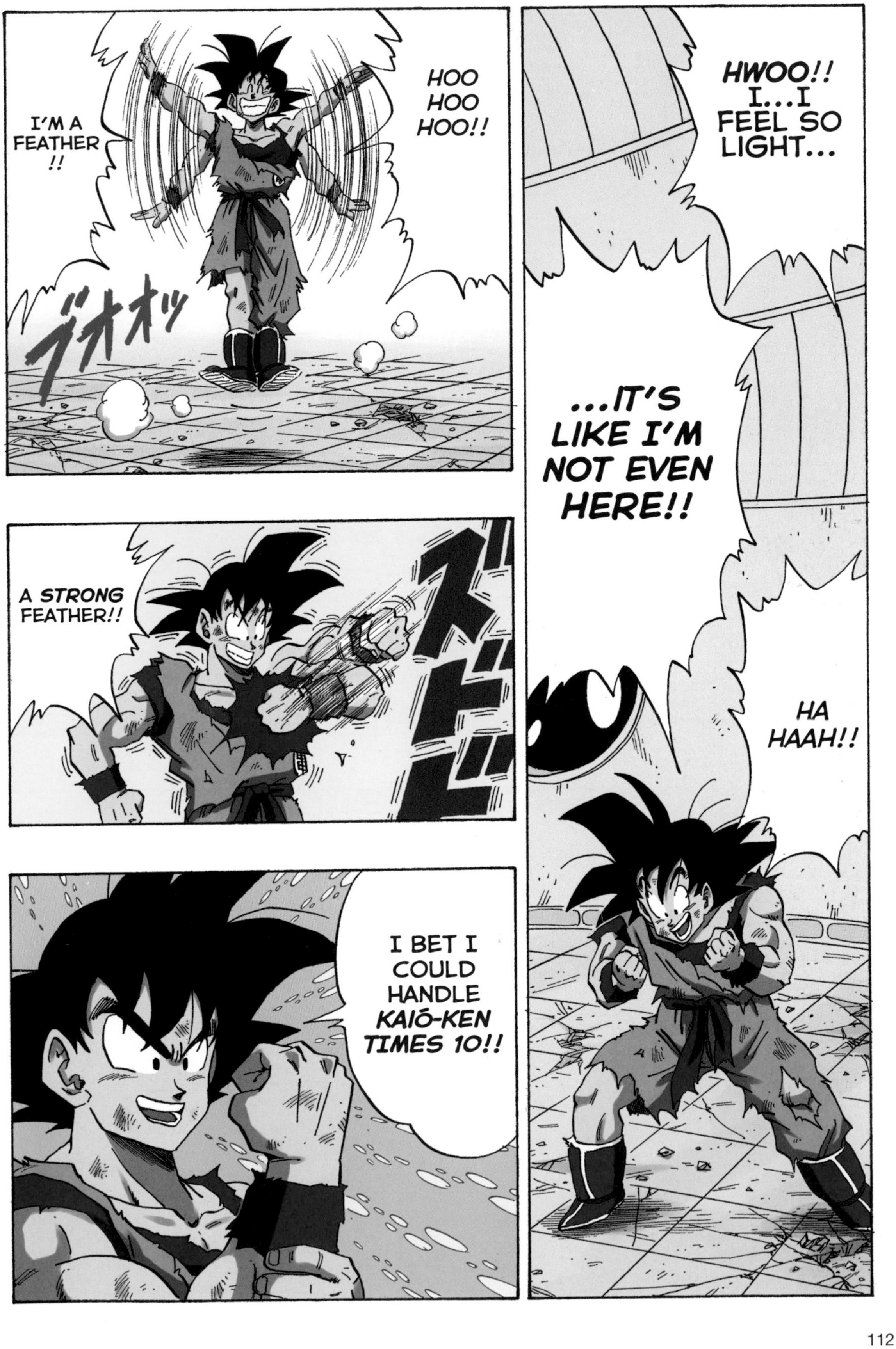
HWOO!! I...I FEEL SO LIGHT...
...IT'S LIKE I'M NOT EVEN HERE!!
HA HAAH!!
HOO HOO HOO!!
I'M A FEATHER!!
A *STRONG* FEATHER!!
I BET I COULD HANDLE *KAIŌ-KEN TIMES 10!!*

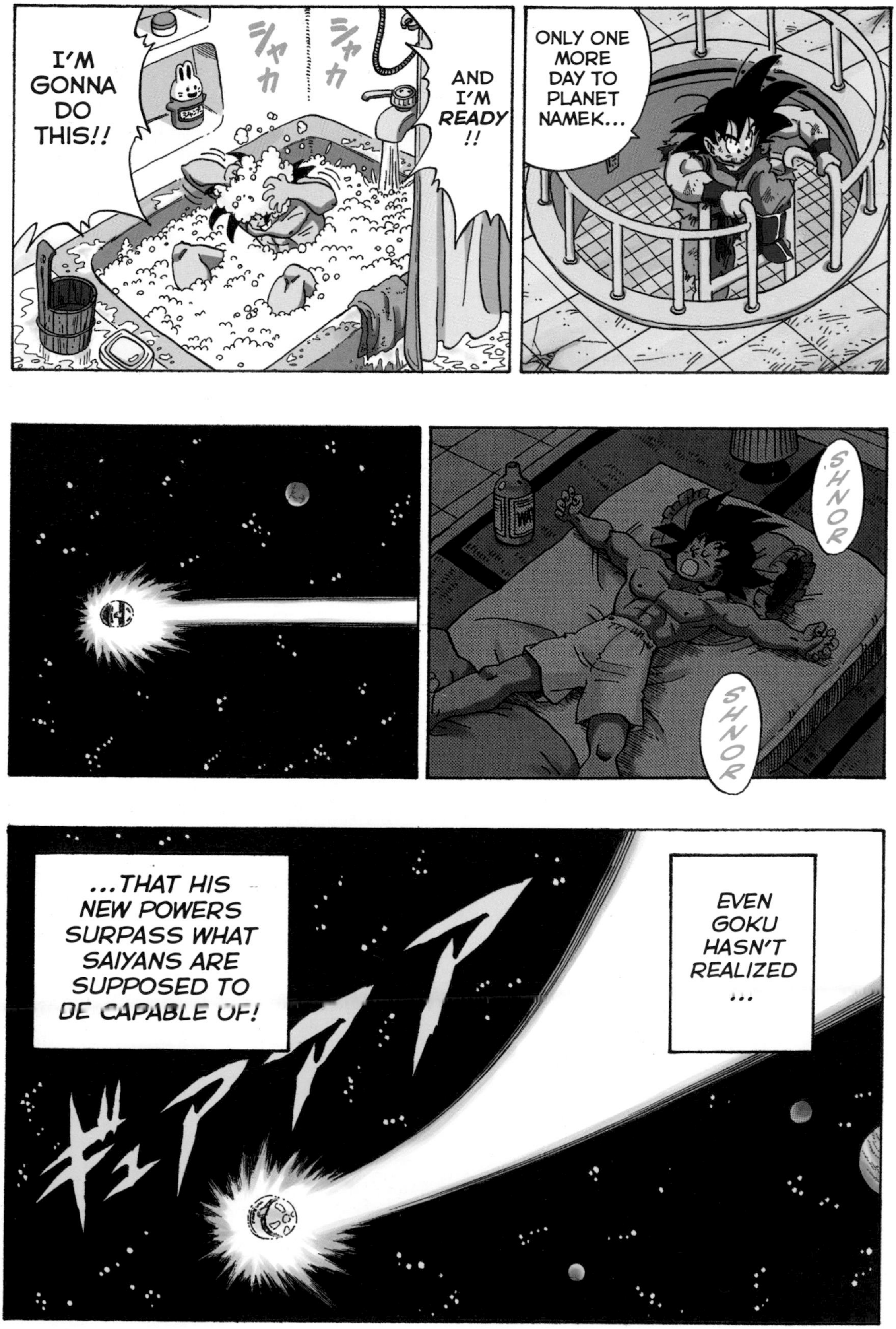
ONLY ONE MORE DAY TO PLANET NAMEK...
I'M GONNA DO THIS!!
シャカ
シャカ
AND I'M *READY*!!
SHNOR
SHNOR
EVEN GOKU HASN'T REALIZED...
...THAT HIS NEW POWERS SURPASS WHAT SAIYANS ARE SUPPOSED TO BE CAPABLE OF!
ギュアアアア

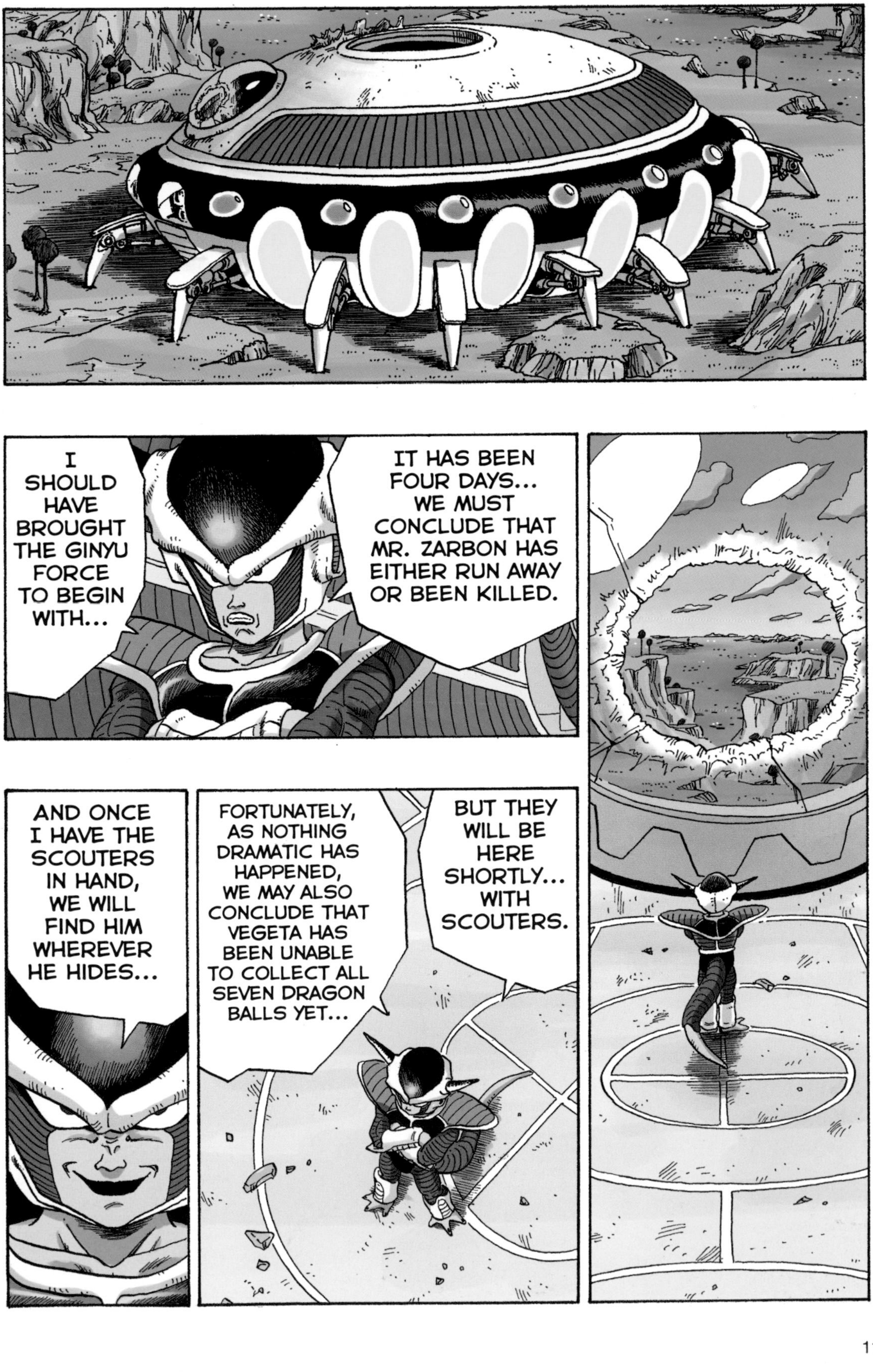
IT HAS BEEN FOUR DAYS... WE MUST CONCLUDE THAT MR. ZARBON HAS EITHER RUN AWAY OR BEEN KILLED.
I SHOULD HAVE BROUGHT THE GINYU FORCE TO BEGIN WITH...
BUT THEY WILL BE HERE SHORTLY... WITH SCOUTERS.
FORTUNATELY, AS NOTHING DRAMATIC HAS HAPPENED, WE MAY ALSO CONCLUDE THAT VEGETA HAS BEEN UNABLE TO COLLECT ALL SEVEN DRAGON BALLS YET...
AND ONCE I HAVE THE SCOUTERS IN HAND, WE WILL FIND HIM WHEREVER HE HIDES...

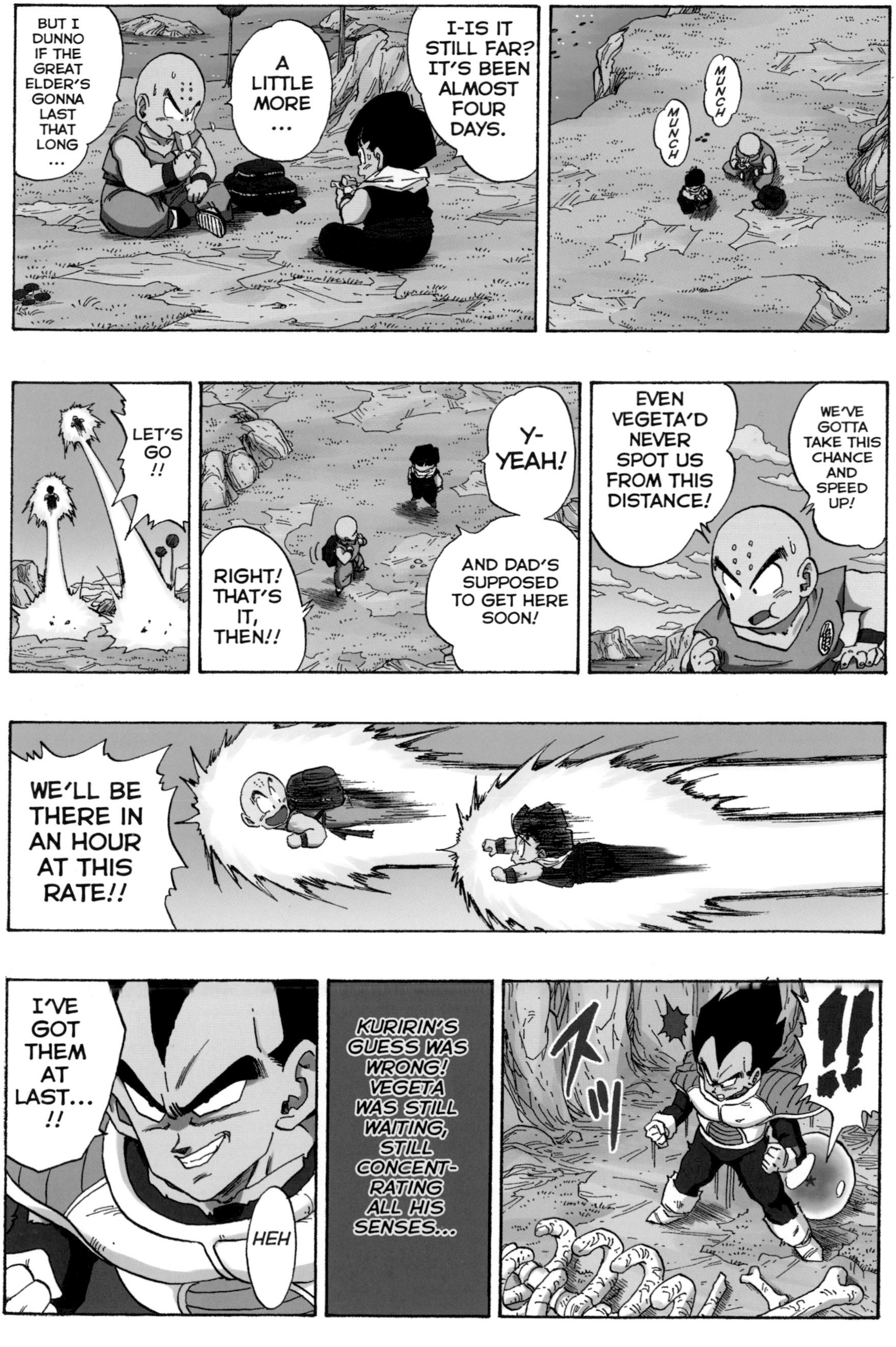
MUNCH
MUNCH
I-IS IT STILL FAR? IT'S BEEN ALMOST FOUR DAYS.
A LITTLE MORE...
BUT I DUNNO IF THE GREAT ELDER'S GONNA LAST THAT LONG...
WE'VE GOTTA TAKE THIS CHANCE AND SPEED UP!
EVEN VEGETA'D NEVER SPOT US FROM THIS DISTANCE!
Y-YEAH!
AND DAD'S SUPPOSED TO GET HERE SOON!
RIGHT! THAT'S IT, THEN!!
LET'S GO!!
WE'LL BE THERE IN AN HOUR AT THIS RATE!!
!!
ズッ
KURIRIN'S GUESS WAS WRONG! VEGETA WAS STILL WAITING, STILL CONCENT-RATING ALL HIS SENSES...
I'VE GOT THEM AT LAST...!!
HEH

Chapter 26 • The Enemy of My Enemy

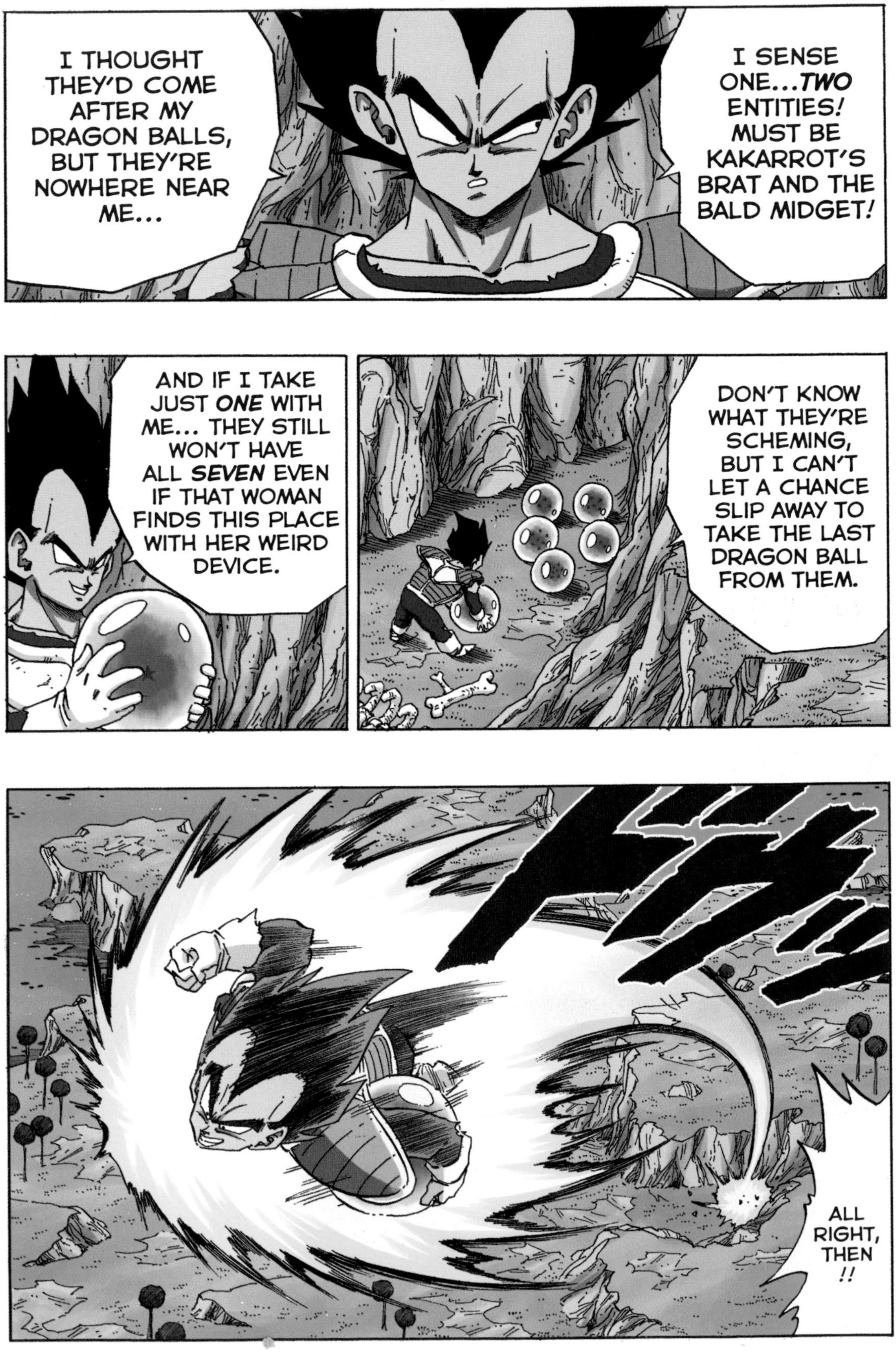
I SENSE ONE...*TWO* ENTITIES! MUST BE KAKARROT'S BRAT AND THE BALD MIDGET!
I THOUGHT THEY'D COME AFTER MY DRAGON BALLS, BUT THEY'RE NOWHERE NEAR ME...
DON'T KNOW WHAT THEY'RE SCHEMING, BUT I CAN'T LET A CHANCE SLIP AWAY TO TAKE THE LAST DRAGON BALL FROM THEM.
AND IF I TAKE JUST *ONE* WITH ME... THEY STILL WON'T HAVE ALL *SEVEN* EVEN IF THAT WOMAN FINDS THIS PLACE WITH HER WEIRD DEVICE.
ALL RIGHT, THEN!!

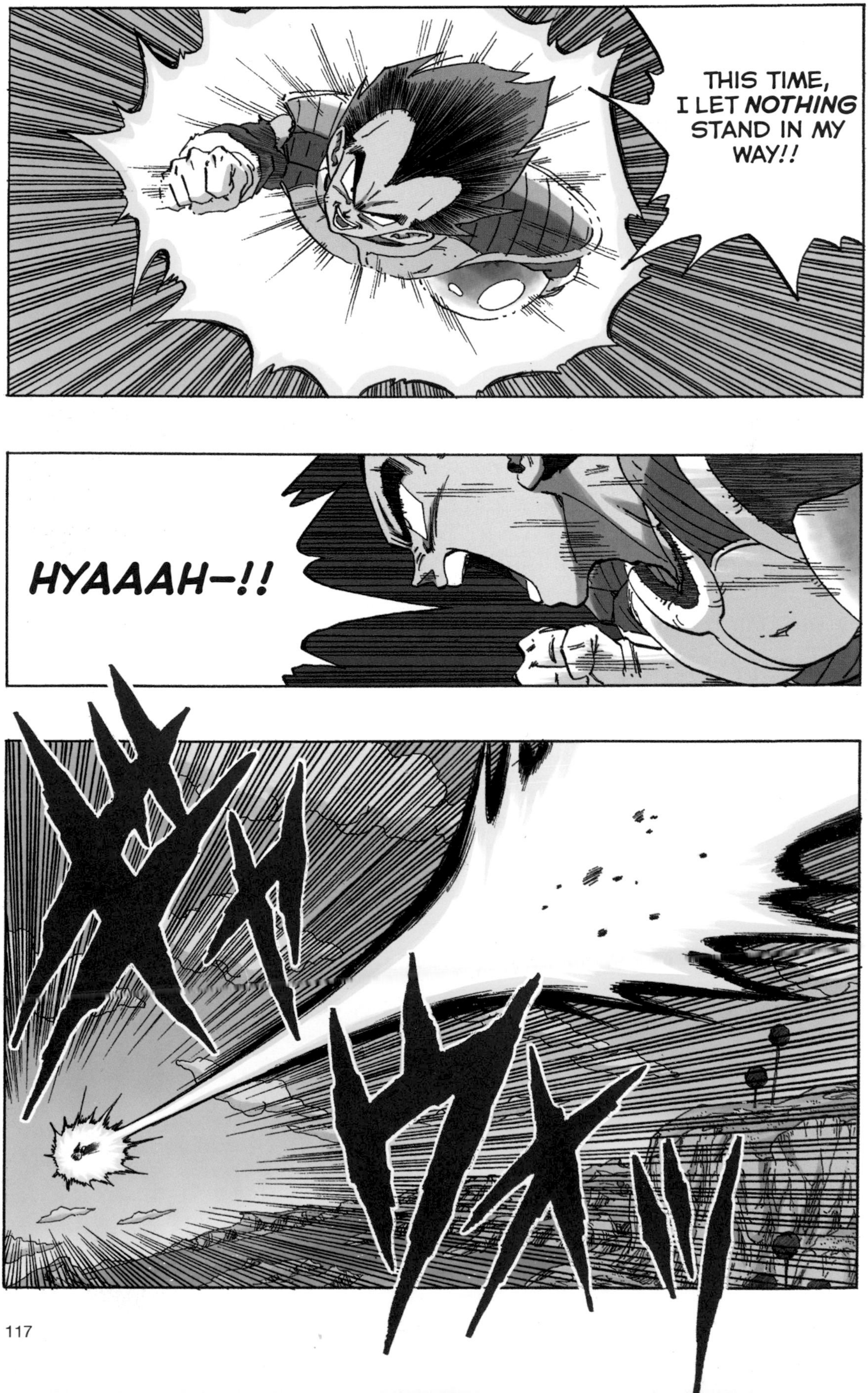
THIS TIME, I LET *NOTHING* STAND IN MY WAY!!
HYAAAH-!!

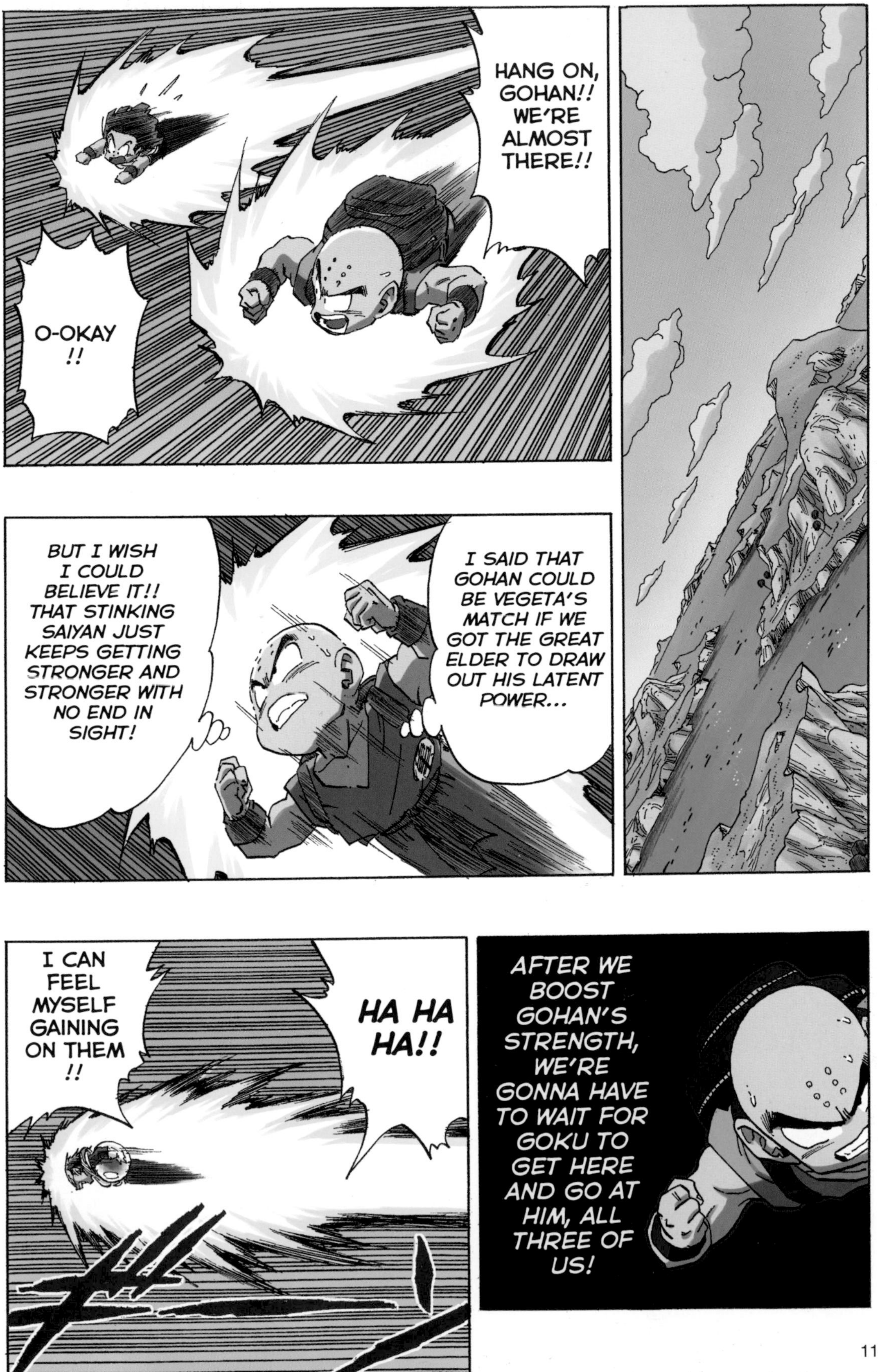
HANG ON, GOHAN!! WE'RE ALMOST THERE!!
O-OKAY!!
I SAID THAT GOHAN COULD BE VEGETA'S MATCH IF WE GOT THE GREAT ELDER TO DRAW OUT HIS LATENT POWER...
BUT I WISH I COULD BELIEVE IT!! THAT STINKING SAIYAN JUST KEEPS GETTING STRONGER AND STRONGER WITH NO END IN SIGHT!
AFTER WE BOOST GOHAN'S STRENGTH, WE'RE GONNA HAVE TO WAIT FOR GOKU TO GET HERE AND GO AT HIM, ALL THREE OF US!
HA HA HA!!
I CAN FEEL MYSELF GAINING ON THEM!!

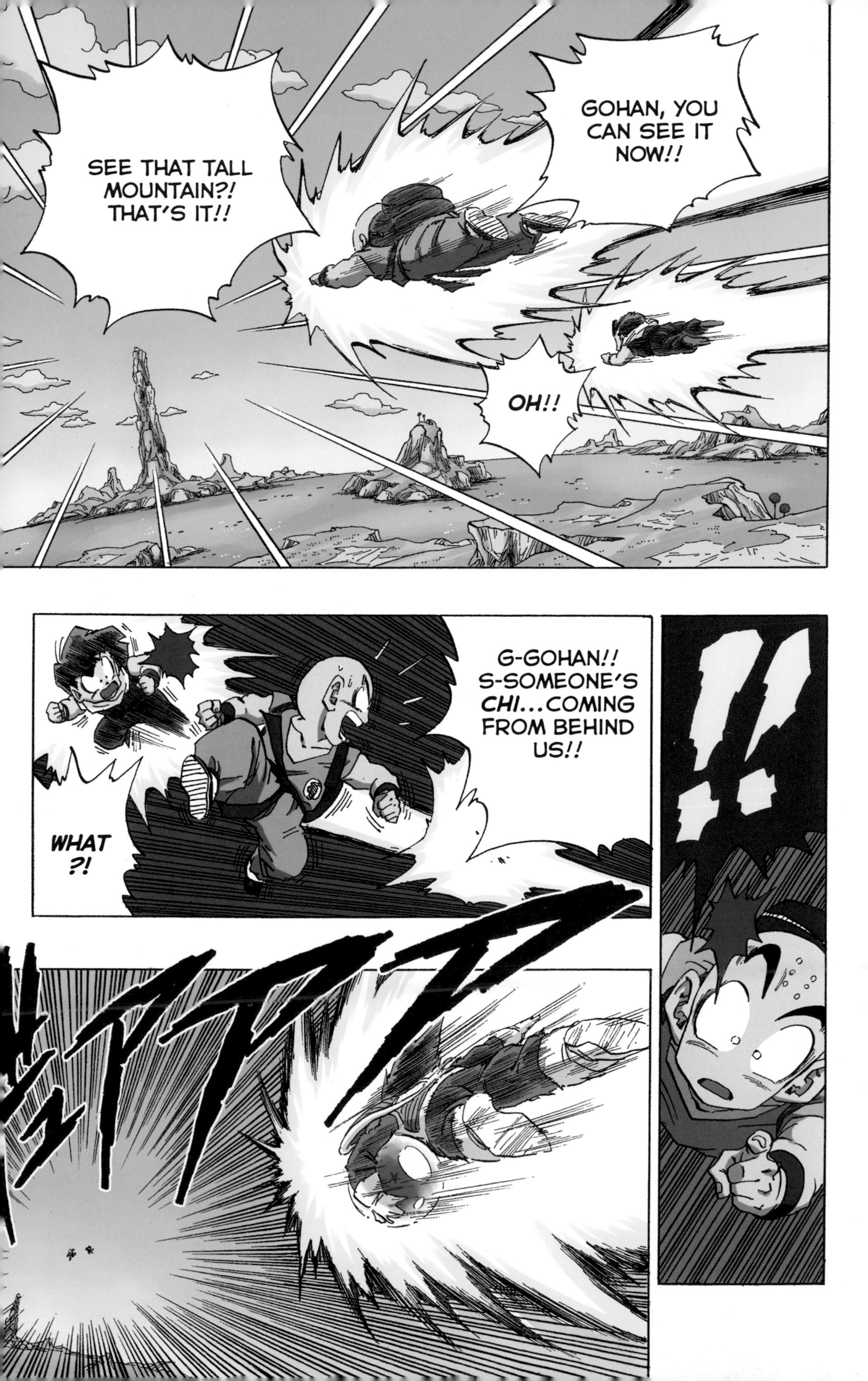
GOHAN, YOU CAN SEE IT NOW!!
OH!!
SEE THAT TALL MOUNTAIN?! THAT'S IT!!
!!
G-GOHAN!! S-SOMEONE'S *CHI*...COMING FROM BEHIND US!!
WHAT?!

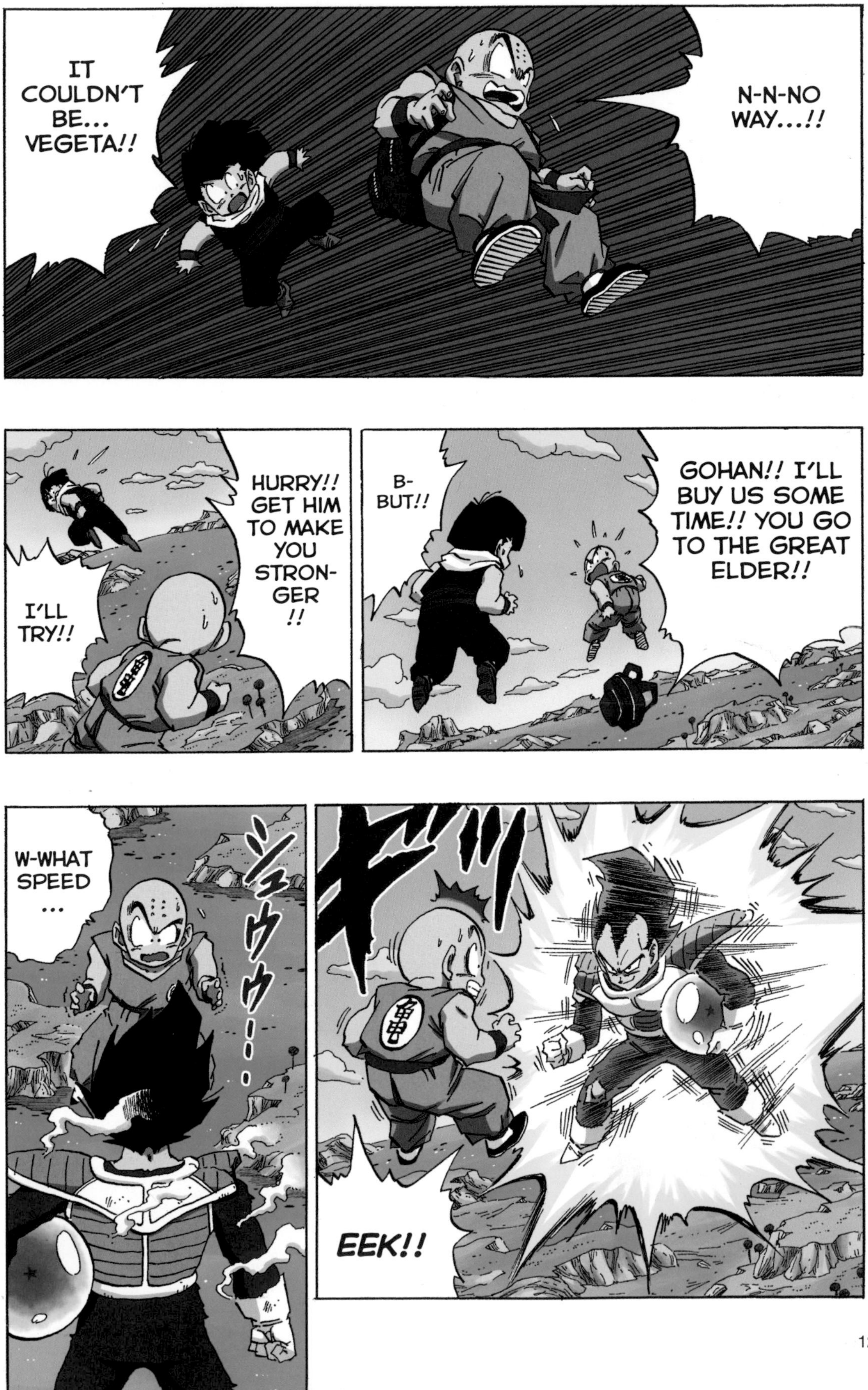
N-N-NO WAY...!!
IT COULDN'T BE... VEGETA!!
GOHAN!! I'LL BUY US SOME TIME!! YOU GO TO THE GREAT ELDER!!
B-BUT!!
HURRY!! GET HIM TO MAKE YOU STRONGER!!
I'LL TRY!!
EEK!!
W-WHAT SPEED...

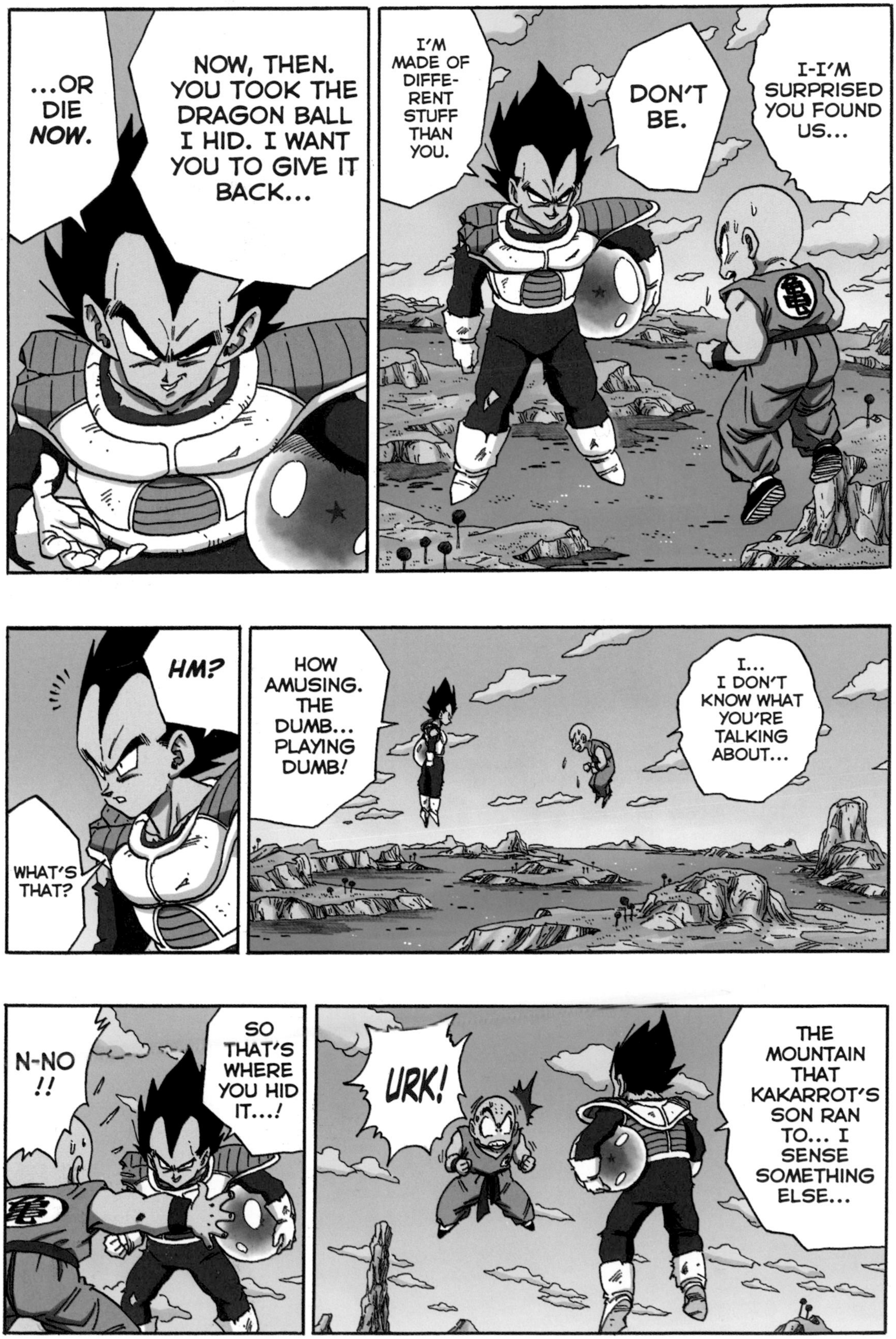
I-I'M SURPRISED YOU FOUND US...
DON'T BE.
I'M MADE OF DIFFERENT STUFF THAN YOU.
NOW, THEN. YOU TOOK THE DRAGON BALL I HID. I WANT YOU TO GIVE IT BACK...
...OR DIE *NOW*.
I... I DON'T KNOW WHAT YOU'RE TALKING ABOUT...
HOW AMUSING. THE DUMB... PLAYING DUMB!
HM?
WHAT'S THAT?
THE MOUNTAIN THAT KAKAROT'S SON RAN TO... I SENSE SOMETHING ELSE...
URK!
SO THAT'S WHERE YOU HID IT...!
N-NO!!

HEY!!

S-
STOP!!

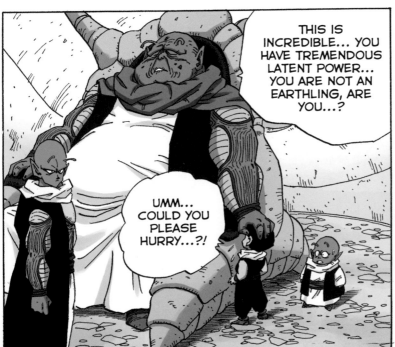

THIS IS INCREDIBLE... YOU HAVE TREMENDOUS LATENT POWER... YOU ARE NOT AN EARTHLING, ARE YOU...?

UMM... COULD YOU PLEASE HURRY...?!

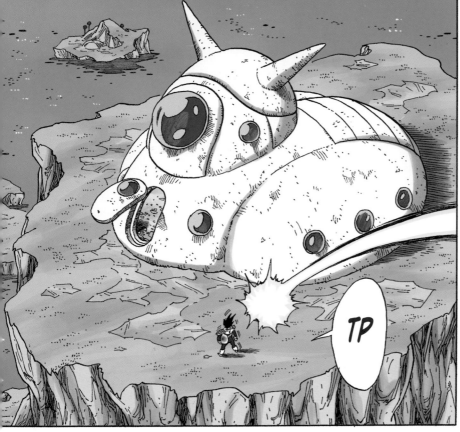

TP

HE'S HERE.

WAIT, VEGETA!! IT'S NOT *THERE*!!

ダッ

WHAT IS THIS...?

I AM NOT LETTING YOU GO IN.

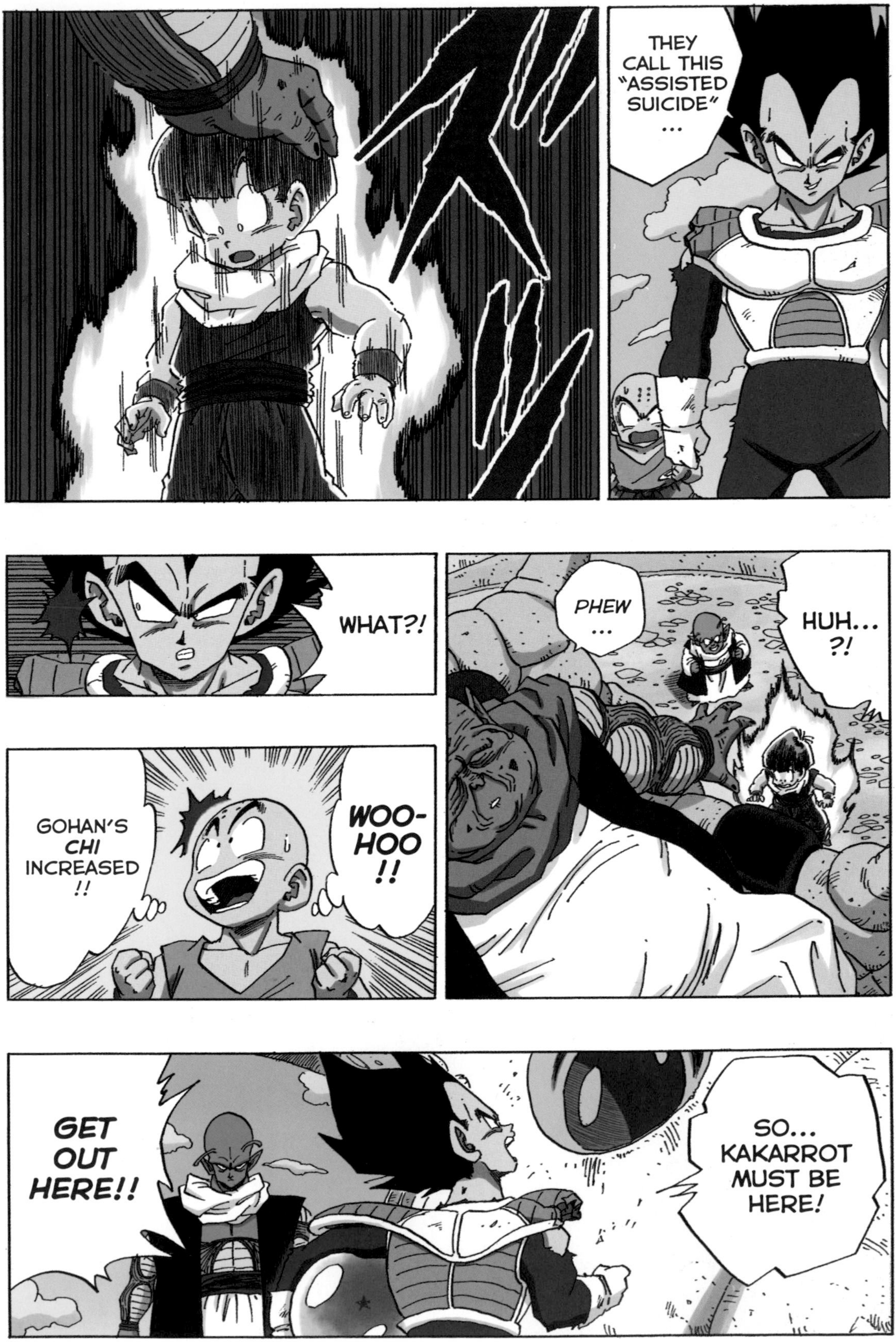
THEY CALL THIS "ASSISTED SUICIDE" ...
HUH... ?!
PHEW ...
WHAT?!
WOO-HOO !!
GOHAN'S CHI INCREASED !!
SO... KAKARROT MUST BE HERE!
GET OUT HERE!!

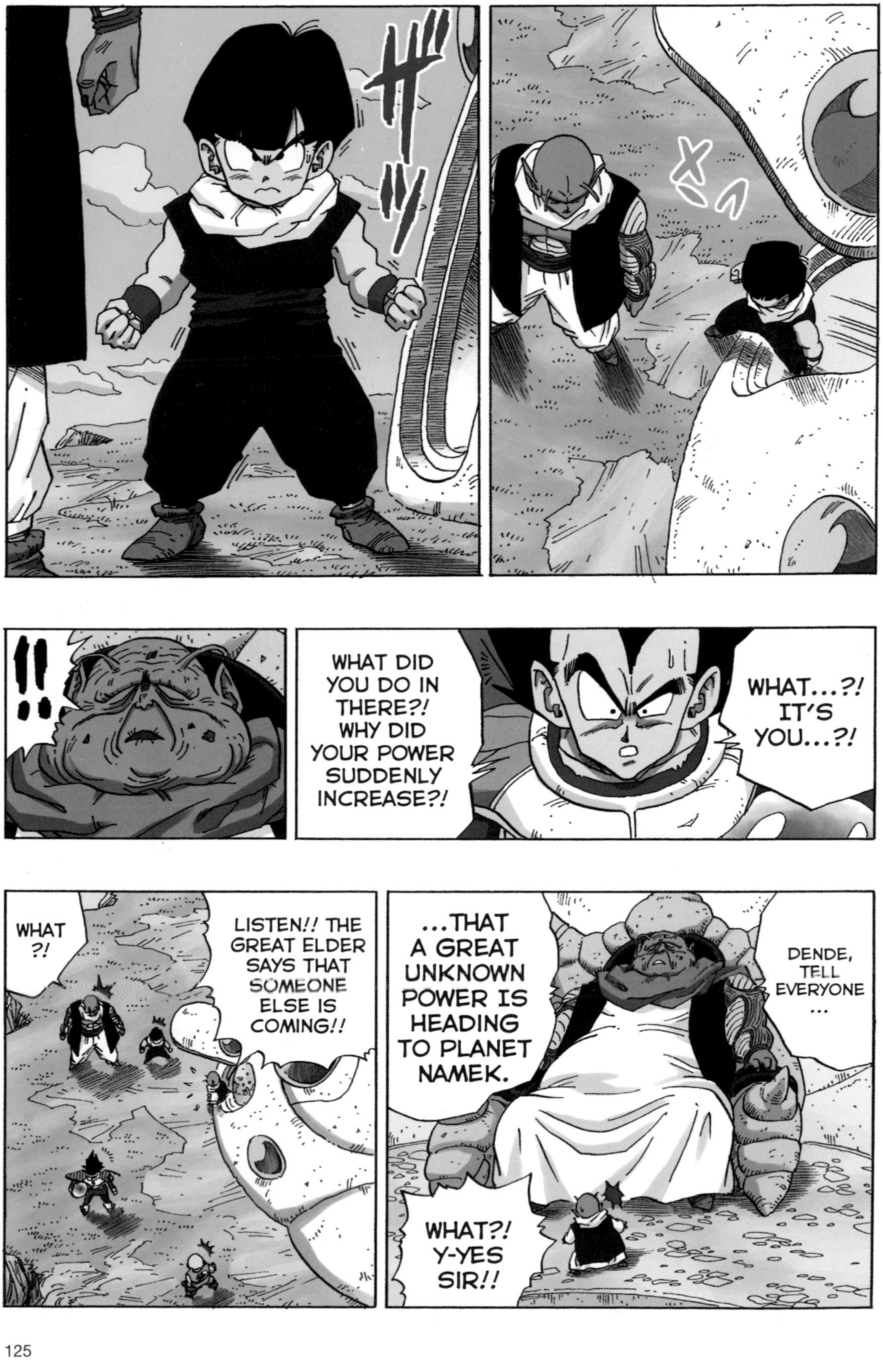
ザッ
WHAT...?! IT'S YOU...?!
WHAT DID YOU DO IN THERE?! WHY DID YOUR POWER SUDDENLY INCREASE?!
!!
DENDE, TELL EVERYONE ...
...THAT A GREAT UNKNOWN POWER IS HEADING TO PLANET NAMEK.
WHAT?! Y-YES SIR!!
LISTEN!! THE GREAT ELDER SAYS THAT SOMEONE ELSE IS COMING!!
WHAT ?!

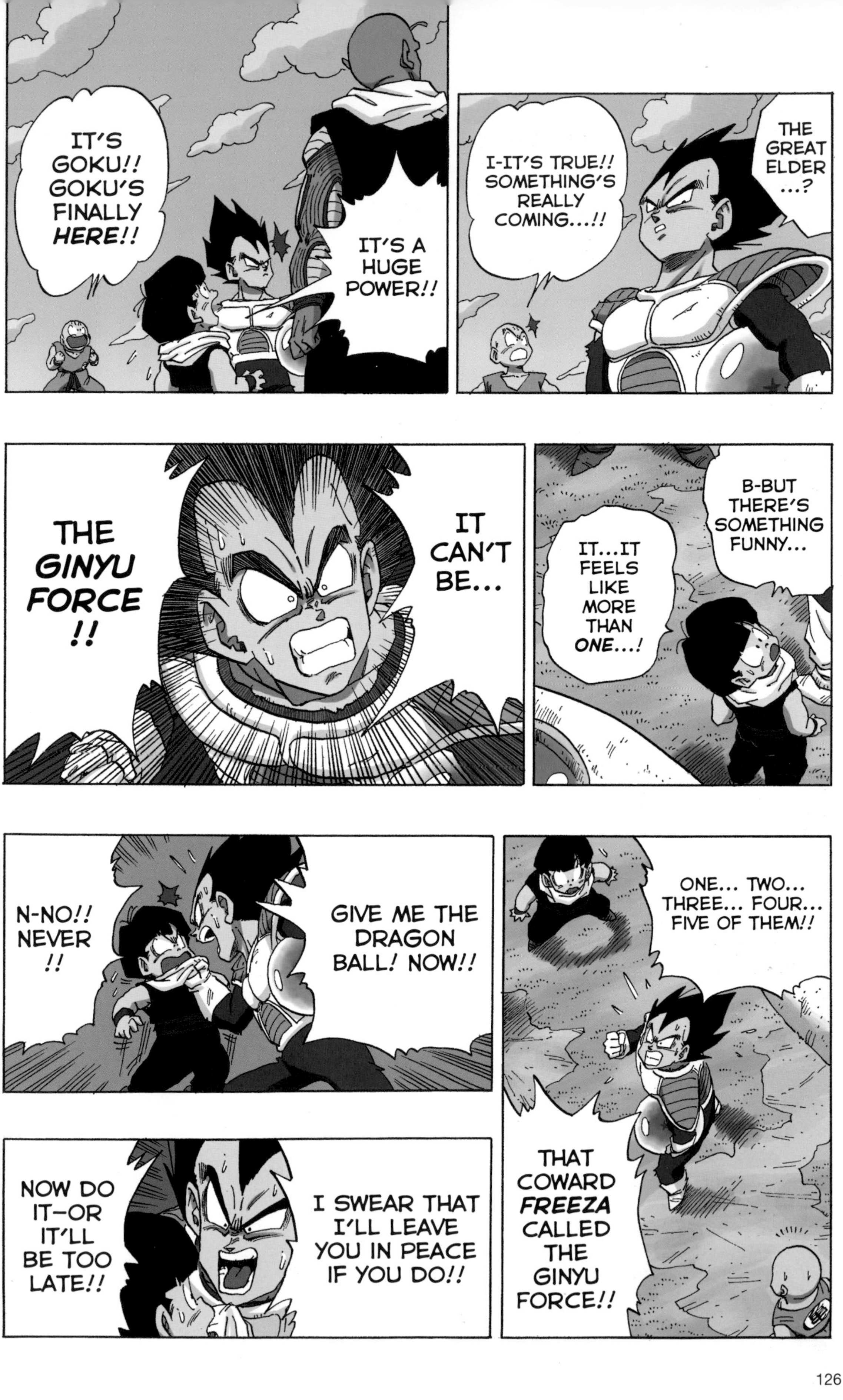
THE GREAT ELDER...?
I-IT'S TRUE!! SOMETHING'S REALLY COMING...!!
IT'S A HUGE POWER!!
IT'S GOKU!! GOKU'S FINALLY HERE!!
B-BUT THERE'S SOMETHING FUNNY...
IT...IT FEELS LIKE MORE THAN ONE...!
IT CAN'T BE...
THE GINYU FORCE!!
ONE... TWO... THREE... FOUR... FIVE OF THEM!!
THAT COWARD FREEZA CALLED THE GINYU FORCE!!
GIVE ME THE DRAGON BALL! NOW!!
N-NO!! NEVER!!
I SWEAR THAT I'LL LEAVE YOU IN PEACE IF YOU DO!!
NOW DO IT—OR IT'LL BE TOO LATE!!

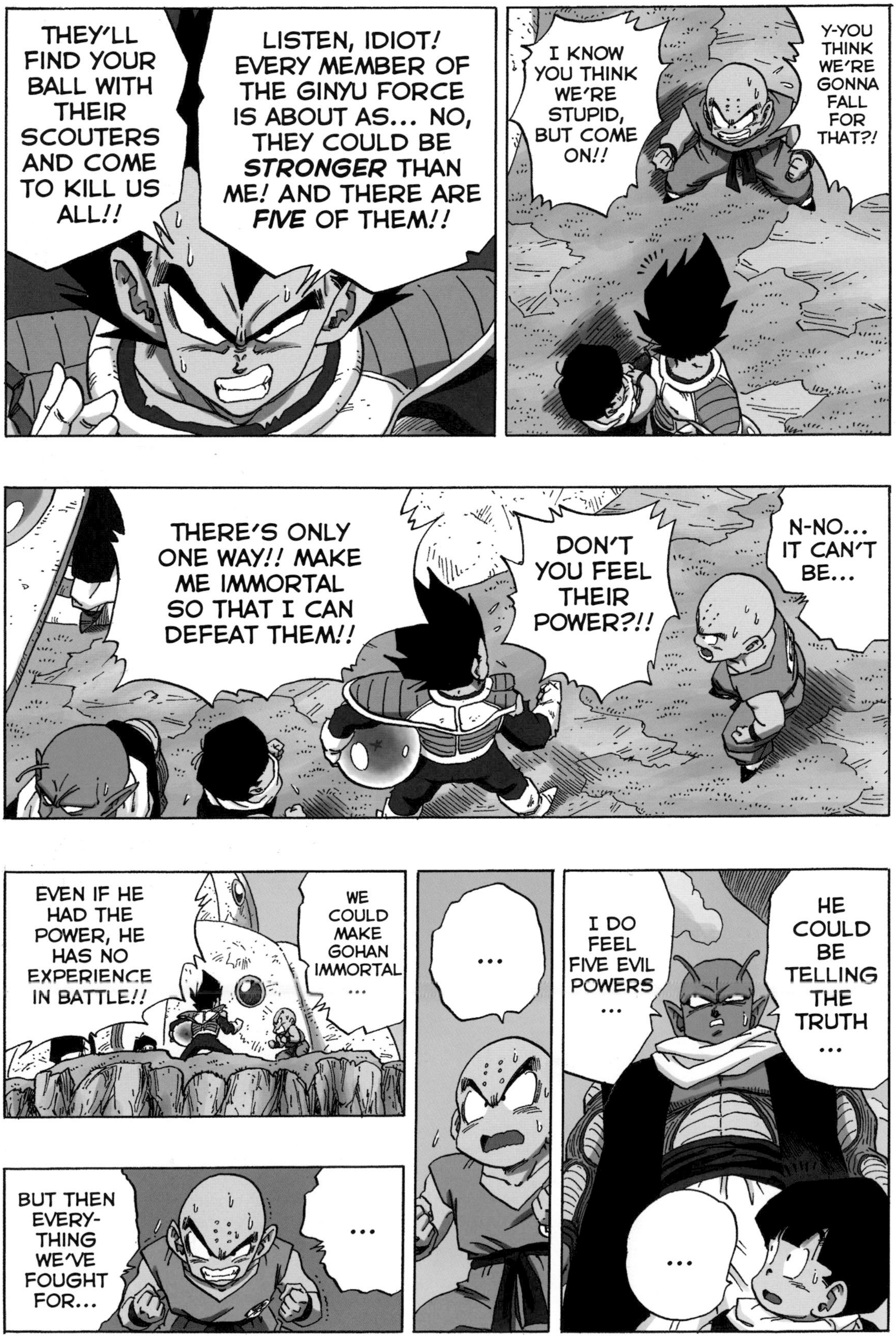
Y-YOU THINK WE'RE GONNA FALL FOR THAT?!
I KNOW YOU THINK WE'RE STUPID, BUT COME ON!!
LISTEN, IDIOT! EVERY MEMBER OF THE GINYU FORCE IS ABOUT AS... NO, THEY COULD BE *STRONGER* THAN ME! AND THERE ARE *FIVE* OF THEM!!
THEY'LL FIND YOUR BALL WITH THEIR SCOUTERS AND COME TO KILL US ALL!!
N-NO... IT CAN'T BE...
DON'T YOU FEEL THEIR POWER?!!
THERE'S ONLY ONE WAY!! MAKE ME IMMORTAL SO THAT I CAN DEFEAT THEM!!
HE COULD BE TELLING THE TRUTH...
I DO FEEL FIVE EVIL POWERS...
...
...
WE COULD MAKE GOHAN IMMORTAL...
EVEN IF HE HAD THE POWER, HE HAS NO EXPERIENCE IN BATTLE!!
...
BUT THEN EVERY-THING WE'VE FOUGHT FOR...

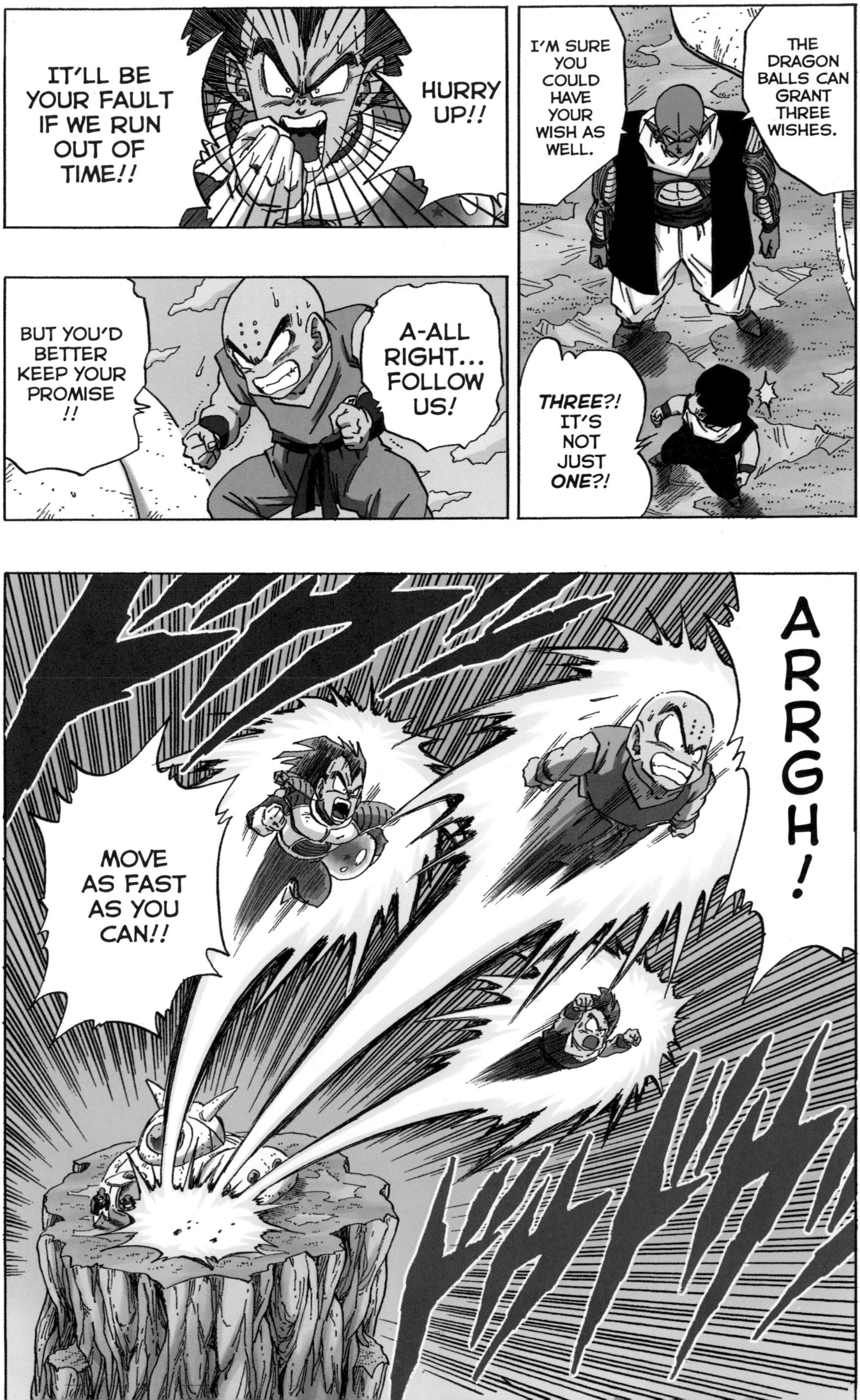
THE DRAGON BALLS CAN GRANT THREE WISHES.
I'M SURE YOU COULD HAVE YOUR WISH AS WELL.
THREE?! IT'S NOT JUST ONE?!
HURRY UP!!
IT'LL BE YOUR FAULT IF WE RUN OUT OF TIME!!
A-ALL RIGHT... FOLLOW US!
BUT YOU'D BETTER KEEP YOUR PROMISE!!
ARRGH!
MOVE AS FAST AS YOU CAN!!

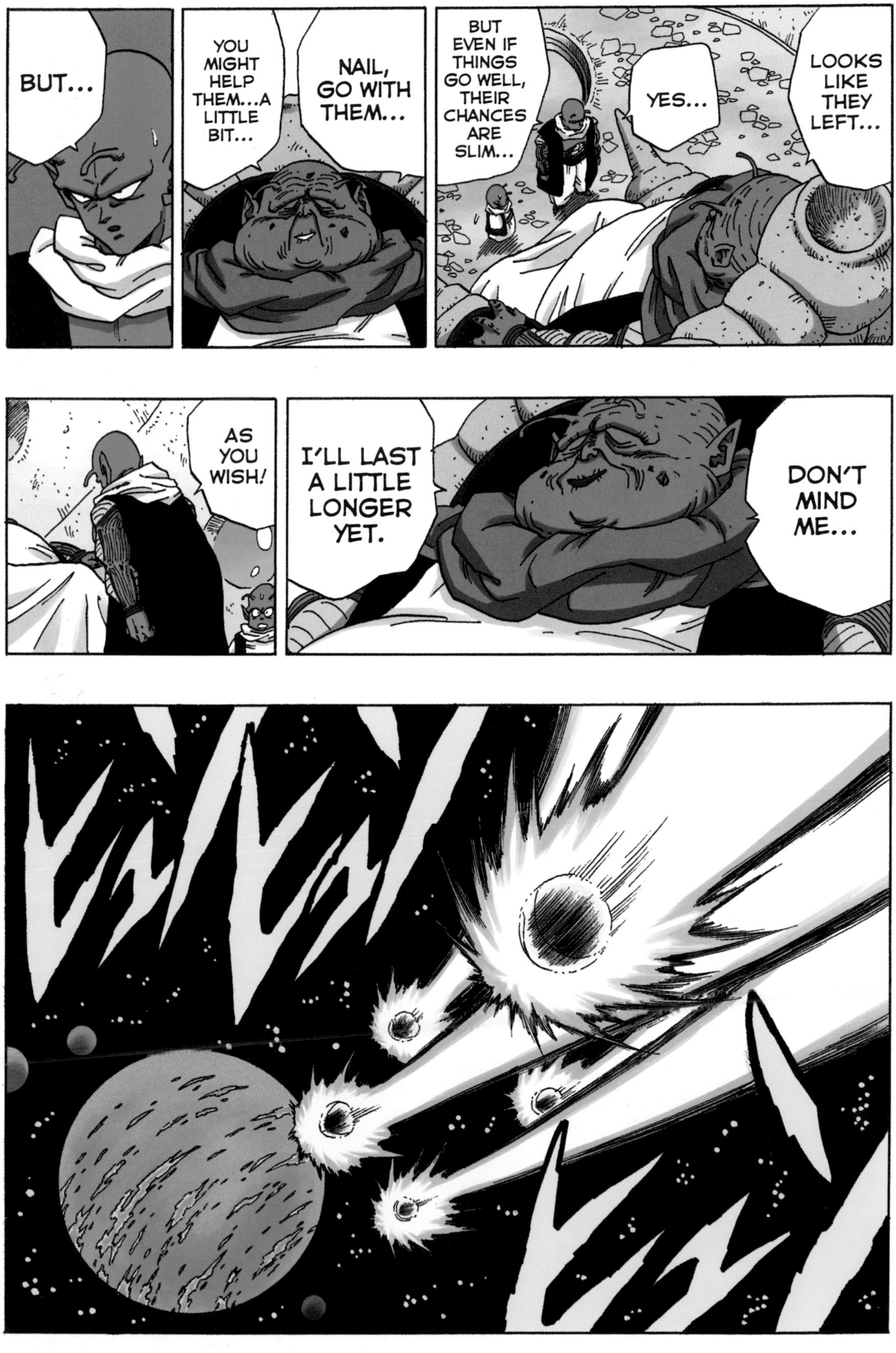
LOOKS LIKE THEY LEFT...
YES...
BUT EVEN IF THINGS GO WELL, THEIR CHANCES ARE SLIM...
NAIL, GO WITH THEM...
YOU MIGHT HELP THEM...A LITTLE BIT...
BUT...
DON'T MIND ME...
I'LL LAST A LITTLE LONGER YET.
AS YOU WISH!

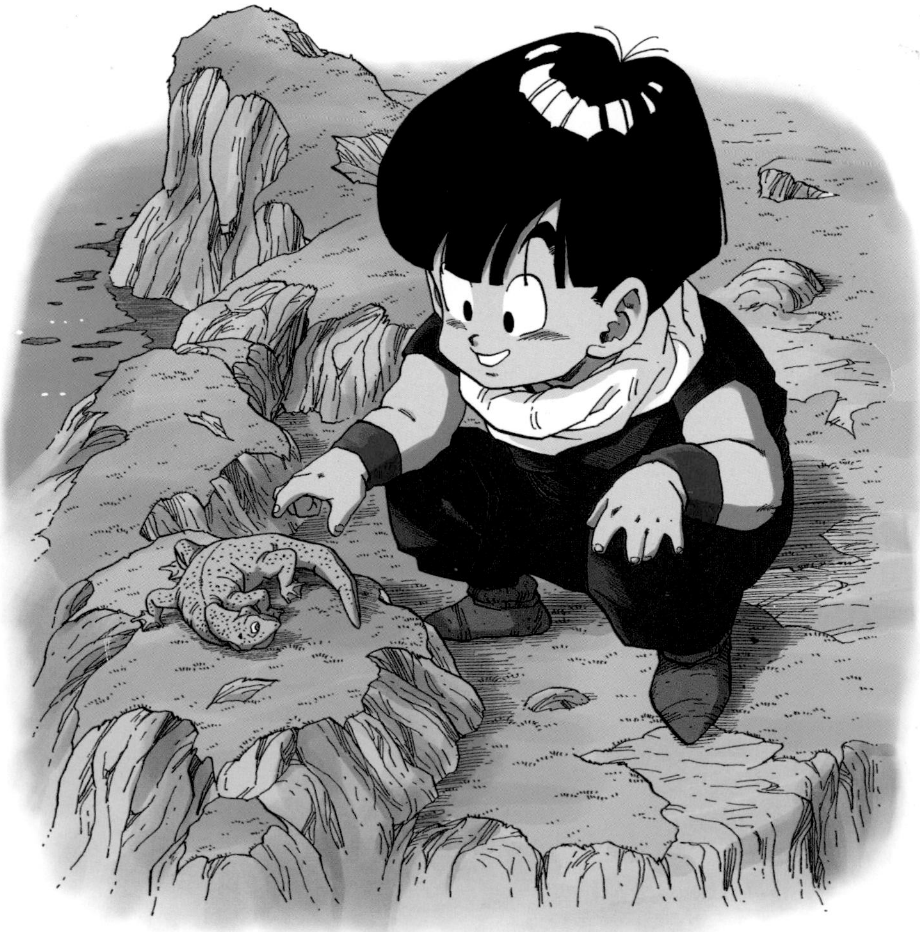

DRAGON BALL FULL COLOR FREEZA ARC

DRAGON BALL
ドラゴンボール

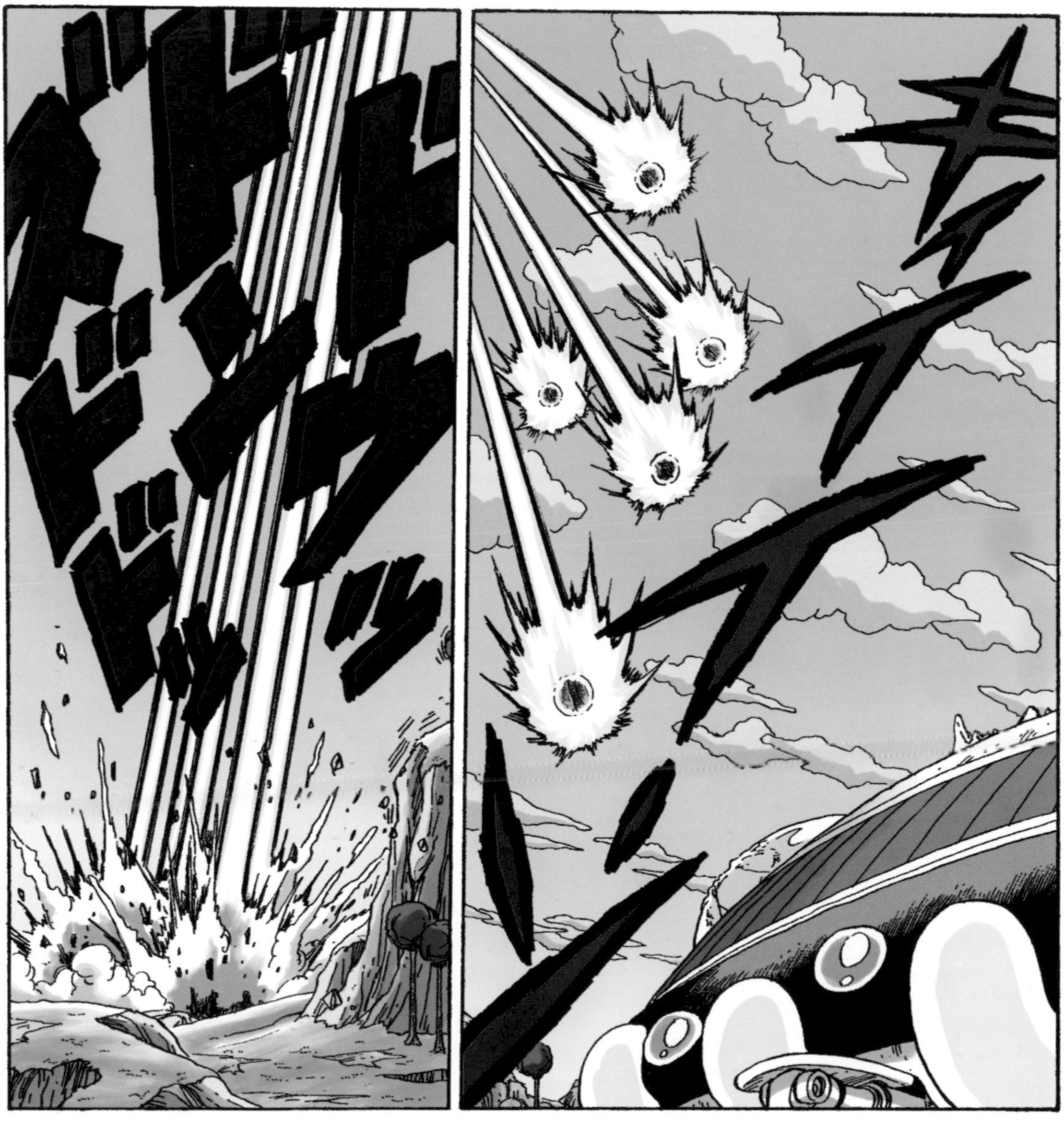
キィイイン
ズドドドドドドドッ

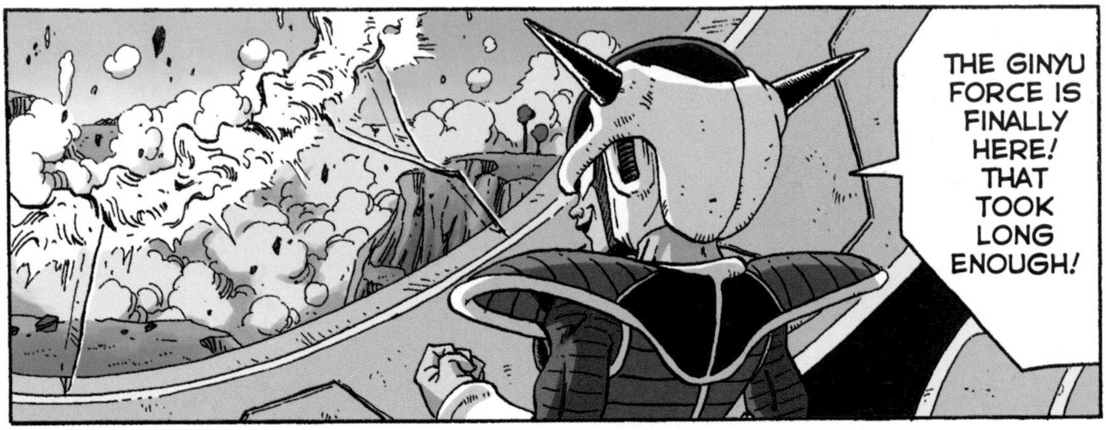
THE GINYU FORCE IS FINALLY HERE! THAT TOOK LONG ENOUGH!

Chapter 27 • The Ginyu Force

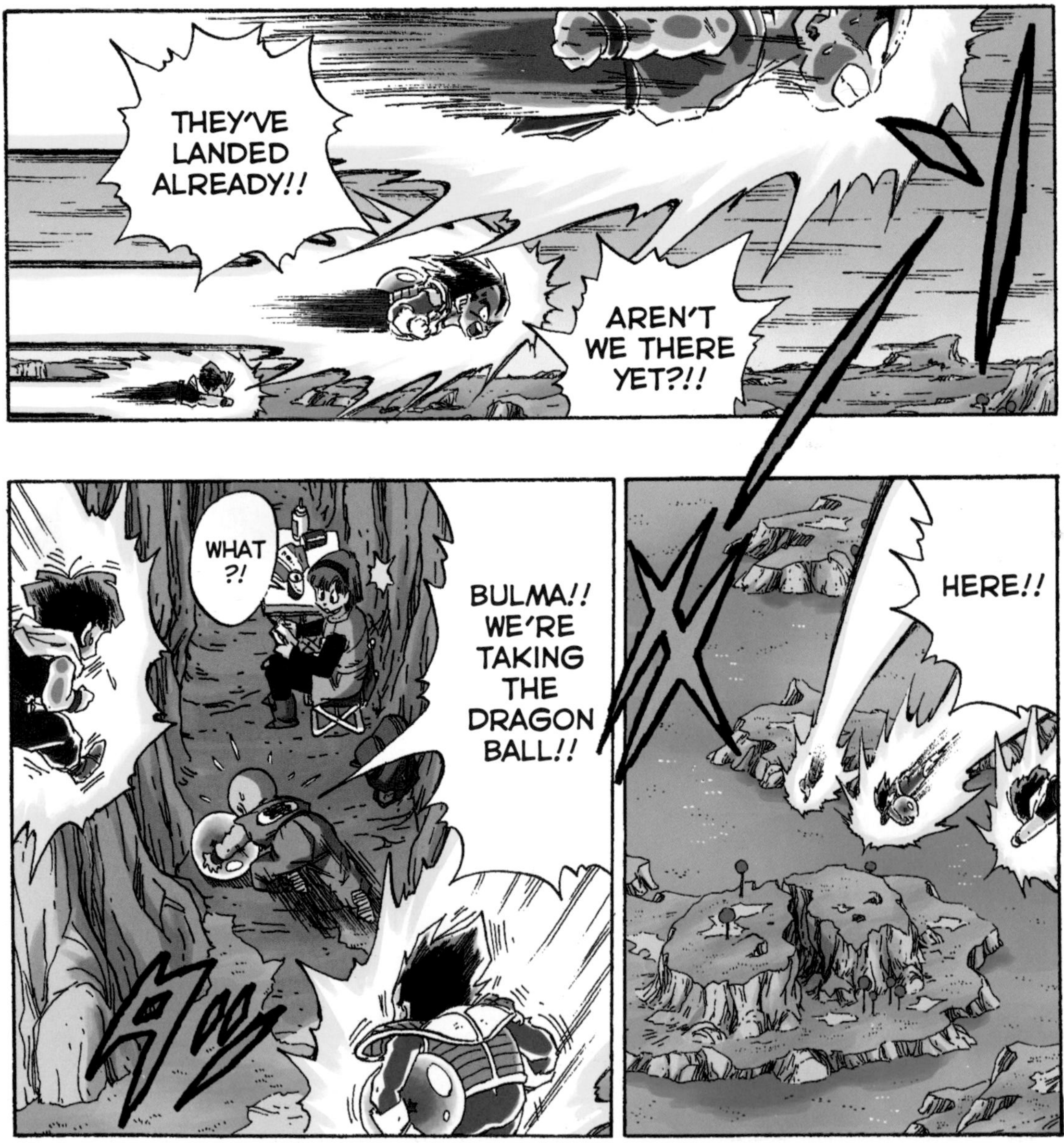
THEY'VE LANDED ALREADY!!
AREN'T WE THERE YET?!!
HERE!!
BULMA!! WE'RE TAKING THE DRAGON BALL!!
WHAT ?!

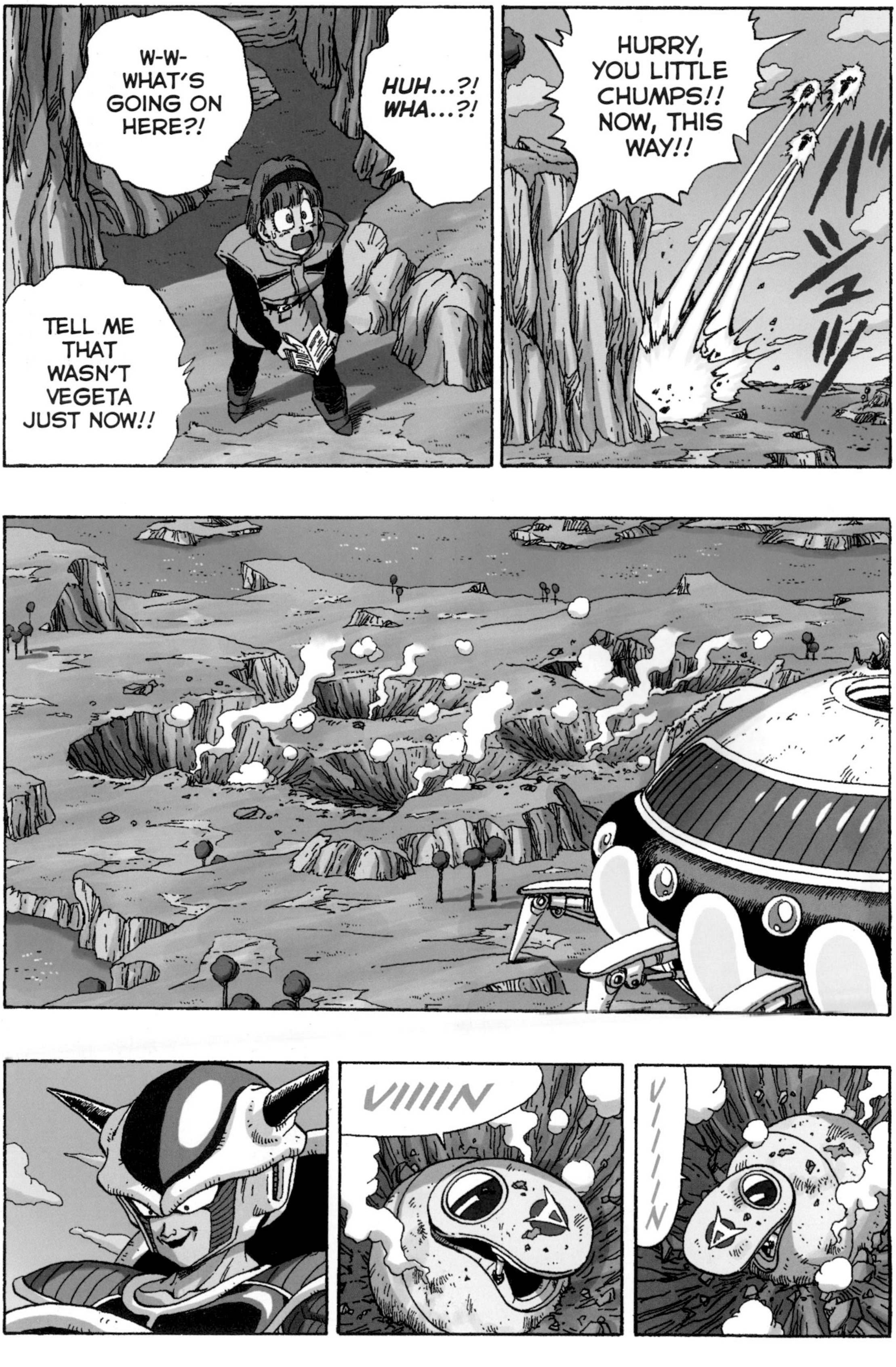
HURRY, YOU LITTLE CHUMPS!! NOW, THIS WAY!!
HUH...?! WHA...?!
W-W- WHAT'S GOING ON HERE?!
TELL ME THAT WASN'T VEGETA JUST NOW!!
VIIIIN
VIIIN

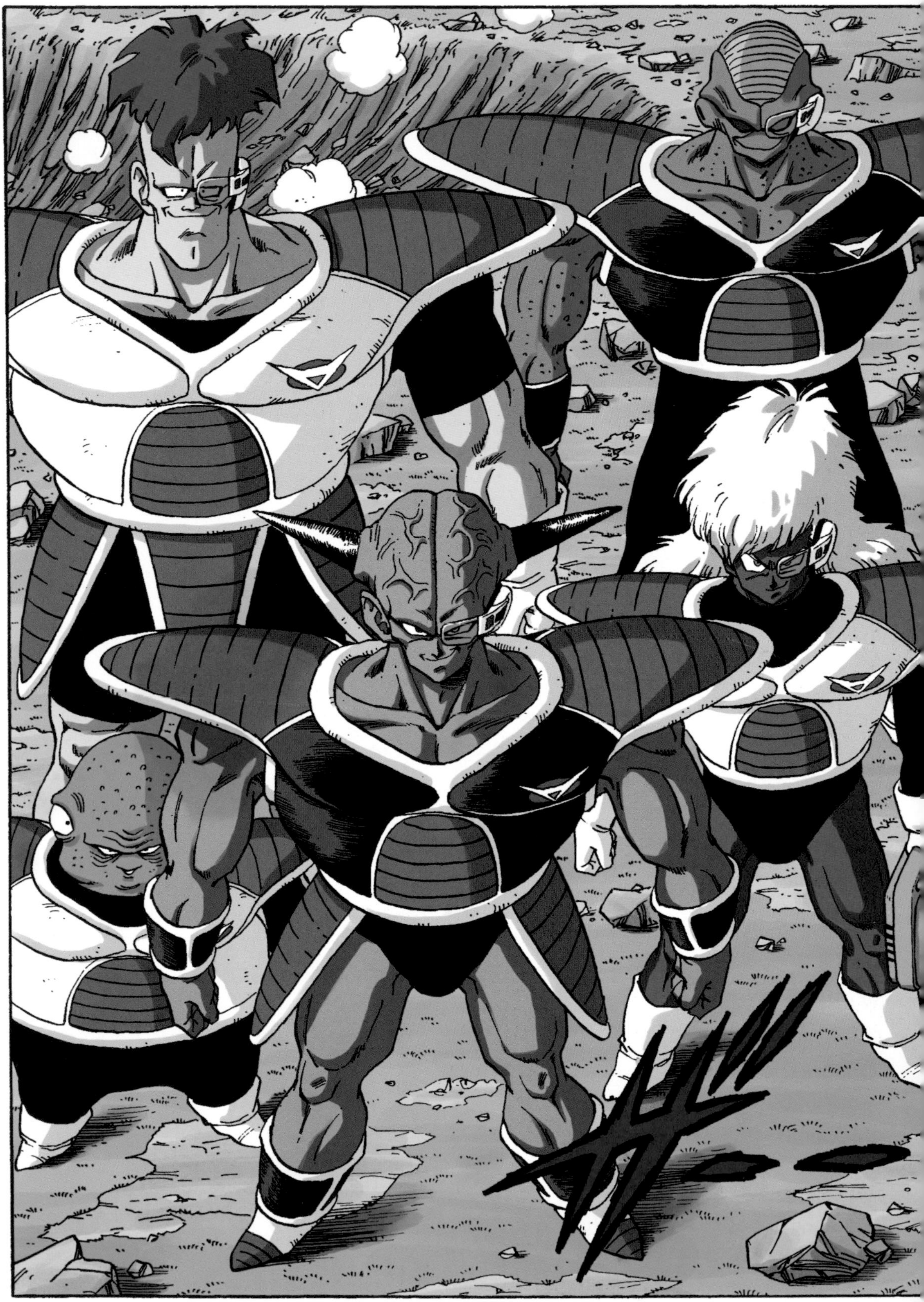

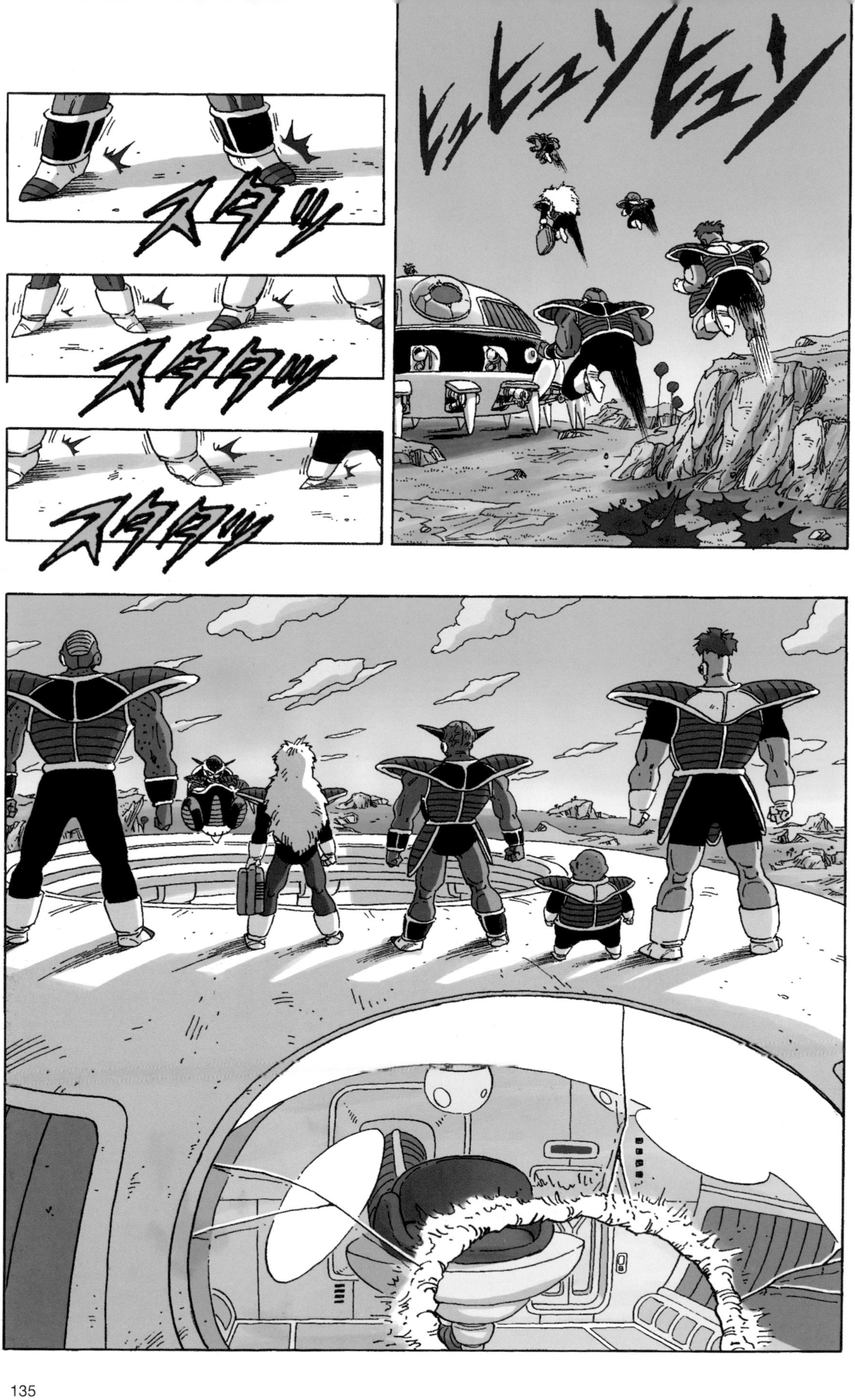
ヒュッヒュンヒュン
スタッ
スタタッ
スタタッ

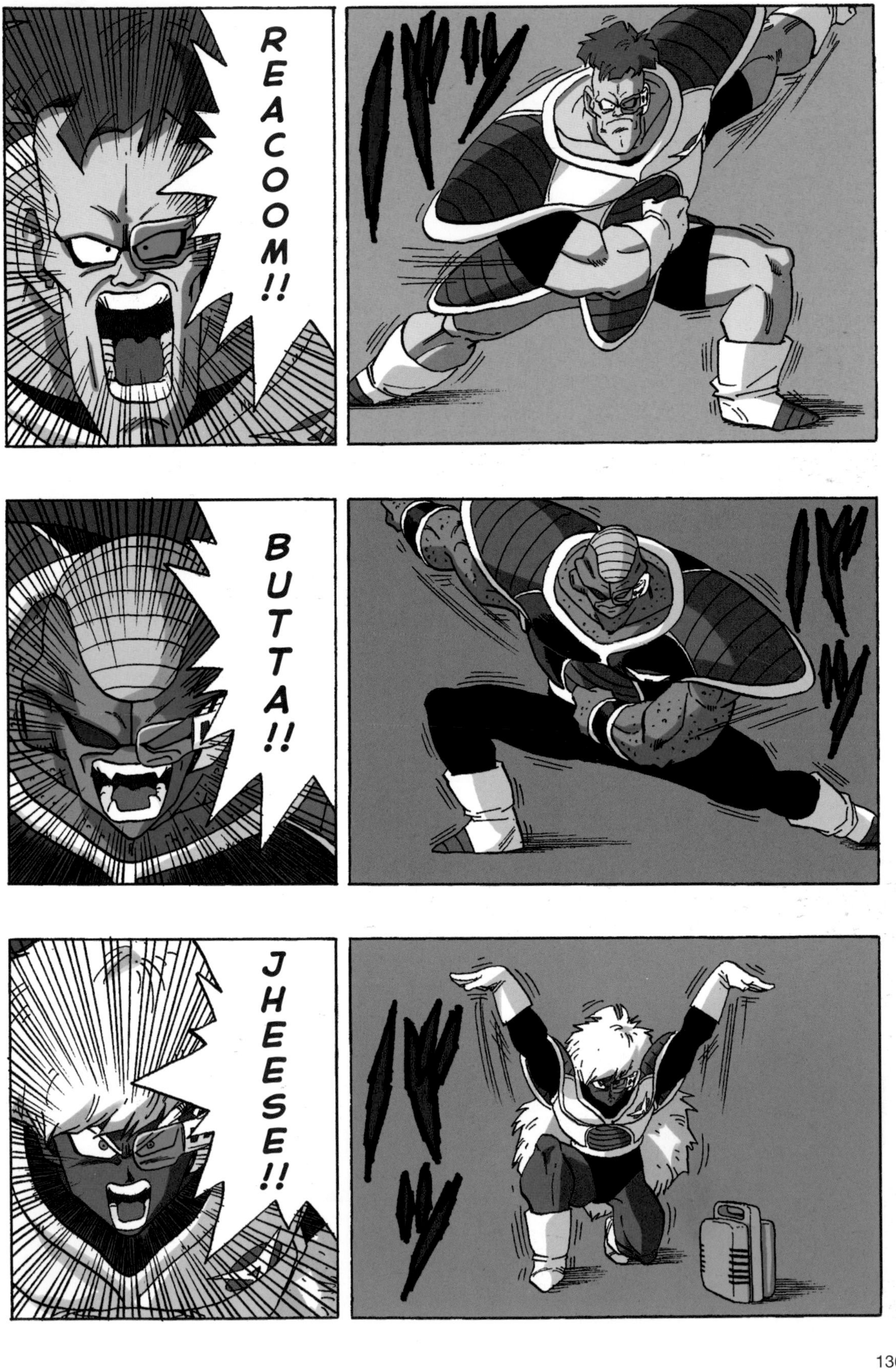
REACOOM!!
BUTTA!!
JHEESE!!

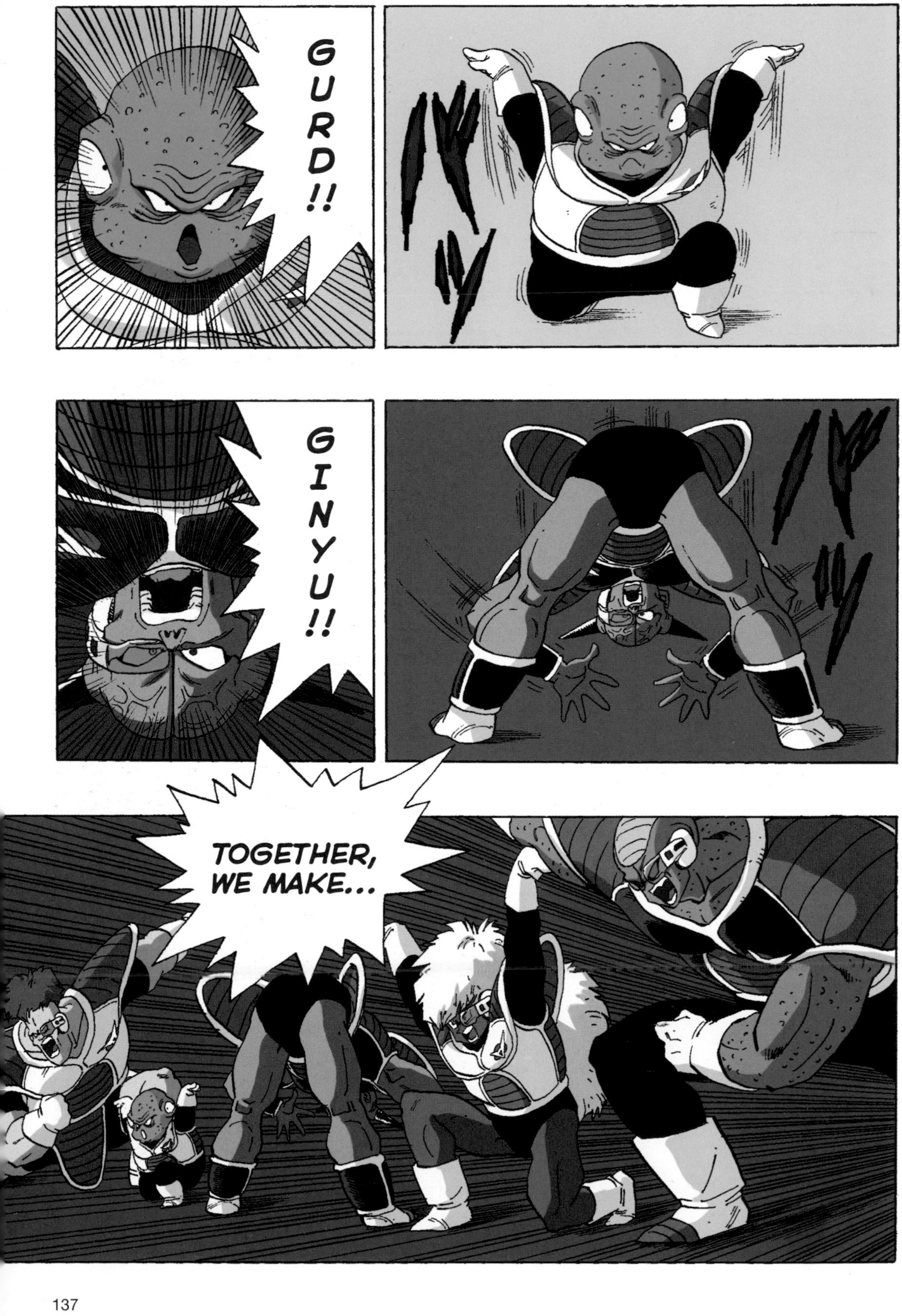
GURD!!
GINYU!!
TOGETHER, WE MAKE...

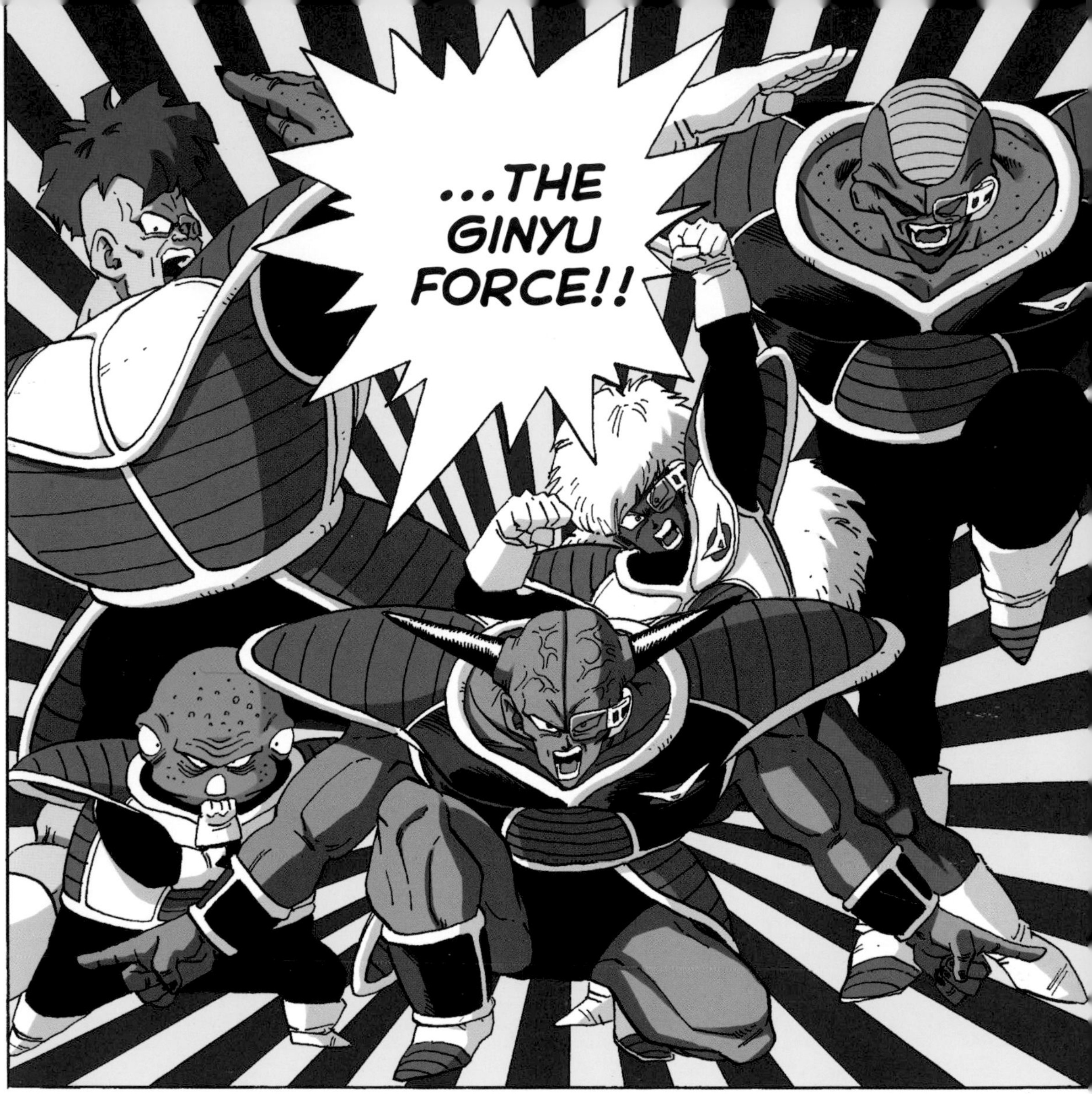
...THE GINYU FORCE!!

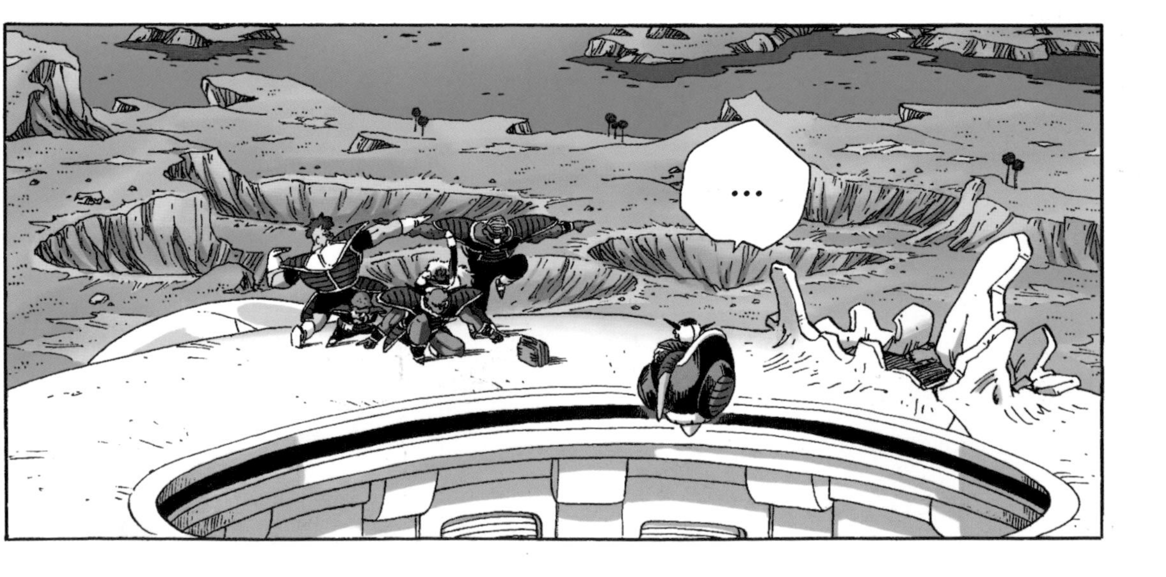
...

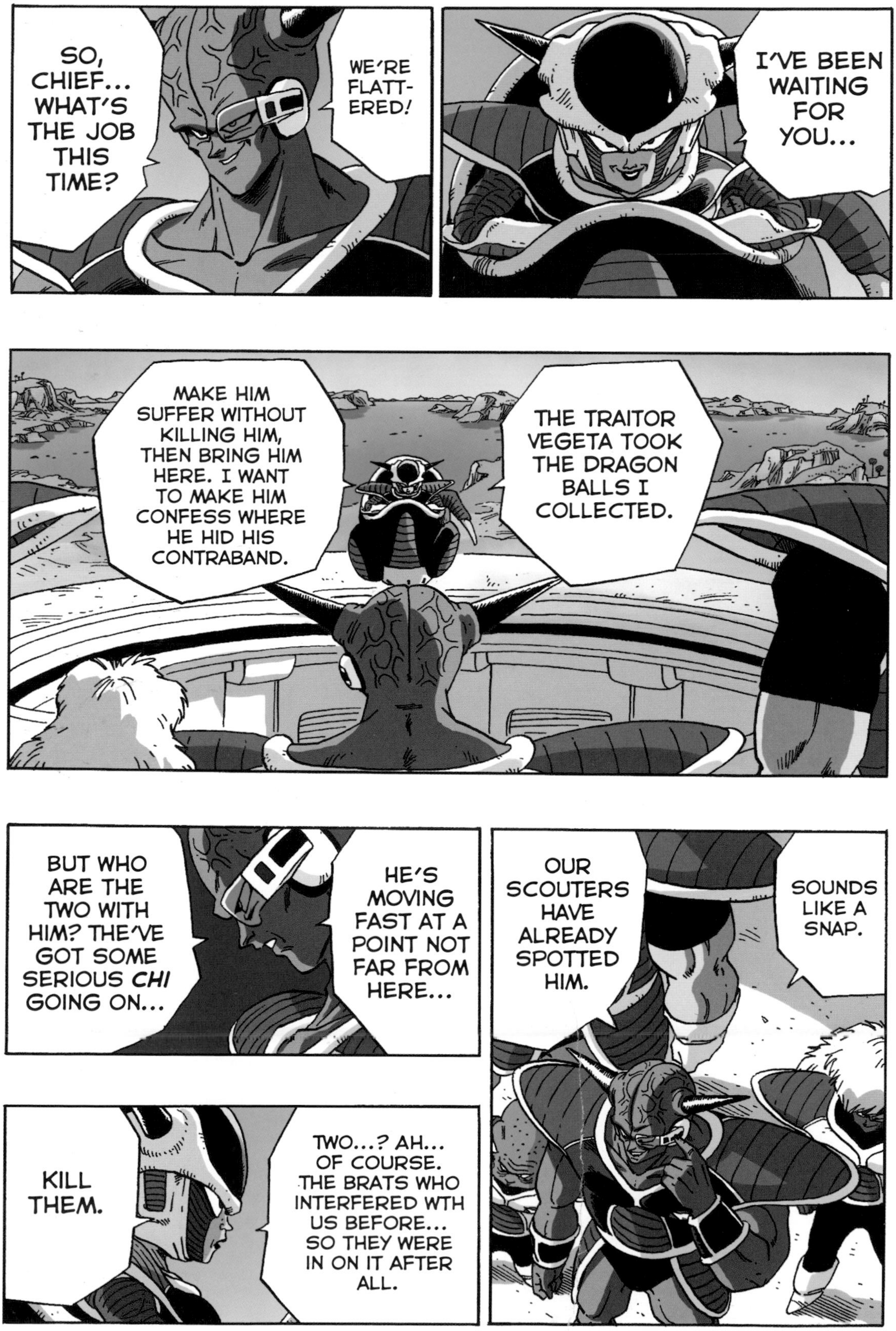
I'VE BEEN WAITING FOR YOU...
WE'RE FLATT-ERED!
SO, CHIEF... WHAT'S THE JOB THIS TIME?
THE TRAITOR VEGETA TOOK THE DRAGON BALLS I COLLECTED.
MAKE HIM SUFFER WITHOUT KILLING HIM, THEN BRING HIM HERE. I WANT TO MAKE HIM CONFESS WHERE HE HID HIS CONTRABAND.
SOUNDS LIKE A SNAP.
OUR SCOUTERS HAVE ALREADY SPOTTED HIM.
HE'S MOVING FAST AT A POINT NOT FAR FROM HERE...
BUT WHO ARE THE TWO WITH HIM? THE'VE GOT SOME SERIOUS *CHI* GOING ON...
TWO...? AH... OF COURSE. THE BRATS WHO INTERFERED WTH US BEFORE... SO THEY WERE IN ON IT AFTER ALL.
KILL THEM.

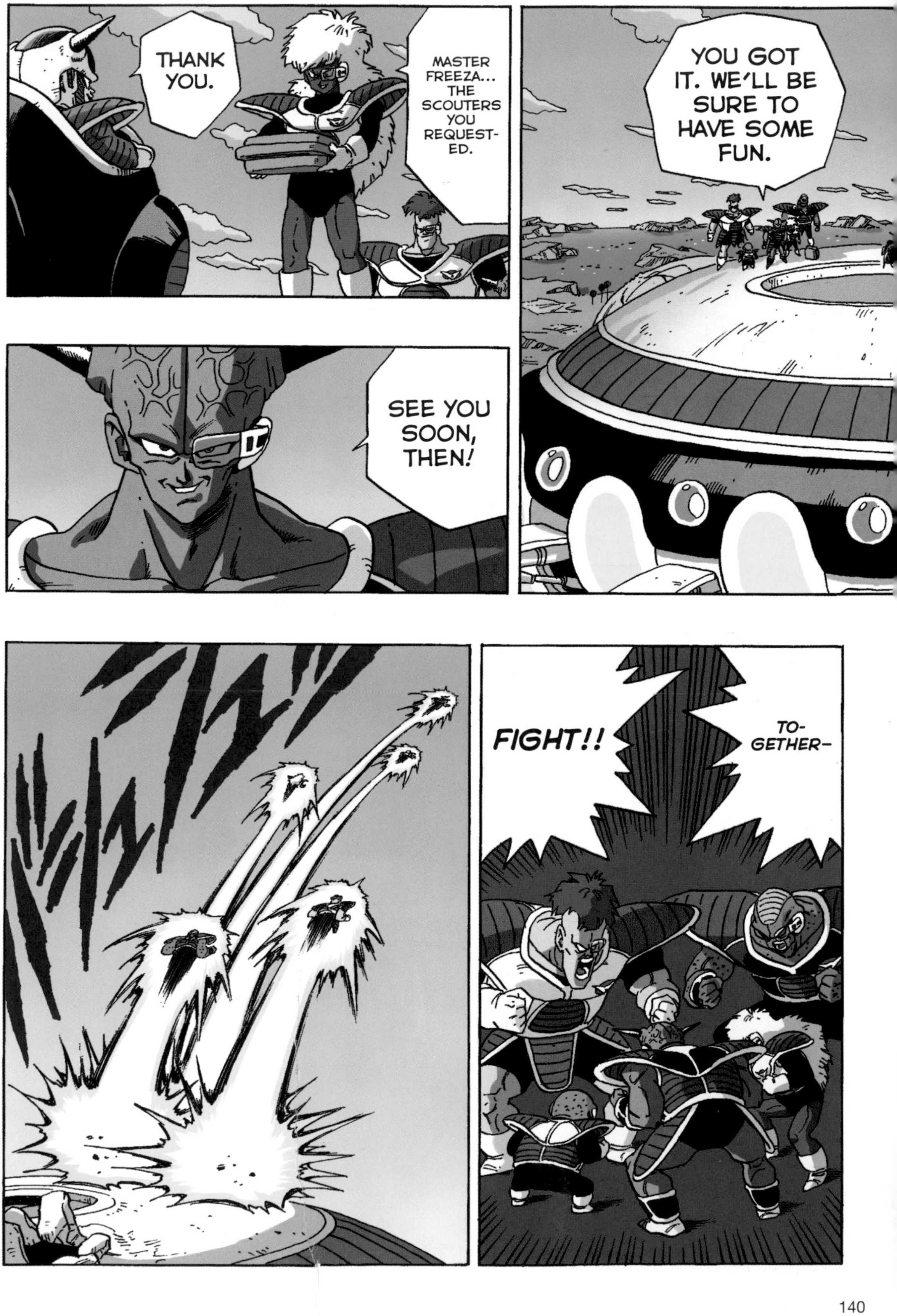
YOU GOT IT. WE'LL BE SURE TO HAVE SOME FUN.
MASTER FREEZA... THE SCOUTERS YOU REQUEST-ED.
THANK YOU.
SEE YOU SOON, THEN!
TO-GETHER-
FIGHT!!

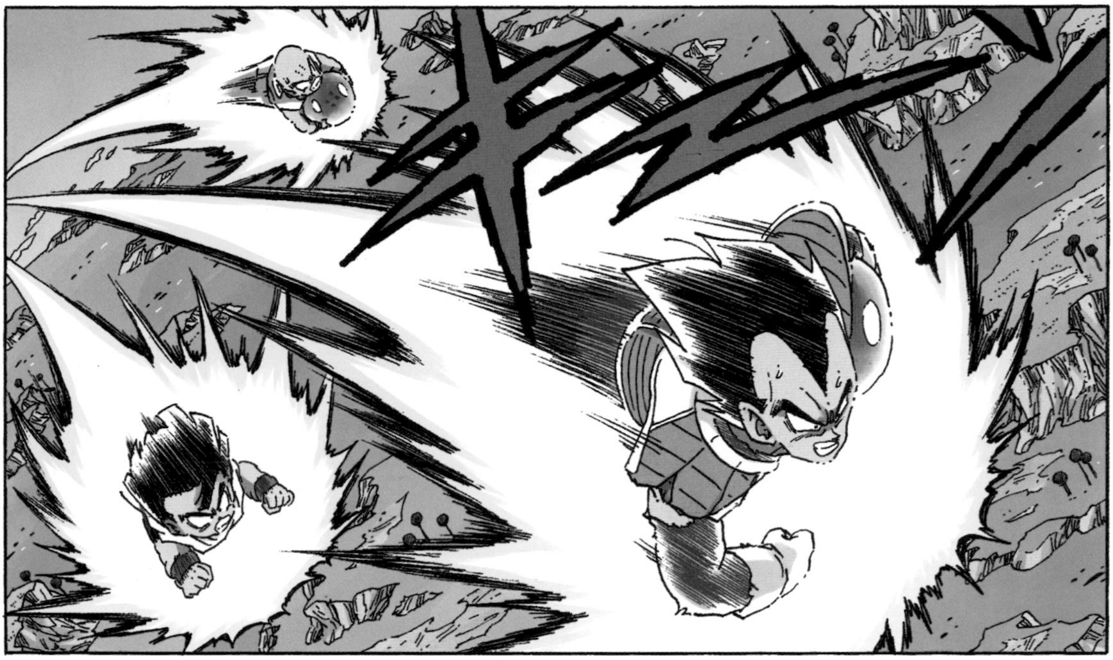

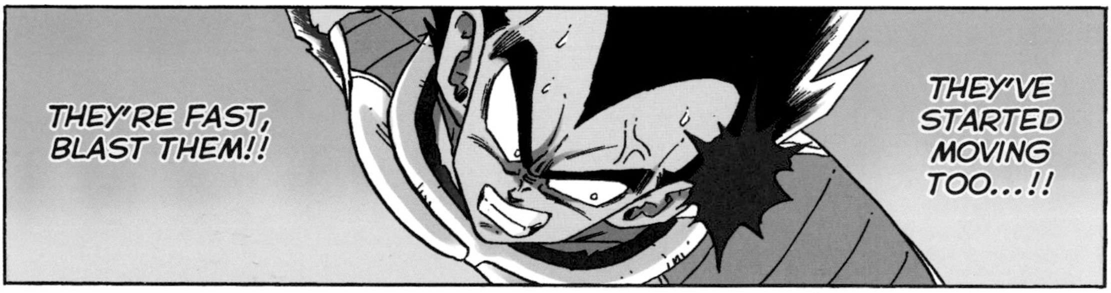
THEY'VE STARTED MOVING TOO...!!
THEY'RE FAST, BLAST THEM!!

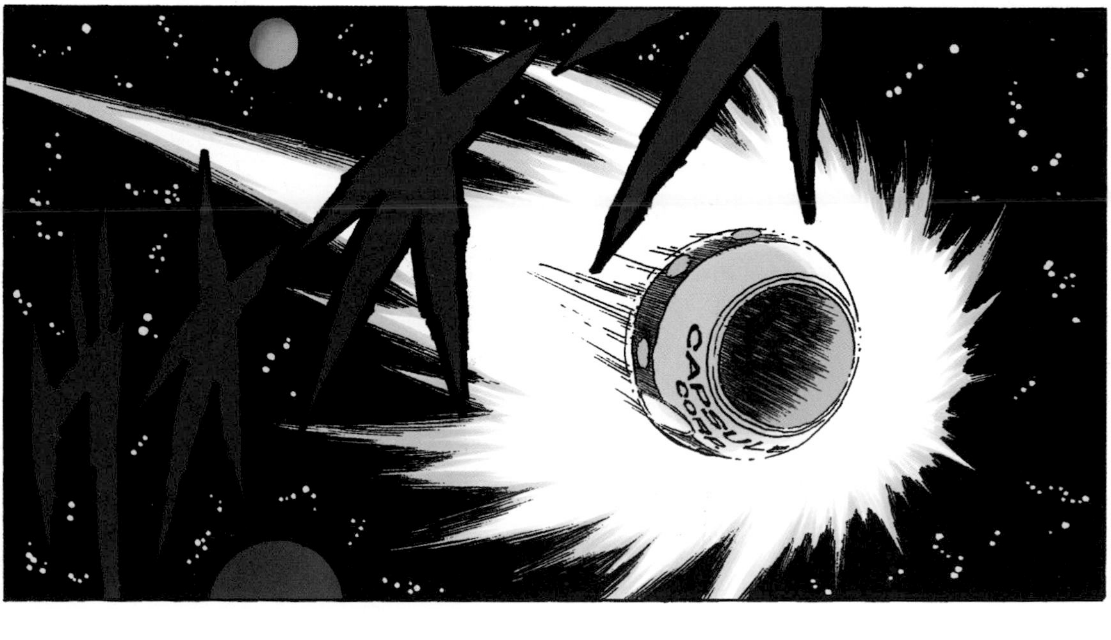
CAPSULE

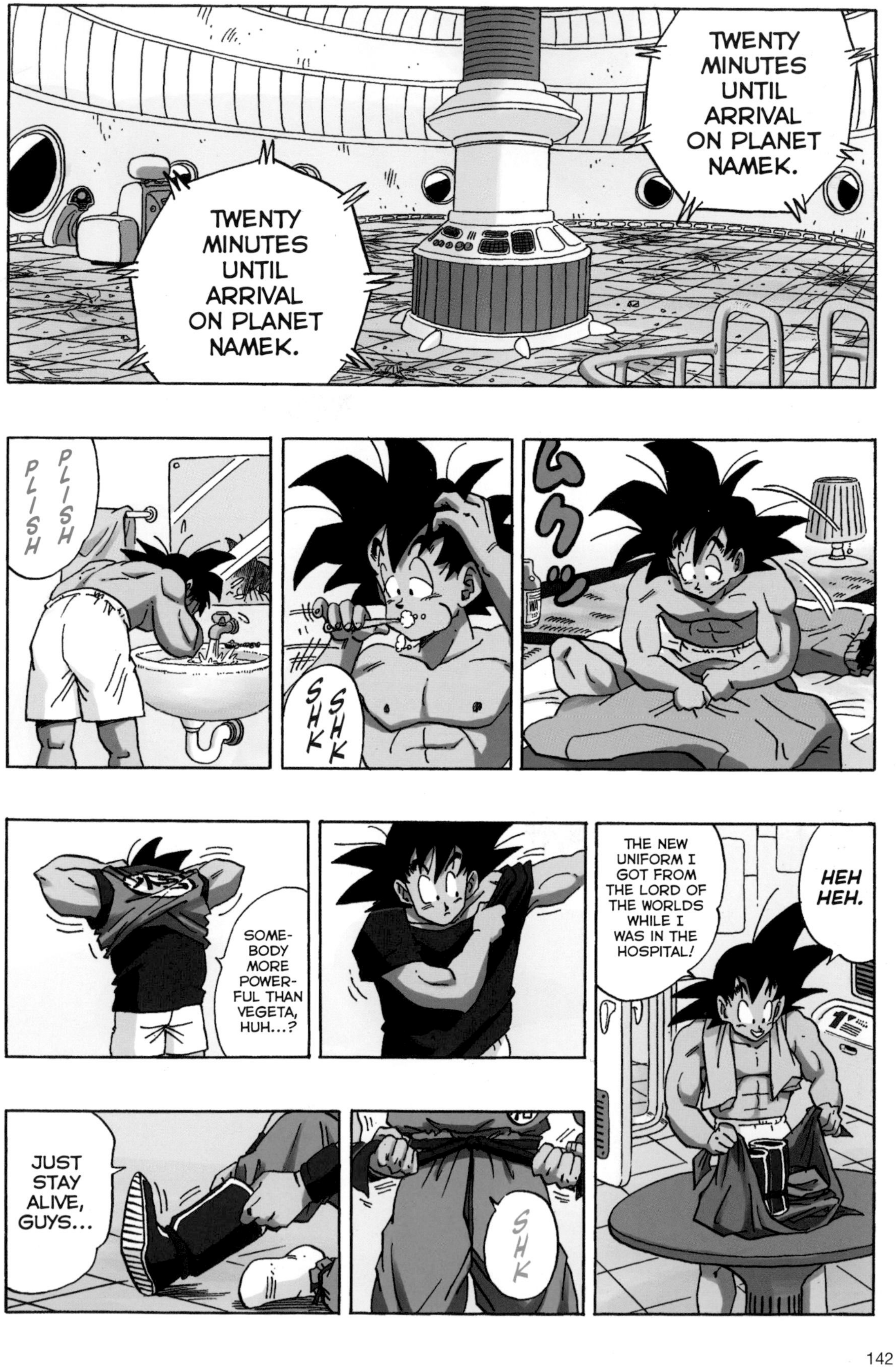
TWENTY MINUTES UNTIL ARRIVAL ON PLANET NAMEK.
TWENTY MINUTES UNTIL ARRIVAL ON PLANET NAMEK.
ムクッ
SHK SHK
PLISH PLISH
HEH HEH.
THE NEW UNIFORM I GOT FROM THE LORD OF THE WORLDS WHILE I WAS IN THE HOSPITAL!
SOME-BODY MORE POWER-FUL THAN VEGETA, HUH...?
SHK
JUST STAY ALIVE, GUYS...

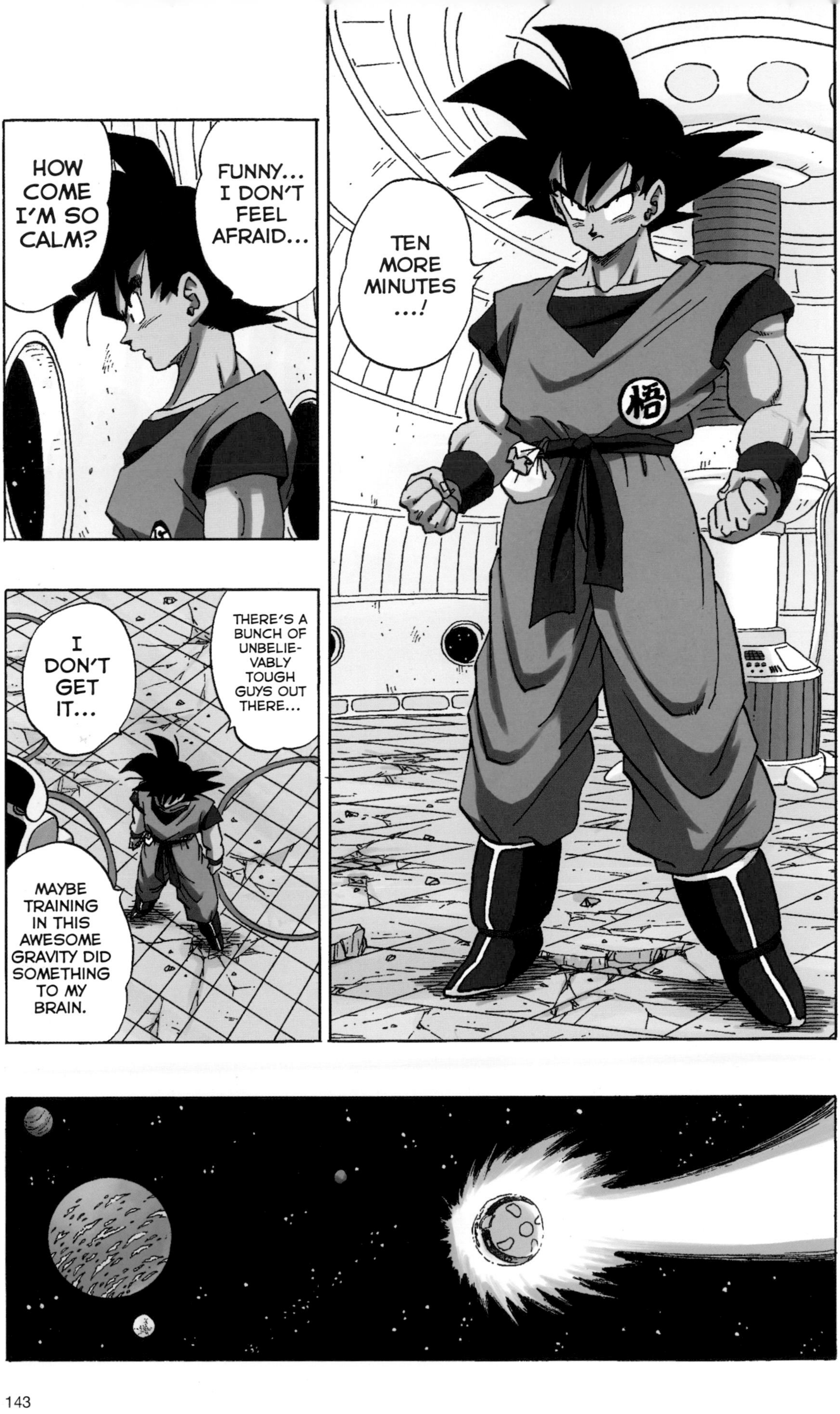
TEN MORE MINUTES ...!
FUNNY... I DON'T FEEL AFRAID...
HOW COME I'M SO CALM?
THERE'S A BUNCH OF UNBELIEVABLY TOUGH GUYS OUT THERE...
I DON'T GET IT...
MAYBE TRAINING IN THIS AWESOME GRAVITY DID SOMETHING TO MY BRAIN.

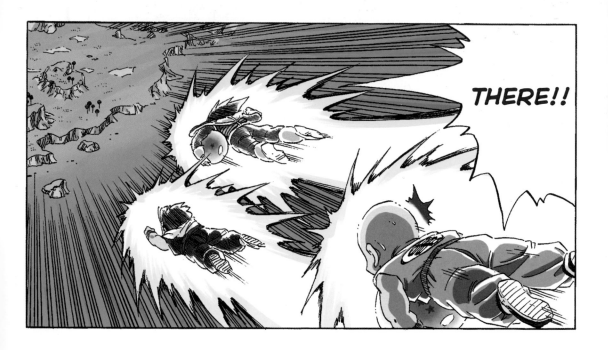

THERE!!

WE GOT THEM ALL!!

UNH!!

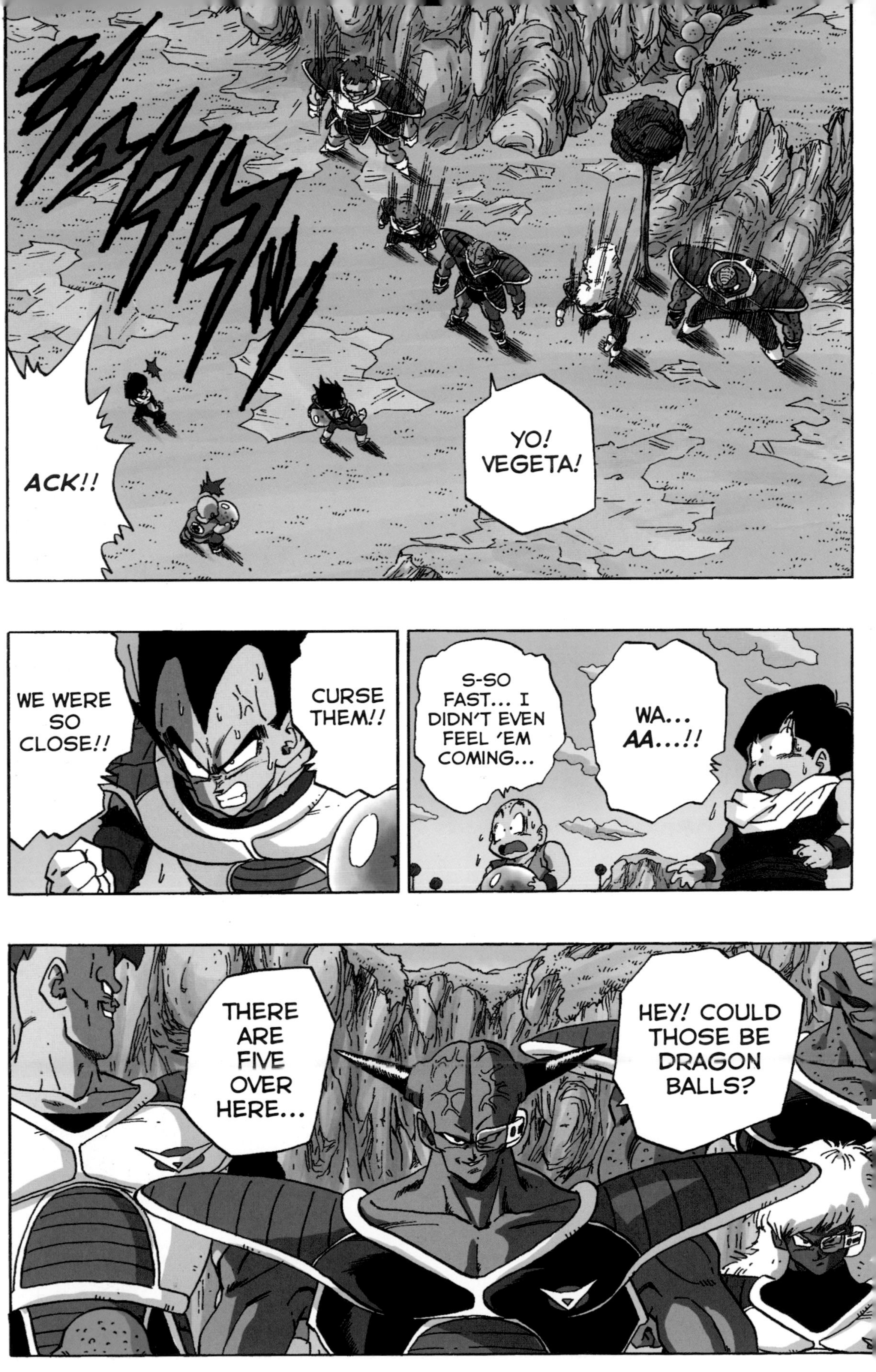
YO! VEGETA!
ACK!!
WA... AA...!!
S-SO FAST... I DIDN'T EVEN FEEL 'EM COMING...
CURSE THEM!!
WE WERE SO CLOSE!!
HEY! COULD THOSE BE DRAGON BALLS?
THERE ARE FIVE OVER HERE...

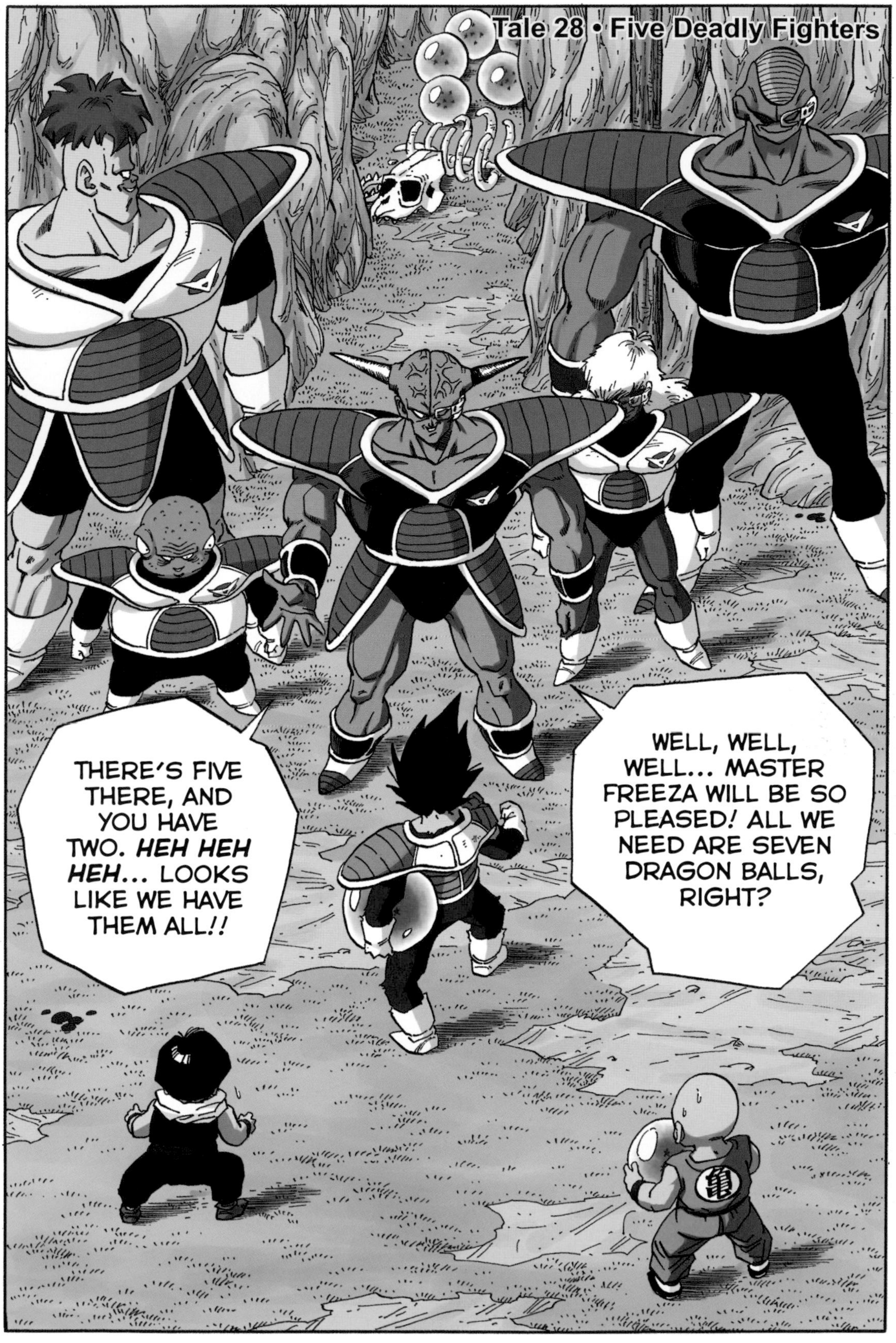
Tale 28 • Five Deadly Fighters
WELL, WELL, WELL... MASTER FREEZA WILL BE SO PLEASED! ALL WE NEED ARE SEVEN DRAGON BALLS, RIGHT?
THERE'S FIVE THERE, AND YOU HAVE TWO. *HEH HEH HEH*... LOOKS LIKE WE HAVE THEM ALL!!

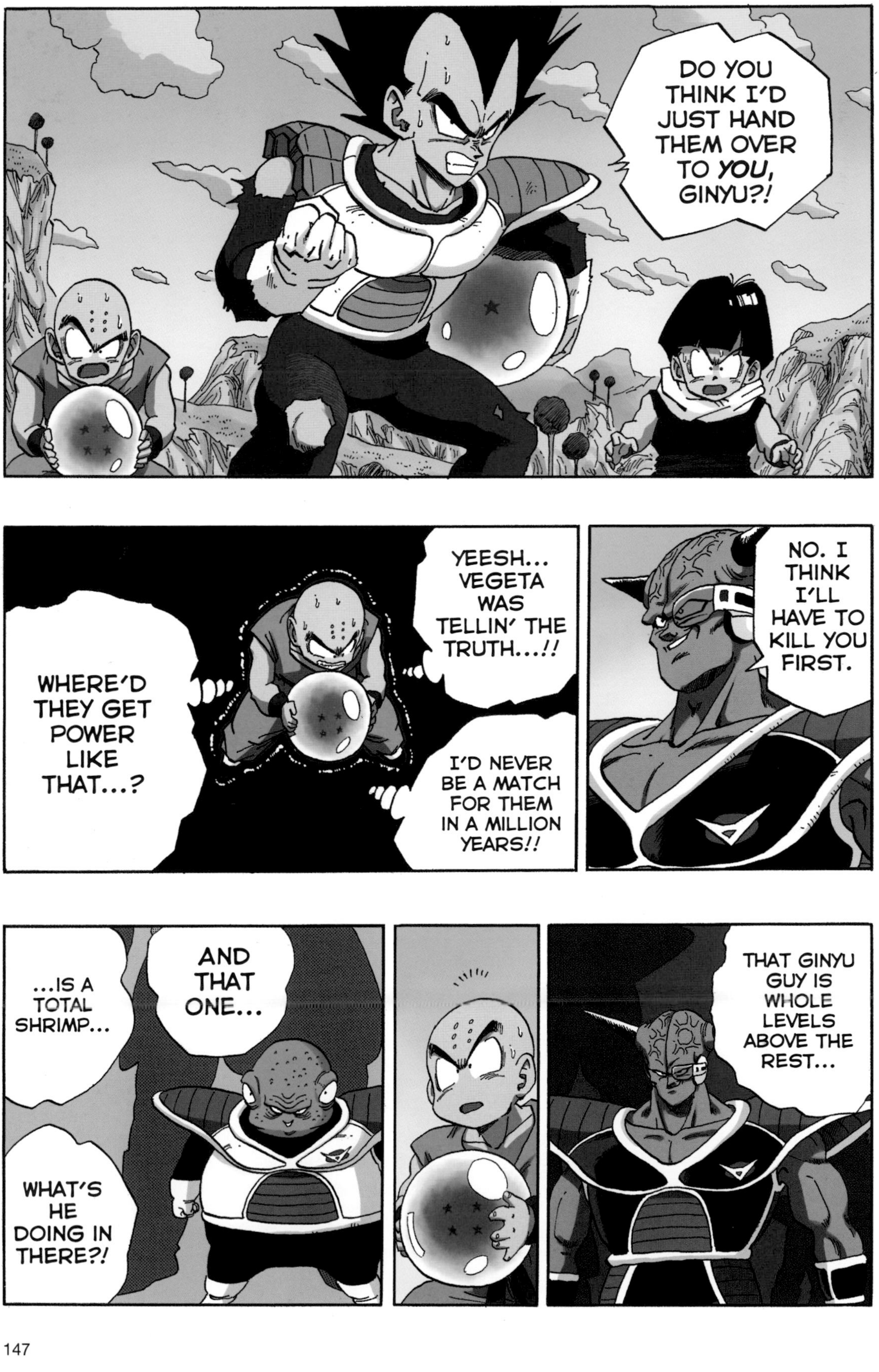
DO YOU THINK I'D JUST HAND THEM OVER TO *YOU*, GINYU?!
NO. I THINK I'LL HAVE TO KILL YOU FIRST.
YEESH... VEGETA WAS TELLIN' THE TRUTH...!!
I'D NEVER BE A MATCH FOR THEM IN A MILLION YEARS!!
WHERE'D THEY GET POWER LIKE THAT...?
THAT GINYU GUY IS WHOLE LEVELS ABOVE THE REST...
AND THAT ONE...
...IS A TOTAL SHRIMP...
WHAT'S HE DOING IN THERE?!

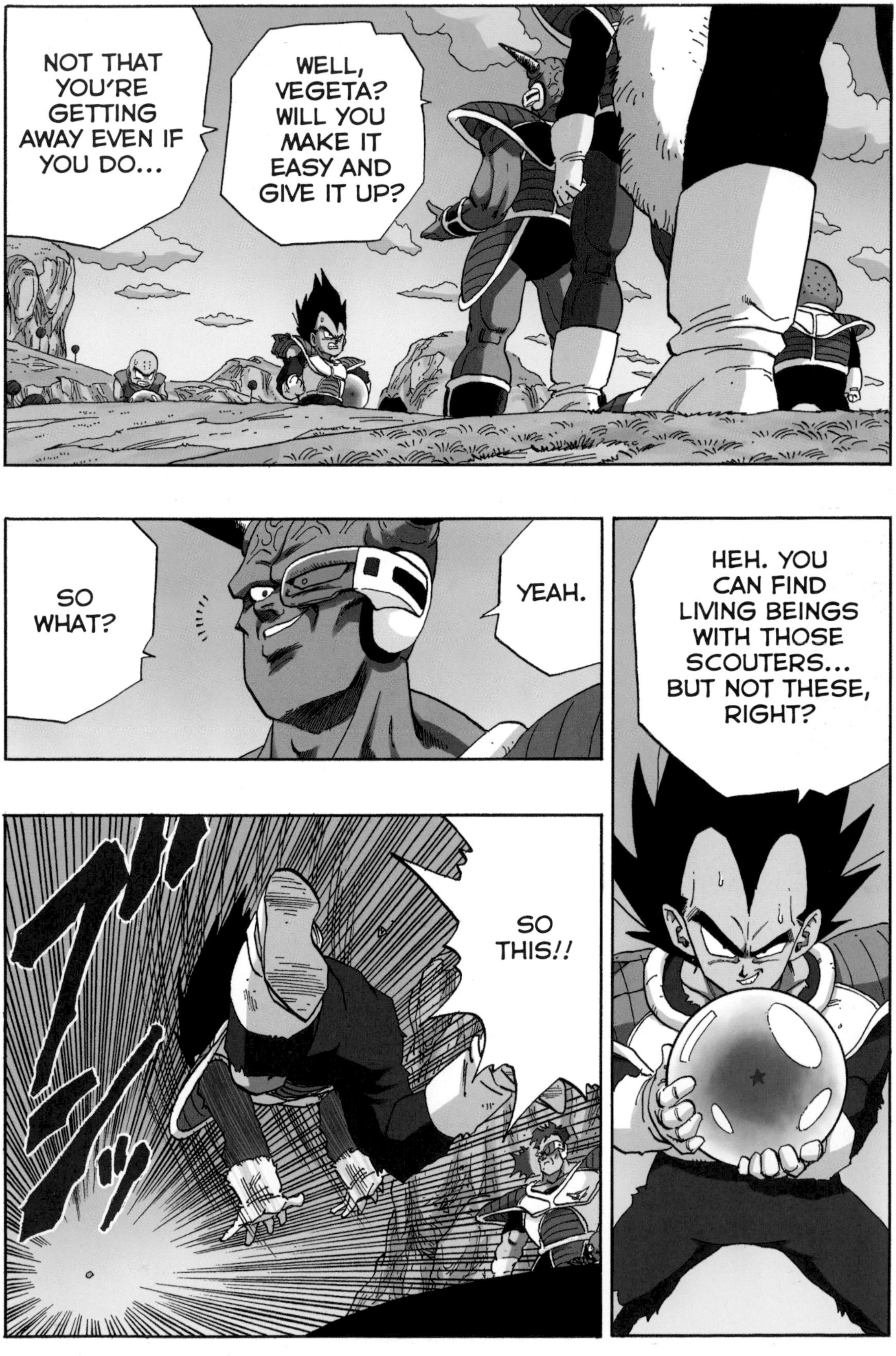
WELL, VEGETA? WILL YOU MAKE IT EASY AND GIVE IT UP?
NOT THAT YOU'RE GETTING AWAY EVEN IF YOU DO...
HEH. YOU CAN FIND LIVING BEINGS WITH THOSE SCOUTERS... BUT NOT THESE, RIGHT?
YEAH.
SO WHAT?
SO THIS!!

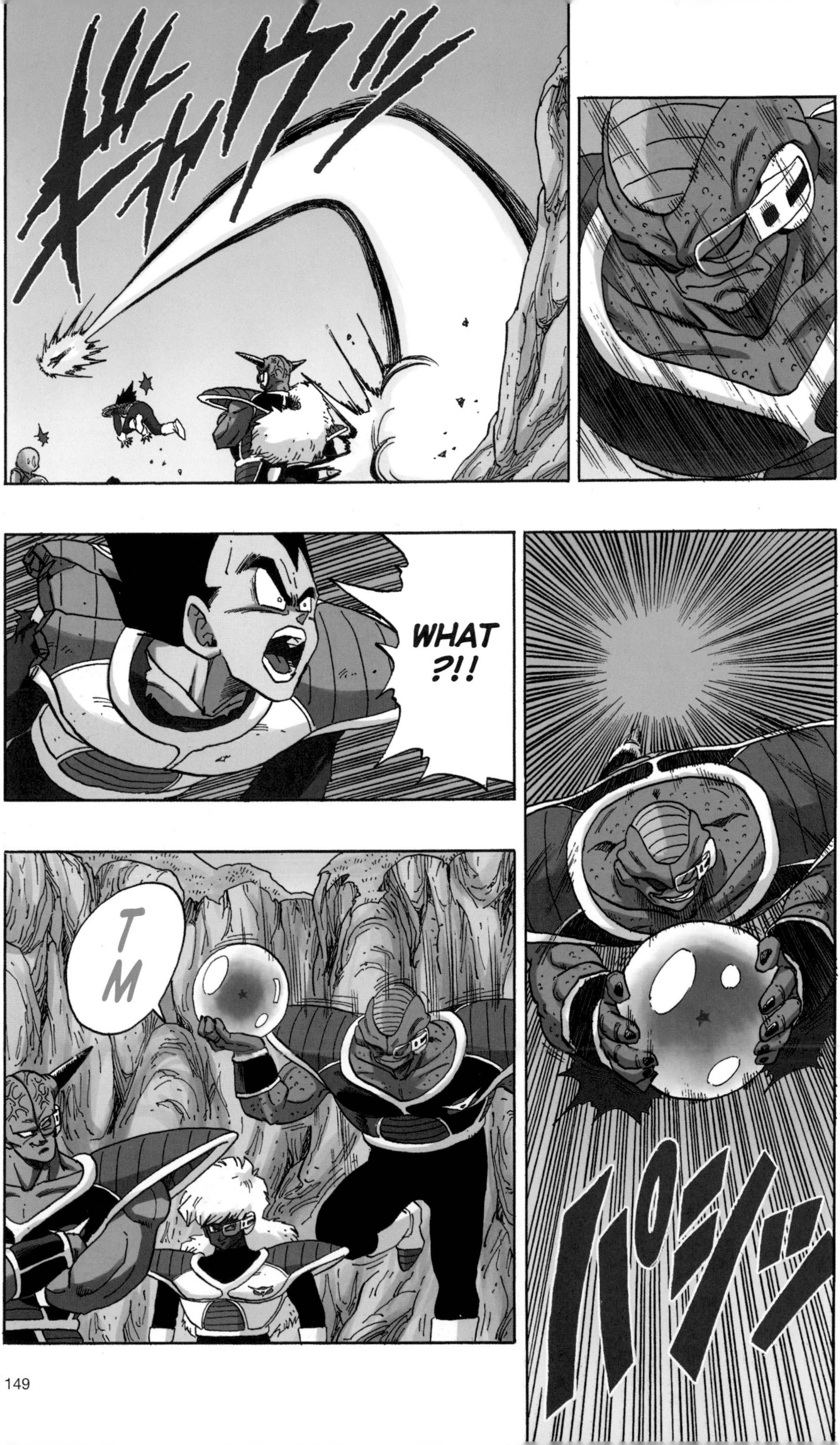
WHAT ?!!
T M

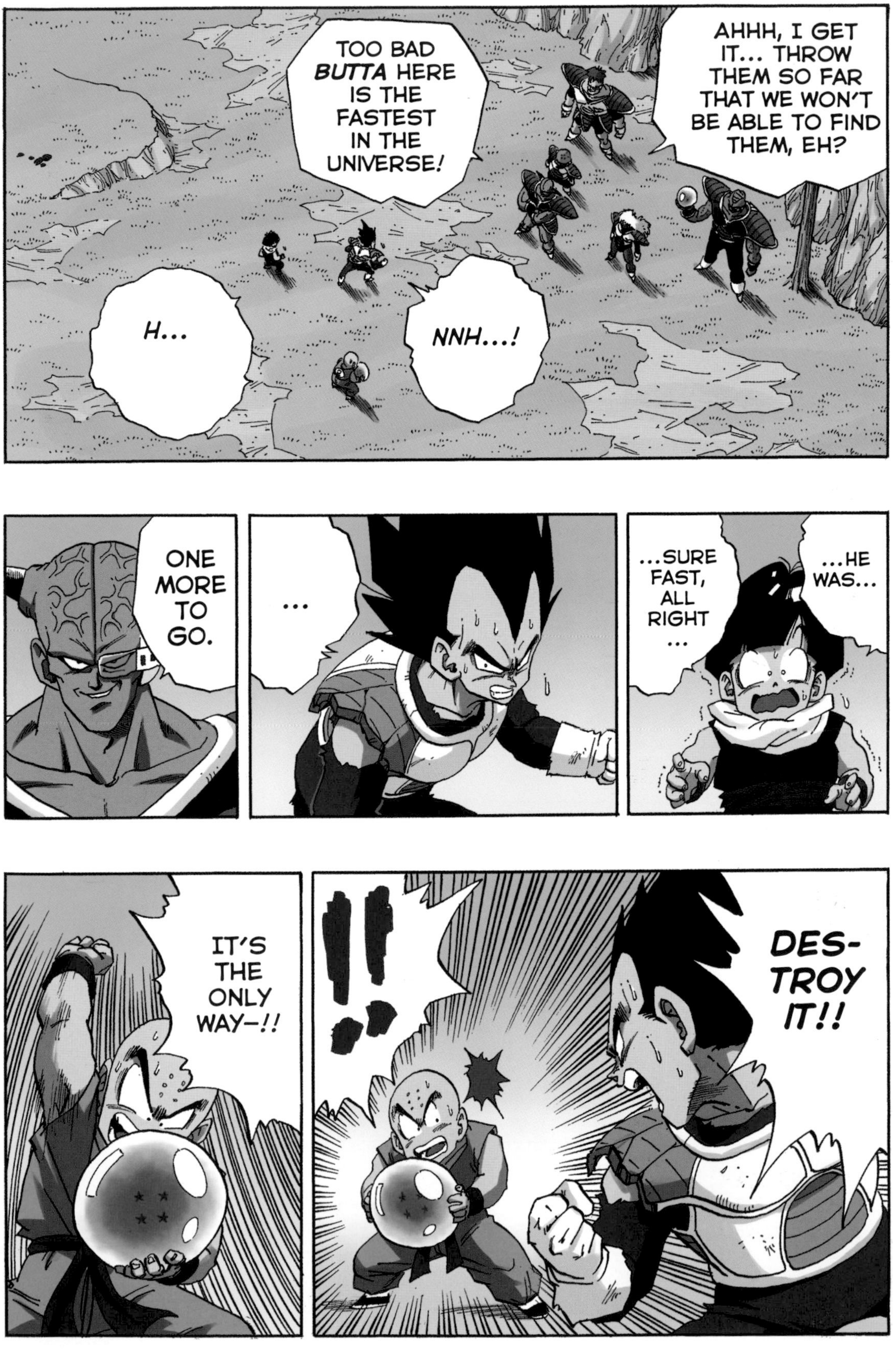
AHHH, I GET IT... THROW THEM SO FAR THAT WE WON'T BE ABLE TO FIND THEM, EH?
TOO BAD *BUTTA* HERE IS THE FASTEST IN THE UNIVERSE!
NNH...!
H...
...HE WAS...
...SURE FAST, ALL RIGHT...
...
ONE MORE TO GO.
DES-TROY IT!!
!!
IT'S THE ONLY WAY–!!

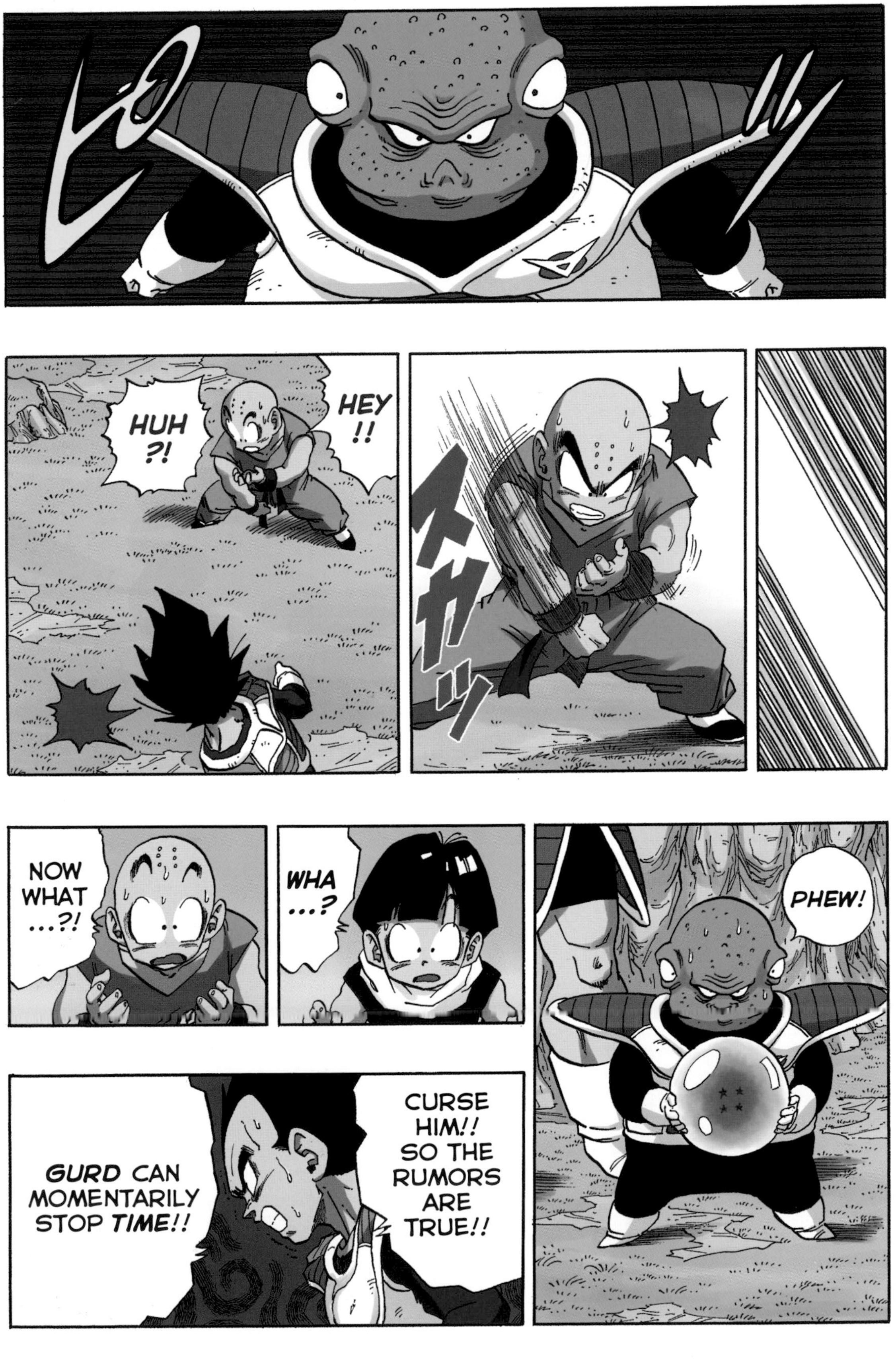
HEY!!
HUH?!
PHEW!
WHA...?
NOW WHAT...?!
CURSE HIM!! SO THE RUMORS ARE TRUE!!
GURD CAN MOMENTARILY STOP TIME!!

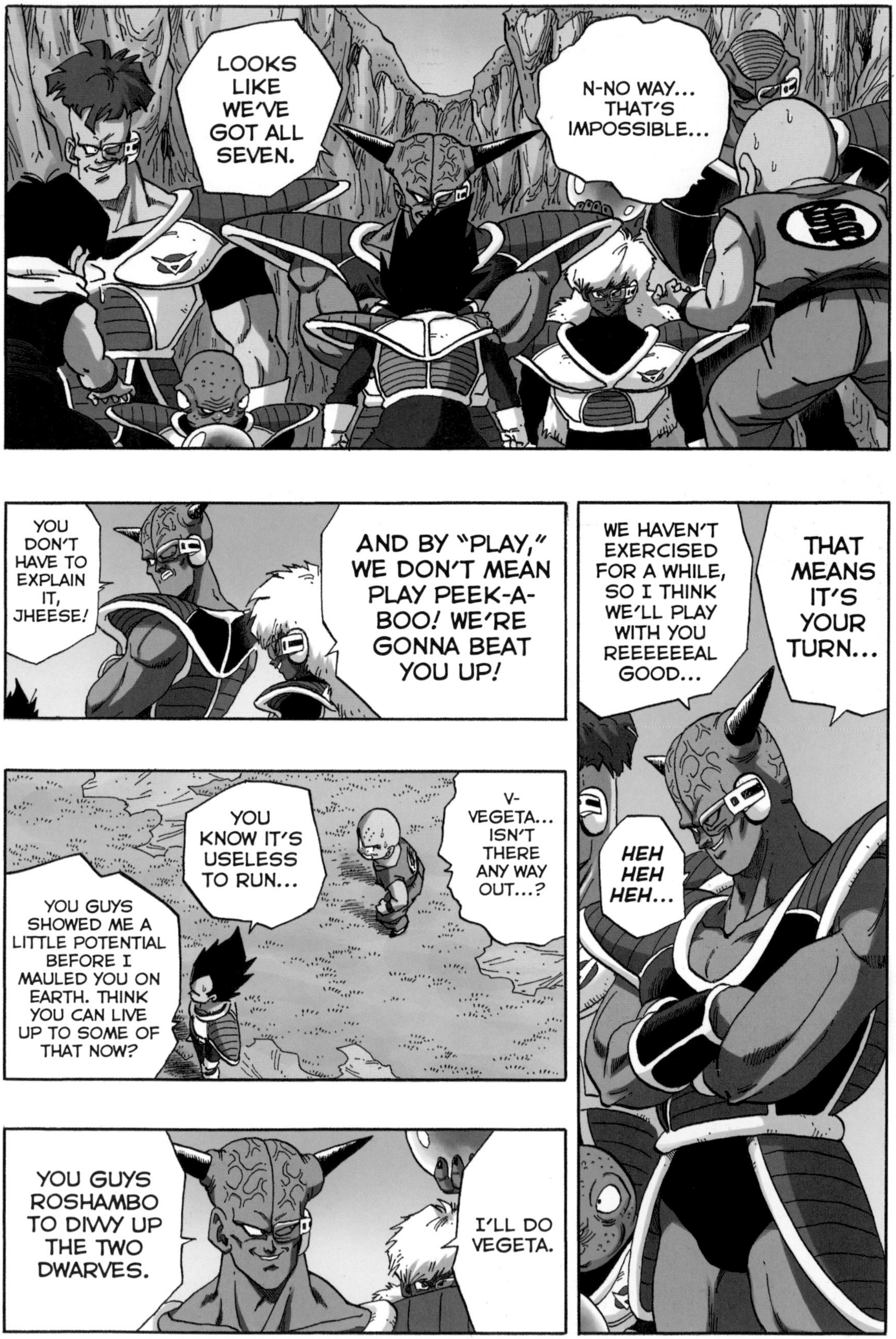
N-NO WAY... THAT'S IMPOSSIBLE...
LOOKS LIKE WE'VE GOT ALL SEVEN.
THAT MEANS IT'S YOUR TURN...
WE HAVEN'T EXERCISED FOR A WHILE, SO I THINK WE'LL PLAY WITH YOU REEEEEEAL GOOD...
HEH HEH HEH...
AND BY "PLAY," WE DON'T MEAN PLAY PEEK-A-BOO! WE'RE GONNA BEAT YOU UP!
YOU DON'T HAVE TO EXPLAIN IT, JHEESE!
V-VEGETA... ISN'T THERE ANY WAY OUT...?
YOU KNOW IT'S USELESS TO RUN...
YOU GUYS SHOWED ME A LITTLE POTENTIAL BEFORE I MAULED YOU ON EARTH. THINK YOU CAN LIVE UP TO SOME OF THAT NOW?
I'LL DO VEGETA.
YOU GUYS ROSHAMBO TO DIVVY UP THE TWO DWARVES.

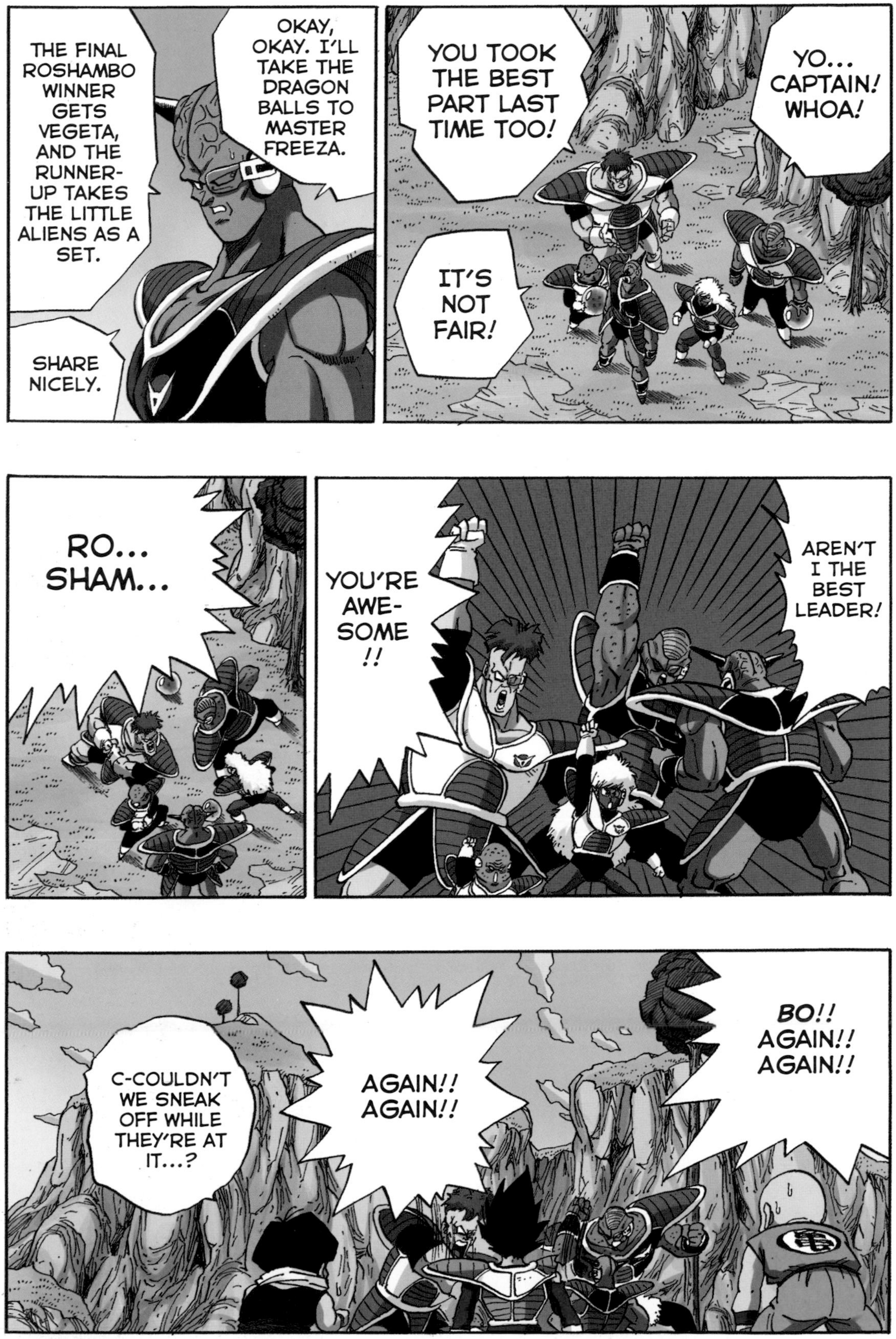
YO... CAPTAIN! WHOA!
YOU TOOK THE BEST PART LAST TIME TOO!
IT'S NOT FAIR!
OKAY, OKAY. I'LL TAKE THE DRAGON BALLS TO MASTER FREEZA.
THE FINAL ROSHAMBO WINNER GETS VEGETA, AND THE RUNNER-UP TAKES THE LITTLE ALIENS AS A SET.
SHARE NICELY.
AREN'T I THE BEST LEADER!
YOU'RE AWE-SOME!!
RO... SHAM...
BO!! AGAIN!! AGAIN!!
AGAIN!! AGAIN!!
C-COULDN'T WE SNEAK OFF WHILE THEY'RE AT IT...?

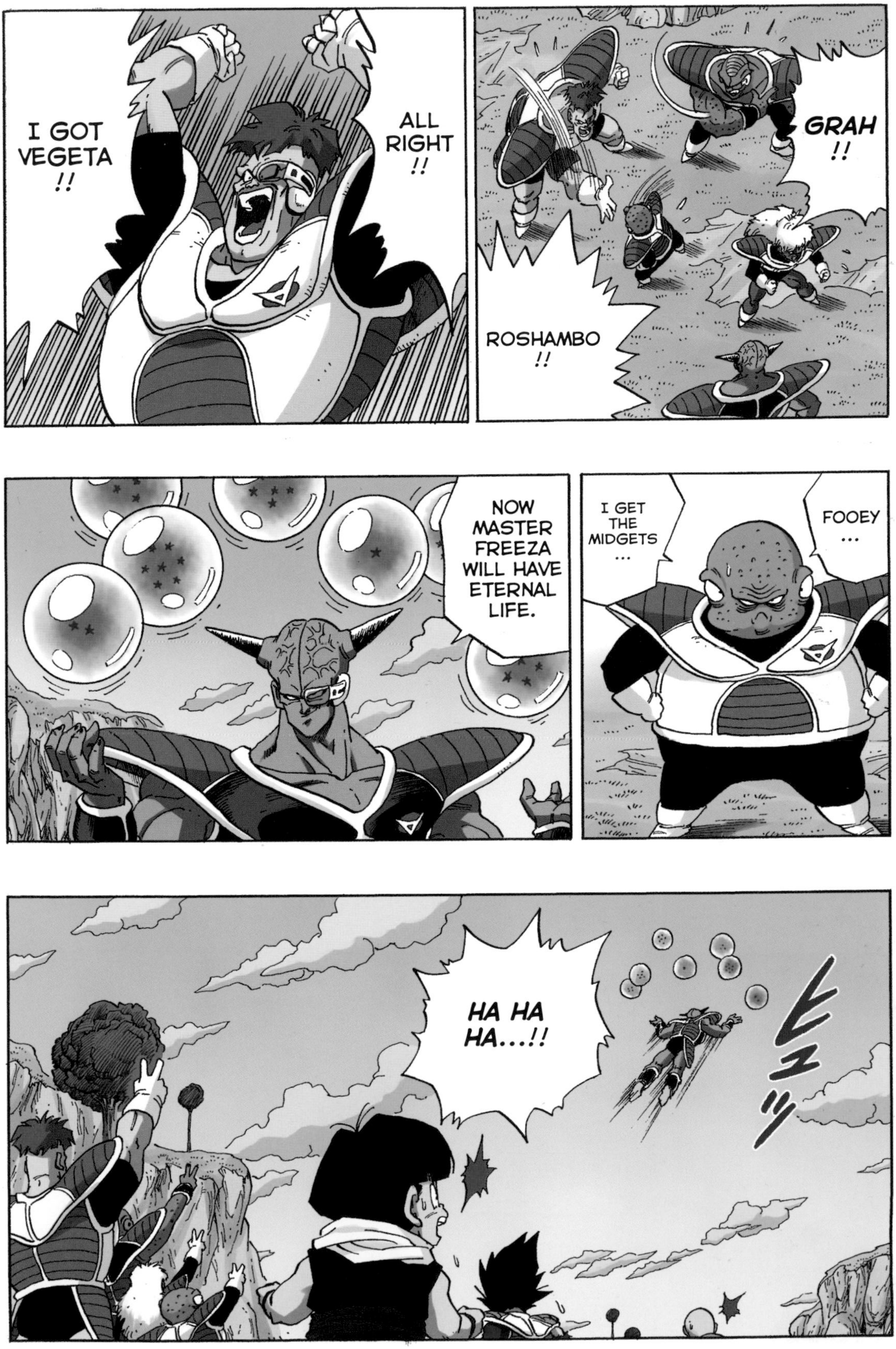
GRAH!!
ROSHAMBO!!
ALL RIGHT!!
I GOT VEGETA!!
FOOEY...
I GET THE MIDGETS...
NOW MASTER FREEZA WILL HAVE ETERNAL LIFE.
ヒュッ
HA HA HA...!!

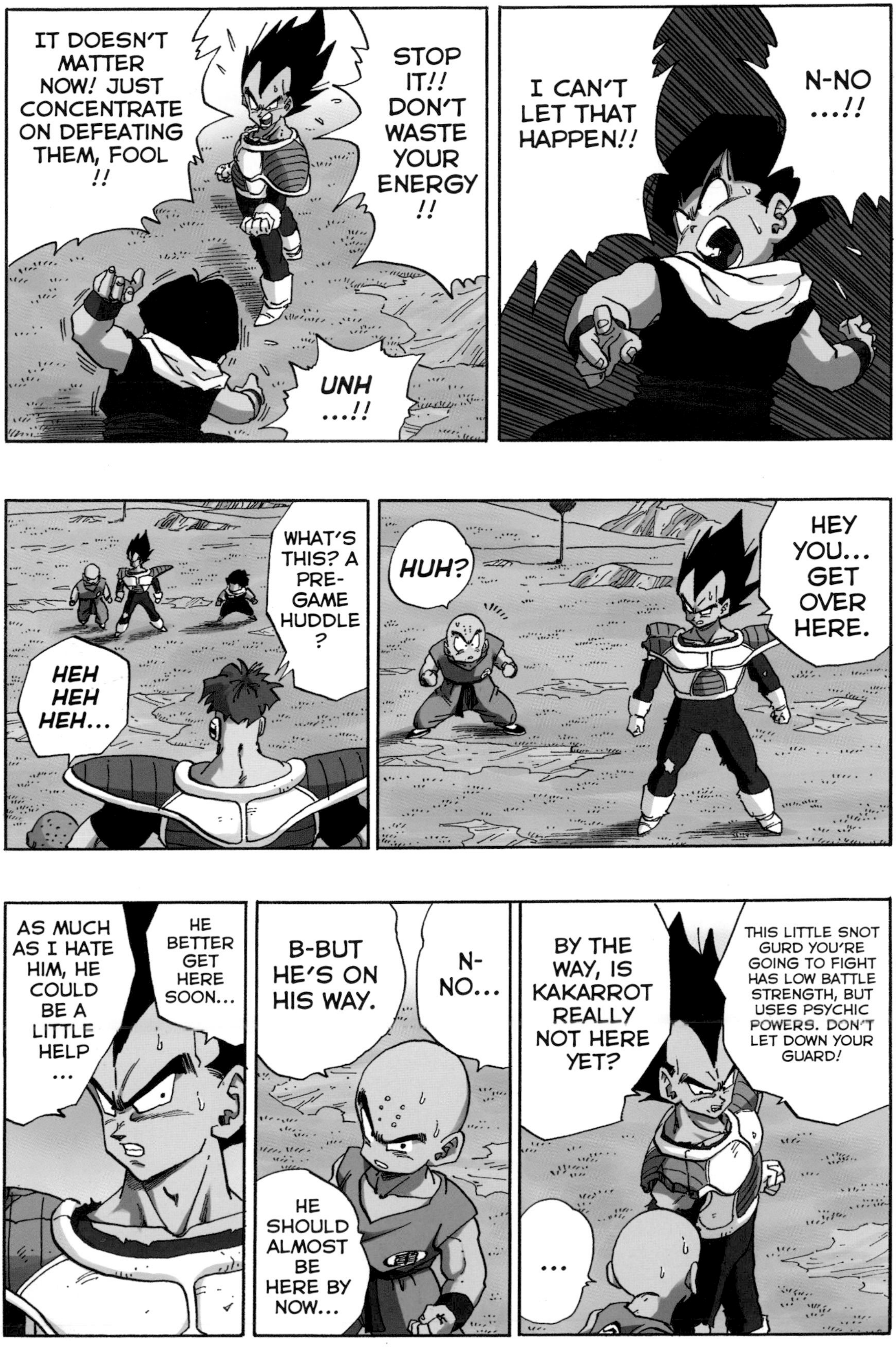
N-NO ...!!
I CAN'T LET THAT HAPPEN!!
STOP IT!! DON'T WASTE YOUR ENERGY!!
IT DOESN'T MATTER NOW! JUST CONCENTRATE ON DEFEATING THEM, FOOL!!
UNH ...!!
HEY YOU... GET OVER HERE.
HUH?
WHAT'S THIS? A PRE-GAME HUDDLE?
HEH HEH HEH...
THIS LITTLE SNOT GURD YOU'RE GOING TO FIGHT HAS LOW BATTLE STRENGTH, BUT USES PSYCHIC POWERS. DON'T LET DOWN YOUR GUARD!
BY THE WAY, IS KAKARROT REALLY NOT HERE YET?
...
N-NO...
B-BUT HE'S ON HIS WAY.
HE SHOULD ALMOST BE HERE BY NOW...
HE BETTER GET HERE SOON...
AS MUCH AS I HATE HIM, HE COULD BE A LITTLE HELP ...

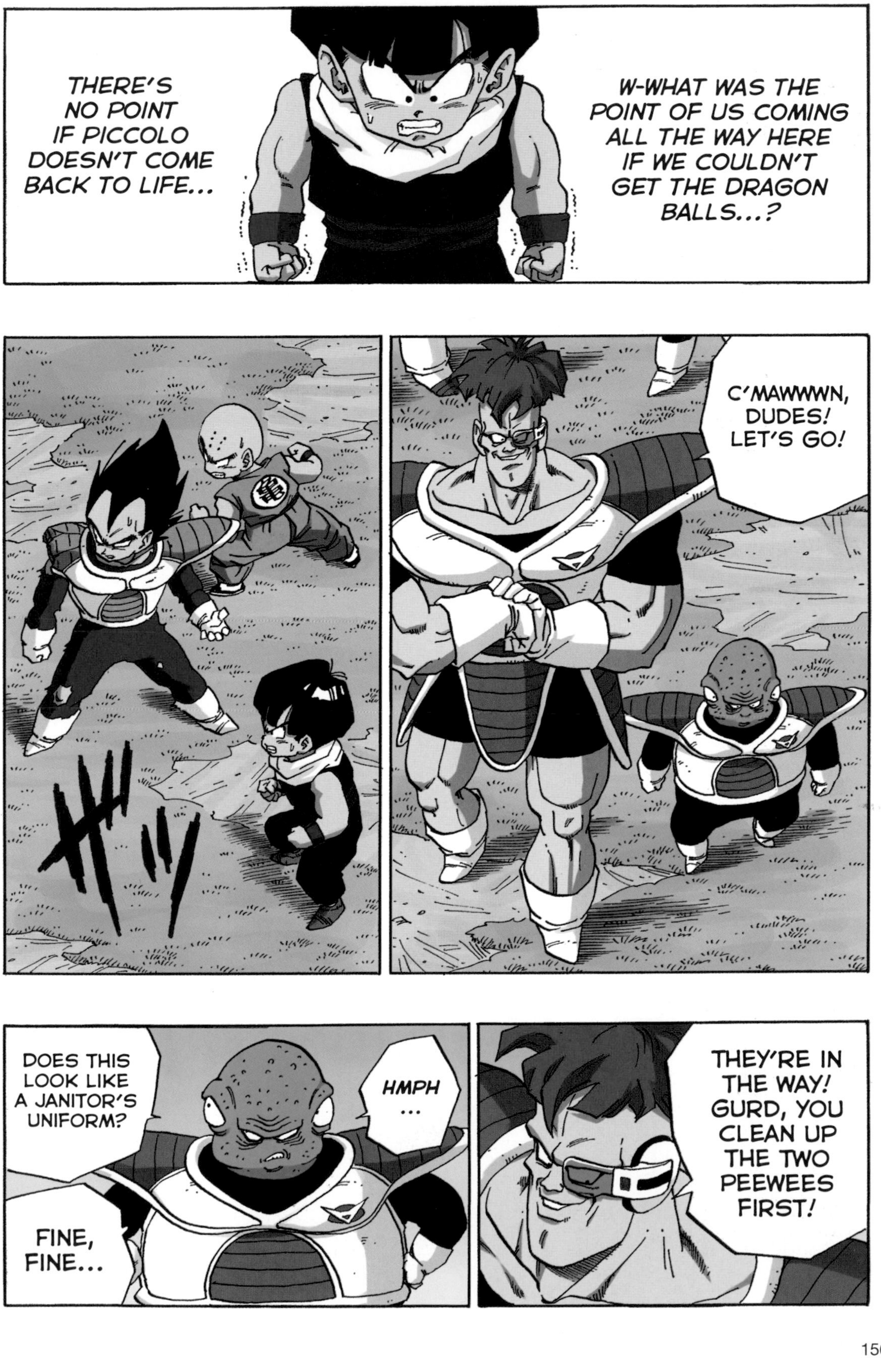
W-WHAT WAS THE POINT OF US COMING ALL THE WAY HERE IF WE COULDN'T GET THE DRAGON BALLS...?
THERE'S NO POINT IF PICCOLO DOESN'T COME BACK TO LIFE...
C'MAWWWN, DUDES! LET'S GO!
THEY'RE IN THE WAY! GURD, YOU CLEAN UP THE TWO PEEWEES FIRST!
HMPH ...
DOES THIS LOOK LIKE A JANITOR'S UNIFORM?
FINE, FINE...

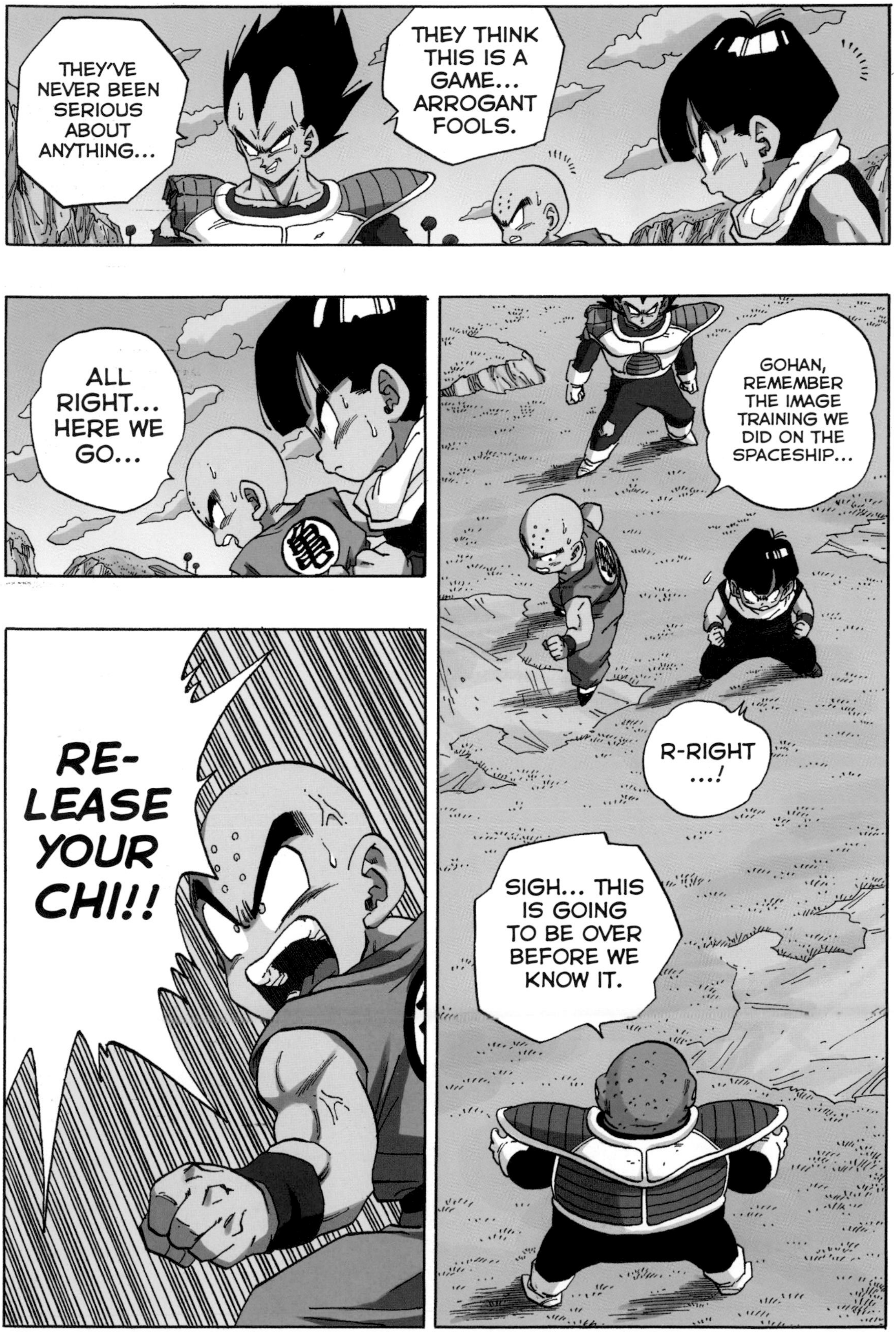
THEY THINK THIS IS A GAME... ARROGANT FOOLS.
THEY'VE NEVER BEEN SERIOUS ABOUT ANYTHING...
GOHAN, REMEMBER THE IMAGE TRAINING WE DID ON THE SPACESHIP...
R-RIGHT ...!
SIGH... THIS IS GOING TO BE OVER BEFORE WE KNOW IT.
ALL RIGHT... HERE WE GO...
RE-LEASE YOUR CHI!!

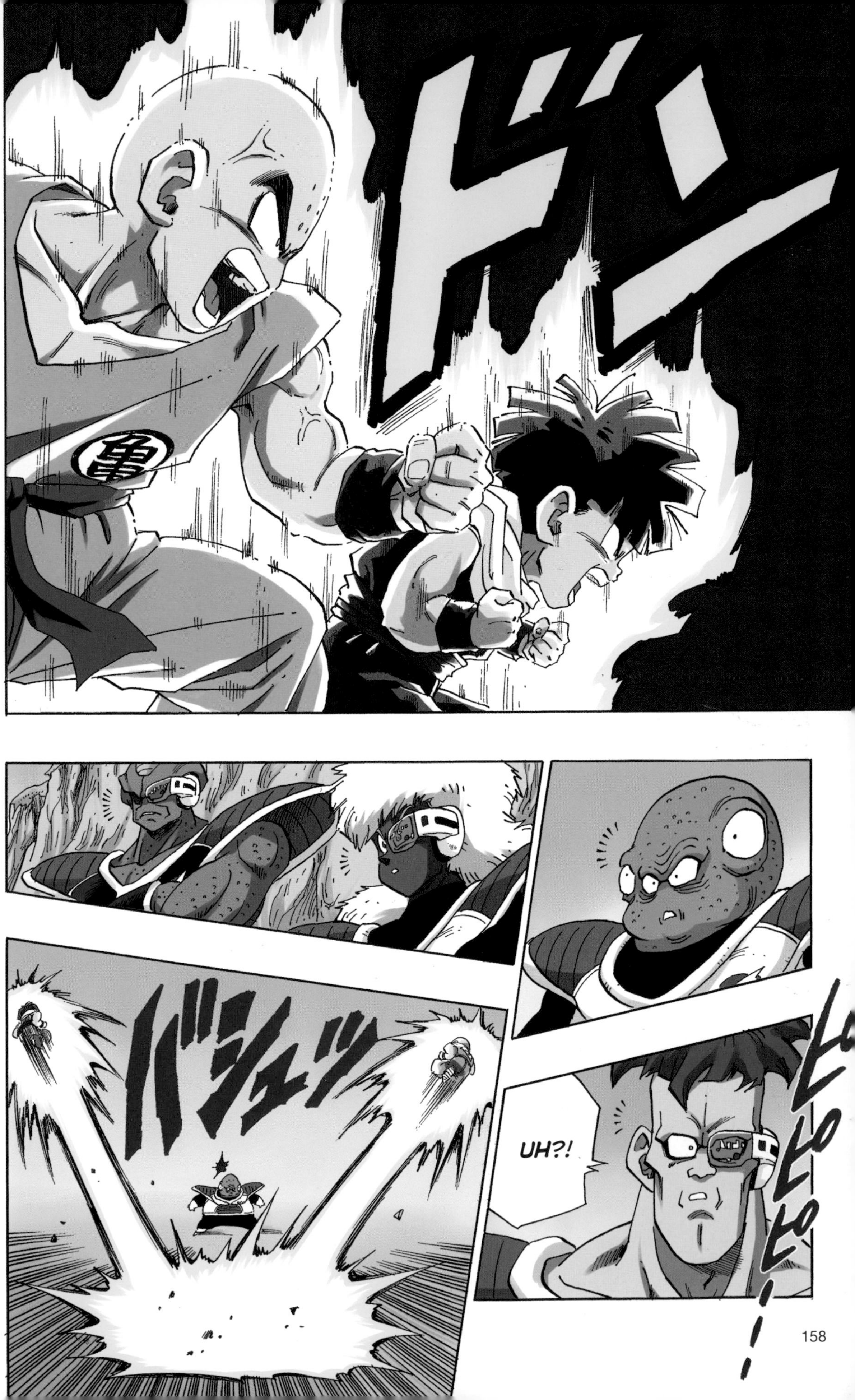
ドン
UH?!
ピピピピピ!!
バシュッ

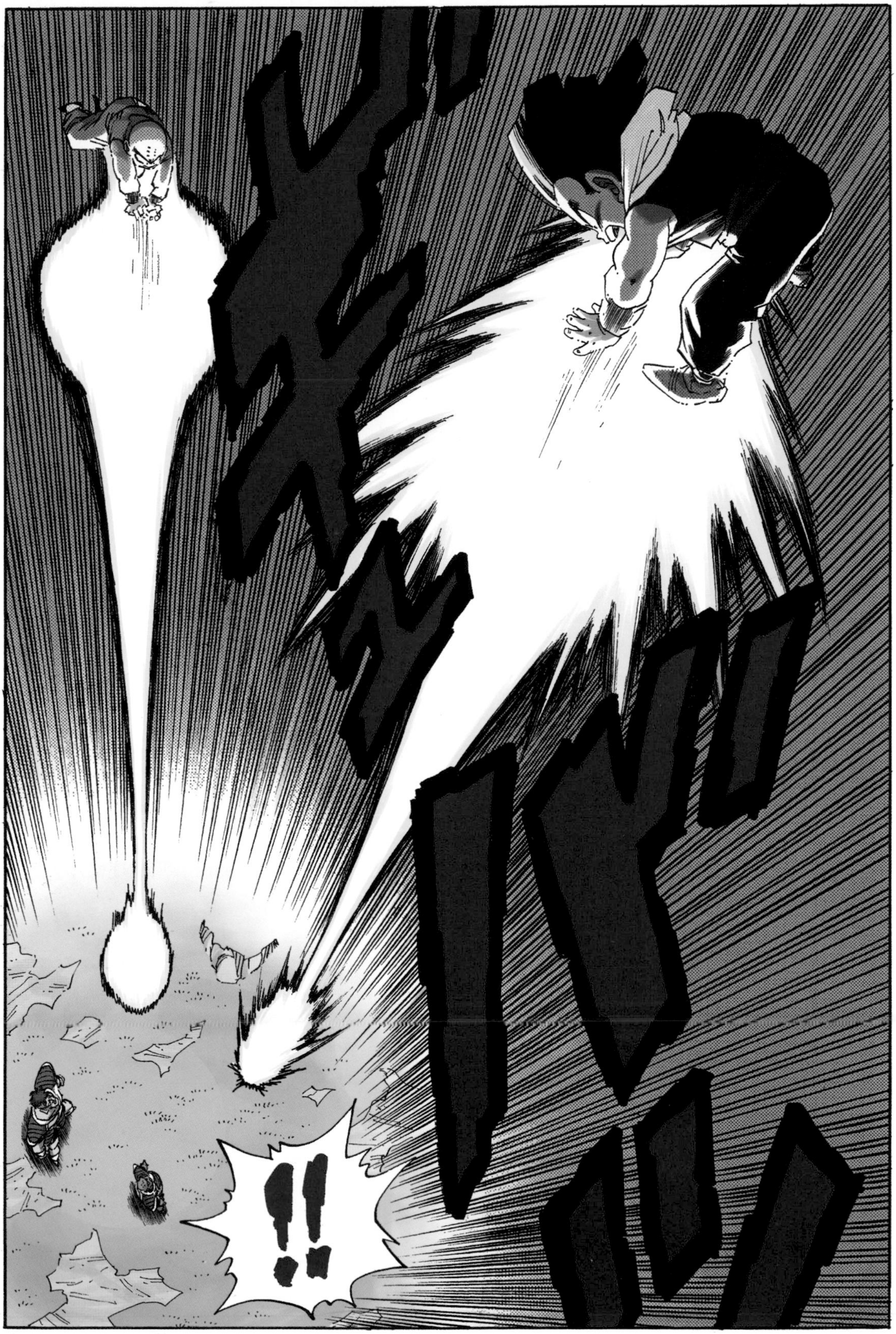
!!

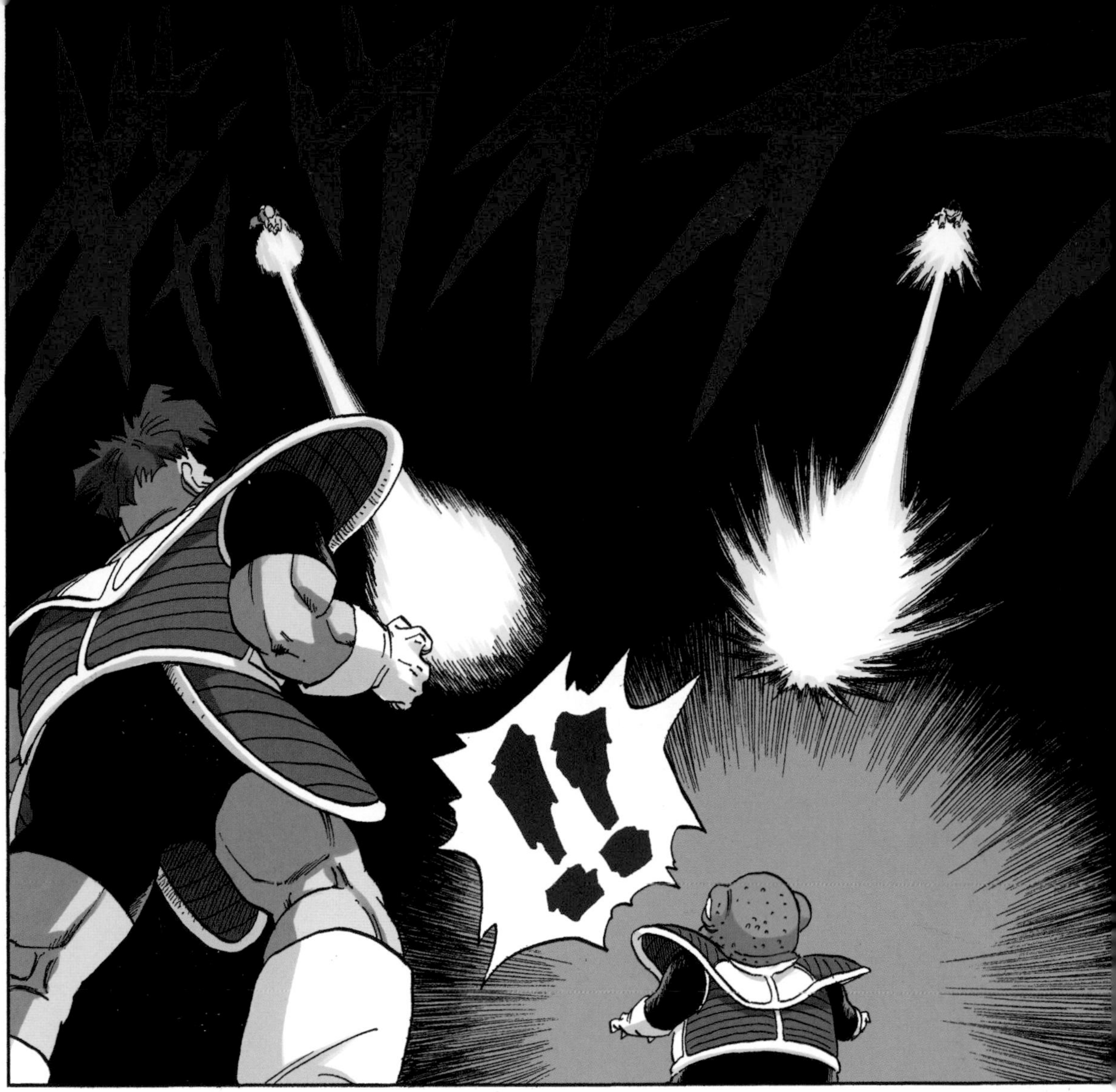
!!

Chapter 29 • Gurd's Psychic Powers

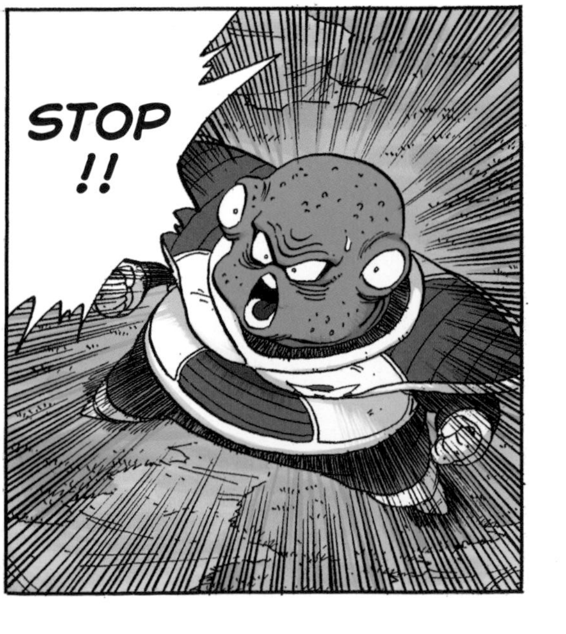
STOP
!!

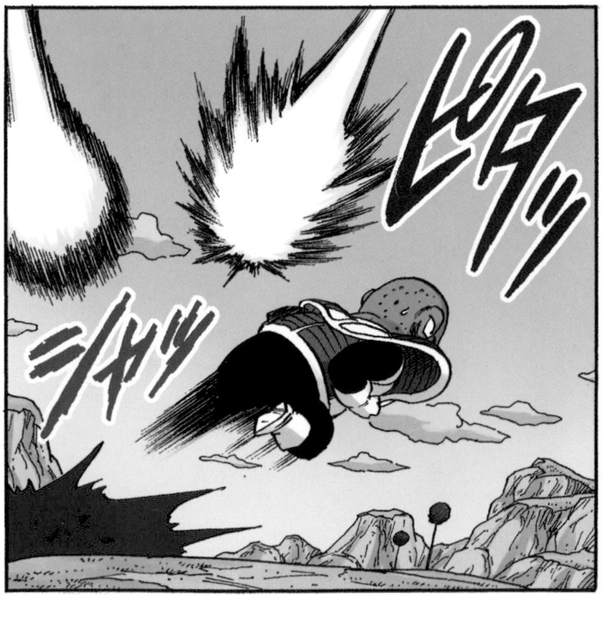
ピタッ
シャッ

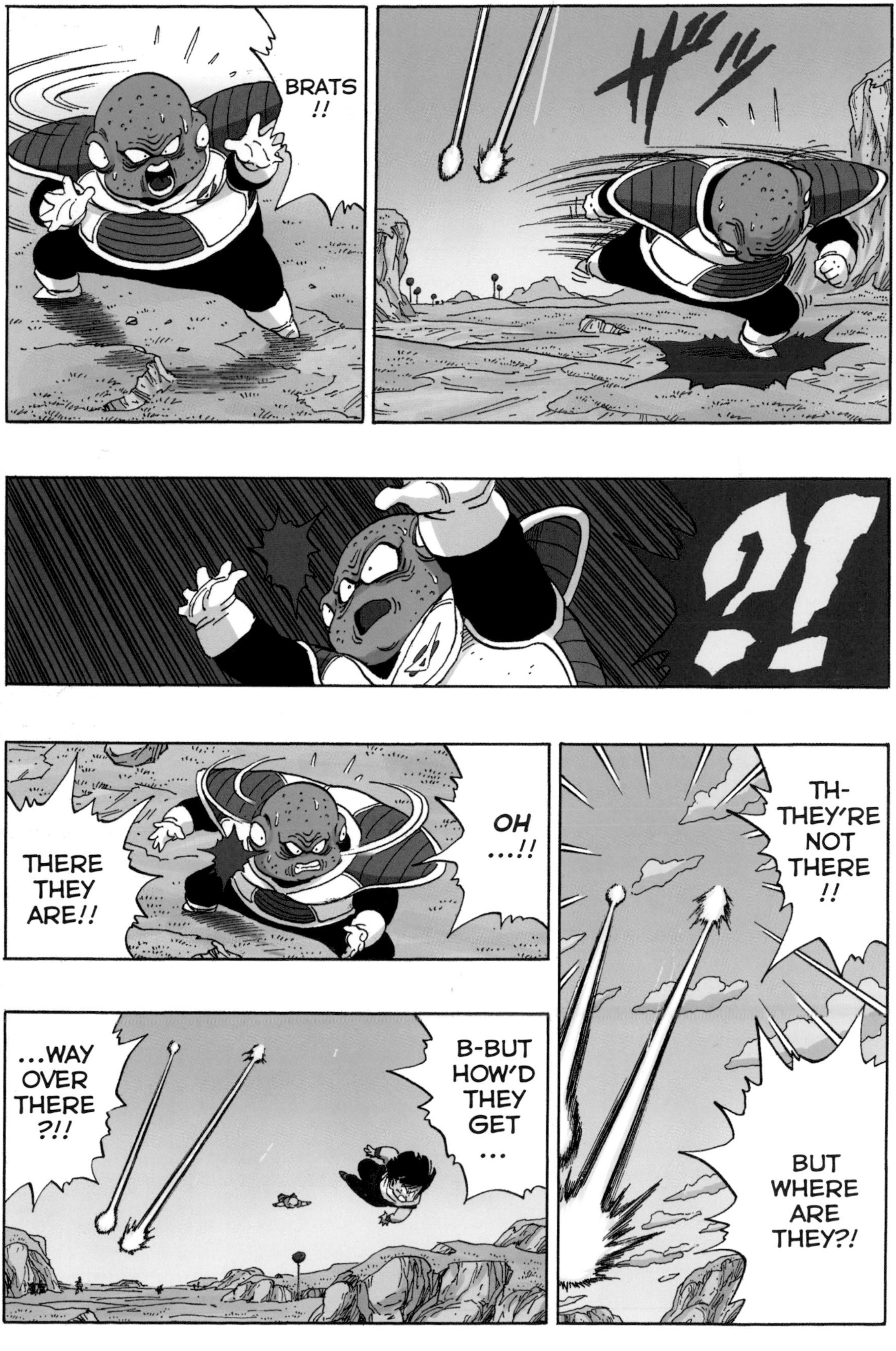
ザッ
BRATS !!
?!
TH-THEY'RE NOT THERE !!
BUT WHERE ARE THEY?!
OH ...!!
THERE THEY ARE!!
B-BUT HOW'D THEY GET ...
...WAY OVER THERE ?!!

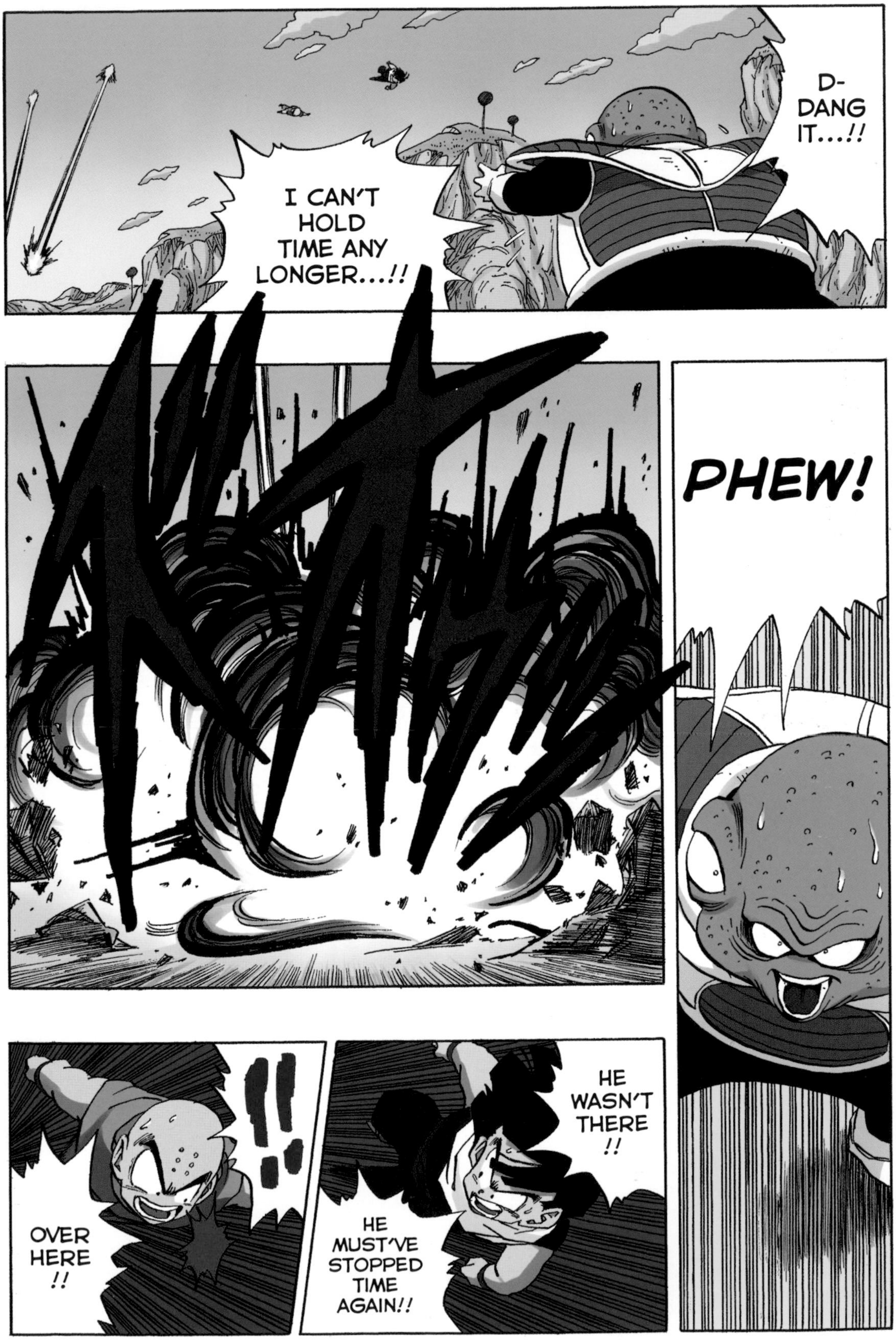
D-DANG IT...!!
I CAN'T HOLD TIME ANY LONGER...!!
PHEW!
HE WASN'T THERE!!
HE MUST'VE STOPPED TIME AGAIN!!
OVER HERE!!

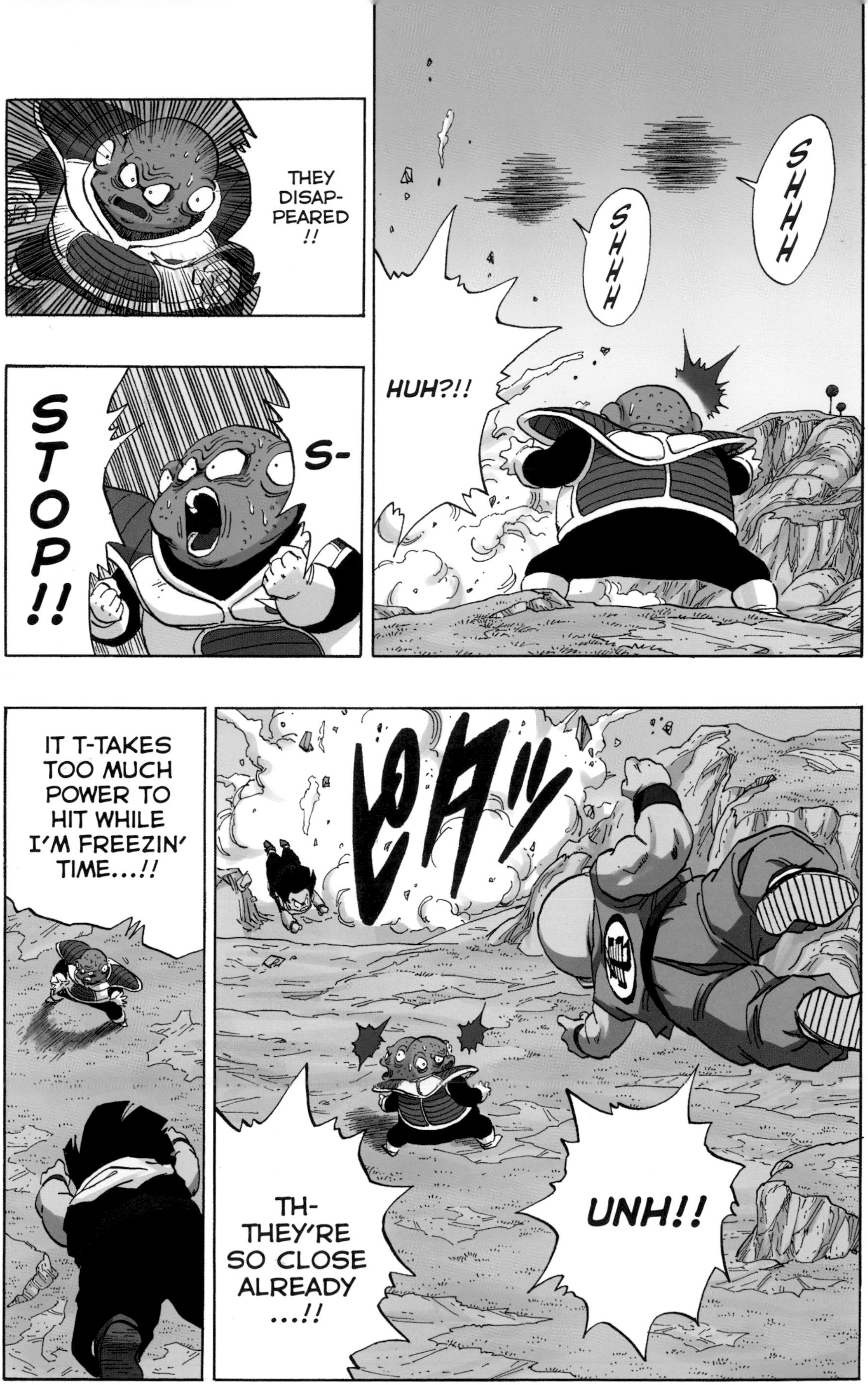
SHHH
SHHH
HUH?!!
THEY DISAPPEARED!!
S- STOP!!
ピタッ
UNH!!
TH- THEY'RE SO CLOSE ALREADY...!!
IT T-TAKES TOO MUCH POWER TO HIT WHILE I'M FREEZIN' TIME...!!

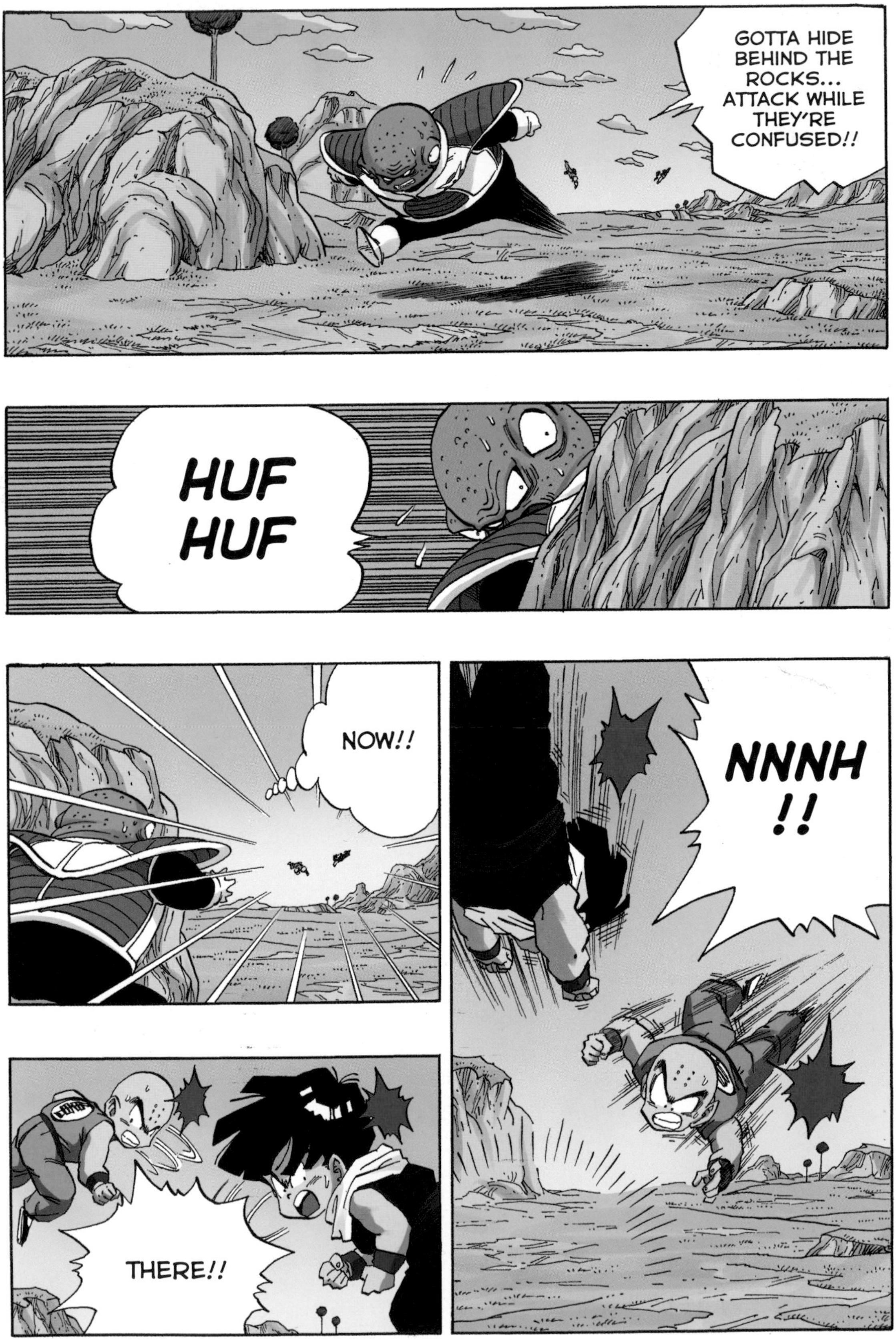
GOTTA HIDE BEHIND THE ROCKS... ATTACK WHILE THEY'RE CONFUSED!!
HUF HUF
NNNH !!
NOW!!
THERE!!

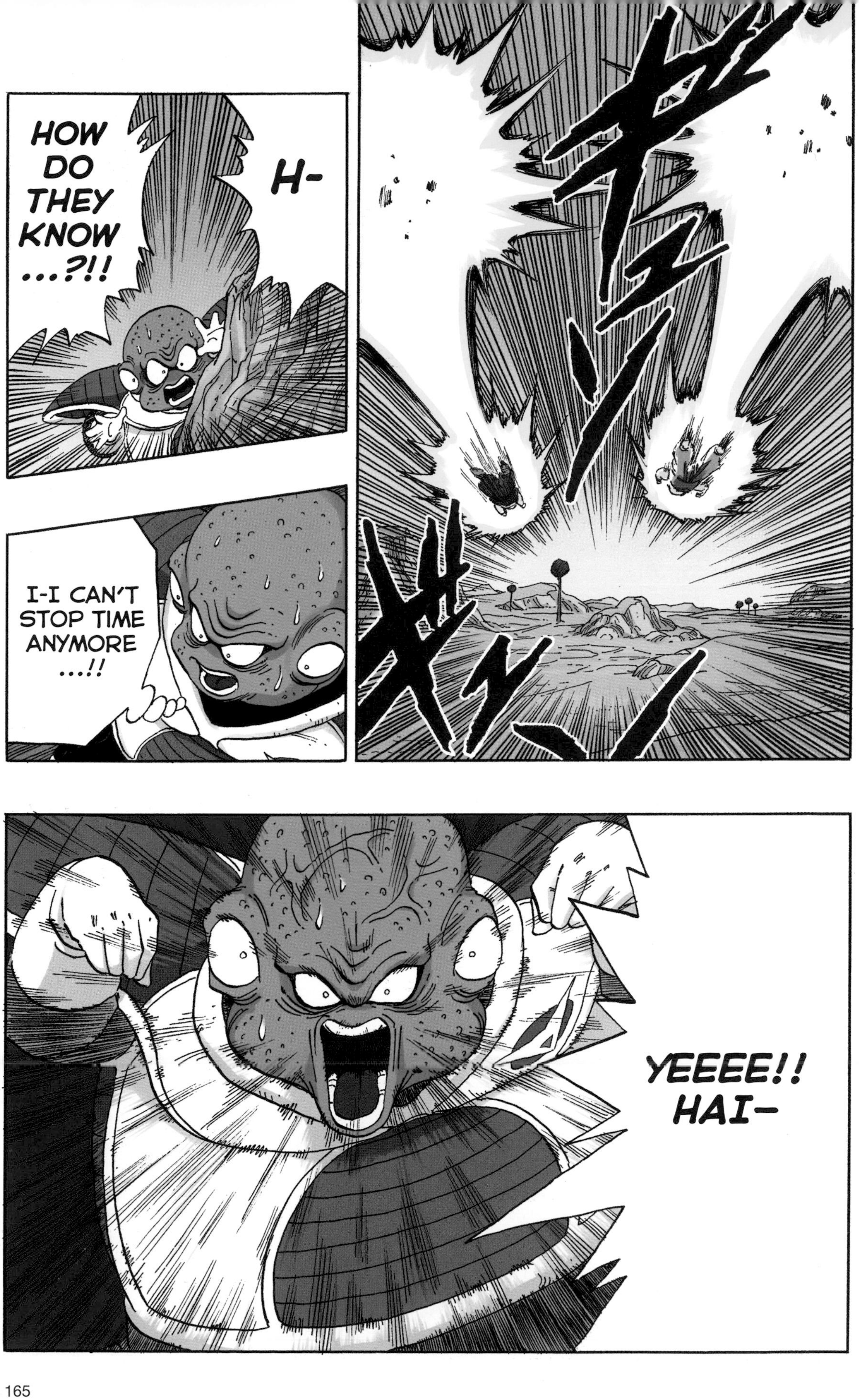
H-
HOW DO THEY KNOW ...?!!
I-I CAN'T STOP TIME ANYMORE ...!!
YEEEE!!
HAI-

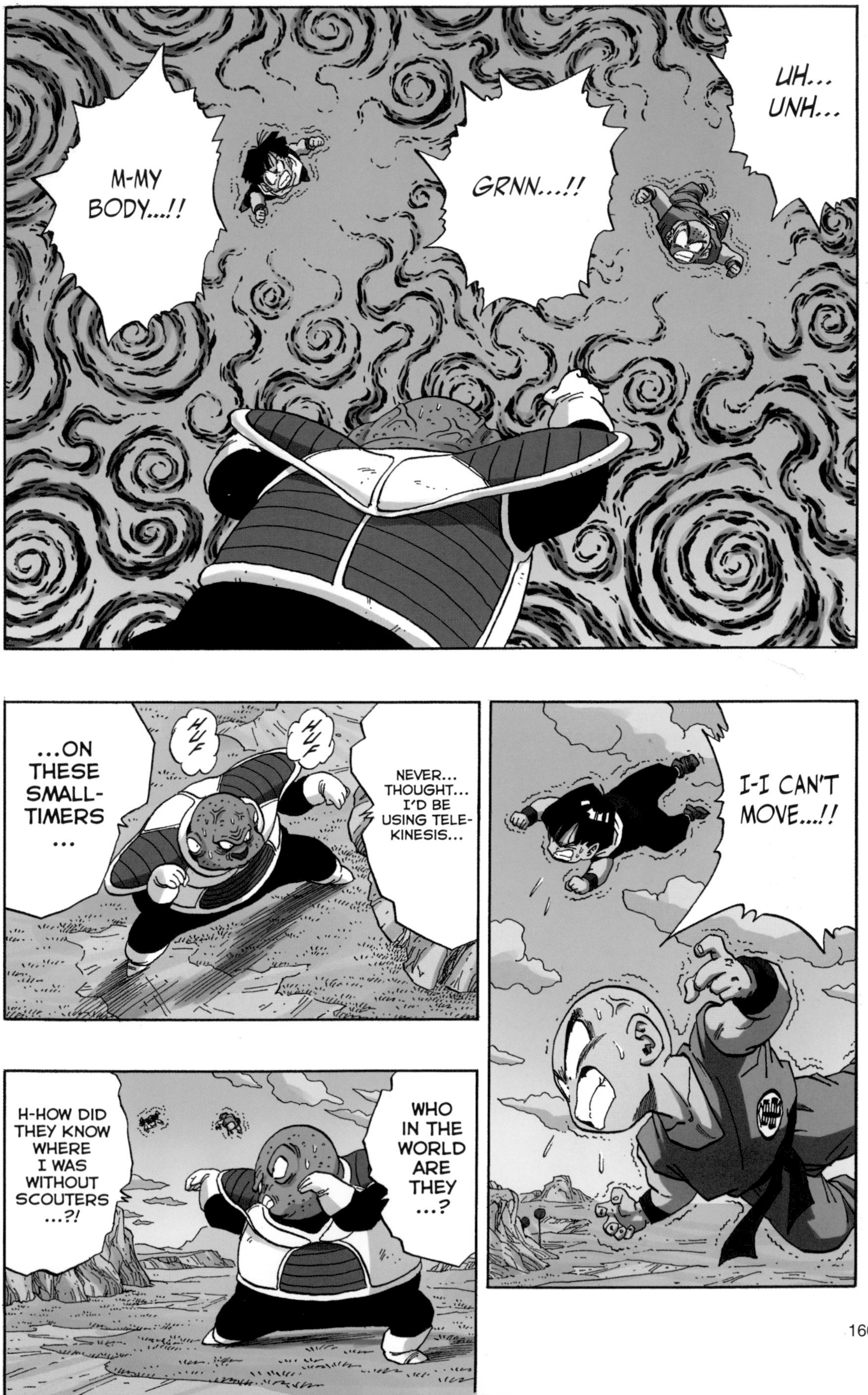
UH... UNH...
GRNN...!!
M-MY BODY...!!
I-I CAN'T MOVE...!!
NEVER... THOUGHT... I'D BE USING TELE-KINESIS...
HUF
HUF
...ON THESE SMALL-TIMERS...
WHO IN THE WORLD ARE THEY...?
H-HOW DID THEY KNOW WHERE I WAS WITHOUT SCOUTERS...?!

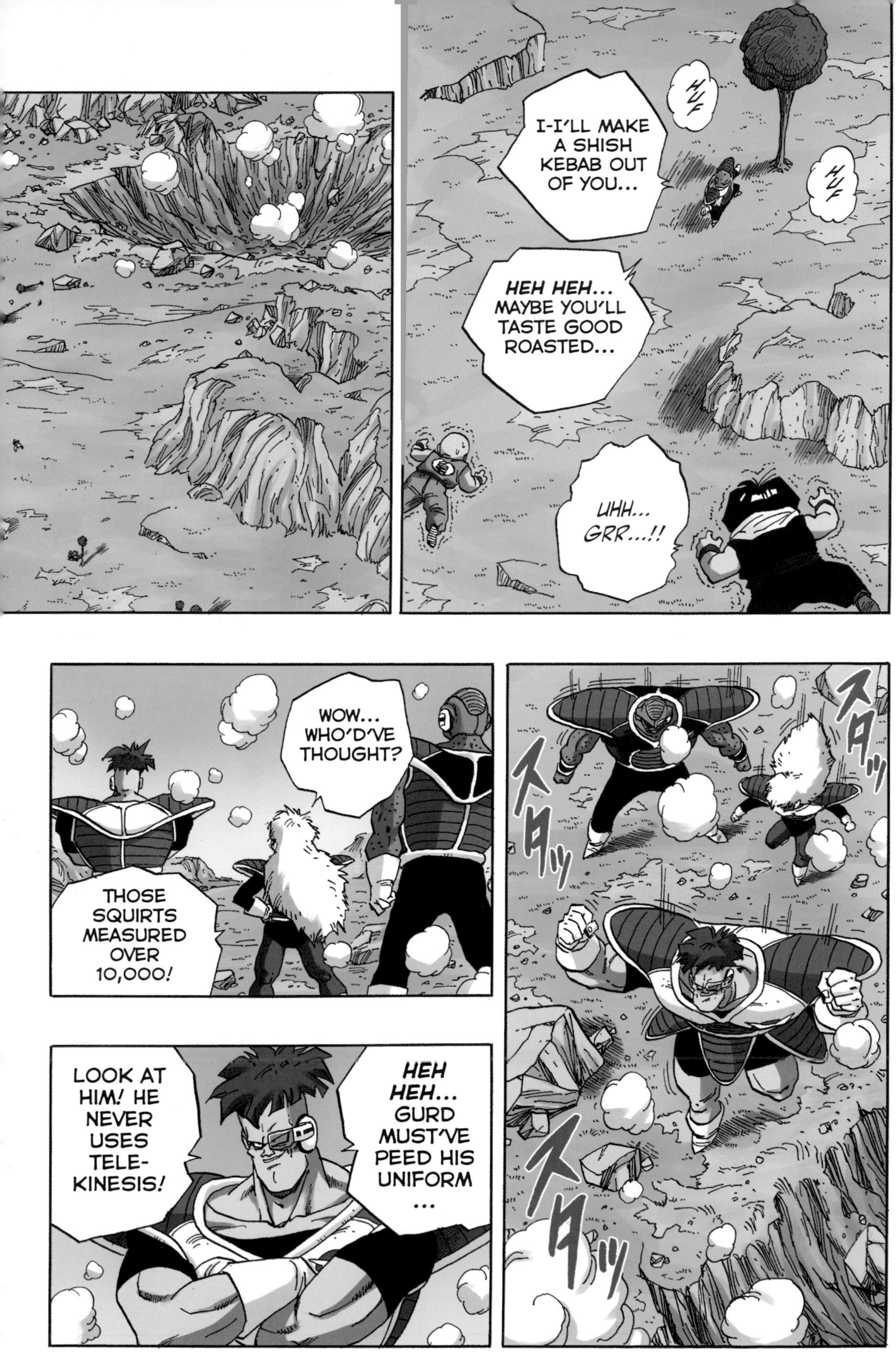
HUF
HUF
I-I'LL MAKE A SHISH KEBAB OUT OF YOU...
HEH HEH... MAYBE YOU'LL TASTE GOOD ROASTED...
UHH... GRR...!!
スタッ
スタッ
スタッ
WOW... WHO'D'VE THOUGHT?
THOSE SQUIRTS MEASURED OVER 10,000!
HEH HEH... GURD MUST'VE PEED HIS UNIFORM...
LOOK AT HIM! HE NEVER USES TELE-KINESIS!

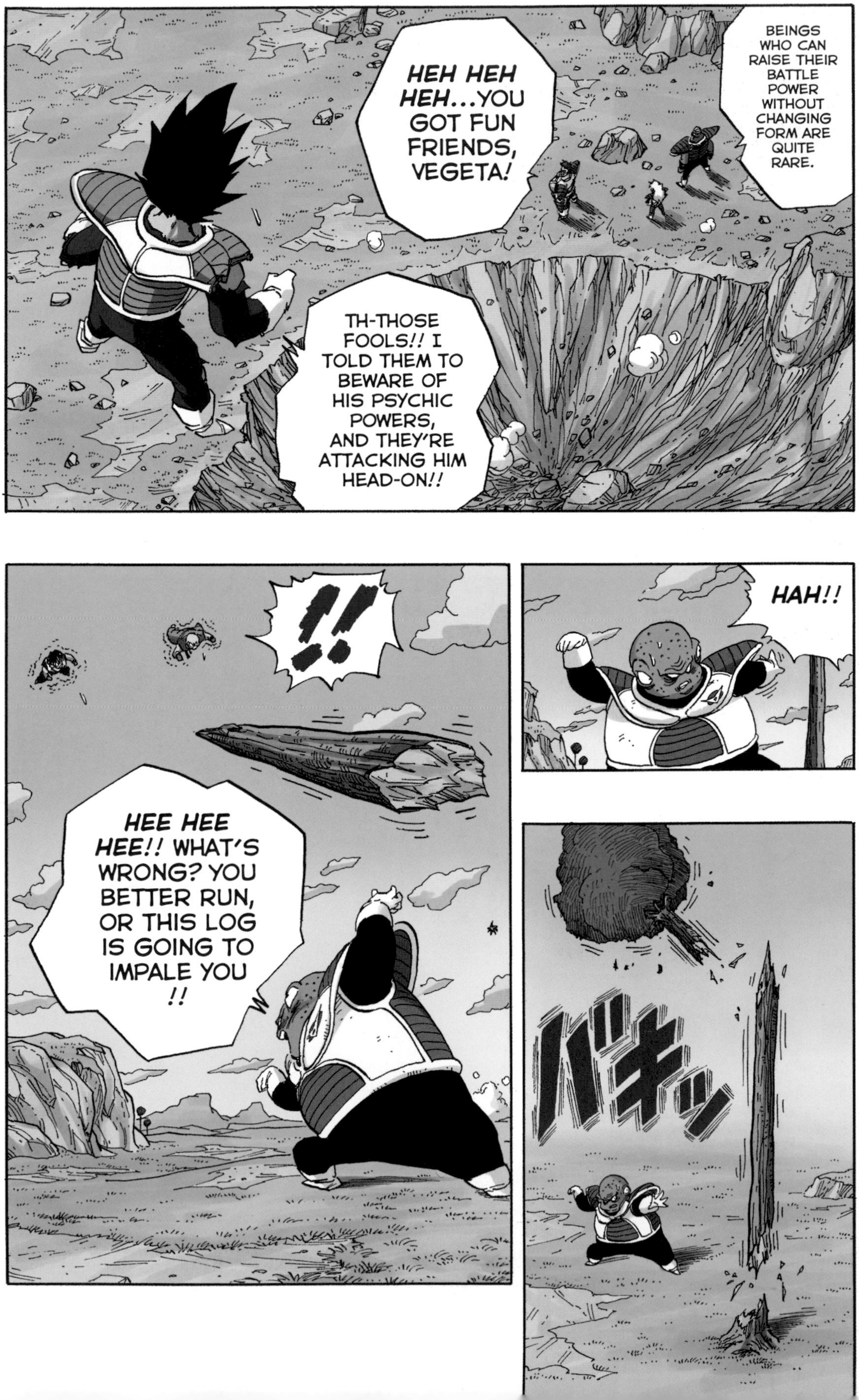
BEINGS WHO CAN RAISE THEIR BATTLE POWER WITHOUT CHANGING FORM ARE QUITE RARE.
HEH HEH HEH...YOU GOT FUN FRIENDS, VEGETA!
TH-THOSE FOOLS!! I TOLD THEM TO BEWARE OF HIS PSYCHIC POWERS, AND THEY'RE ATTACKING HIM HEAD-ON!!
HAH!!
バキッ
!!
HEE HEE HEE!! WHAT'S WRONG? YOU BETTER RUN, OR THIS LOG IS GOING TO IMPALE YOU!!

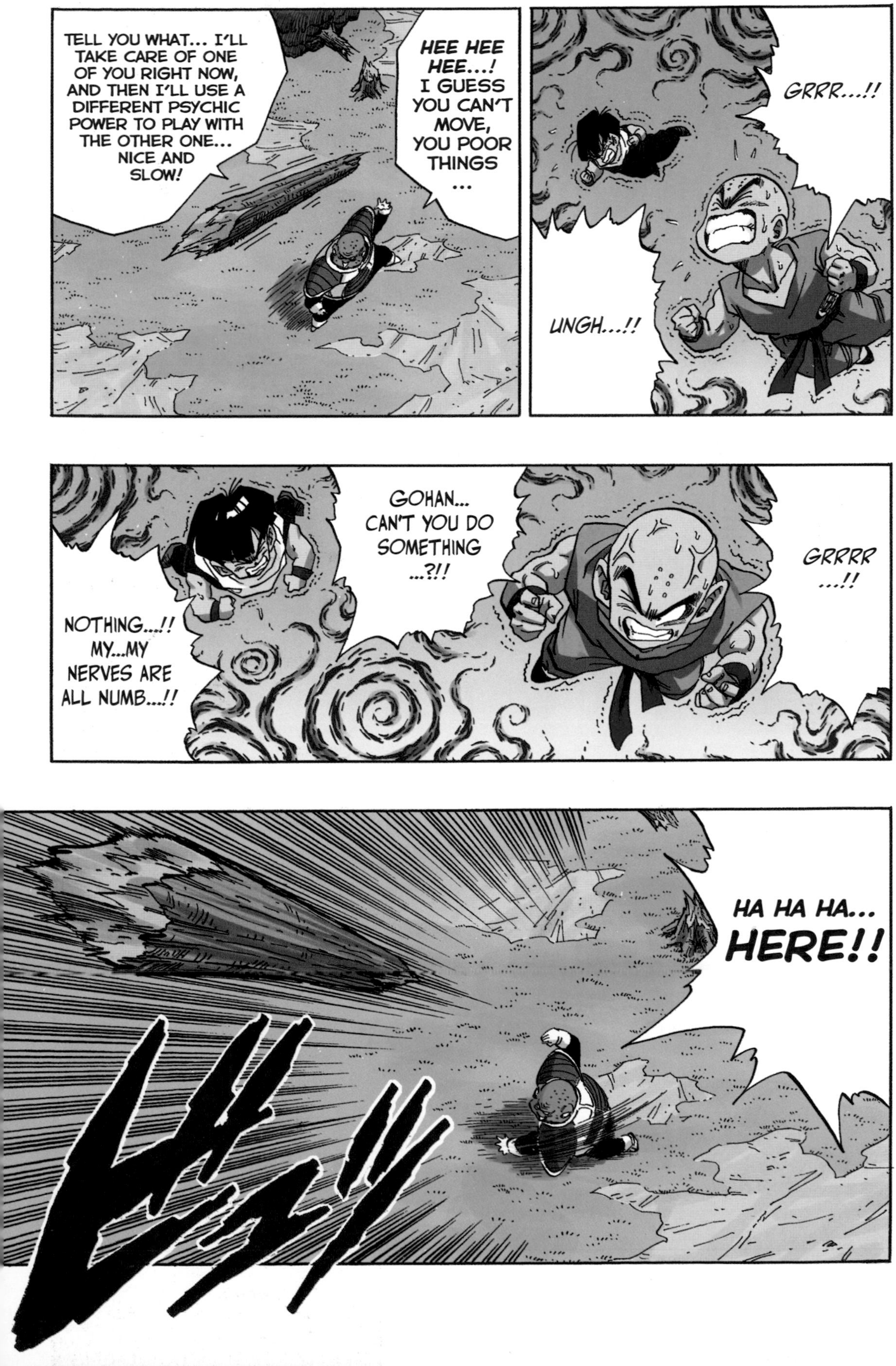

GRRR...!!
UNGH...!!
HEE HEE HEE...! I GUESS YOU CAN'T MOVE, YOU POOR THINGS...
TELL YOU WHAT... I'LL TAKE CARE OF ONE OF YOU RIGHT NOW, AND THEN I'LL USE A DIFFERENT PSYCHIC POWER TO PLAY WITH THE OTHER ONE... NICE AND SLOW!
GRRRR...!!
GOHAN... CAN'T YOU DO SOMETHING...?!!
NOTHING...!! MY...MY NERVES ARE ALL NUMB...!!
HA HA HA... HERE!!

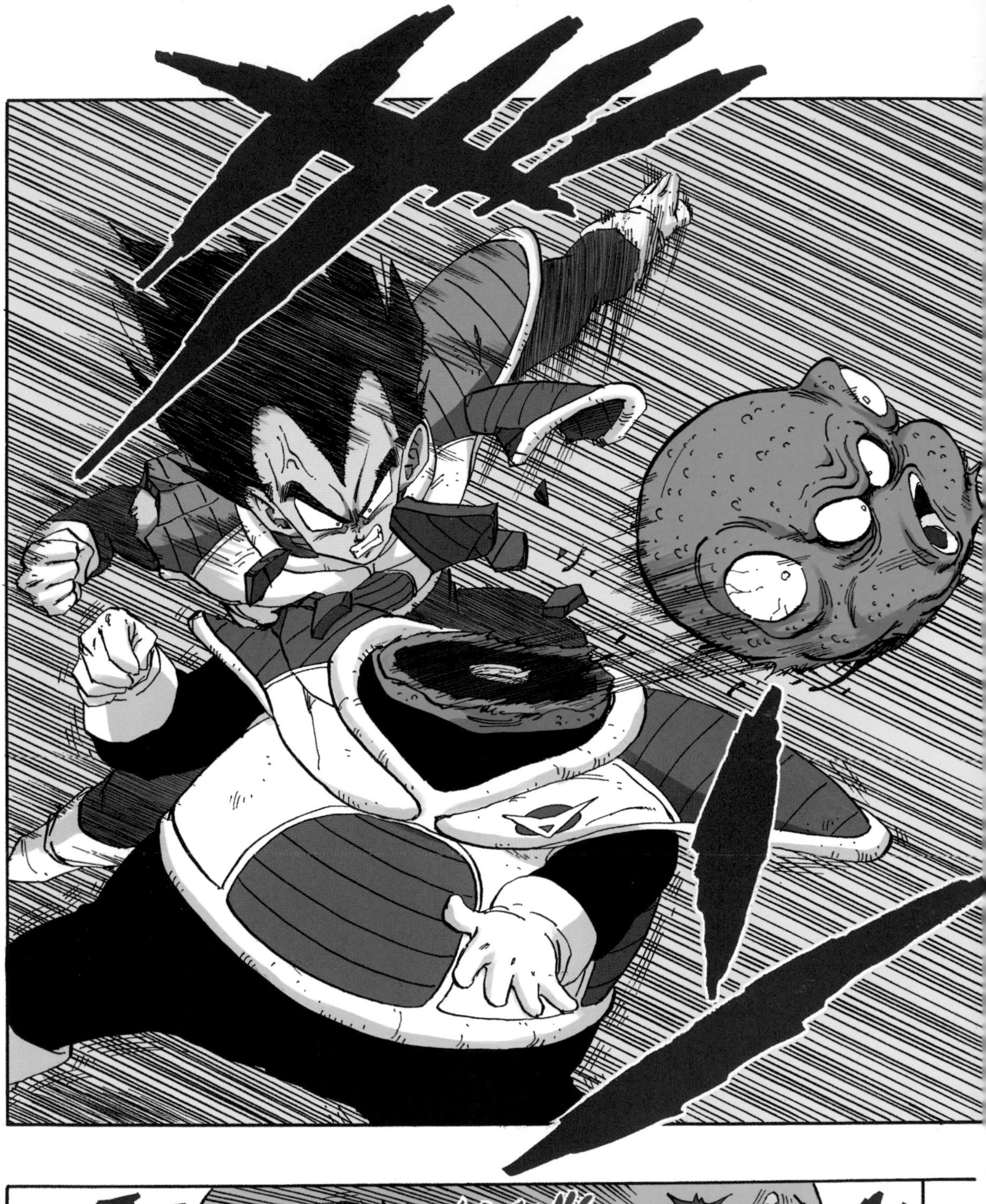
!!
ピクッ
!!

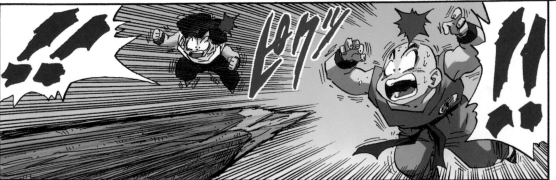

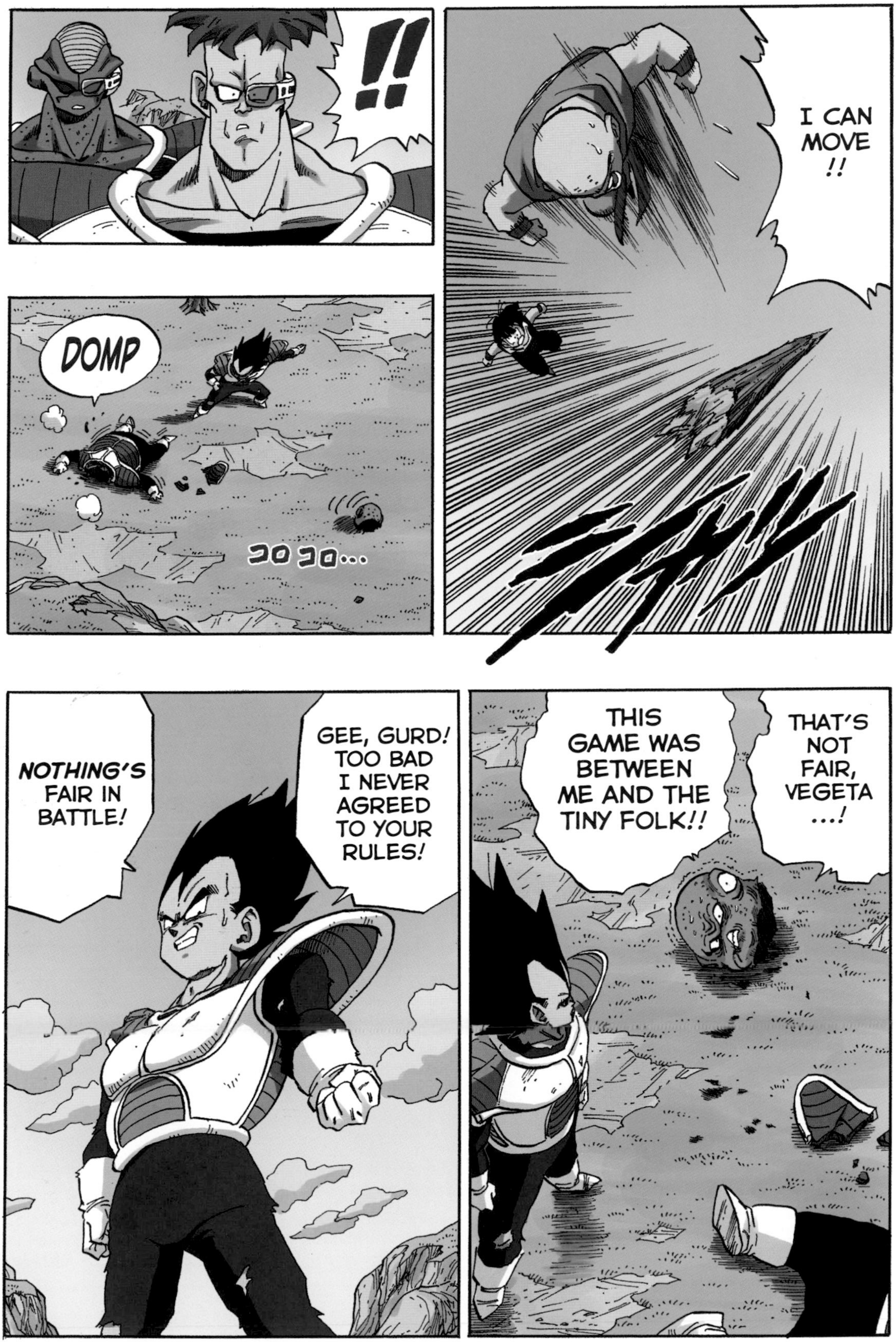
I CAN MOVE!!
!!
DOMP
コロコロ...
THAT'S NOT FAIR, VEGETA...!
THIS GAME WAS BETWEEN ME AND THE TINY FOLK!!
GEE, GURD! TOO BAD I NEVER AGREED TO YOUR RULES!
NOTHING'S FAIR IN BATTLE!

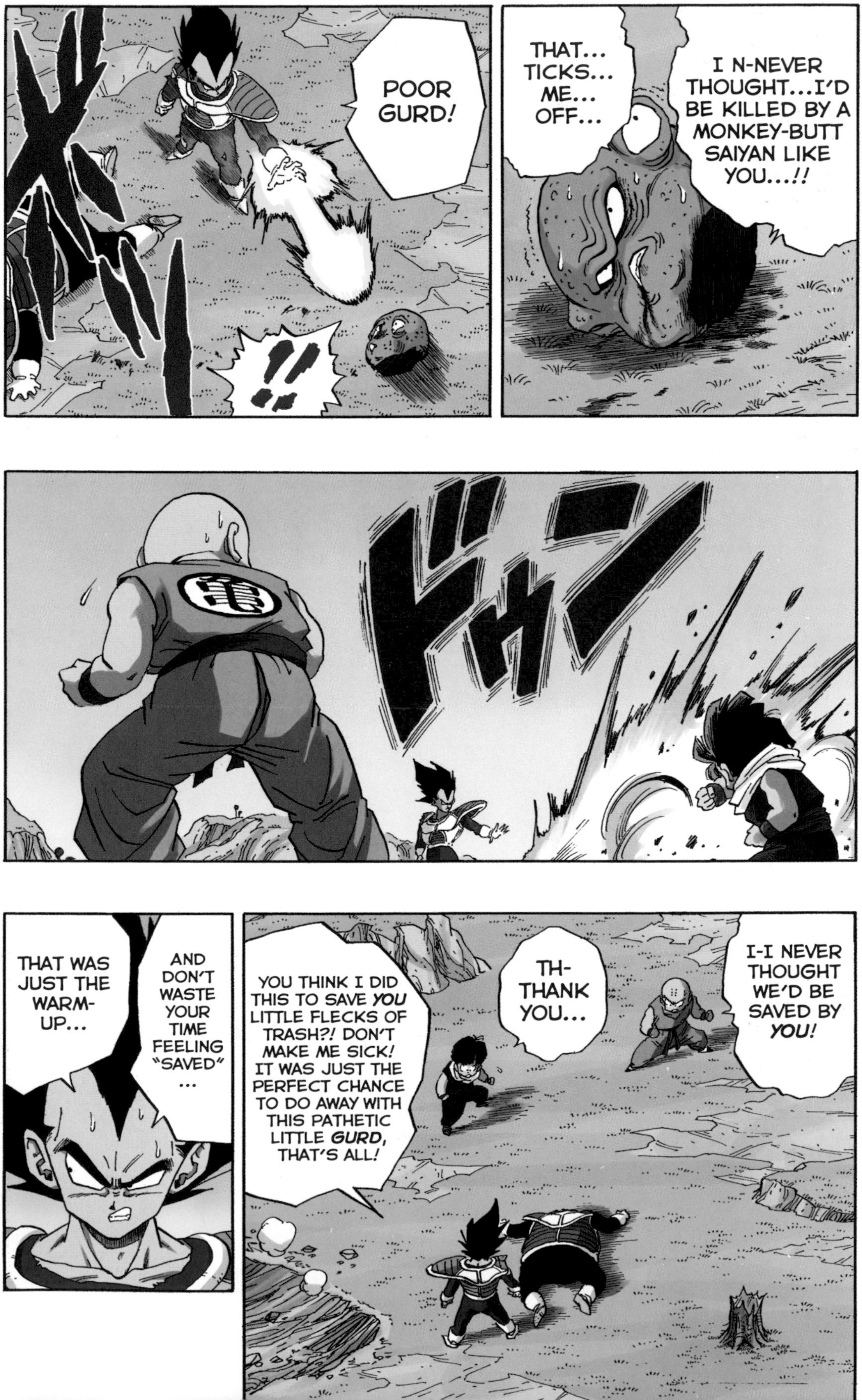
I N-NEVER THOUGHT...I'D BE KILLED BY A MONKEY-BUTT SAIYAN LIKE YOU...!!
THAT... TICKS... ME... OFF...
POOR GURD!
!!
ドゥン
I-I NEVER THOUGHT WE'D BE SAVED BY YOU!
TH-THANK YOU...
YOU THINK I DID THIS TO SAVE YOU LITTLE FLECKS OF TRASH?! DON'T MAKE ME SICK! IT WAS JUST THE PERFECT CHANCE TO DO AWAY WITH THIS PATHETIC LITTLE GURD, THAT'S ALL!
AND DON'T WASTE YOUR TIME FEELING "SAVED"...
THAT WAS JUST THE WARM-UP...

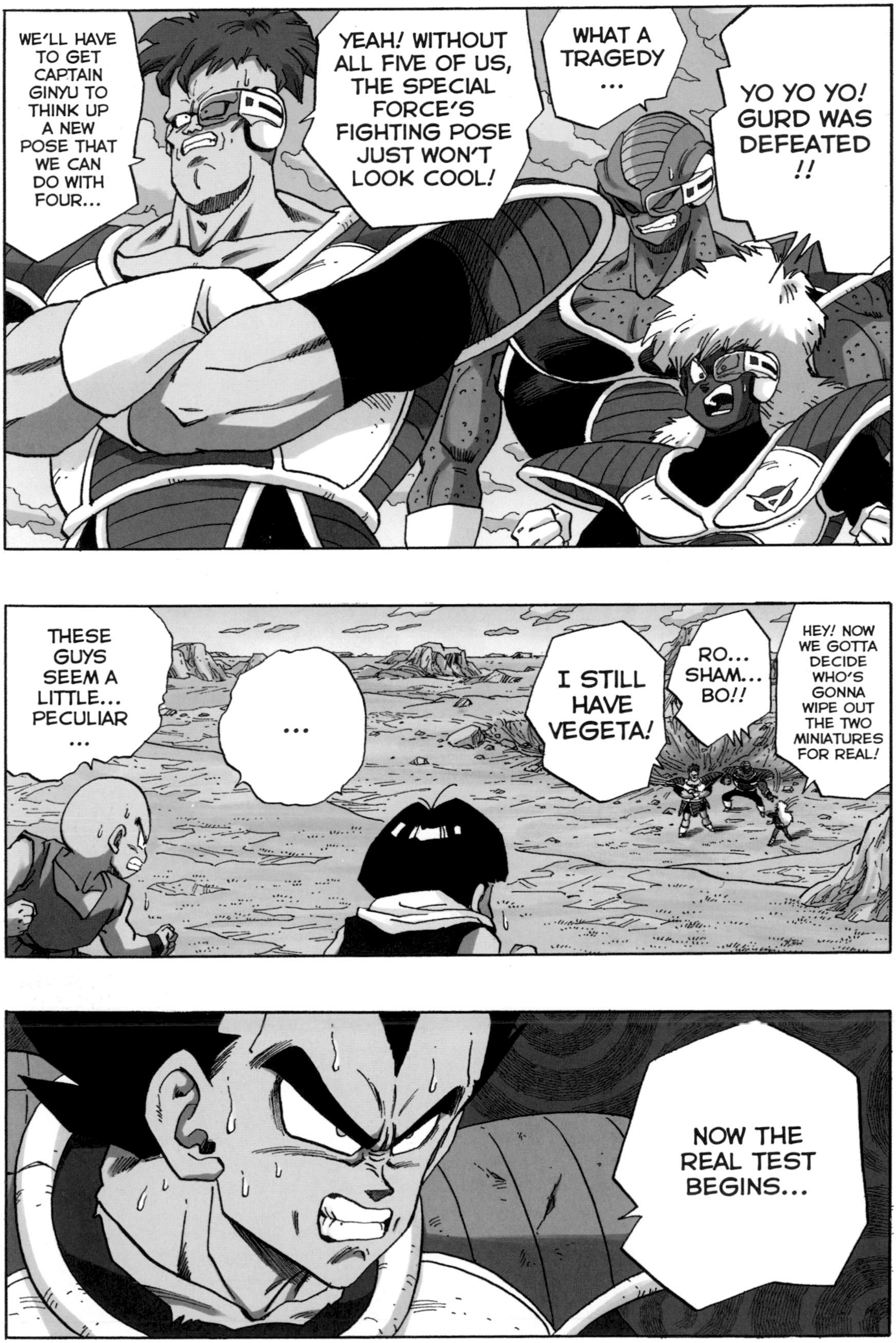
YO YO YO! GURD WAS DEFEATED!!
WHAT A TRAGEDY...
YEAH! WITHOUT ALL FIVE OF US, THE SPECIAL FORCE'S FIGHTING POSE JUST WON'T LOOK COOL!
WE'LL HAVE TO GET CAPTAIN GINYU TO THINK UP A NEW POSE THAT WE CAN DO WITH FOUR...
HEY! NOW WE GOTTA DECIDE WHO'S GONNA WIPE OUT THE TWO MINIATURES FOR REAL!
RO... SHAM... BO!!
I STILL HAVE VEGETA!
...
THESE GUYS SEEM A LITTLE... PECULIAR...
NOW THE REAL TEST BEGINS...

Chapter 30 • Vegeta vs. Reacoom

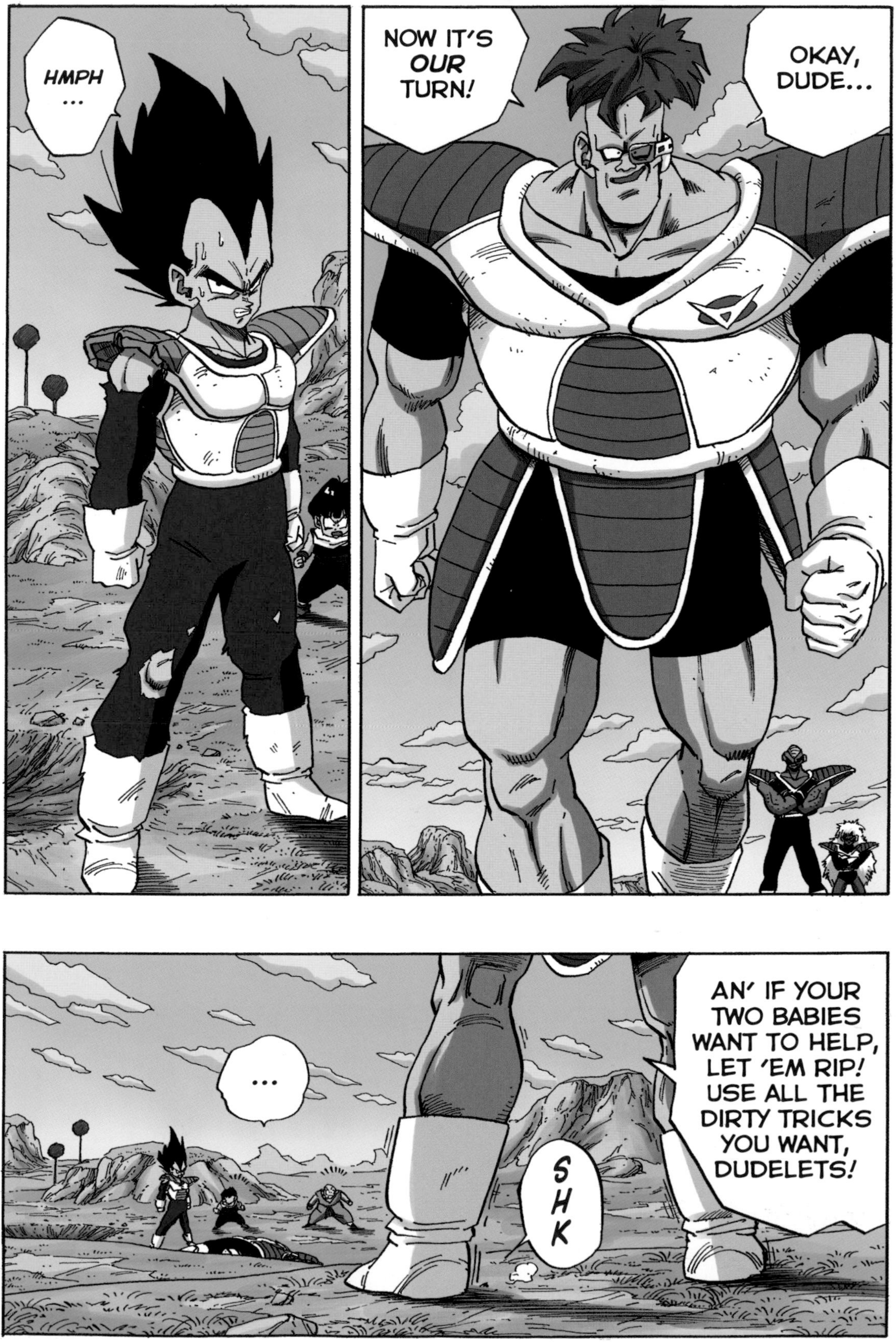
OKAY, DUDE...
NOW IT'S *OUR* TURN!
HMPH ...
AN' IF YOUR TWO BABIES WANT TO HELP, LET 'EM RIP! USE ALL THE DIRTY TRICKS YOU WANT, DUDELETS!
SHK
...

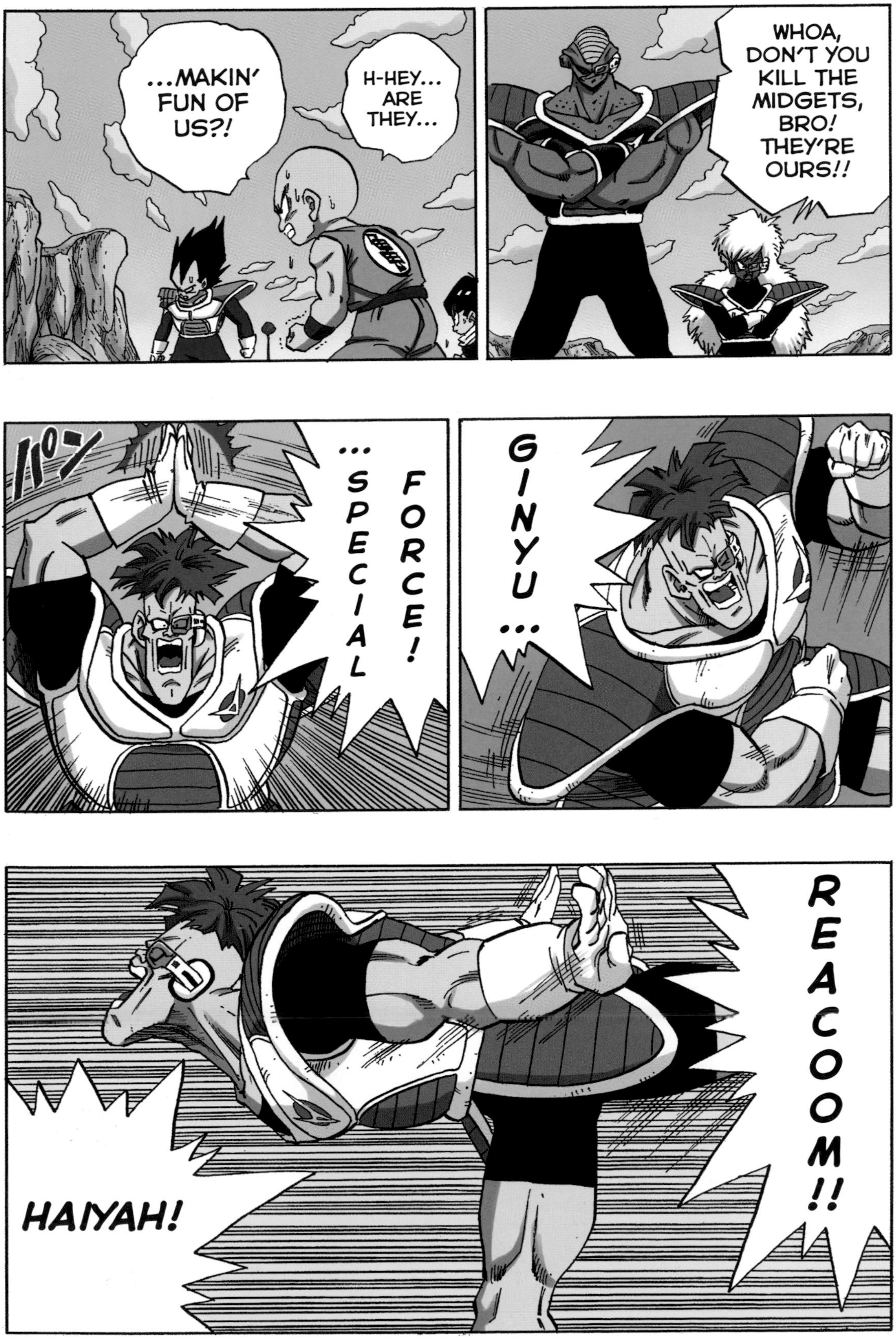
WHOA, DON'T YOU KILL THE MIDGETS, BRO! THEY'RE OURS!!
H-HEY... ARE THEY...
...MAKIN' FUN OF US?!
GINYU...
...SPECIAL FORCE!
REACOOOM!!
HAIYAH!

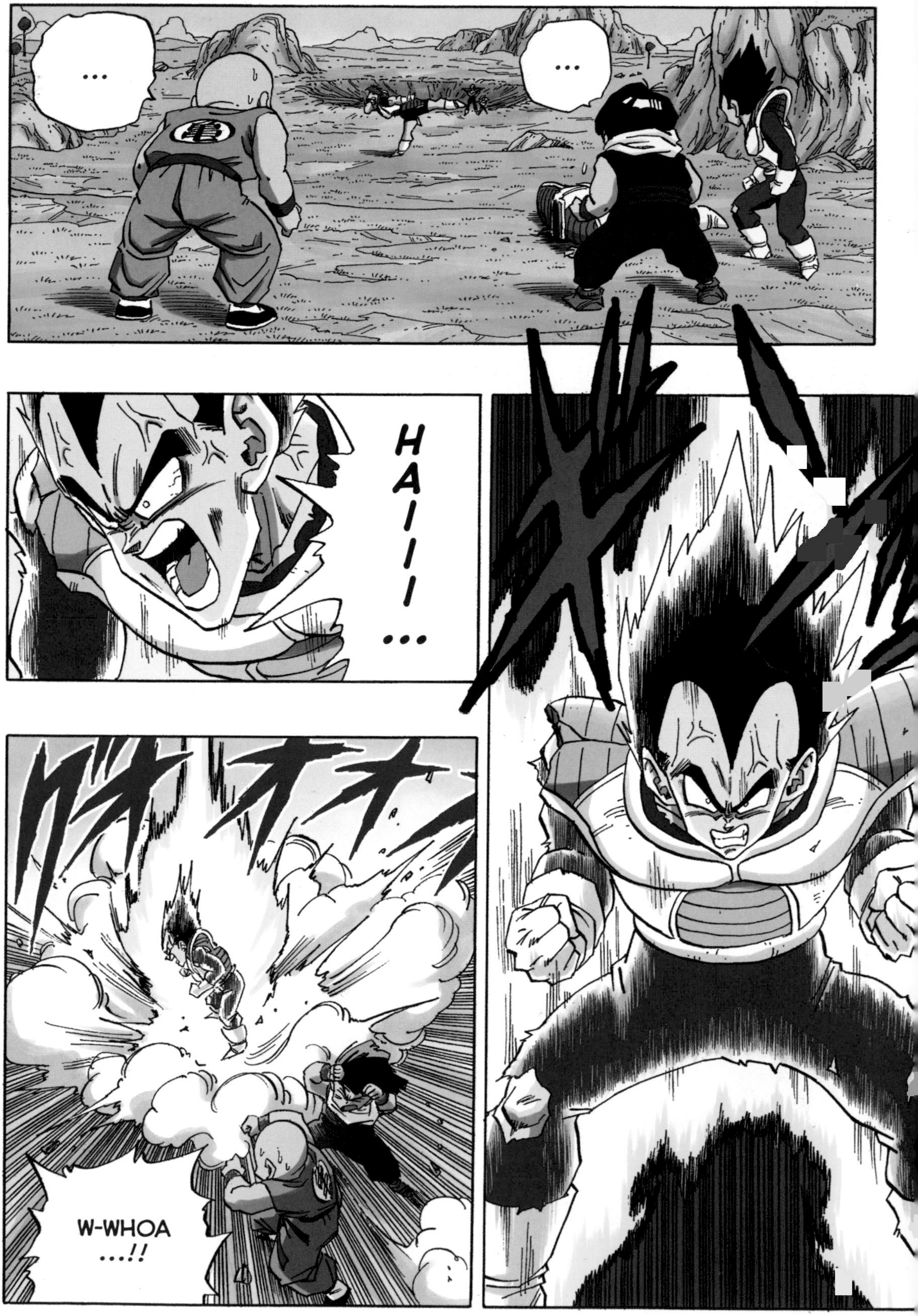
...
...
HAIII...
W-WHOA ...!!

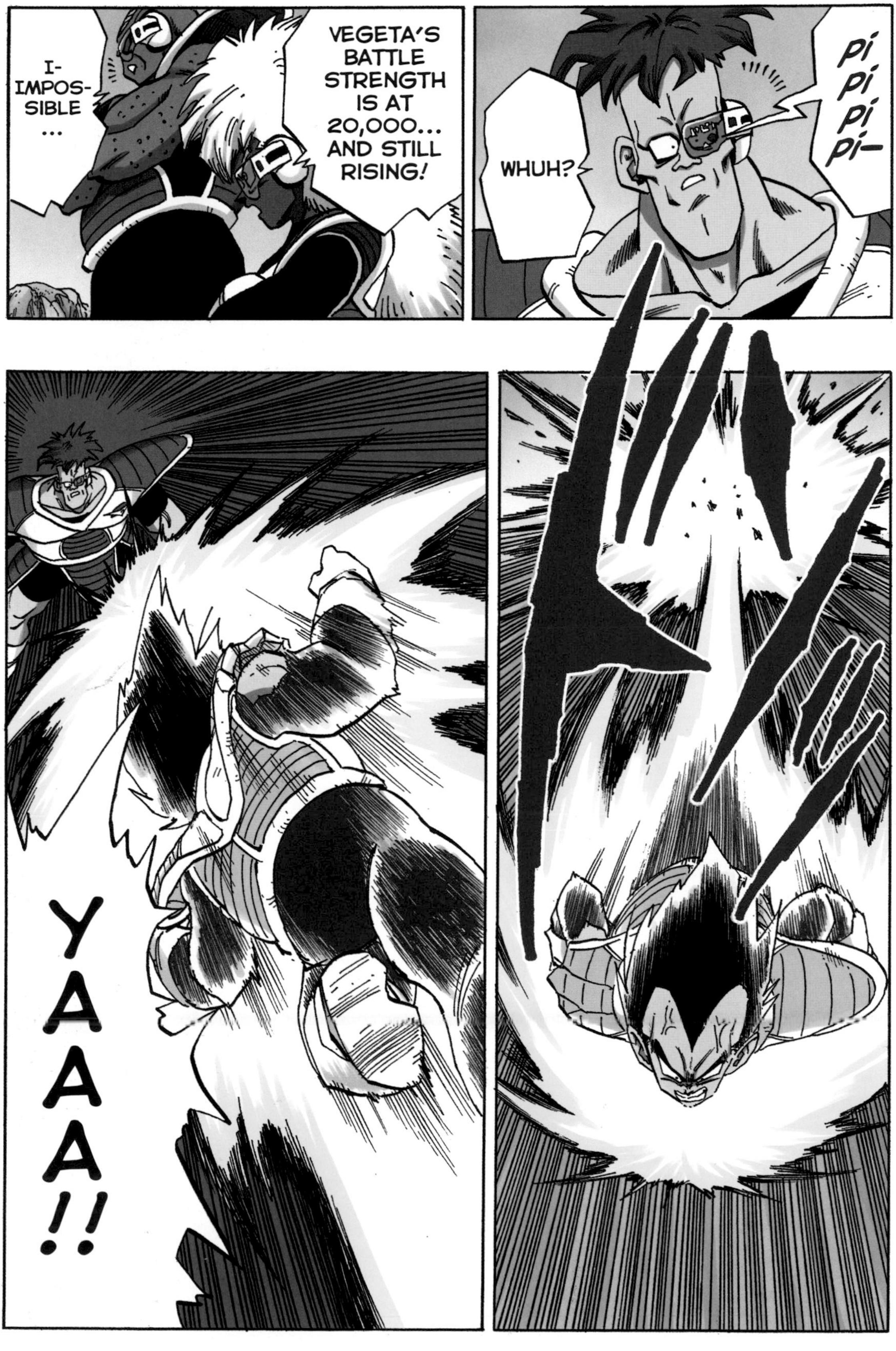
pi pi pi pi–
WHUH?
VEGETA'S BATTLE STRENGTH IS AT 20,000... AND STILL RISING!
I- IMPOSSIBLE ...
YAAAA!!

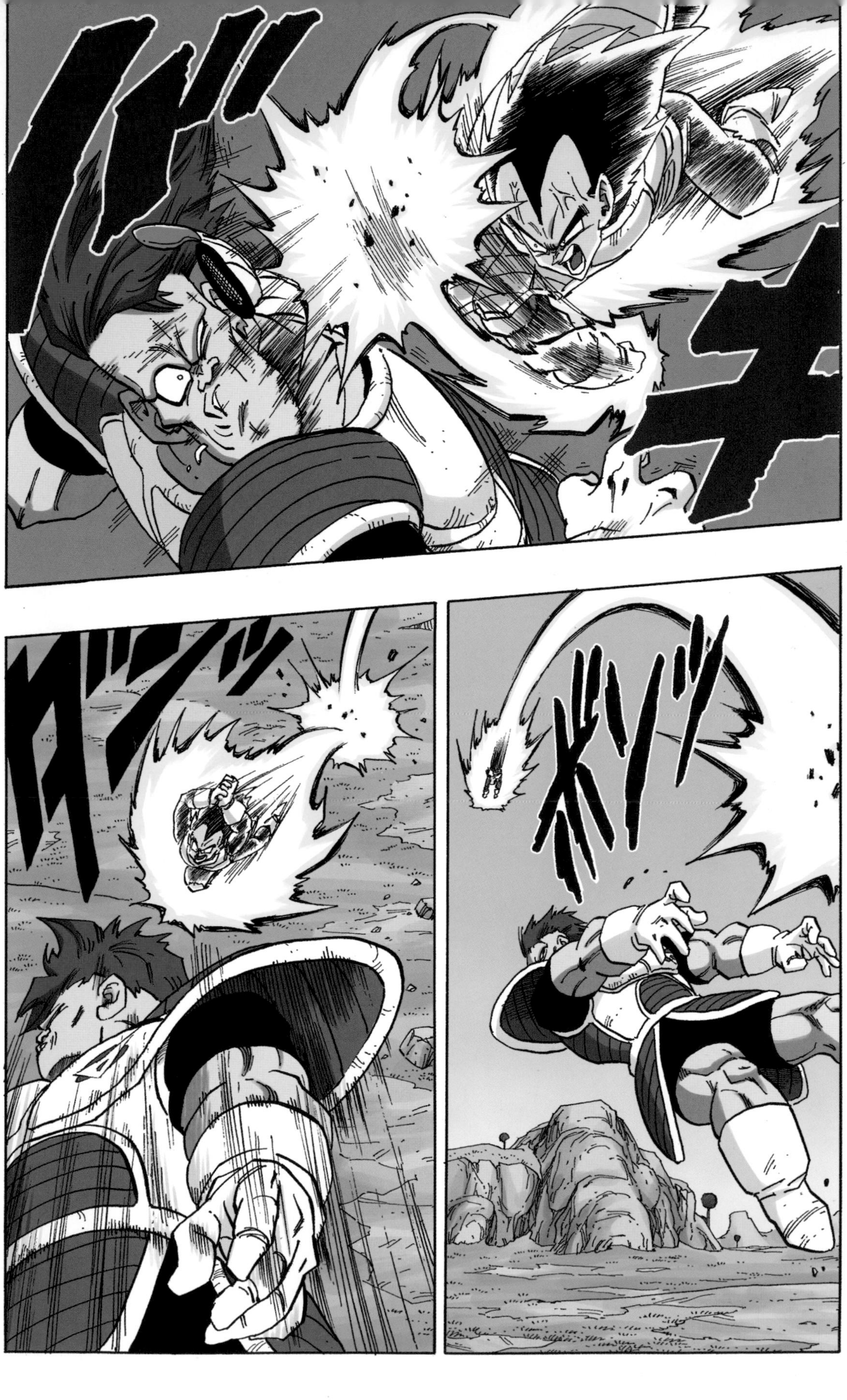

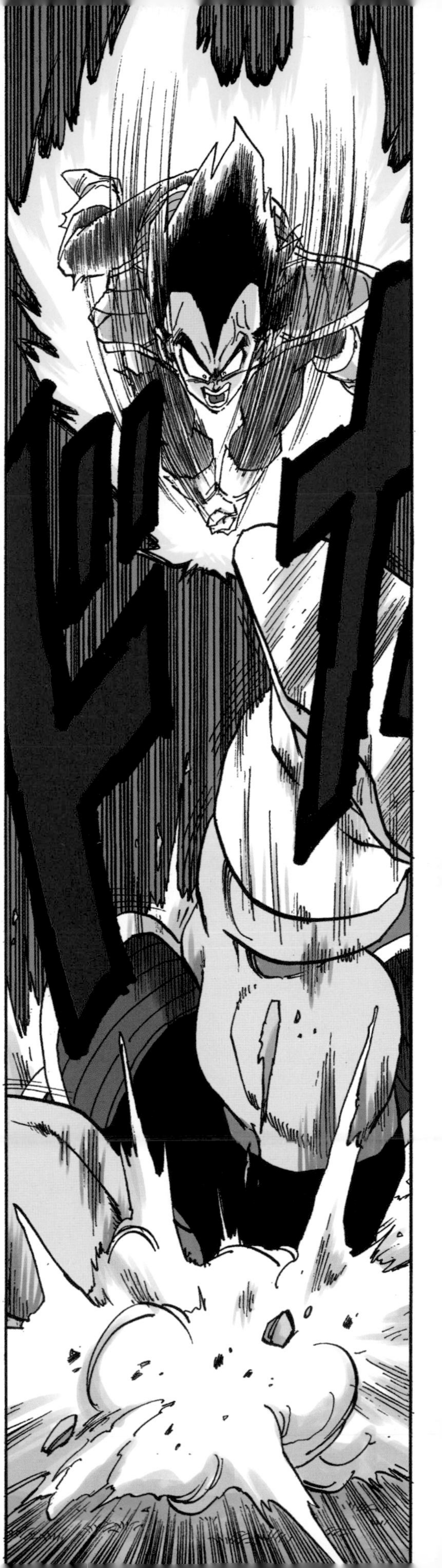

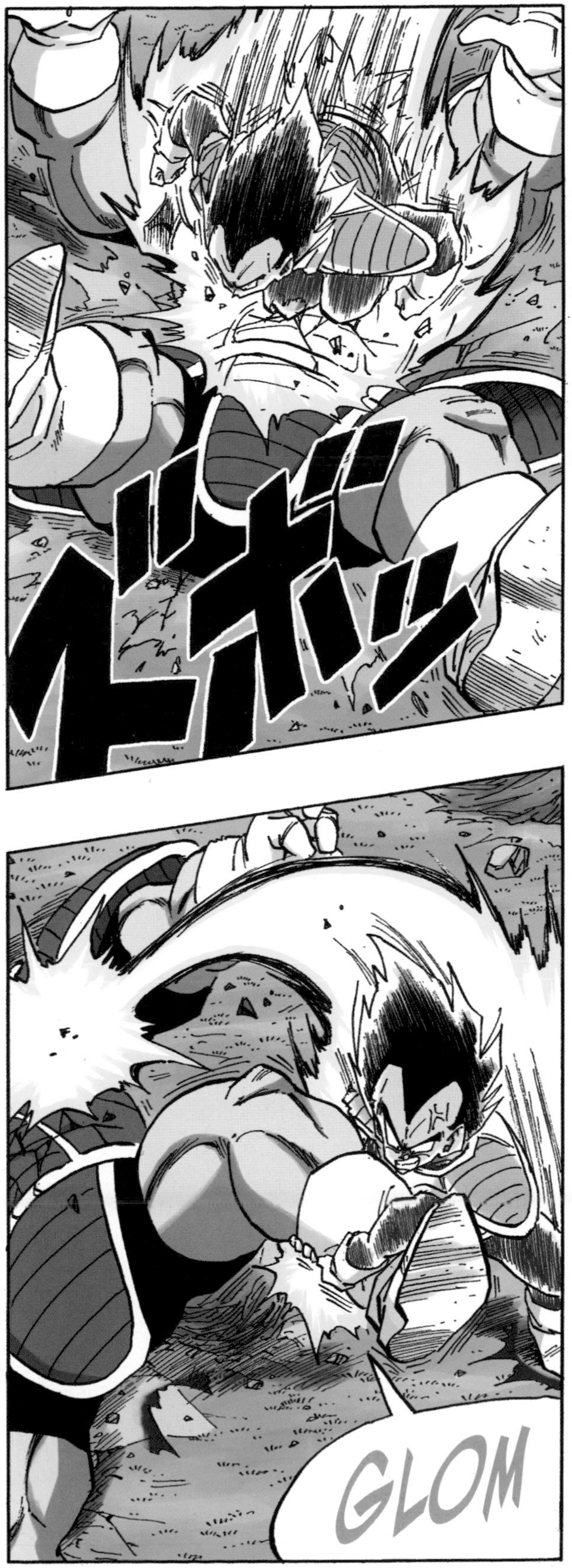
ドボッ
GLOM

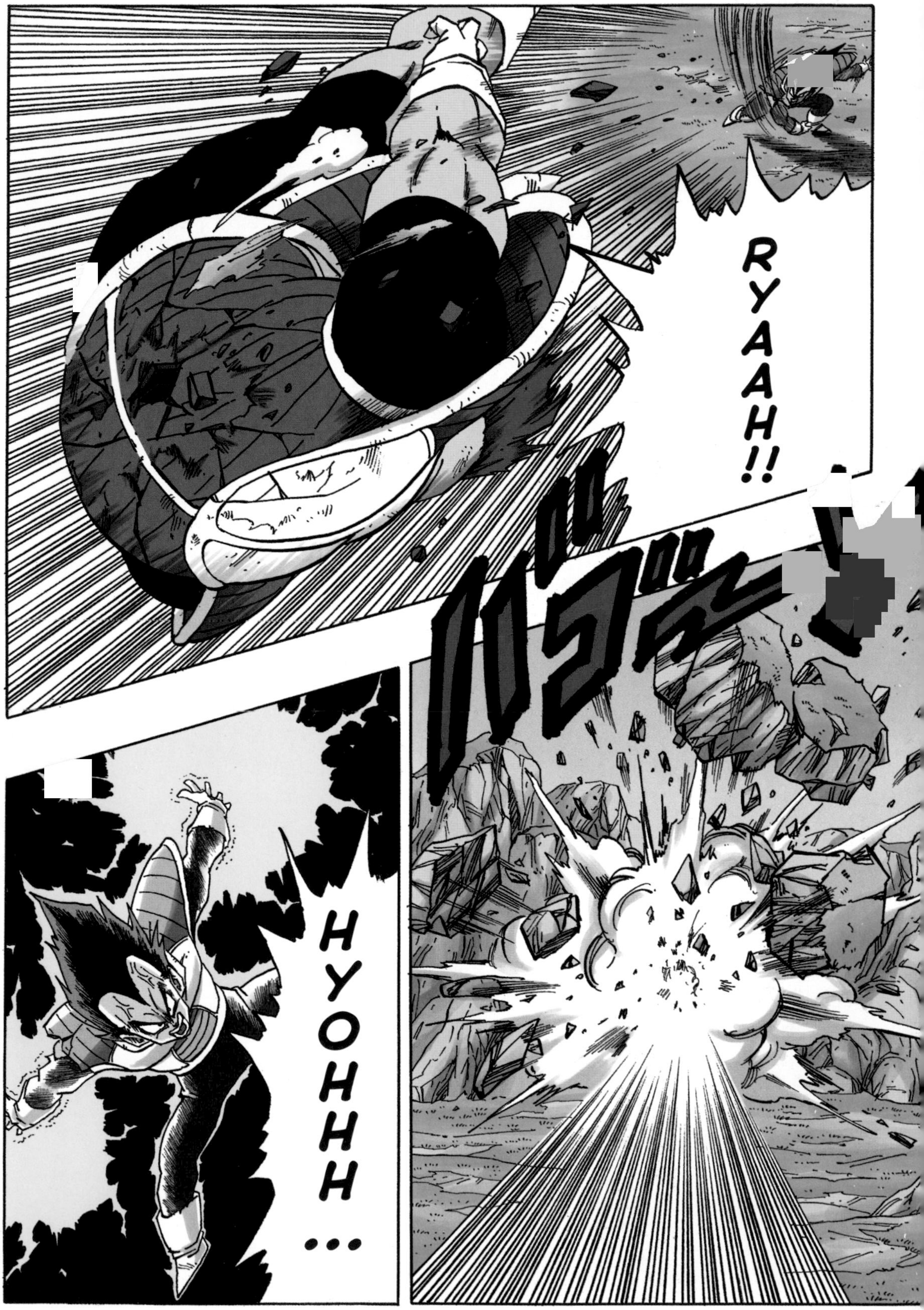
RYAAH!!
HYOHHH...

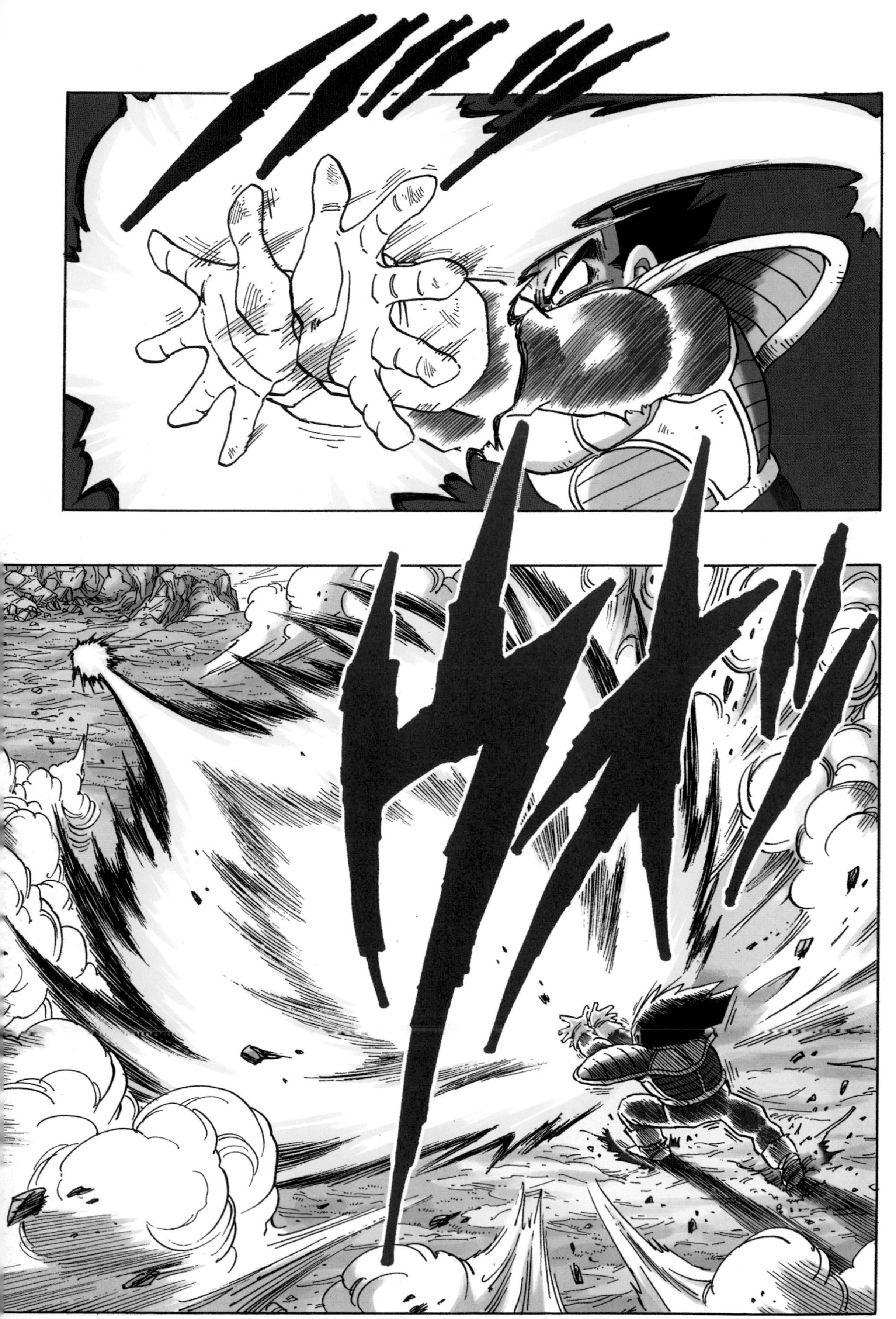

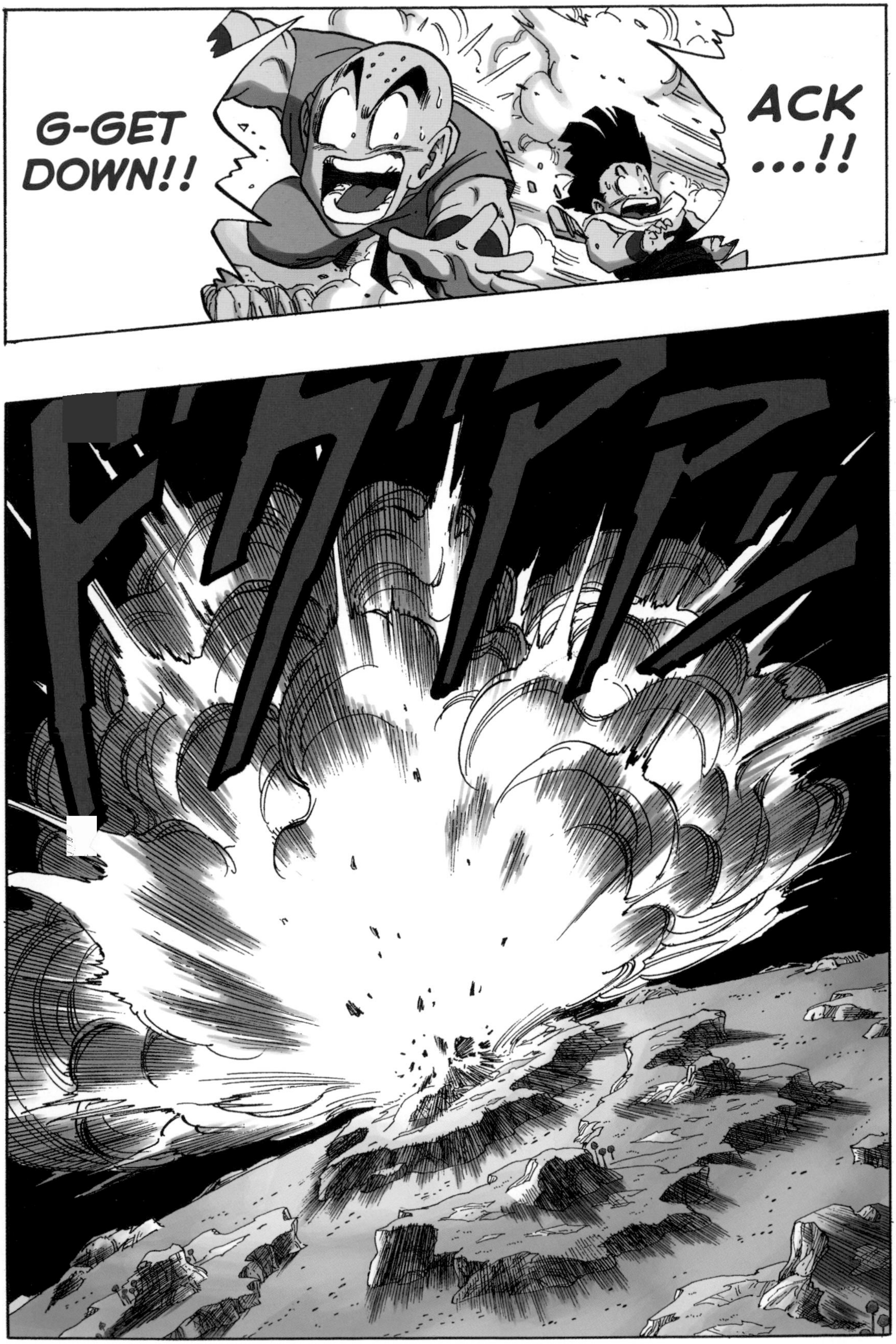
ACK ...!!
G-GET DOWN!!

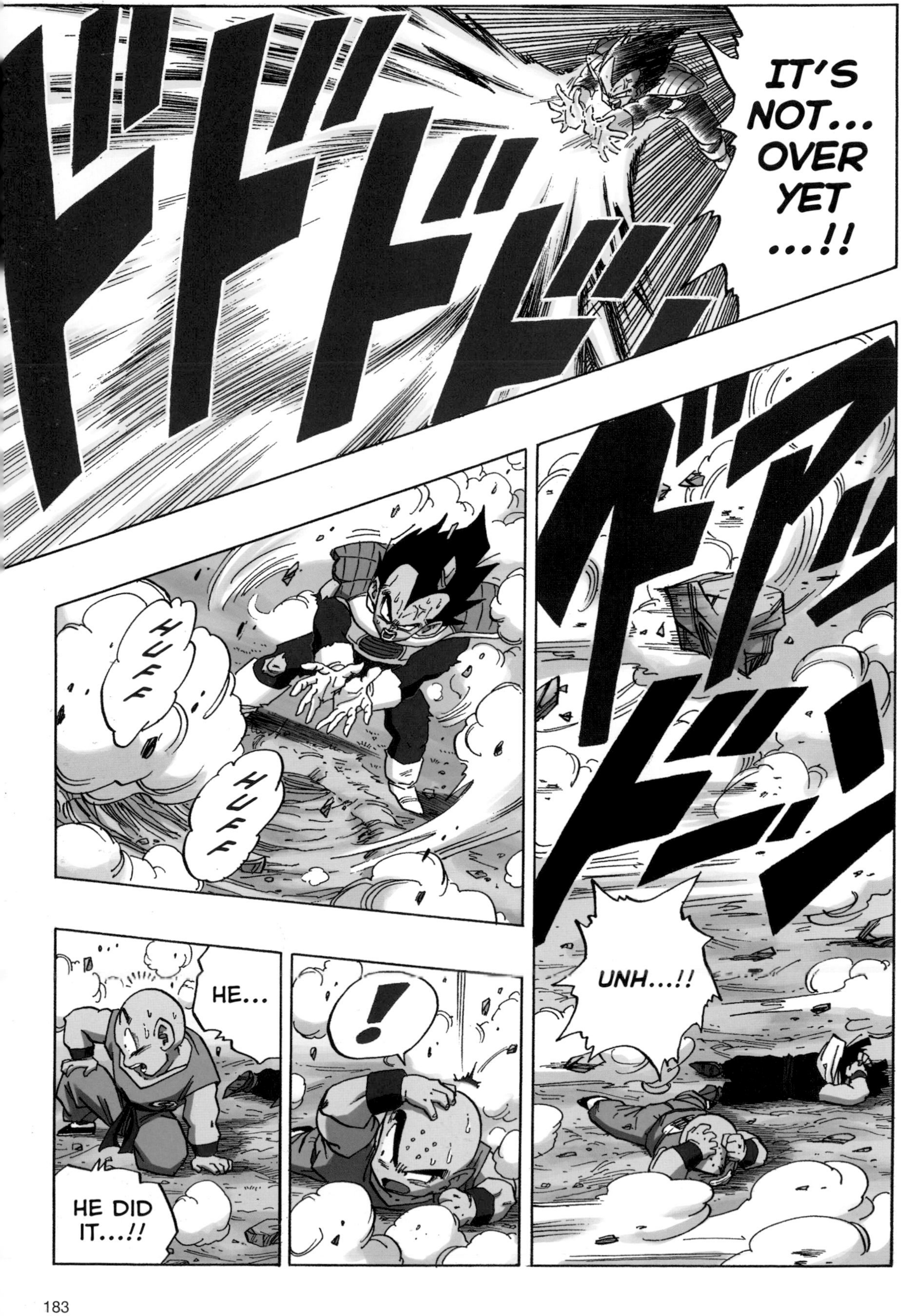
IT'S NOT... OVER YET ...!!
UNH...!!
HUFF
HUFF
!
HE...
HE DID IT...!!

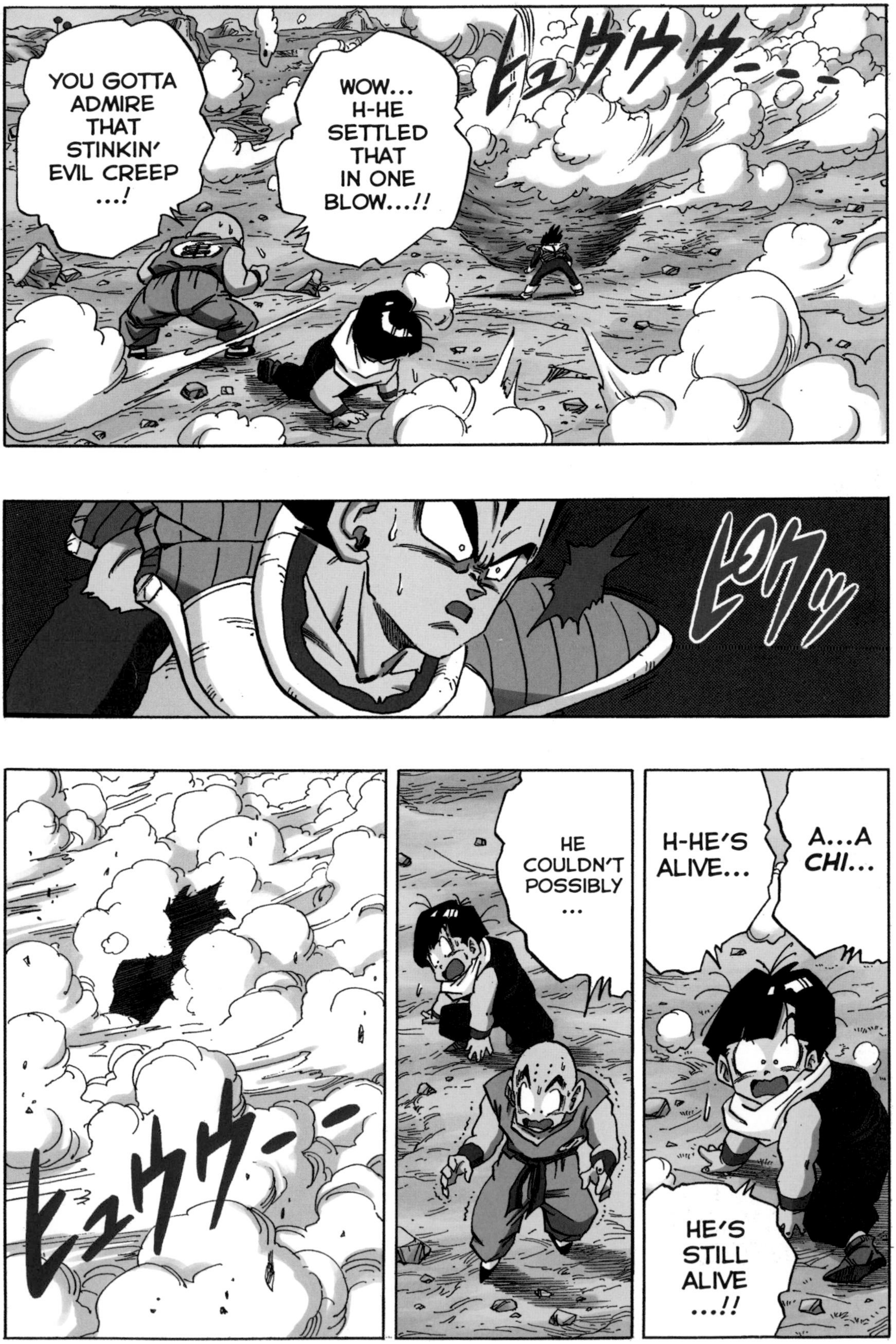
WOW... H-HE SETTLED THAT IN ONE BLOW...!!
YOU GOTTA ADMIRE THAT STINKIN' EVIL CREEP ...!
A...A *CHI*...
H-HE'S ALIVE...
HE'S STILL ALIVE ...!!
HE COULDN'T POSSIBLY ...

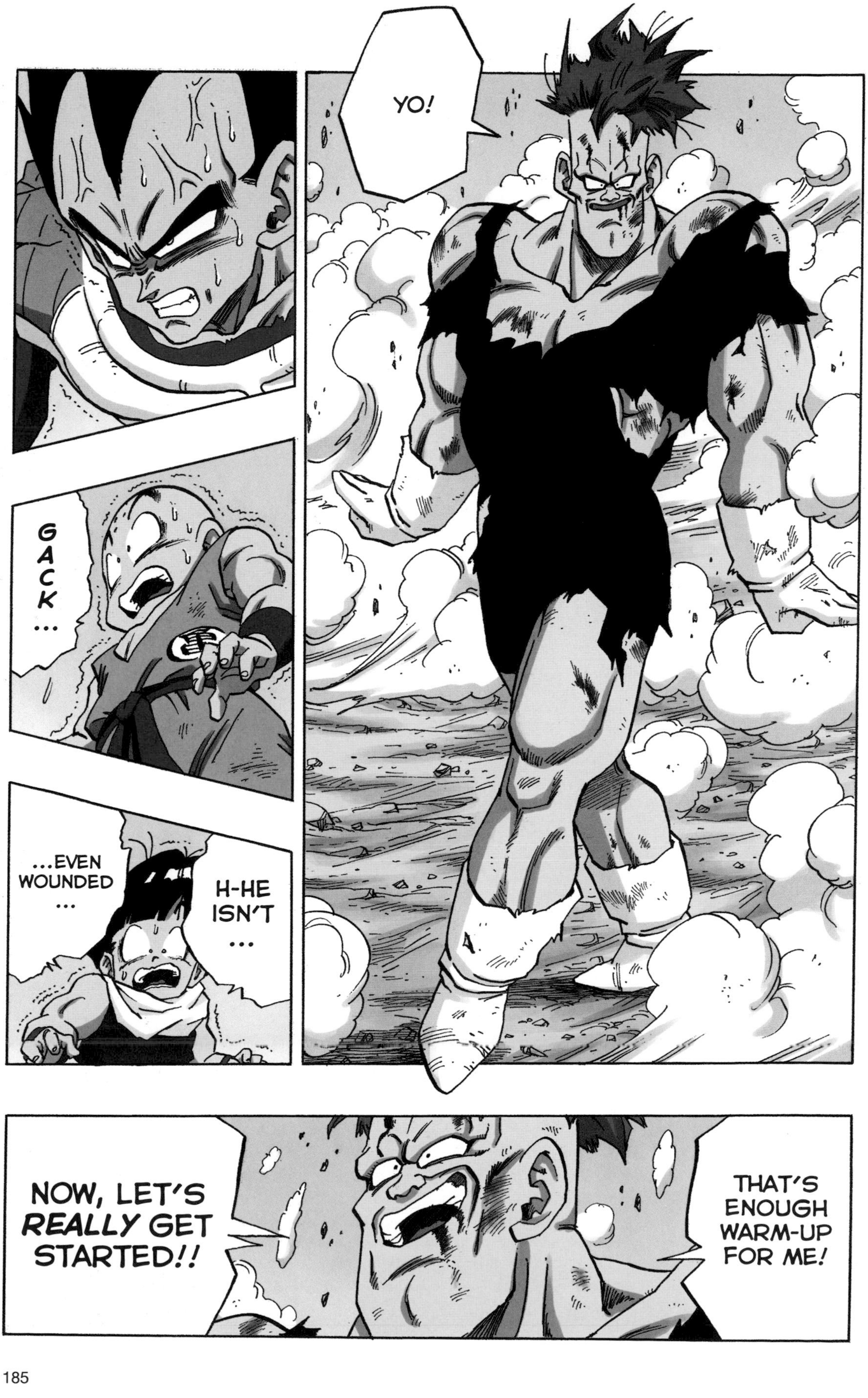
YO!
GACK...
H-HE ISN'T ...
...EVEN WOUNDED ...
THAT'S ENOUGH WARM-UP FOR ME!
NOW, LET'S *REALLY* GET STARTED!!

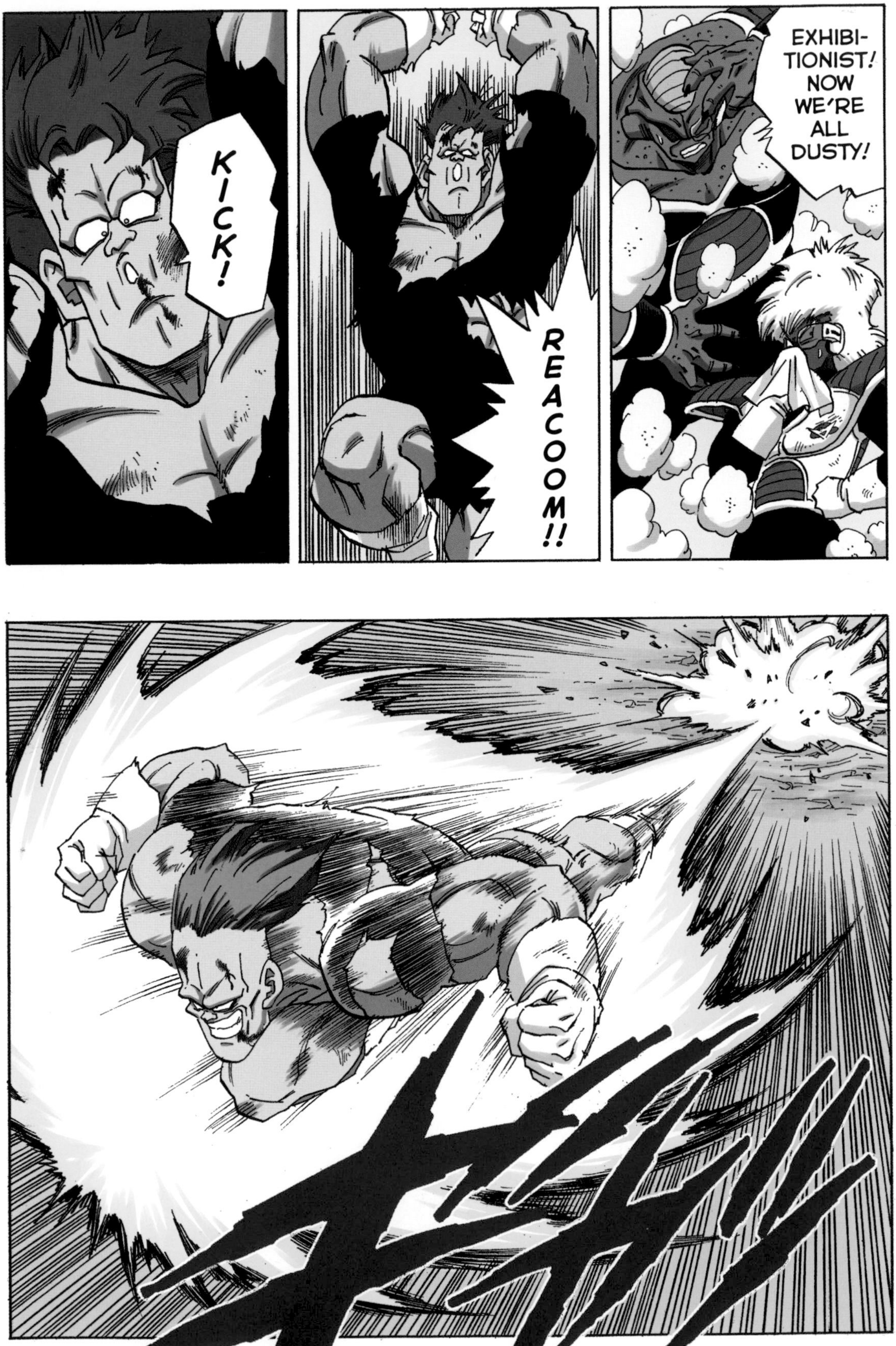
EXHIBITIONIST! NOW WE'RE ALL DUSTY!
REACOOOM!!
KICK!

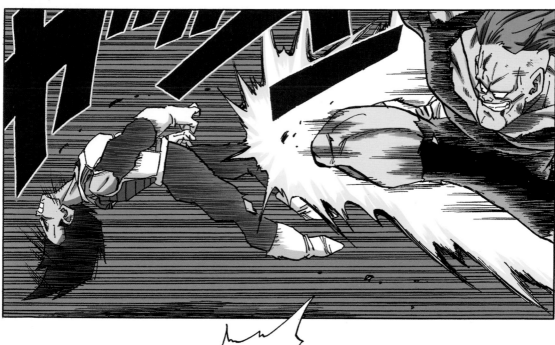

GUH...

Chapter 31 • Vegeta vs. Reacoom, Part 2

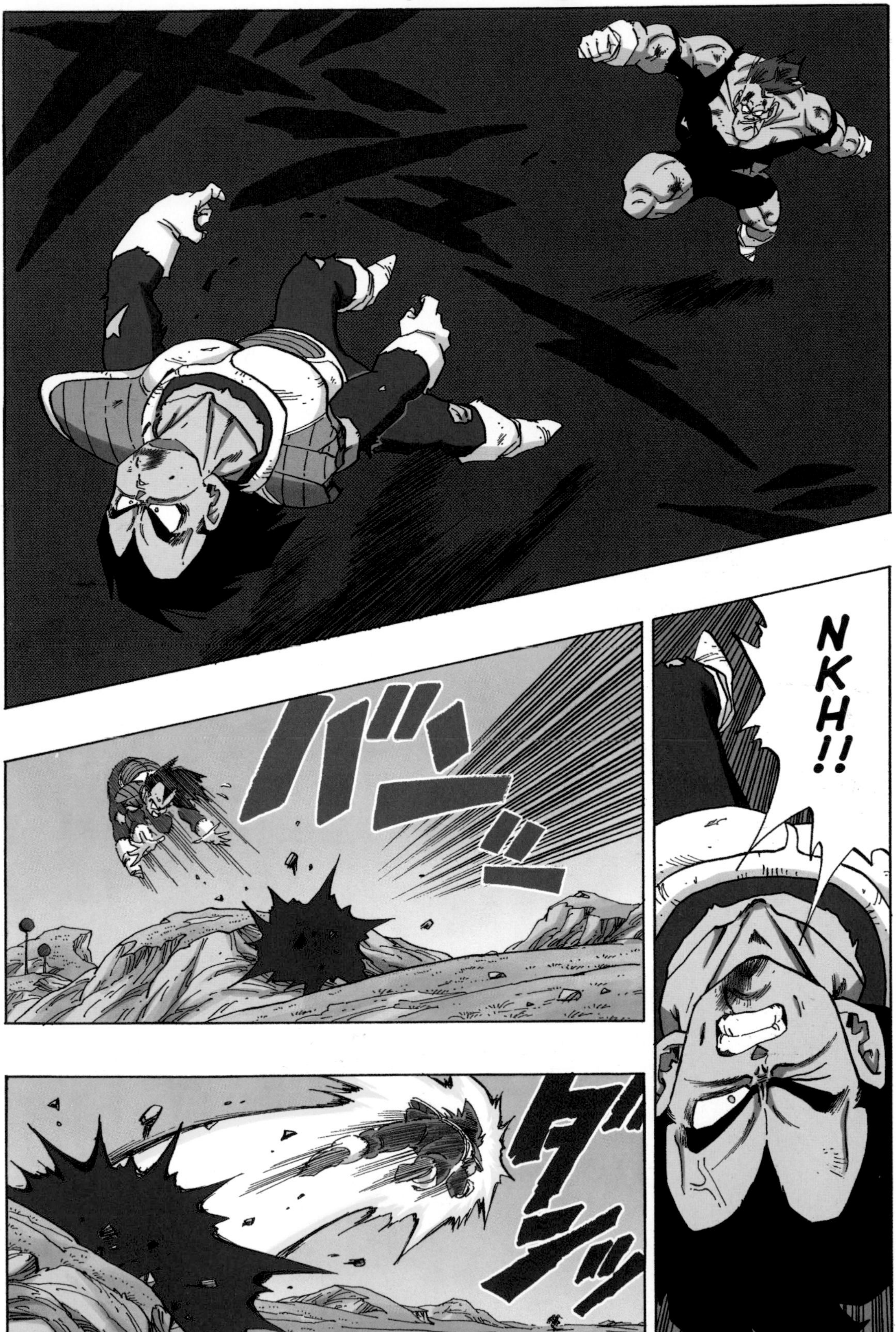
NKH!!

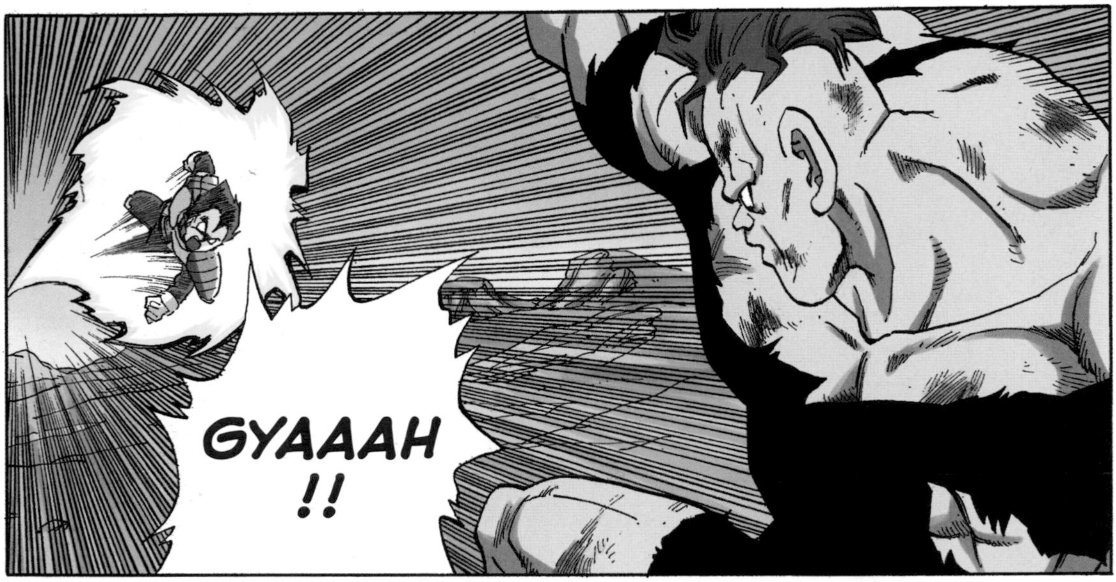
GYAAAH
!!

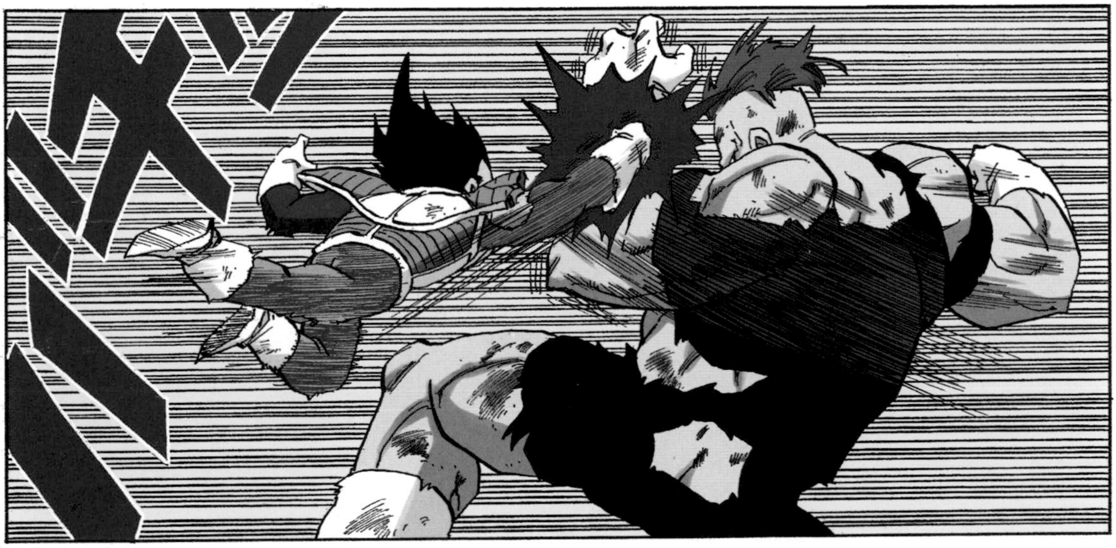

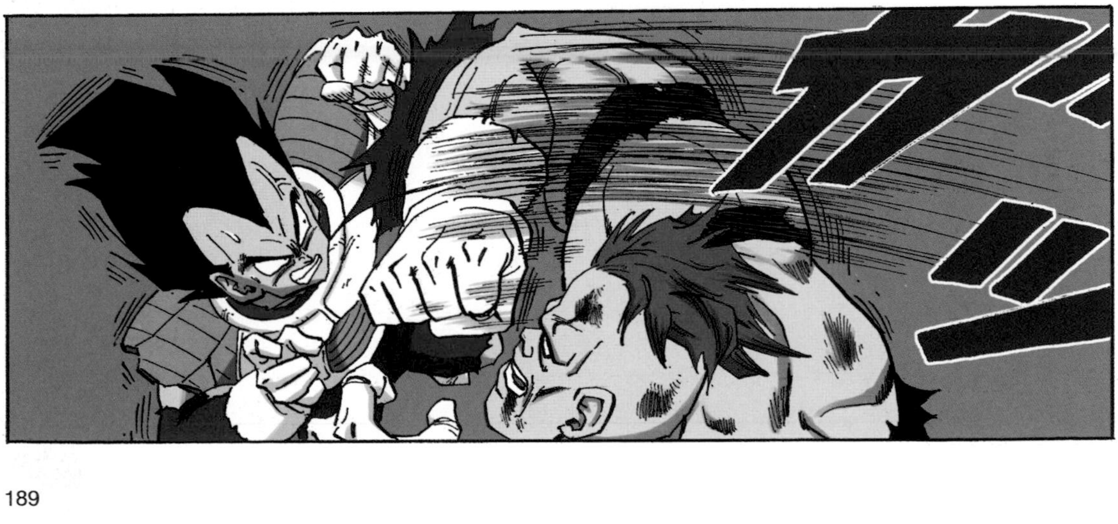

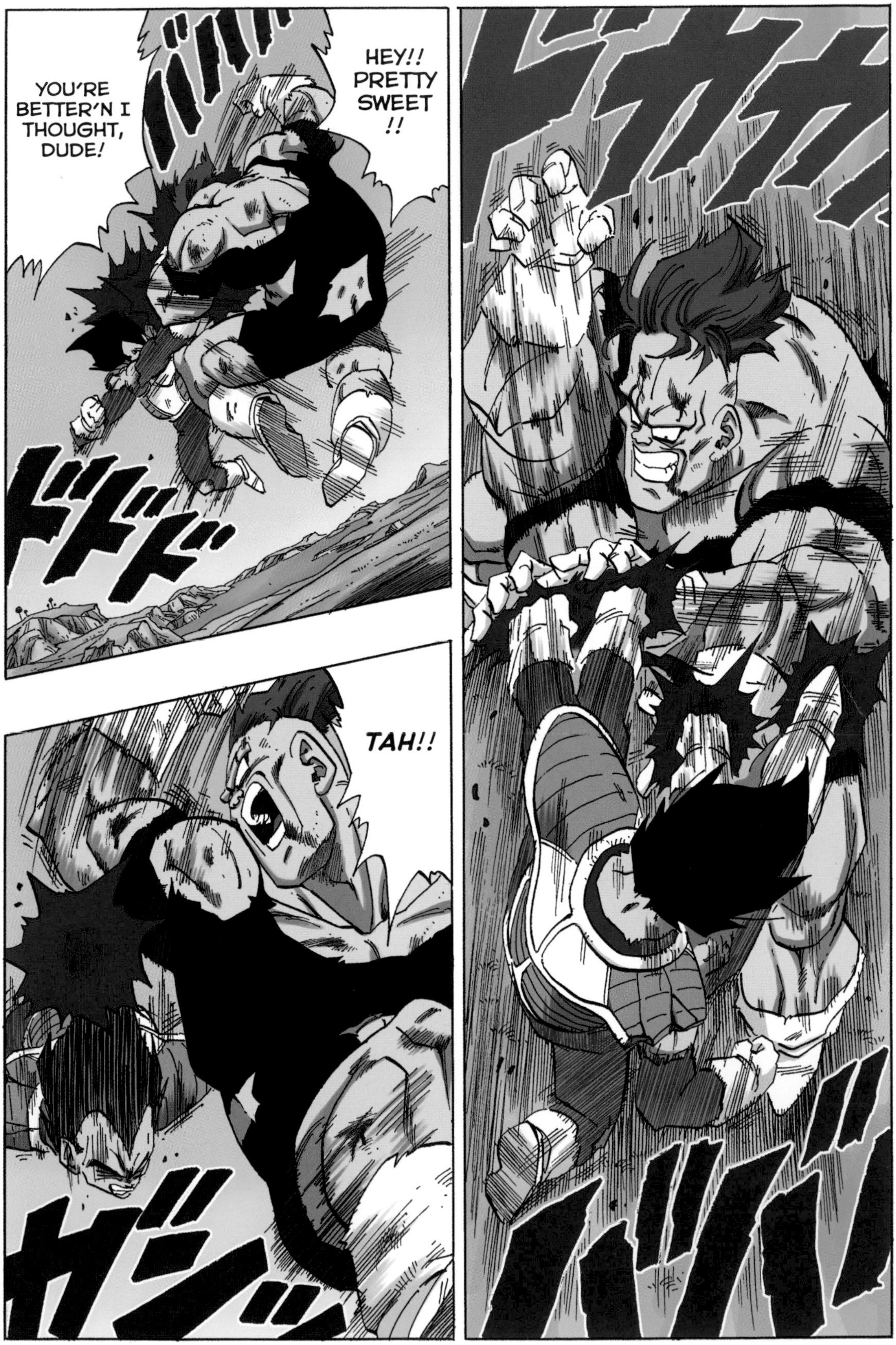
HEY!! PRETTY SWEET!!
YOU'RE BETTER'N I THOUGHT, DUDE!
TAH!!

グシャッ

バチッ

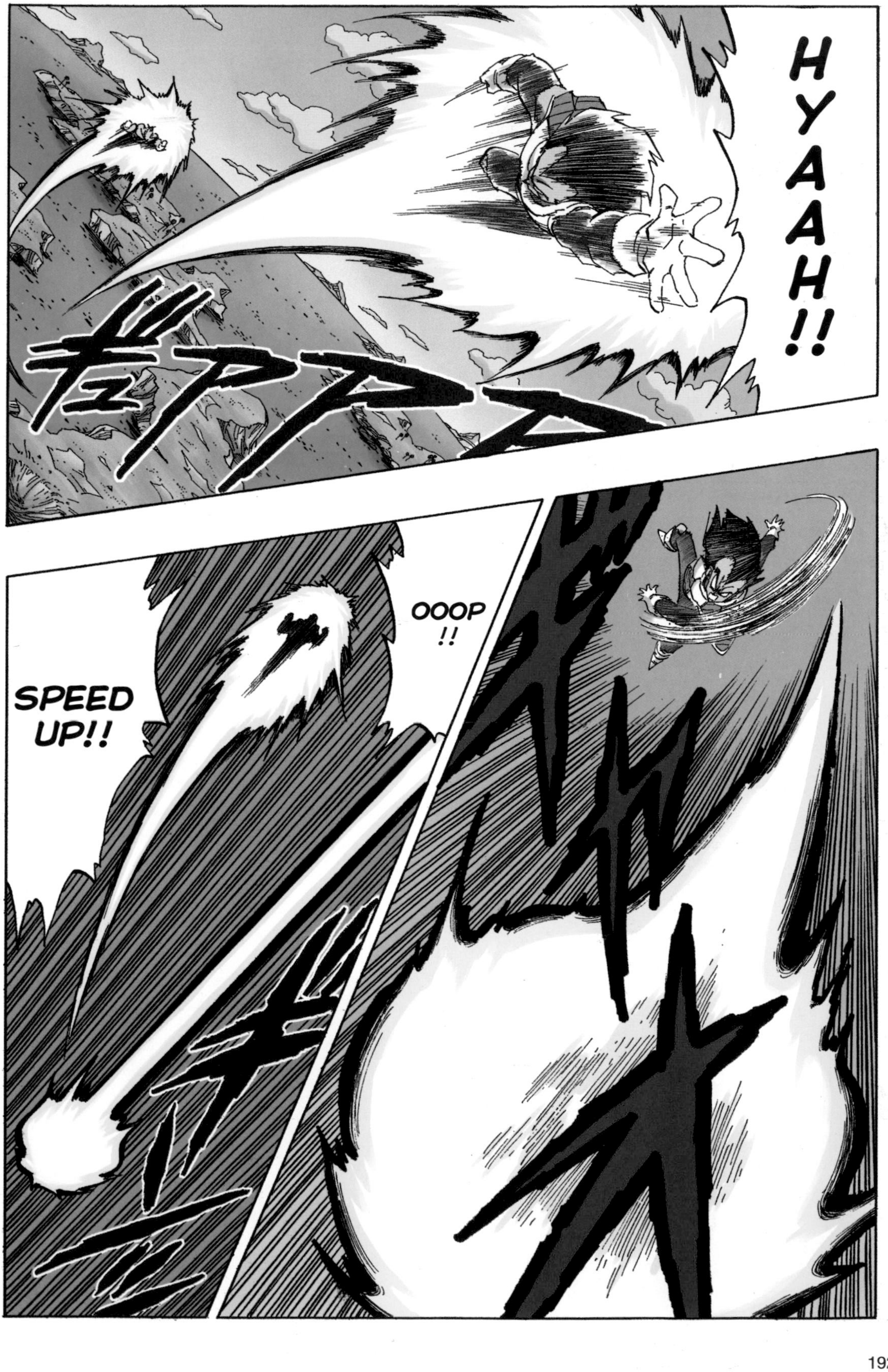
HYAAAH!!
OOOP !!
SPEED UP!!

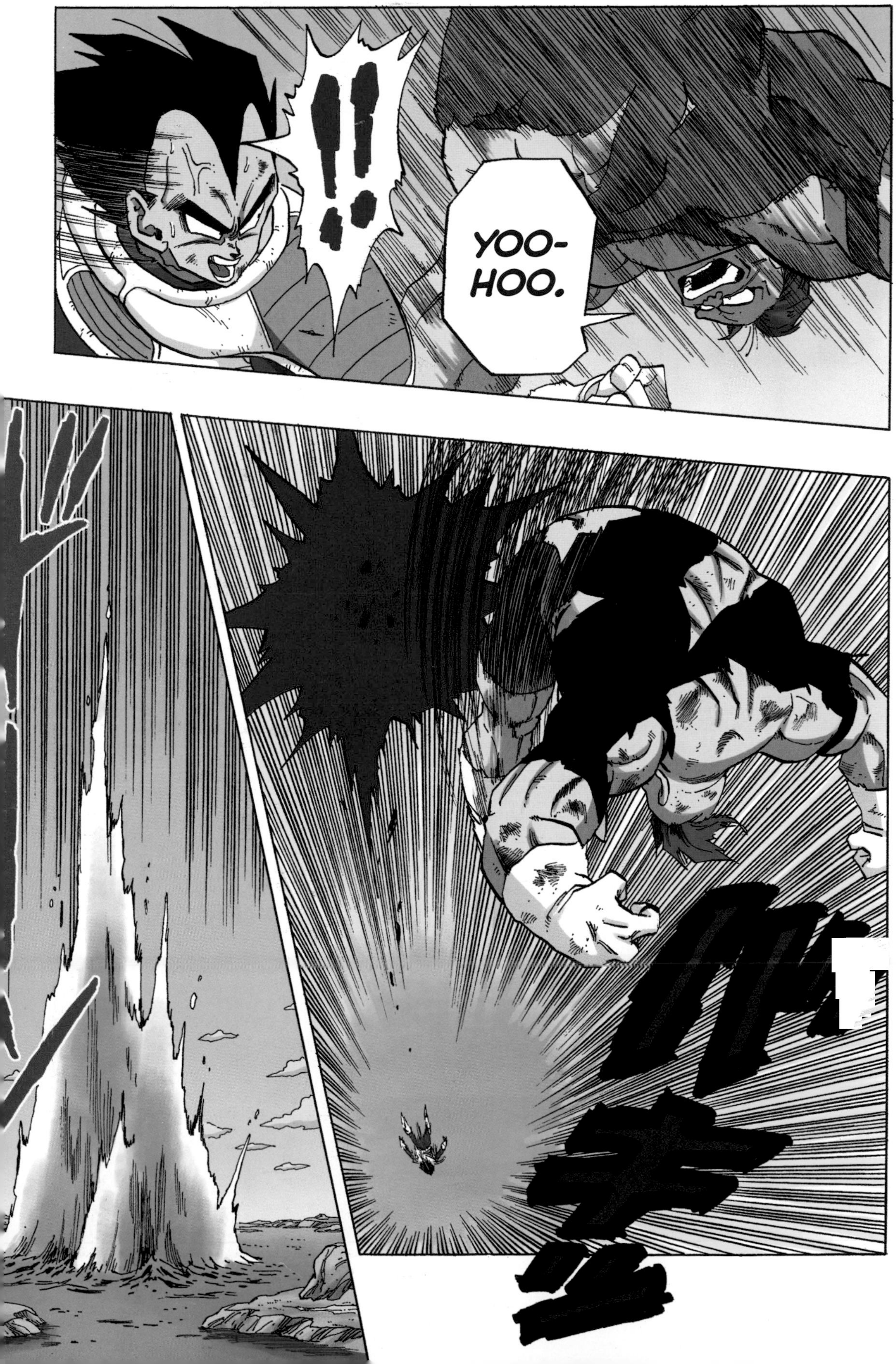
YOO-HOO.
!!

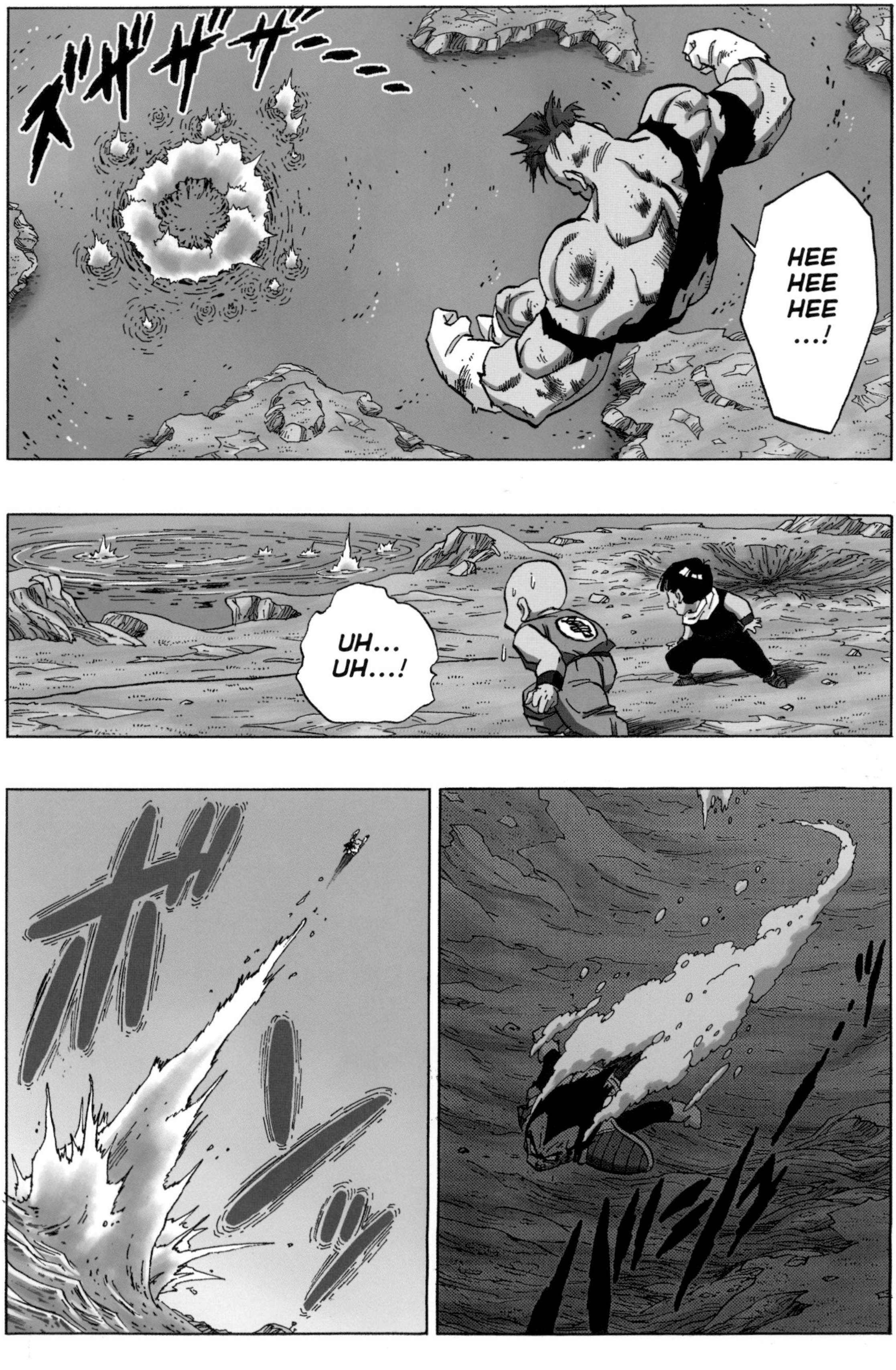
HEE HEE HEE ...!
ズザザザーーー
UH... UH...!

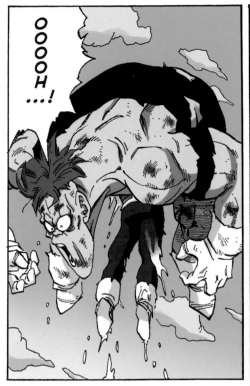

OOOOH ....!

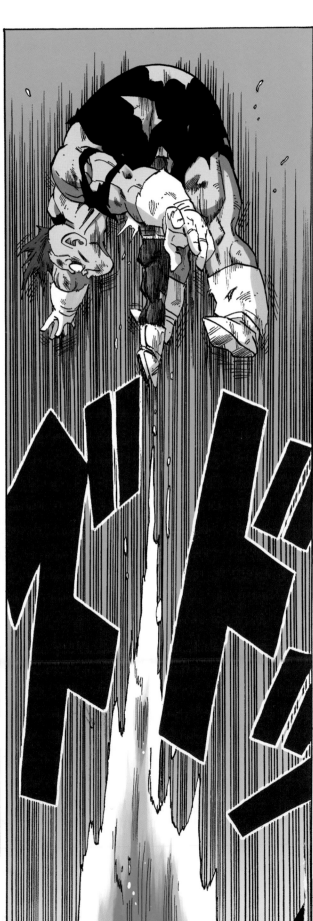

HEH

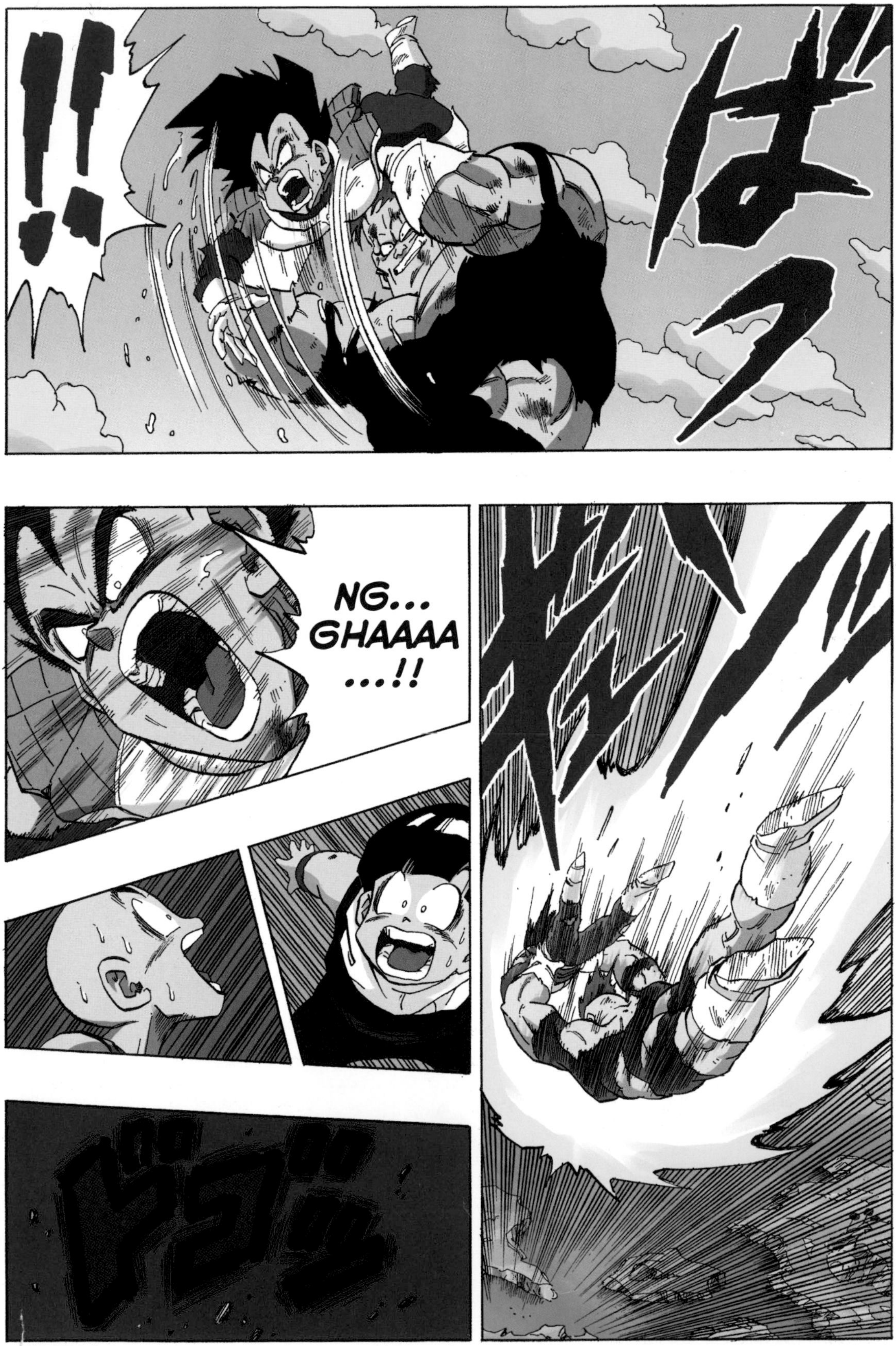
ばっ
!!
NG... GHAAAA ...!!

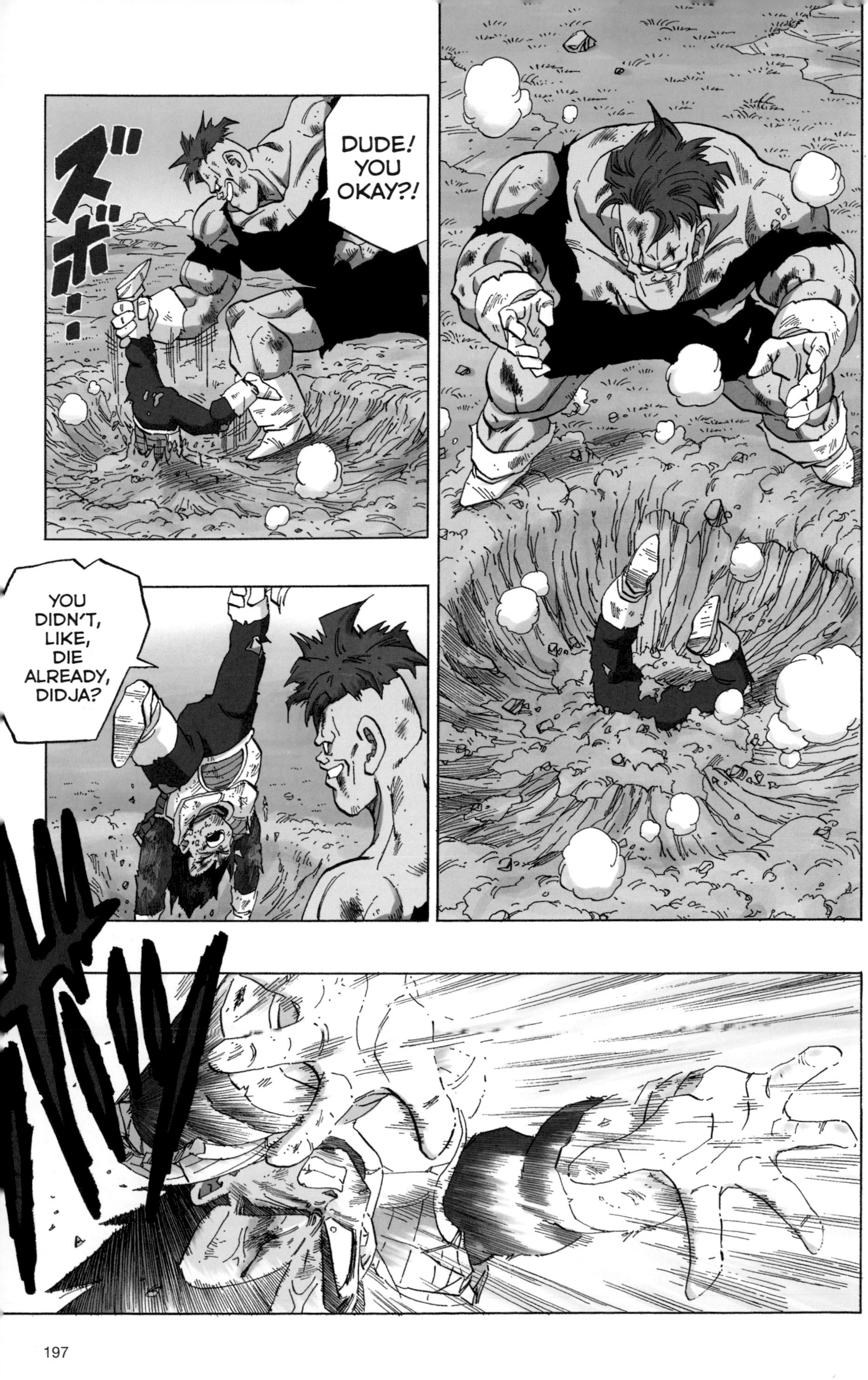
ズボ
DUDE! YOU OKAY?!
YOU DIDN'T, LIKE, DIE ALREADY, DIDJA?

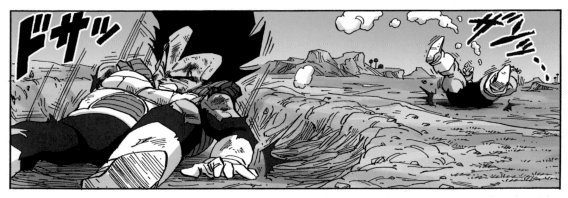

H-HE
DID
IT...?

HUFF

HUFF

NNH...
UHH...

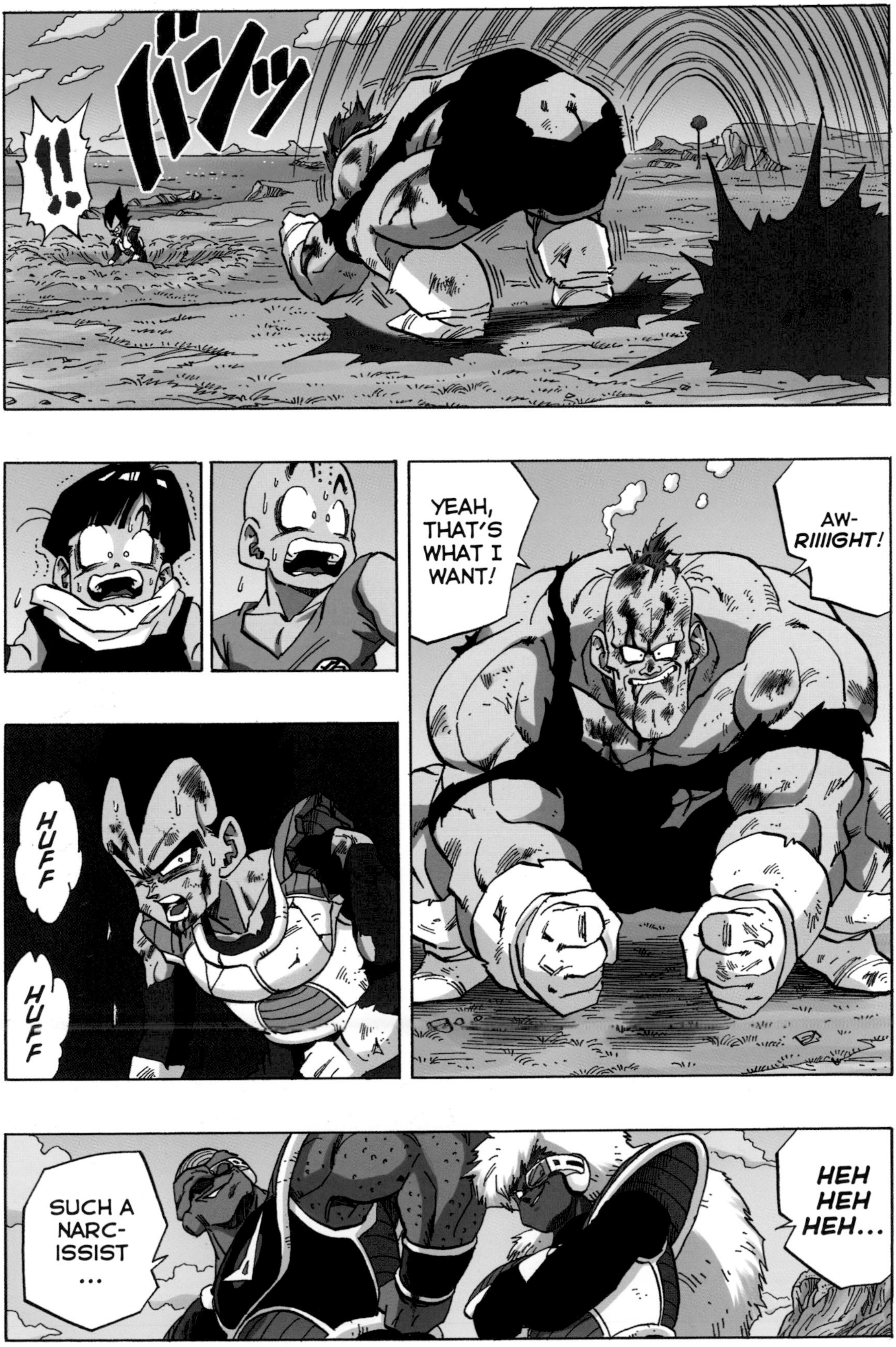
バンッ
!!
AW- RIIIIGHT!
YEAH, THAT'S WHAT I WANT!
HUFF HUFF
HEH HEH HEH...
SUCH A NARC- ISSIST ...

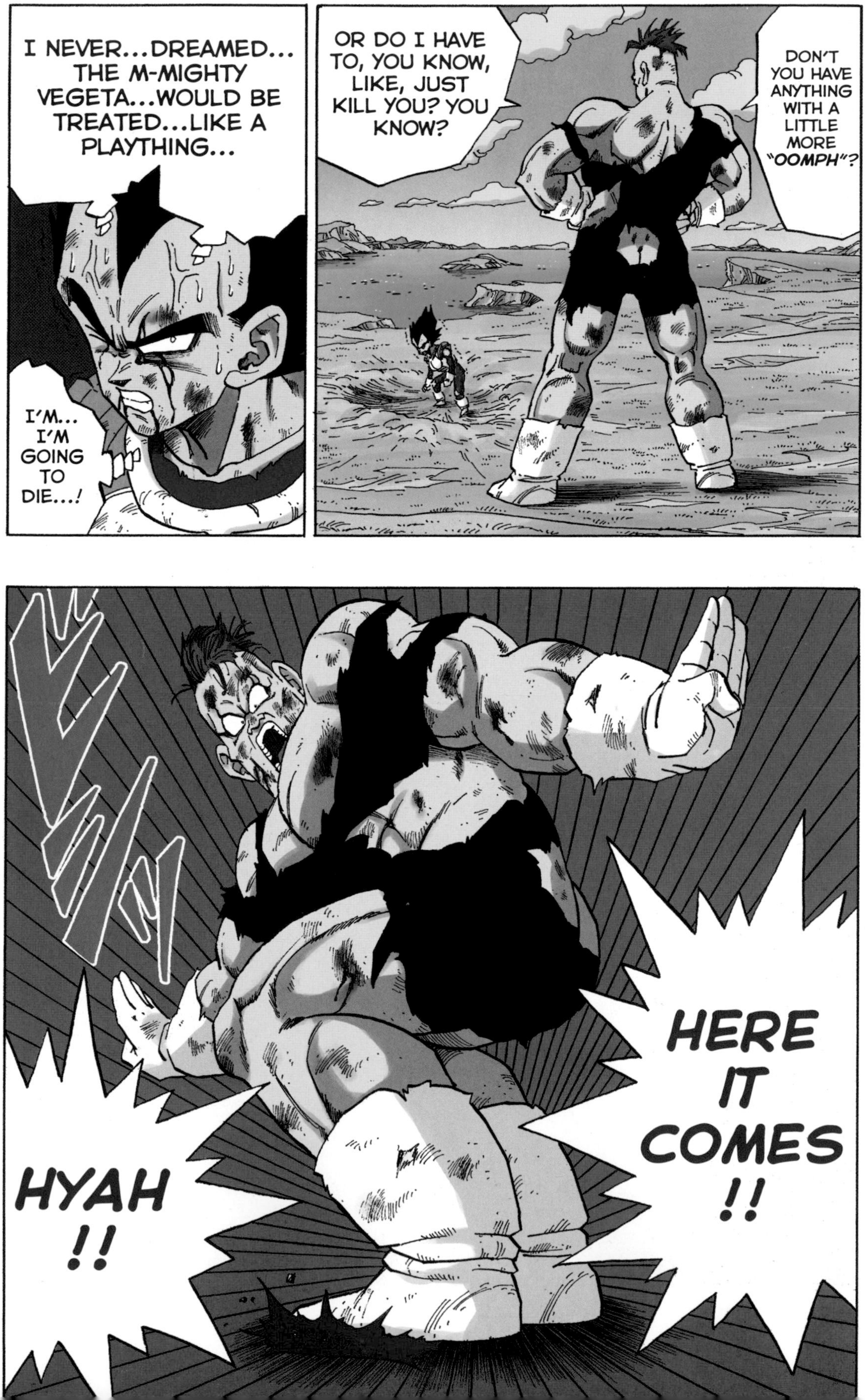
DON'T YOU HAVE ANYTHING WITH A LITTLE MORE "OOMPH"?
OR DO I HAVE TO, YOU KNOW, LIKE, JUST KILL YOU? YOU KNOW?
I NEVER...DREAMED... THE M-MIGHTY VEGETA...WOULD BE TREATED...LIKE A PLAYTHING...
I'M... I'M GOING TO DIE...!
HERE IT COMES!!
HYAH!!

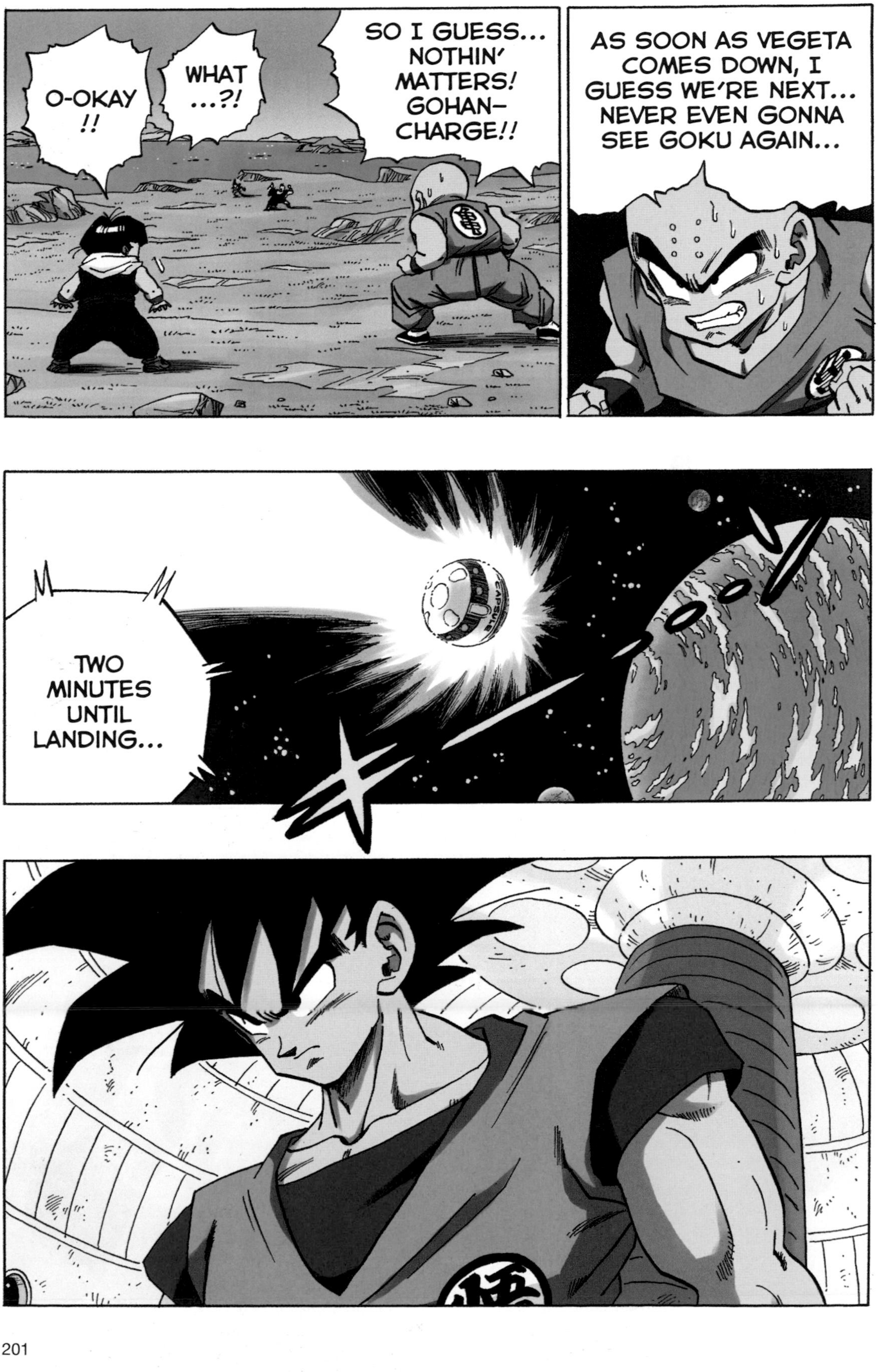
AS SOON AS VEGETA COMES DOWN, I GUESS WE'RE NEXT... NEVER EVEN GONNA SEE GOKU AGAIN...
SO I GUESS... NOTHIN' MATTERS! GOHAN—CHARGE!!
WHAT ...?!
O-OKAY !!
CAPSULE
TWO MINUTES UNTIL LANDING...

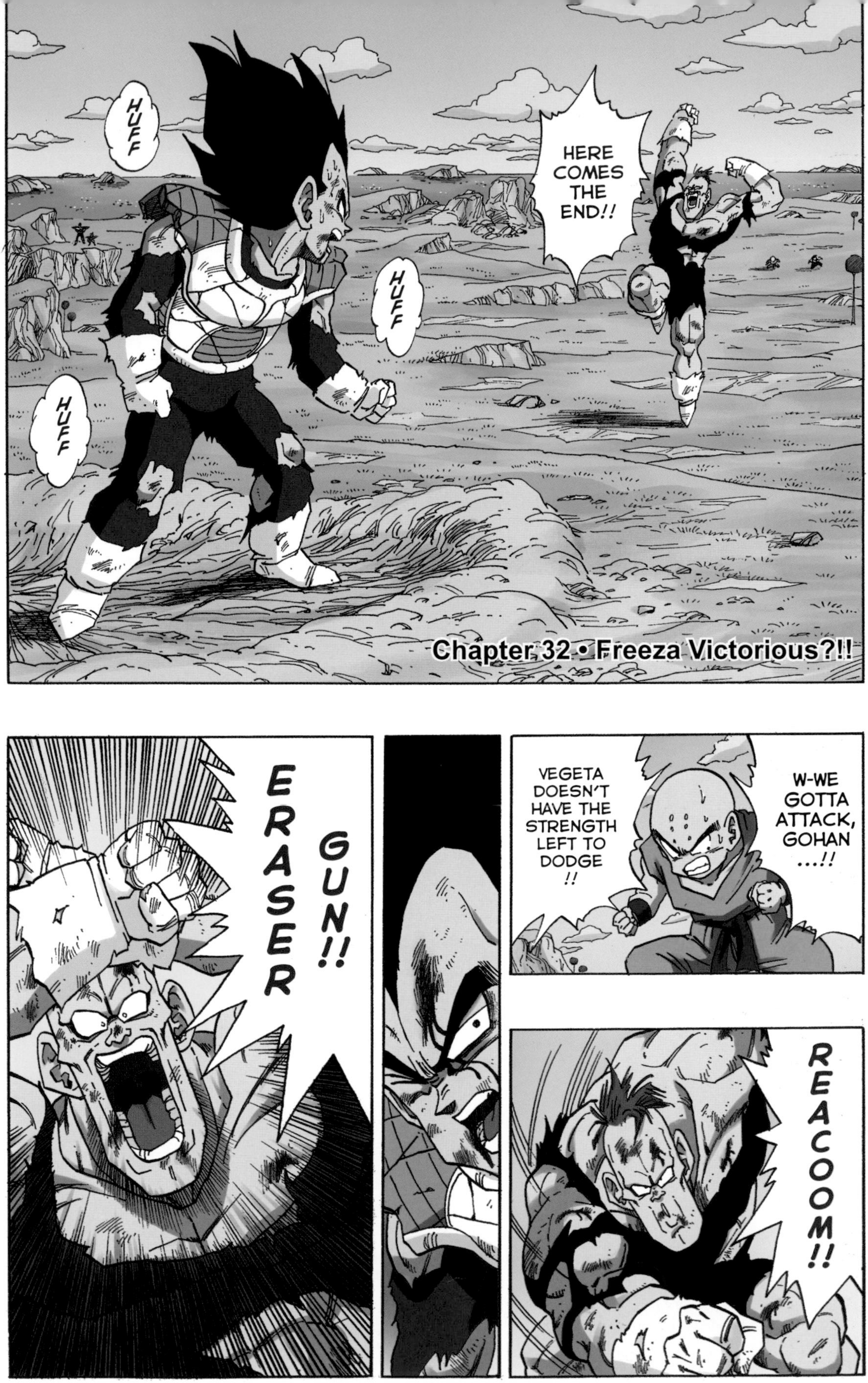
HERE COMES THE END!!
HUFF
HUFF
HUFF
Chapter 32 • Freeza Victorious?!!
W-WE GOTTA ATTACK, GOHAN ...!!
VEGETA DOESN'T HAVE THE STRENGTH LEFT TO DODGE !!
REACOOOM!!
ERASER GUN!!

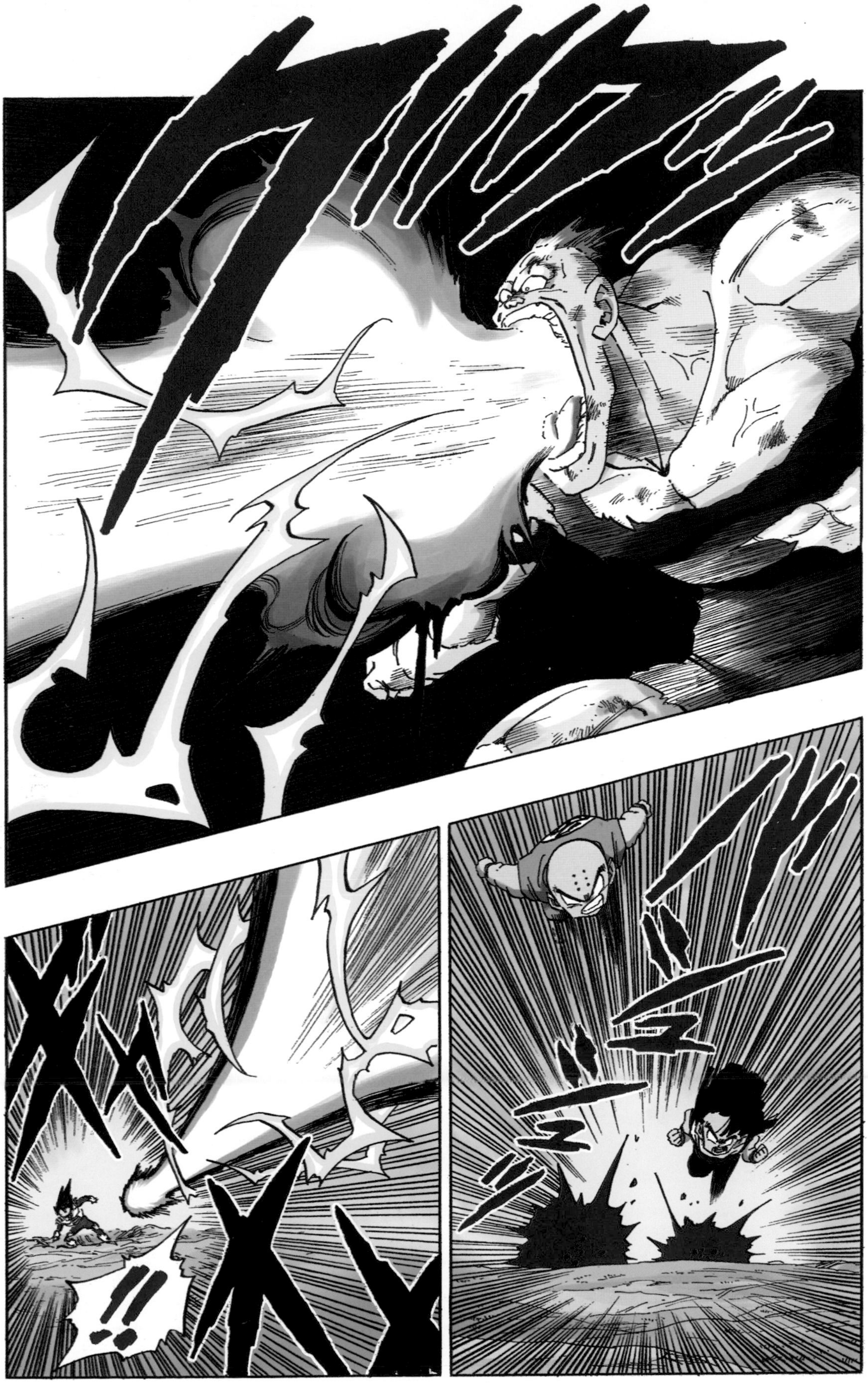
!!

N-K!!

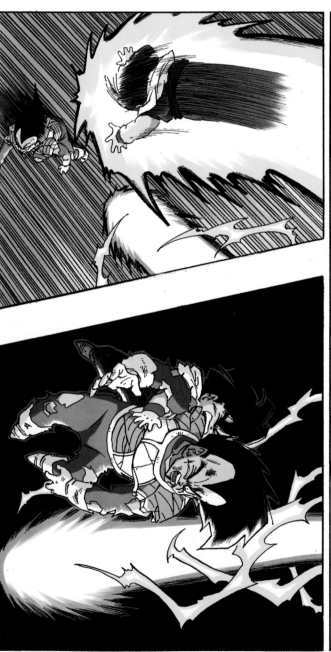

UH!!

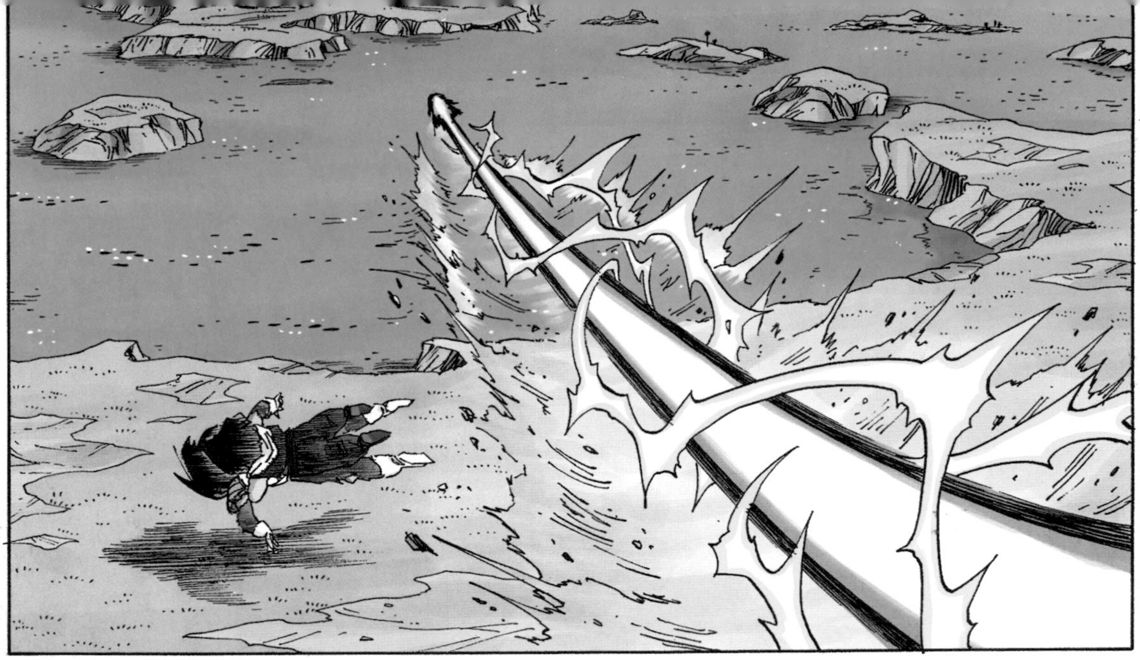

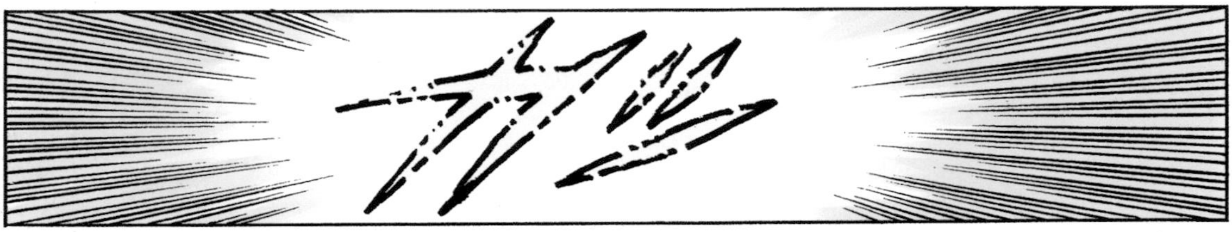

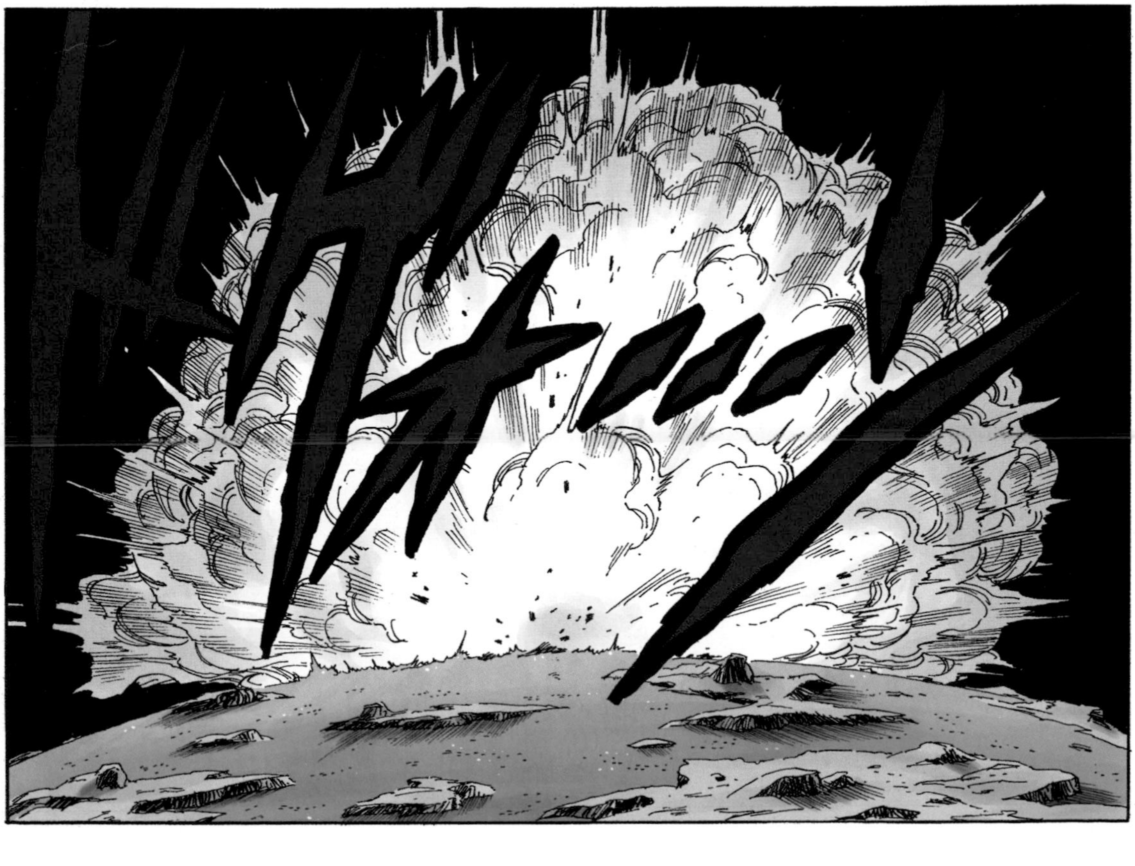

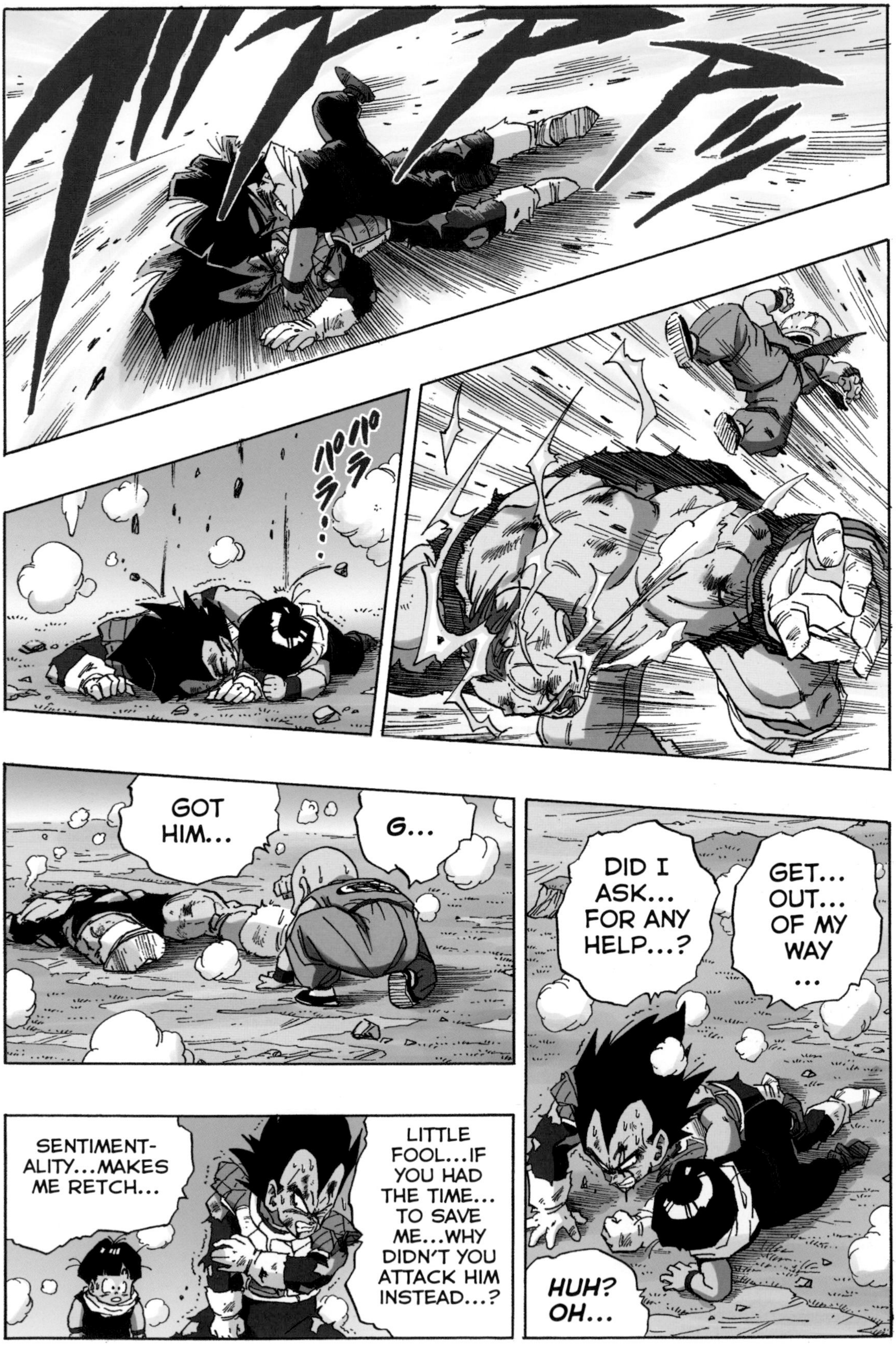
パラパラ…
GET... OUT... OF MY WAY ...
DID I ASK... FOR ANY HELP...?
HUH? OH...
G...
GOT HIM...
LITTLE FOOL...IF YOU HAD THE TIME... TO SAVE ME...WHY DIDN'T YOU ATTACK HIM INSTEAD...?
SENTIMENT-ALITY...MAKES ME RETCH...

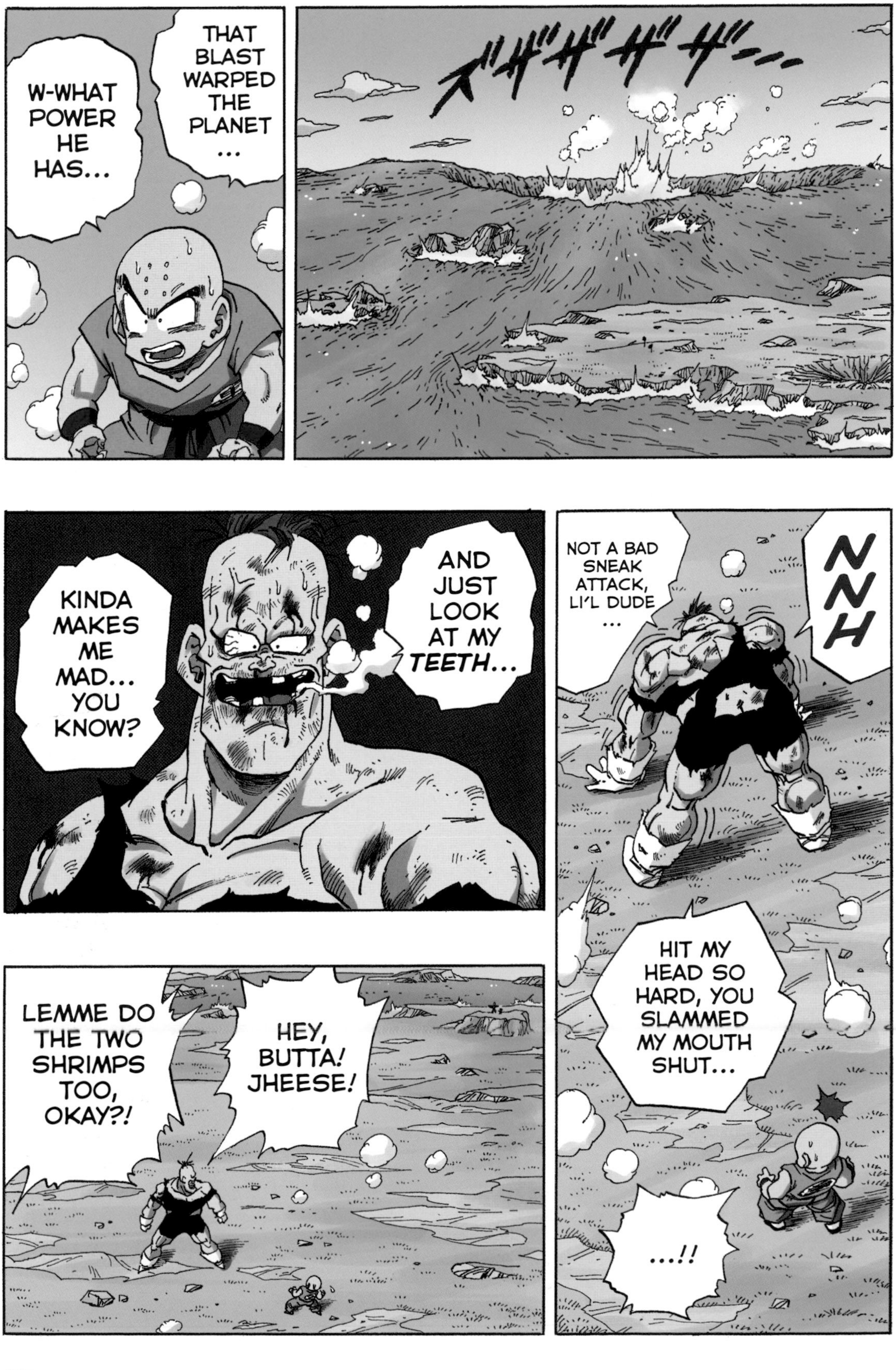
ズザザザザ
THAT BLAST WARPED THE PLANET...
W-WHAT POWER HE HAS...
NNH
NOT A BAD SNEAK ATTACK, LI'L DUDE...
HIT MY HEAD SO HARD, YOU SLAMMED MY MOUTH SHUT...
...!!
AND JUST LOOK AT MY *TEETH*...
KINDA MAKES ME MAD... YOU KNOW?
HEY, BUTTA! JHEESE!
LEMME DO THE TWO SHRIMPS TOO, OKAY?!

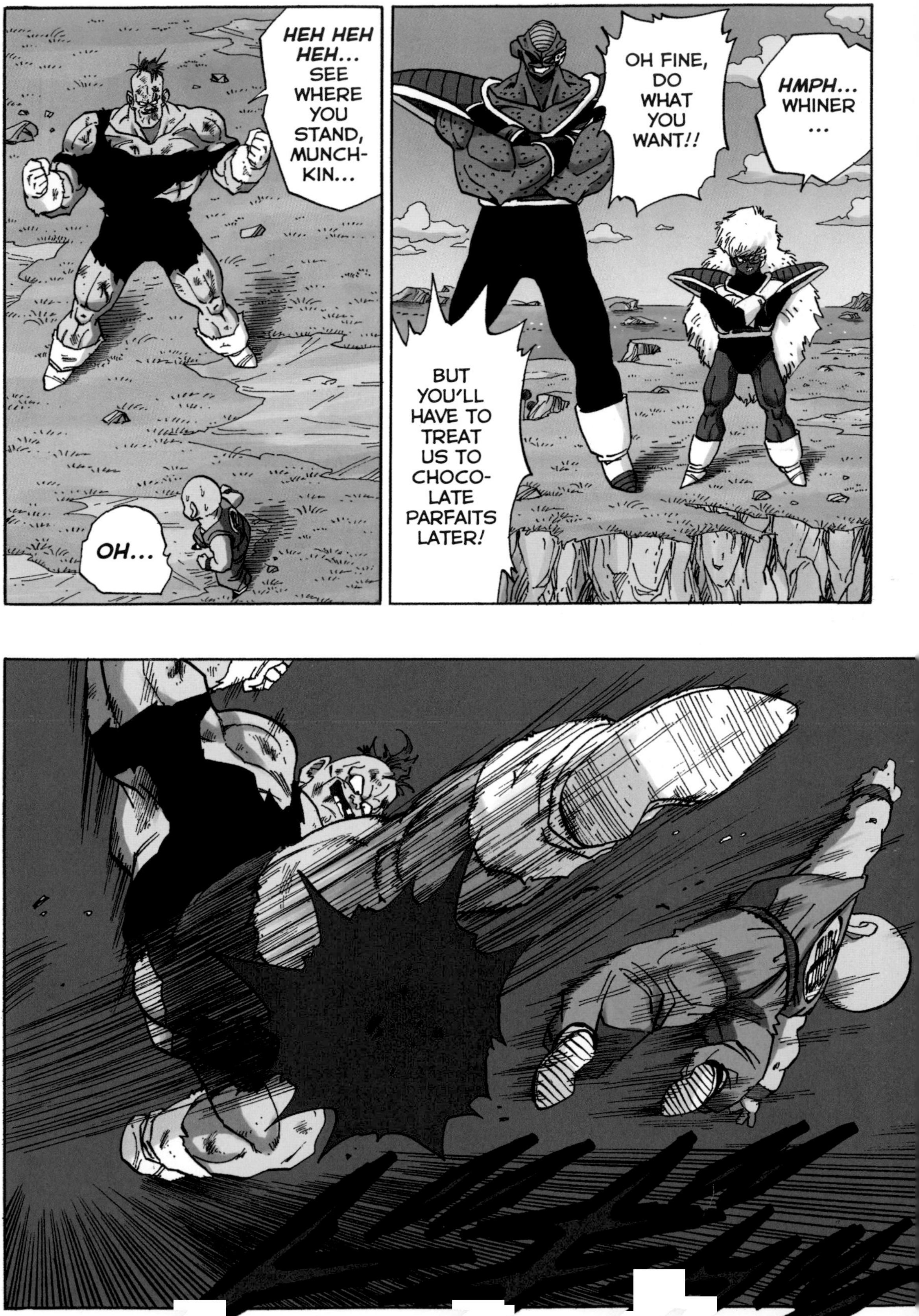
HMPH... WHINER ...
OH FINE, DO WHAT YOU WANT!!
BUT YOU'LL HAVE TO TREAT US TO CHOCOLATE PARFAITS LATER!
HEH HEH HEH... SEE WHERE YOU STAND, MUNCH-KIN...
OH...

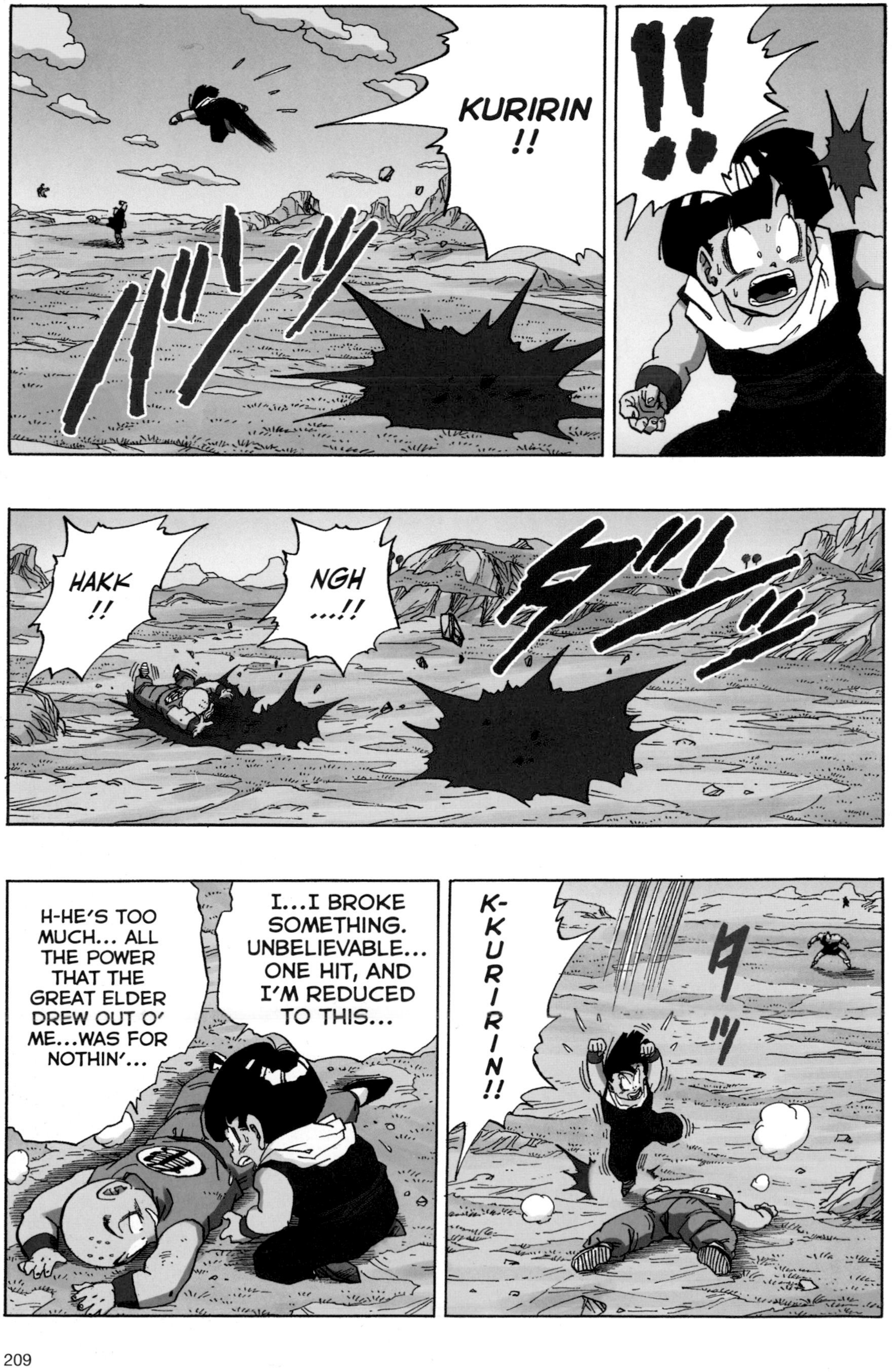
!!
KURIRIN !!
NGH ...!!
HAKK !!
K-KURIRIN!!
I...I BROKE SOMETHING. UNBELIEVABLE... ONE HIT, AND I'M REDUCED TO THIS...
H-HE'S TOO MUCH... ALL THE POWER THAT THE GREAT ELDER DREW OUT O' ME...WAS FOR NOTHIN'...

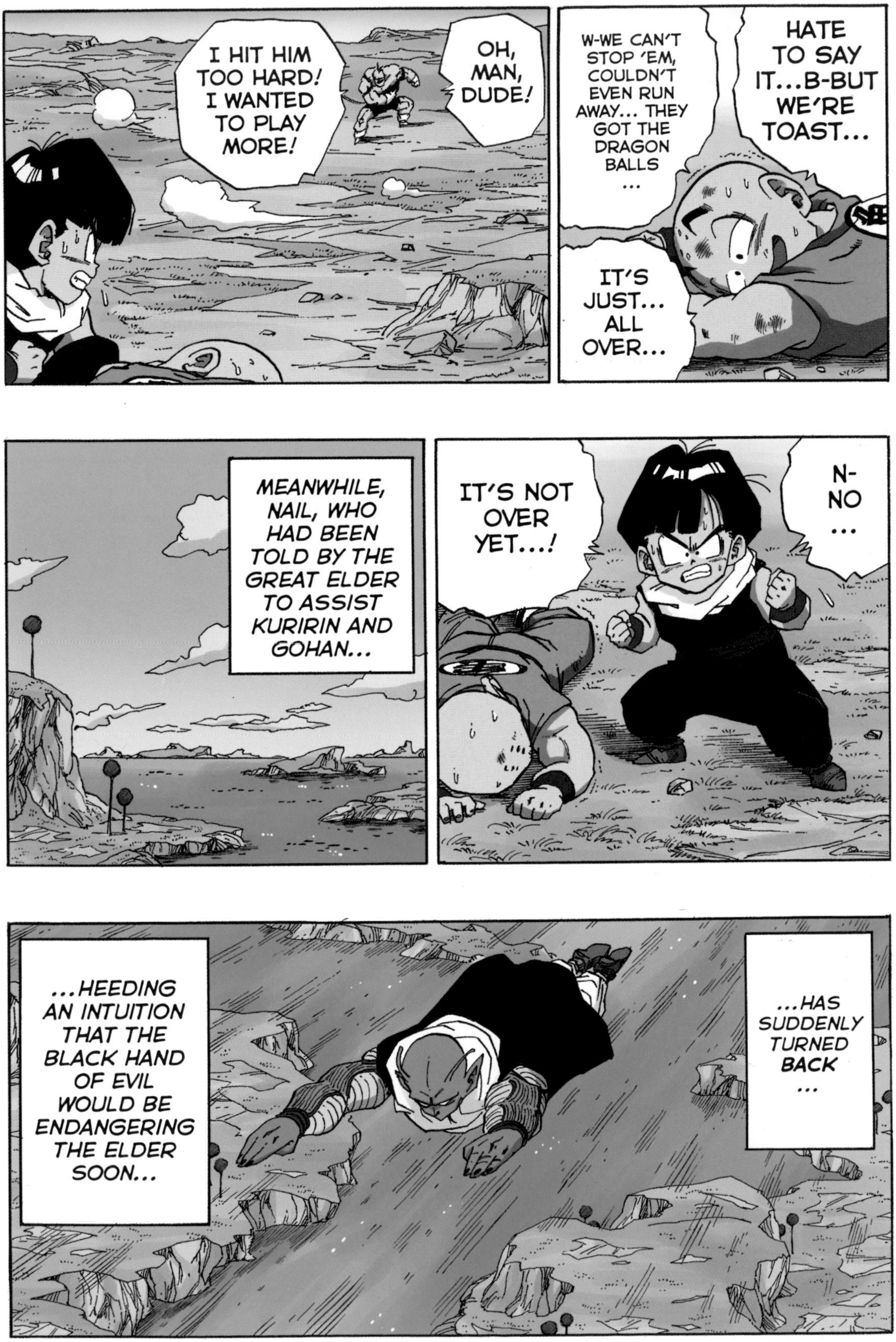
HATE TO SAY IT...B-BUT WE'RE TOAST...
W-WE CAN'T STOP 'EM, COULDN'T EVEN RUN AWAY... THEY GOT THE DRAGON BALLS ...
IT'S JUST... ALL OVER...
OH, MAN, DUDE!
I HIT HIM TOO HARD! I WANTED TO PLAY MORE!
N-NO ...
IT'S NOT OVER YET...!
MEANWHILE, NAIL, WHO HAD BEEN TOLD BY THE GREAT ELDER TO ASSIST KURIRIN AND GOHAN...
...HEEDING AN INTUITION THAT THE BLACK HAND OF EVIL WOULD BE ENDANGERING THE ELDER SOON...
...HAS SUDDENLY TURNED BACK ...

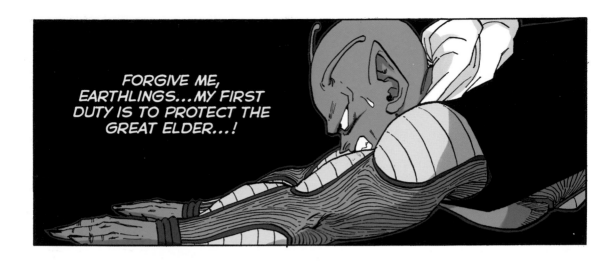

FORGIVE ME, EARTHLINGS...MY FIRST DUTY IS TO PROTECT THE GREAT ELDER...!

N... NNH...!!

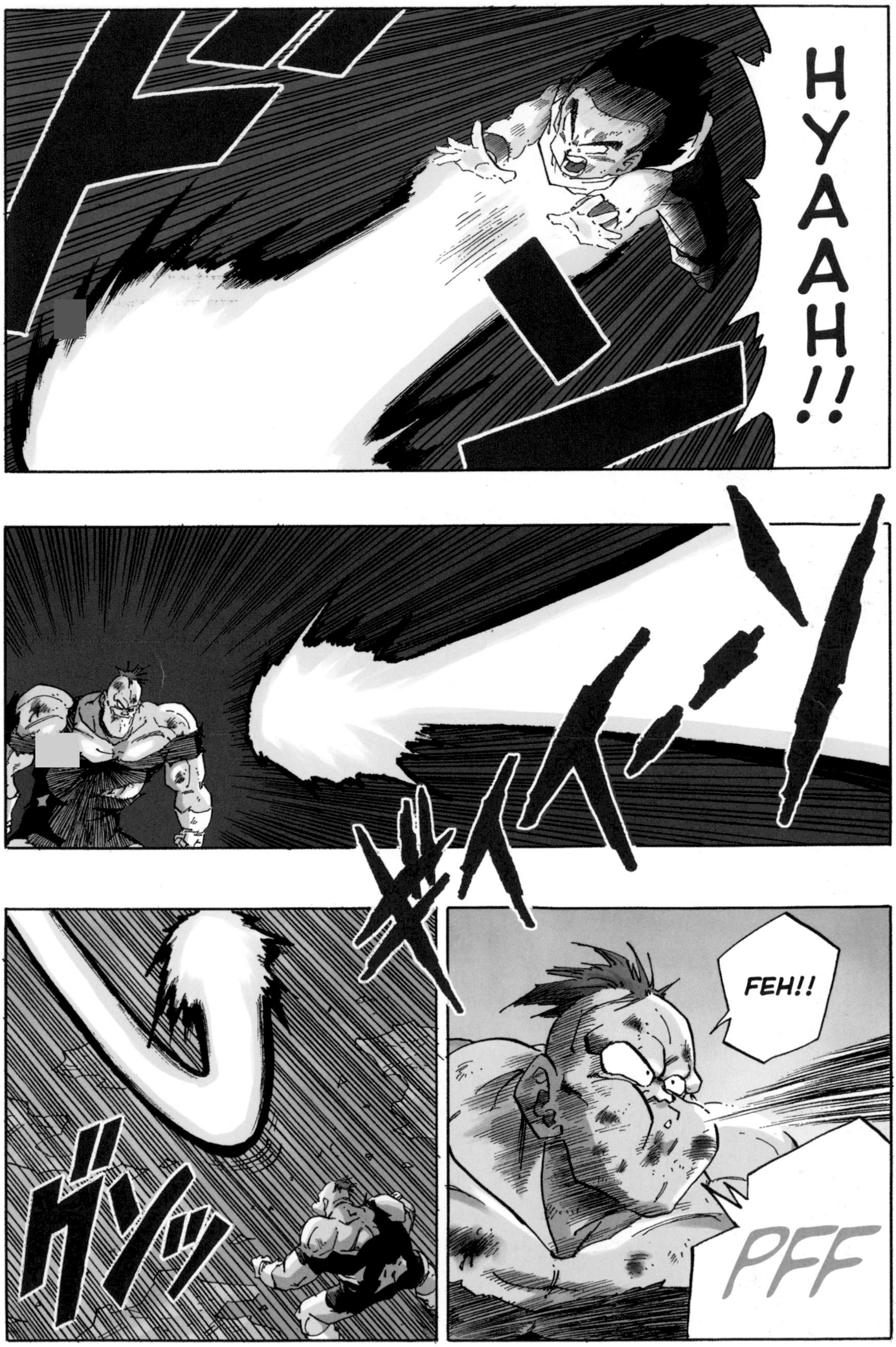
HYAAH!!
FEH!!
PFF
ヴンッ

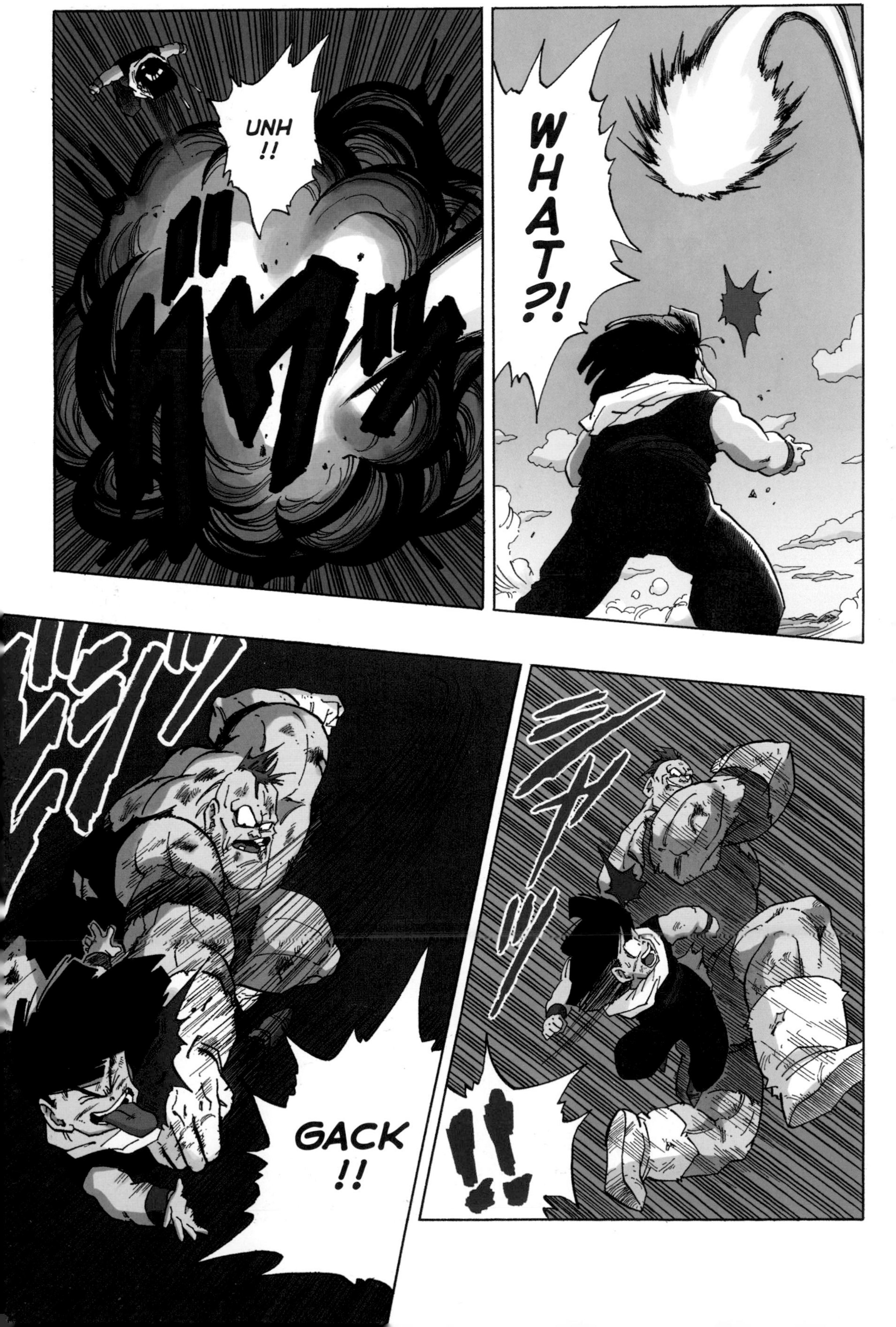
WHAT?!
UNH !!
!!
GACK !!

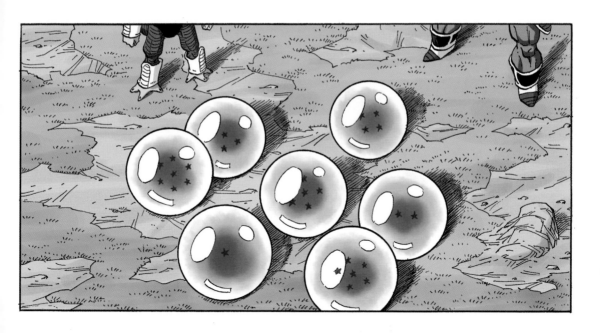

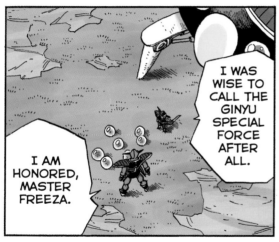

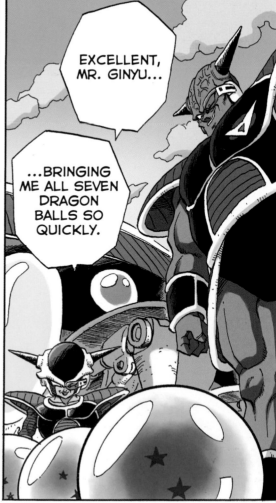

EXCELLENT, MR. GINYU...
...BRINGING ME ALL SEVEN DRAGON BALLS SO QUICKLY.
I WAS WISE TO CALL THE GINYU SPECIAL FORCE AFTER ALL.
I AM HONORED, MASTER FREEZA.
AT LAST, I WILL HAVE ETERNAL LIFE.
WHAT UNSPEAKABLE JOY!

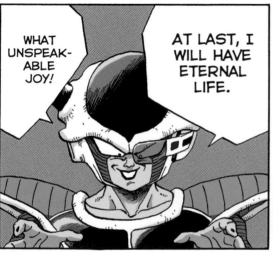

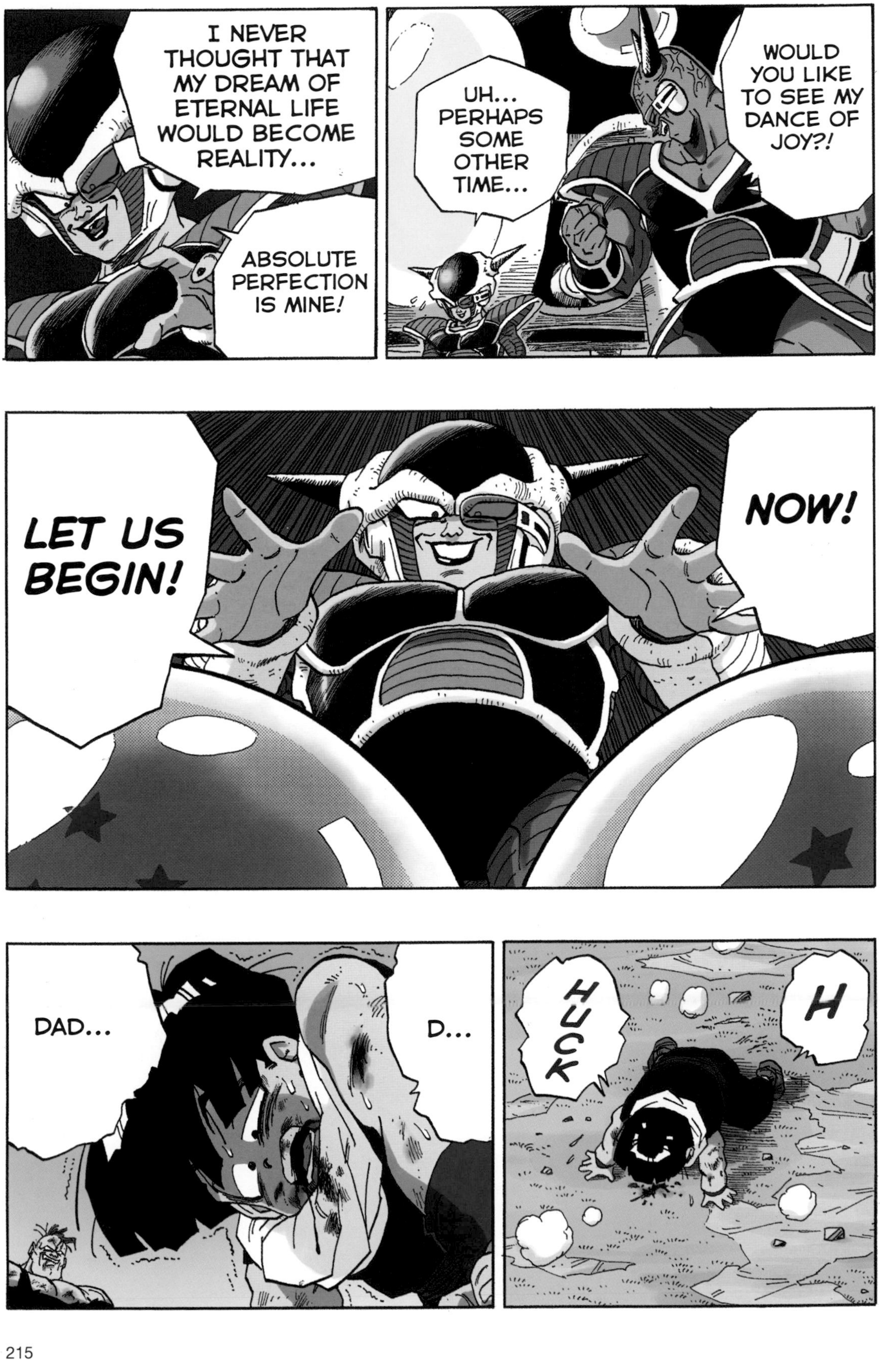
WOULD YOU LIKE TO SEE MY DANCE OF JOY?!
UH... PERHAPS SOME OTHER TIME...
I NEVER THOUGHT THAT MY DREAM OF ETERNAL LIFE WOULD BECOME REALITY...
ABSOLUTE PERFECTION IS MINE!
NOW!
LET US BEGIN!
H
HUCK
D...
DAD...

Chapter 33 • Son Gohan's Last Stand

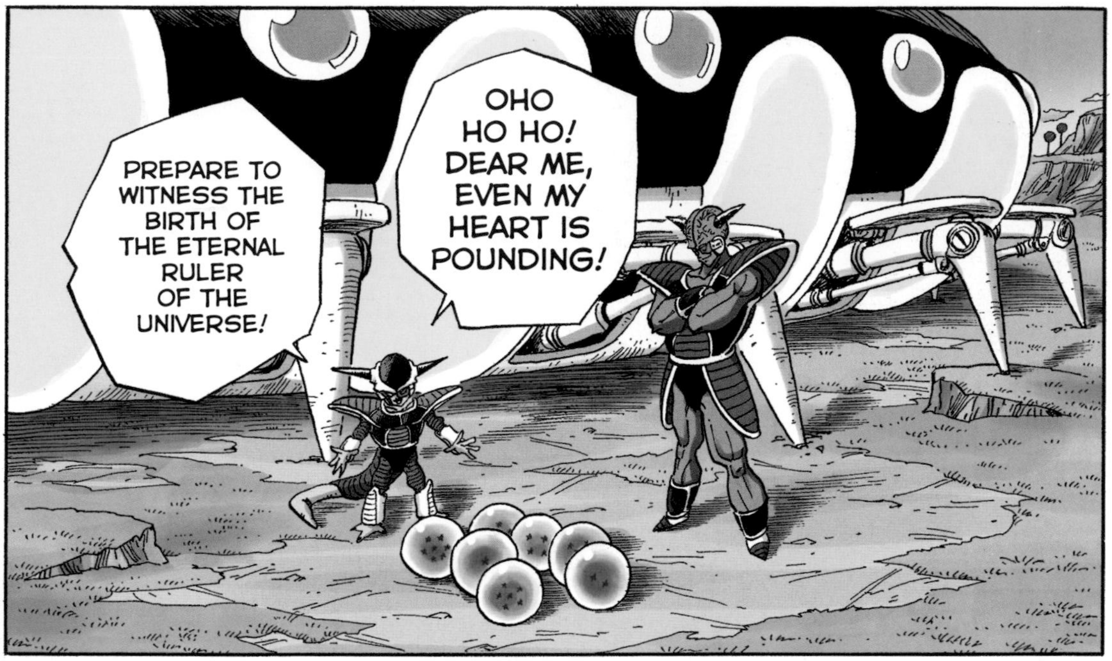
OHO HO HO! DEAR ME, EVEN MY HEART IS POUNDING!
PREPARE TO WITNESS THE BIRTH OF THE ETERNAL RULER OF THE UNIVERSE!

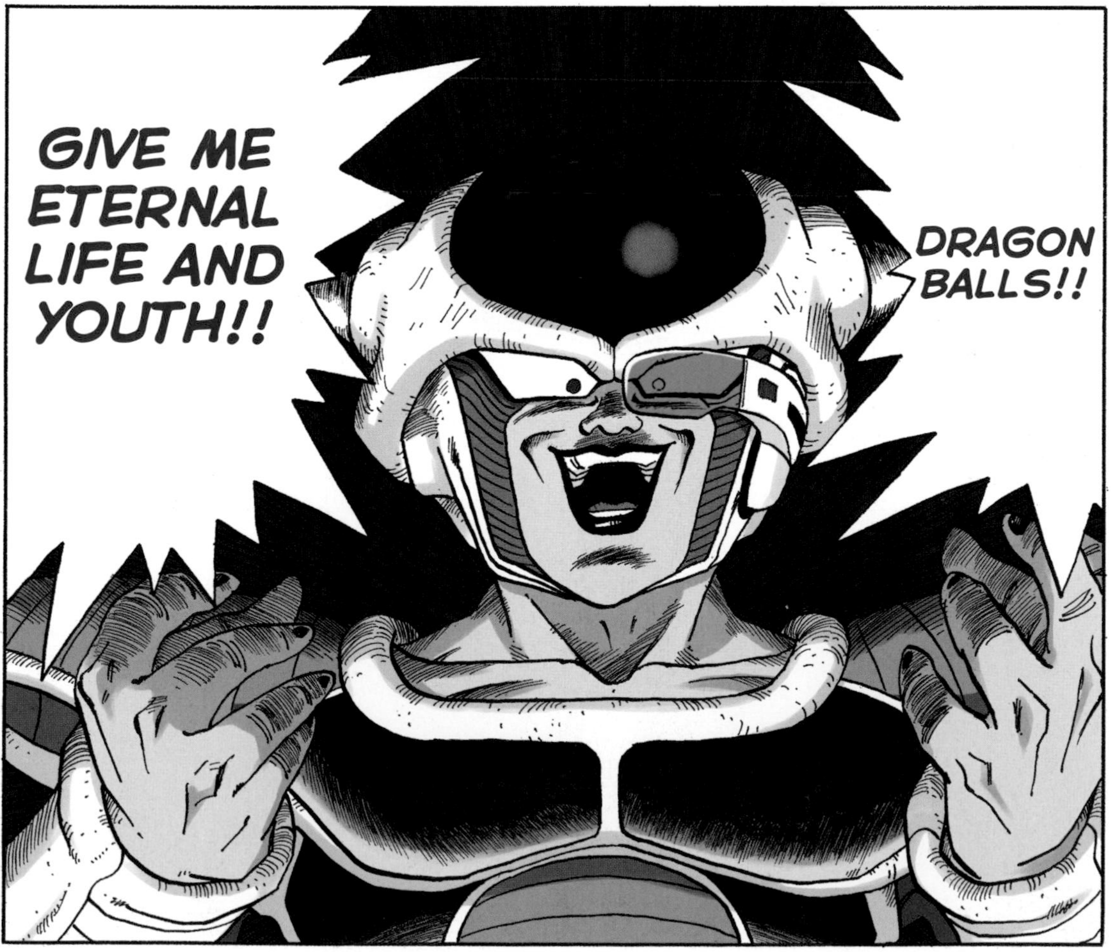
DRAGON BALLS!!
GIVE ME ETERNAL LIFE AND YOUTH!!

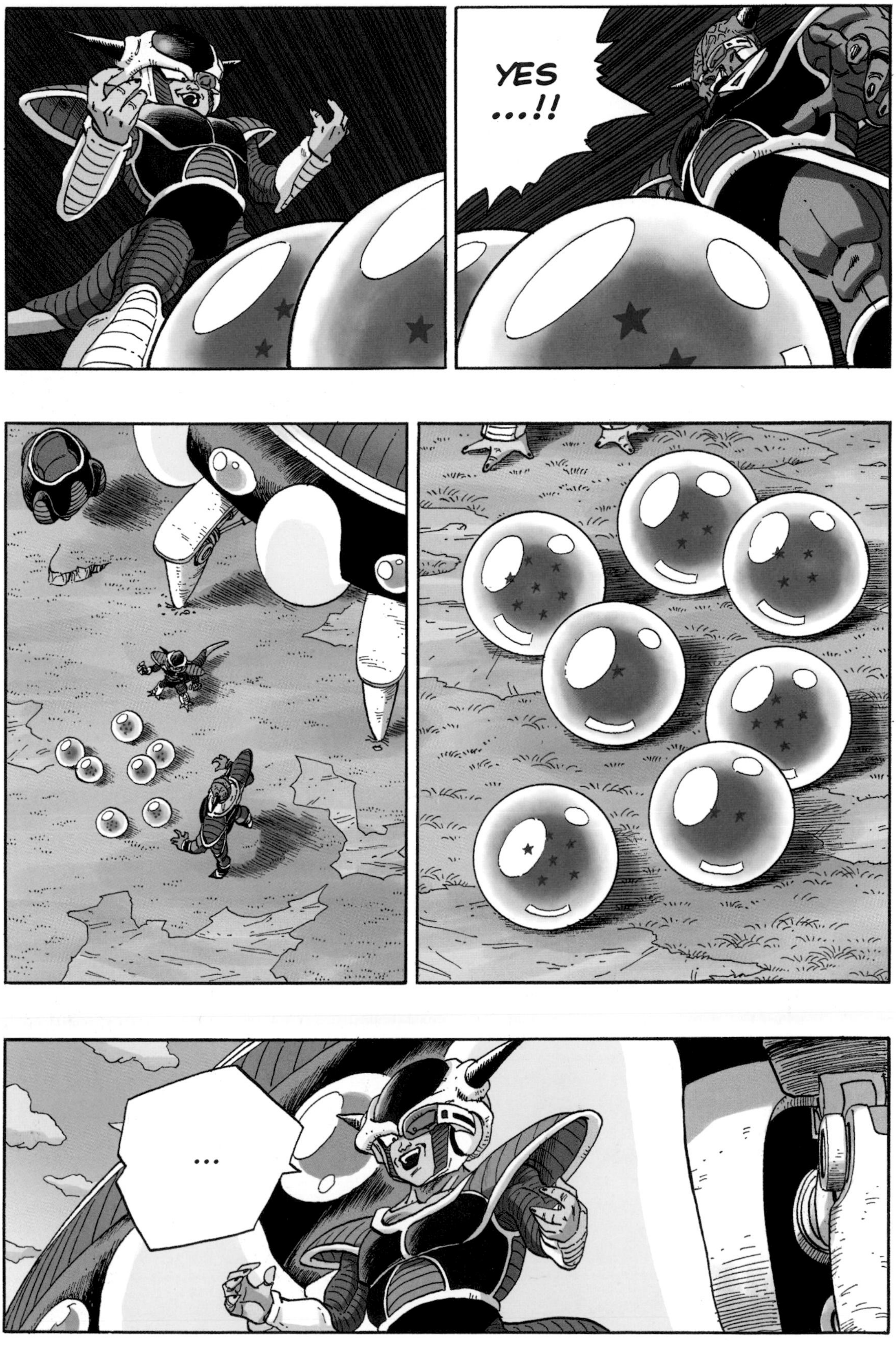
YES
...!!
...

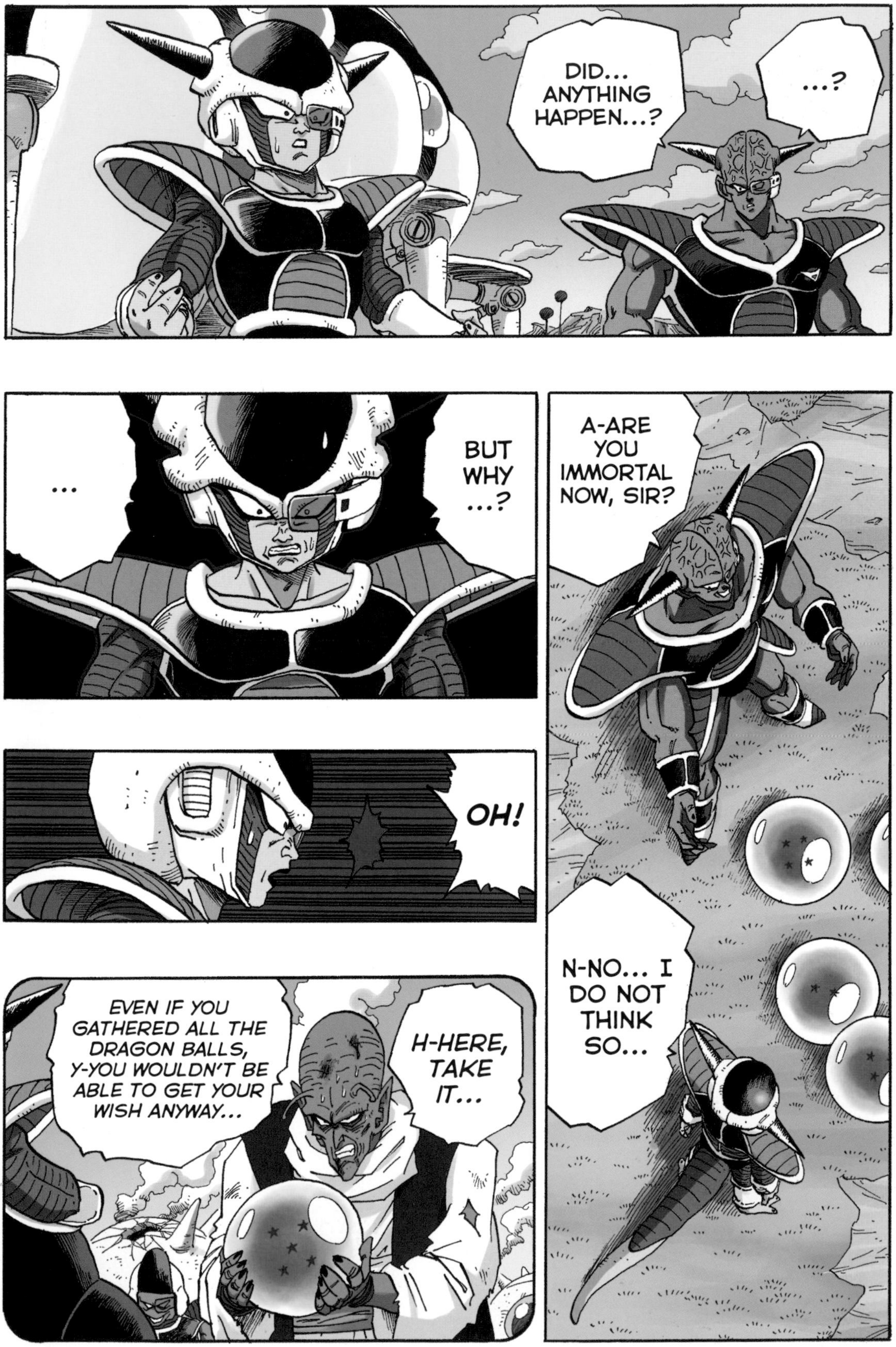
...?
DID... ANYTHING HAPPEN...?
A-ARE YOU IMMORTAL NOW, SIR?
N-NO... I DO NOT THINK SO...
BUT WHY ...?
...
OH!
H-HERE, TAKE IT...
EVEN IF YOU GATHERED ALL THE DRAGON BALLS, Y-YOU WOULDN'T BE ABLE TO GET YOUR WISH ANYWAY...

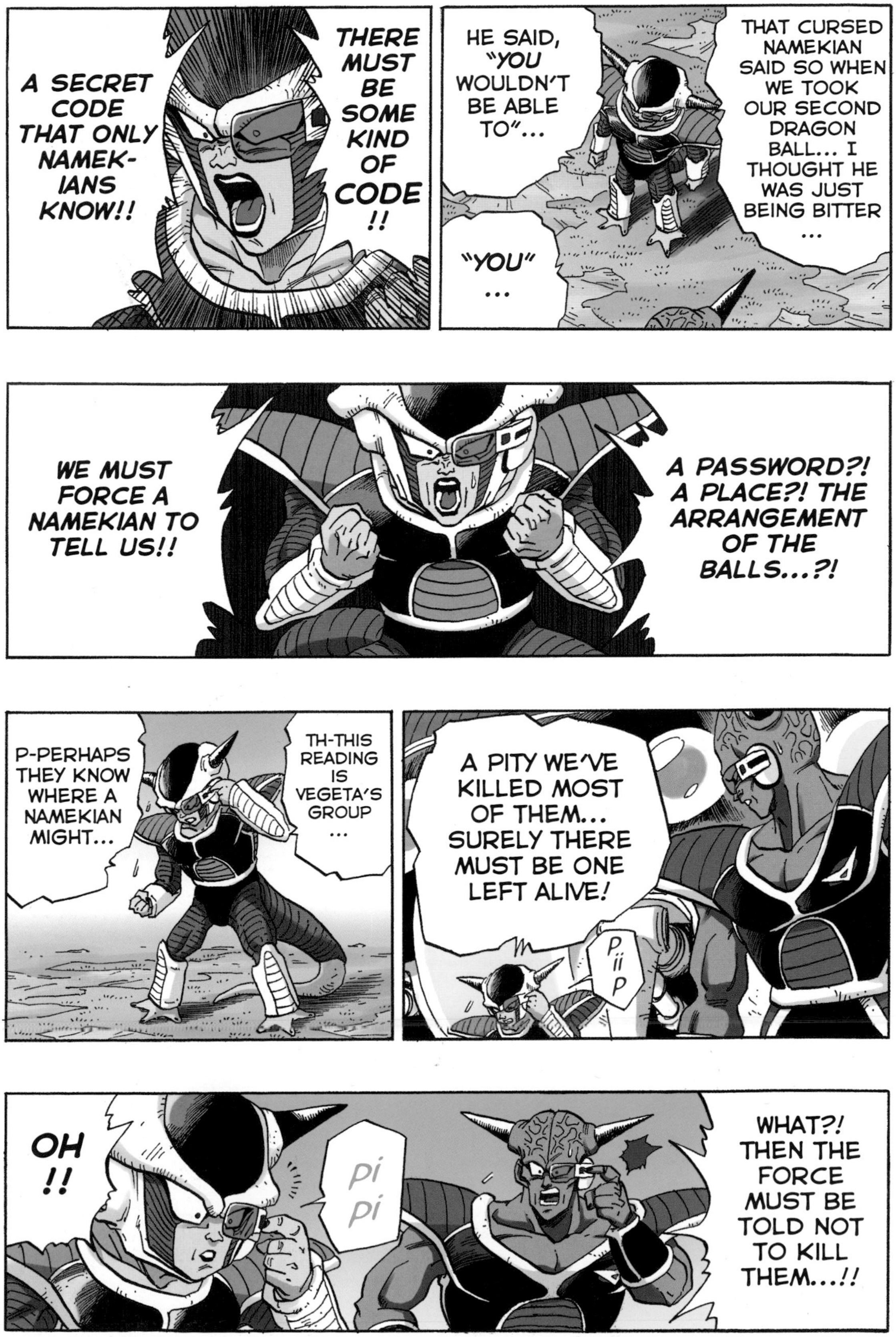
THAT CURSED NAMEKIAN SAID SO WHEN WE TOOK OUR SECOND DRAGON BALL... I THOUGHT HE WAS JUST BEING BITTER ...
HE SAID, "YOU WOULDN'T BE ABLE TO"...
"YOU" ...
THERE MUST BE SOME KIND OF CODE!!
A SECRET CODE THAT ONLY NAMEK-IANS KNOW!!
A PASSWORD?! A PLACE?! THE ARRANGEMENT OF THE BALLS...?!
WE MUST FORCE A NAMEKIAN TO TELL US!!
A PITY WE'VE KILLED MOST OF THEM... SURELY THERE MUST BE ONE LEFT ALIVE!
PiiP
TH-THIS READING IS VEGETA'S GROUP ...
P-PERHAPS THEY KNOW WHERE A NAMEKIAN MIGHT...
WHAT?! THEN THE FORCE MUST BE TOLD NOT TO KILL THEM...!!
pi pi
OH !!

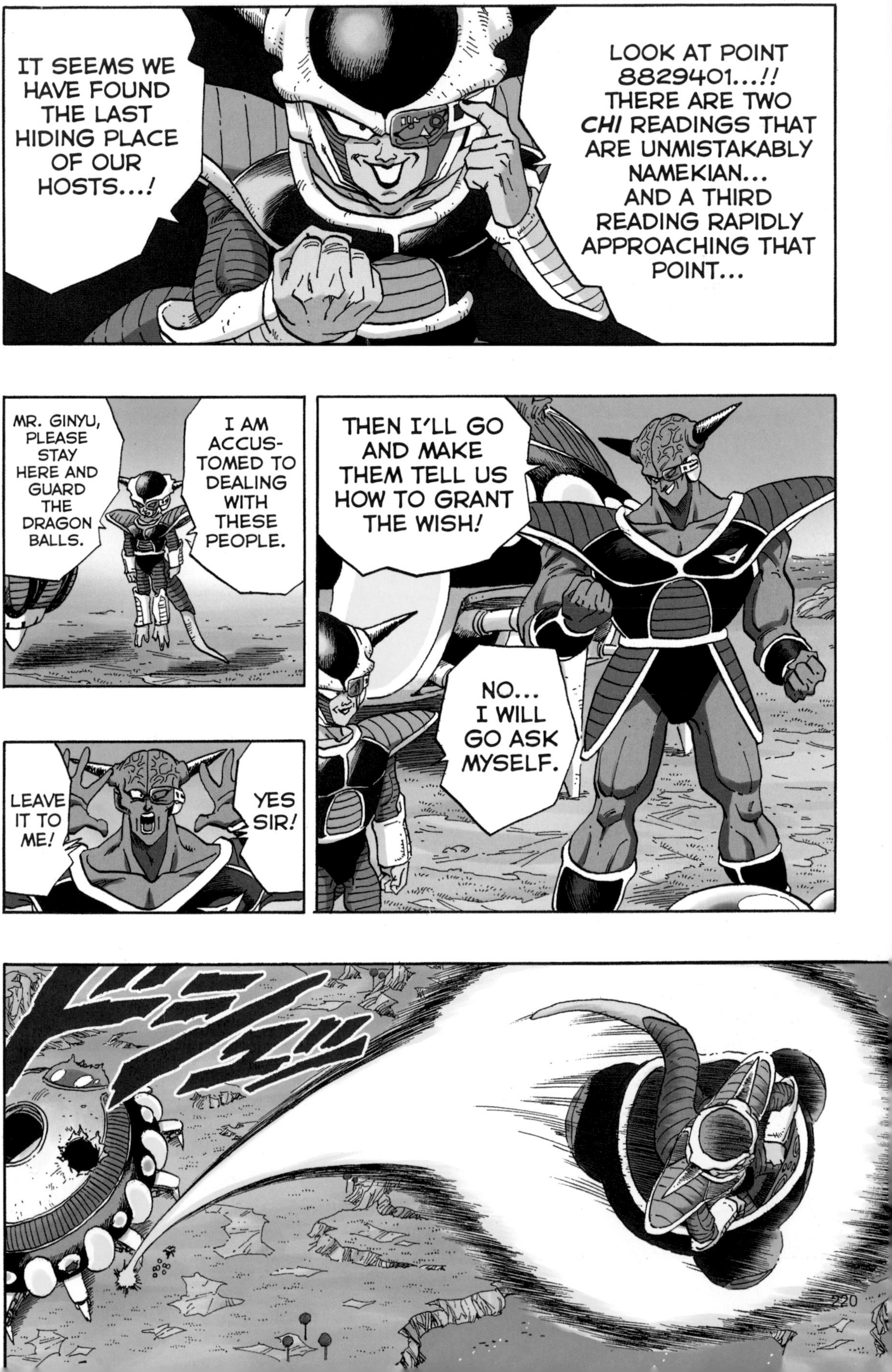
LOOK AT POINT 8829401...!! THERE ARE TWO *CHI* READINGS THAT ARE UNMISTAKABLY NAMEKIAN... AND A THIRD READING RAPIDLY APPROACHING THAT POINT...
IT SEEMS WE HAVE FOUND THE LAST HIDING PLACE OF OUR HOSTS...!
THEN I'LL GO AND MAKE THEM TELL US HOW TO GRANT THE WISH!
NO... I WILL GO ASK MYSELF.
I AM ACCUSTOMED TO DEALING WITH THESE PEOPLE.
MR. GINYU, PLEASE STAY HERE AND GUARD THE DRAGON BALLS.
YES SIR!
LEAVE IT TO ME!

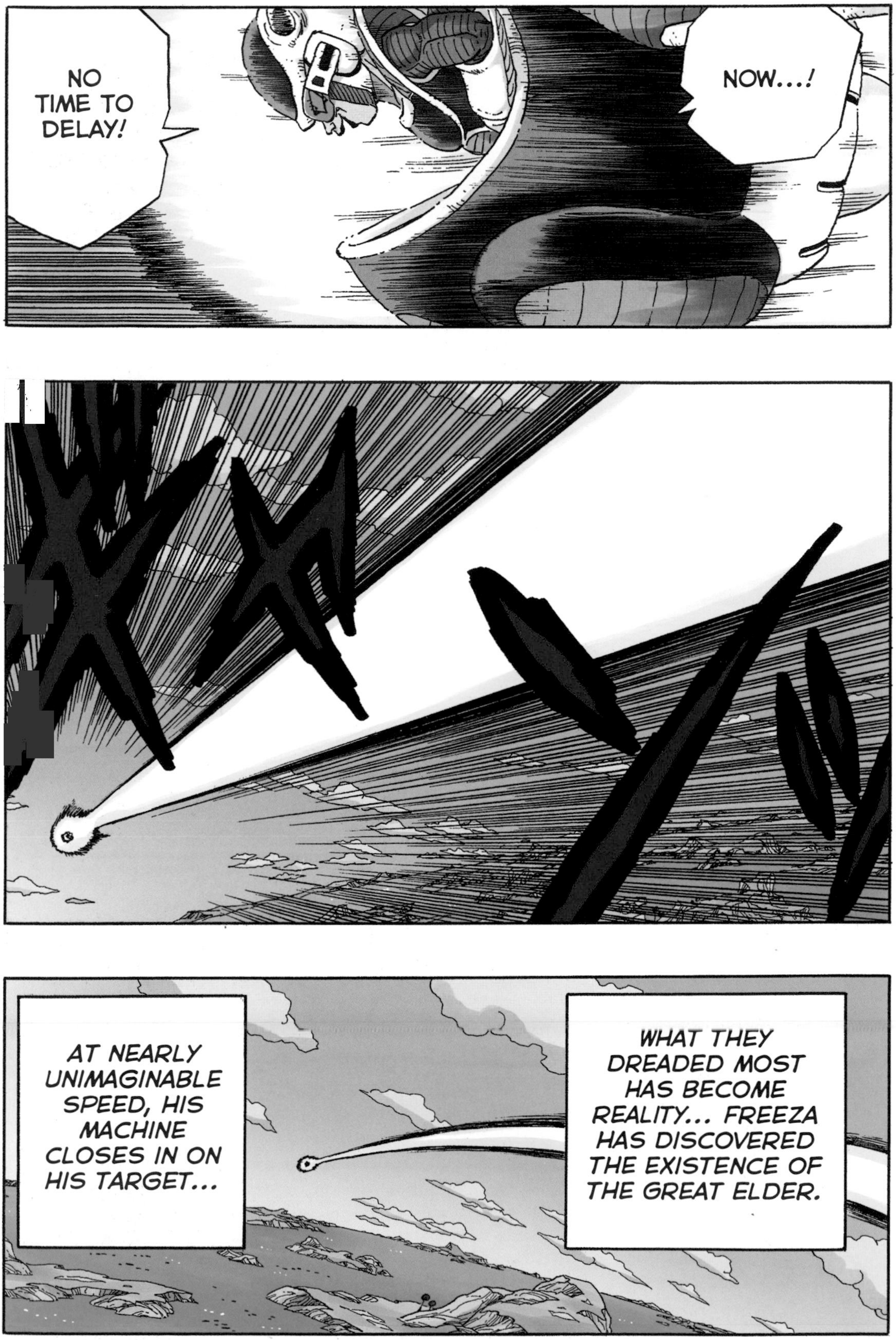
NOW...!
NO TIME TO DELAY!
WHAT THEY DREADED MOST HAS BECOME REALITY... FREEZA HAS DISCOVERED THE EXISTENCE OF THE GREAT ELDER.
AT NEARLY UNIMAGINABLE SPEED, HIS MACHINE CLOSES IN ON HIS TARGET...

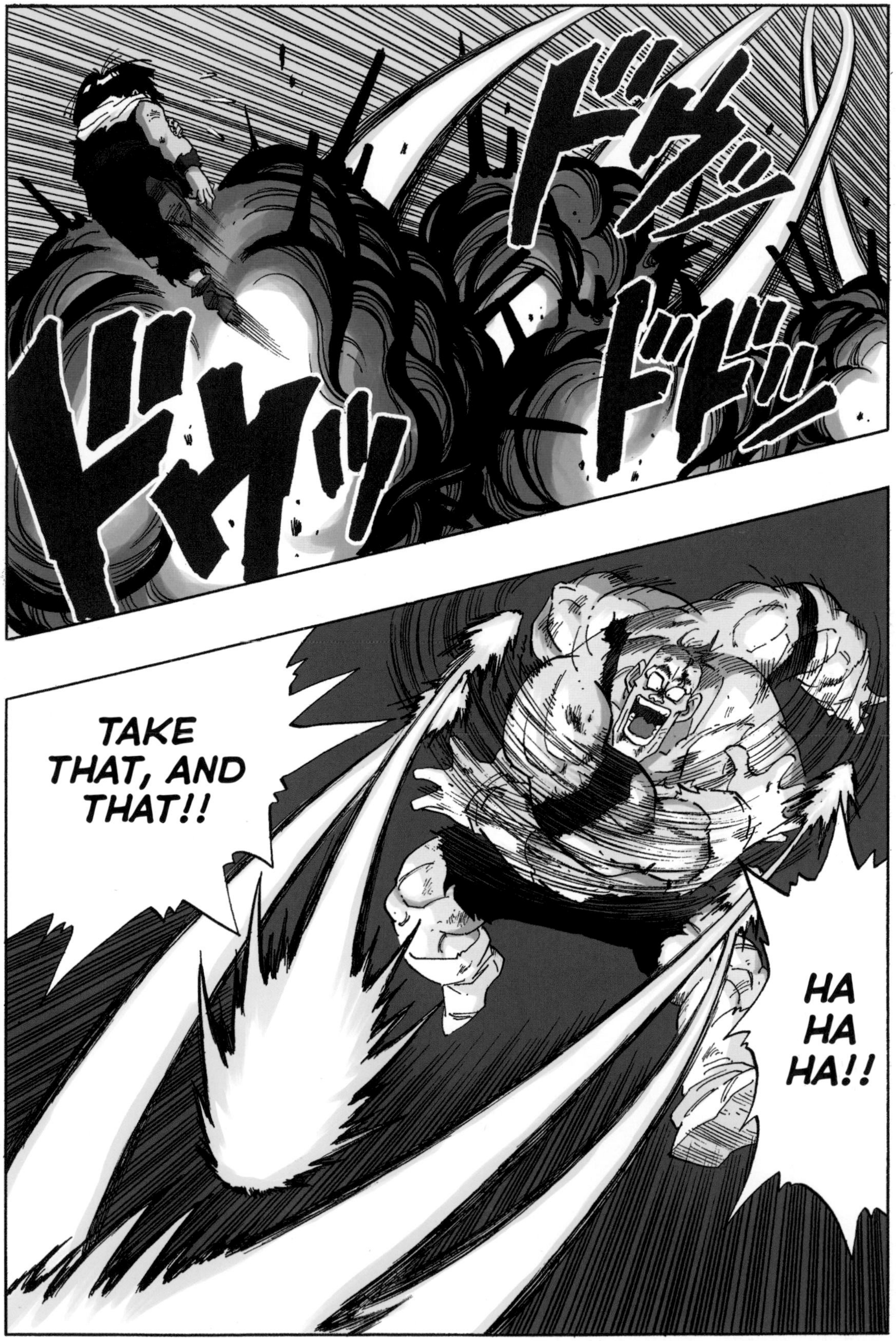
TAKE THAT, AND THAT!!
HA HA HA!!

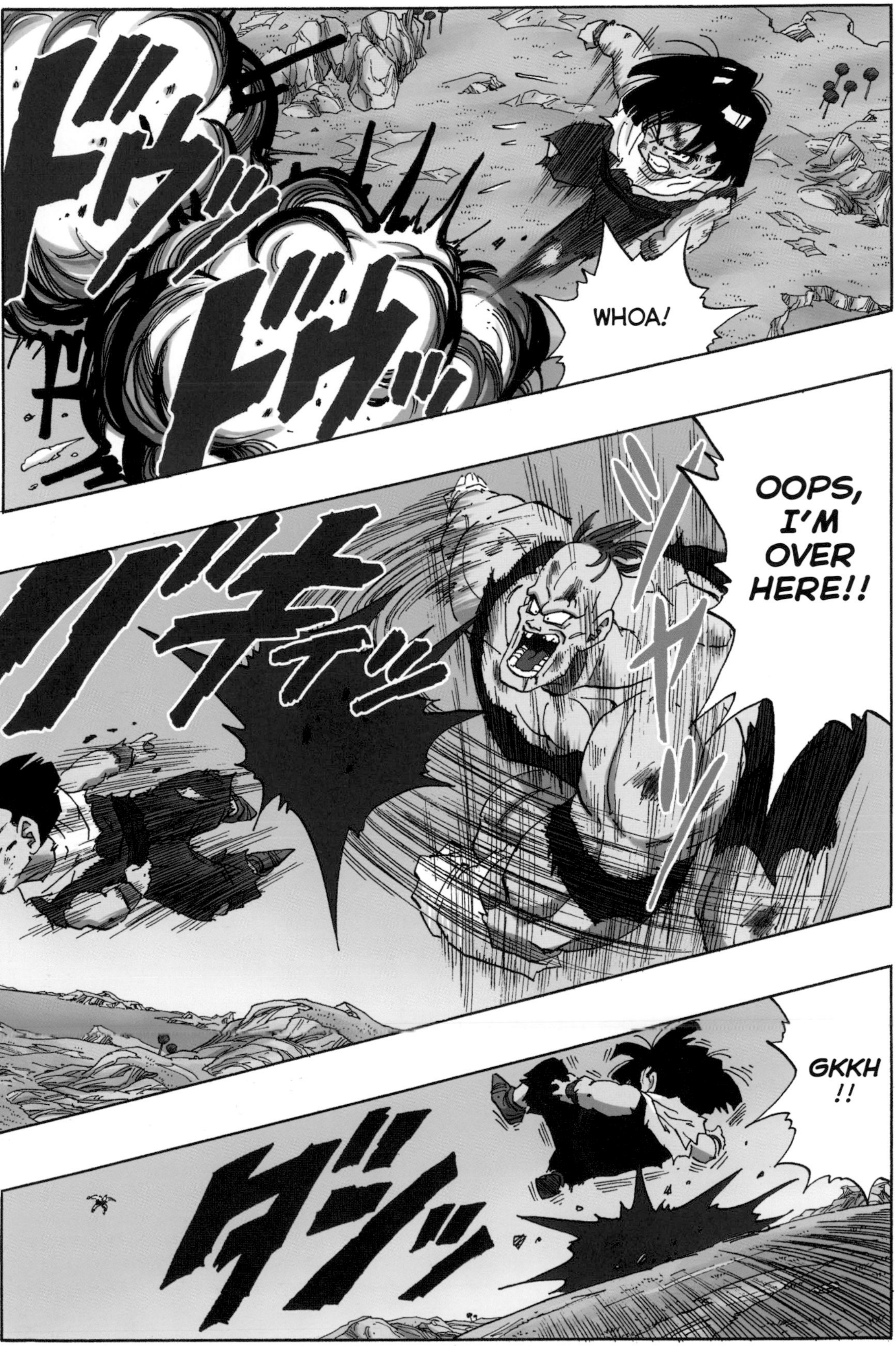
WHOA!
OOPS, I'M OVER HERE!!
GKKH !!

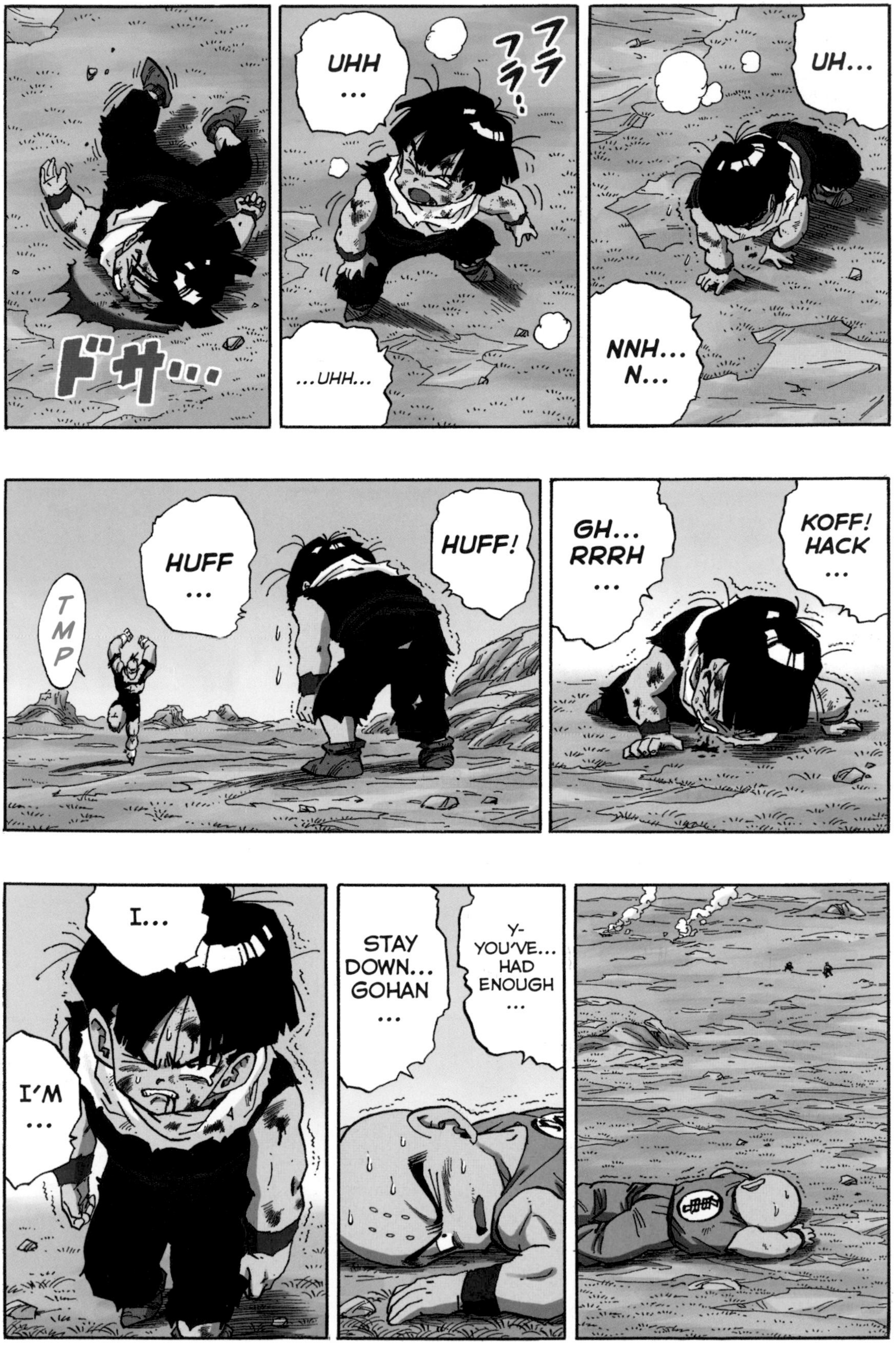
UH...
NNH... N...
フラフラ...
UHH ...
...UHH...
ドサ...
KOFF! HACK ...
GH... RRRH ...
HUFF!
HUFF ...
TMP
Y-YOU'VE... HAD ENOUGH ...
STAY DOWN... GOHAN ...
I...
I'M ...

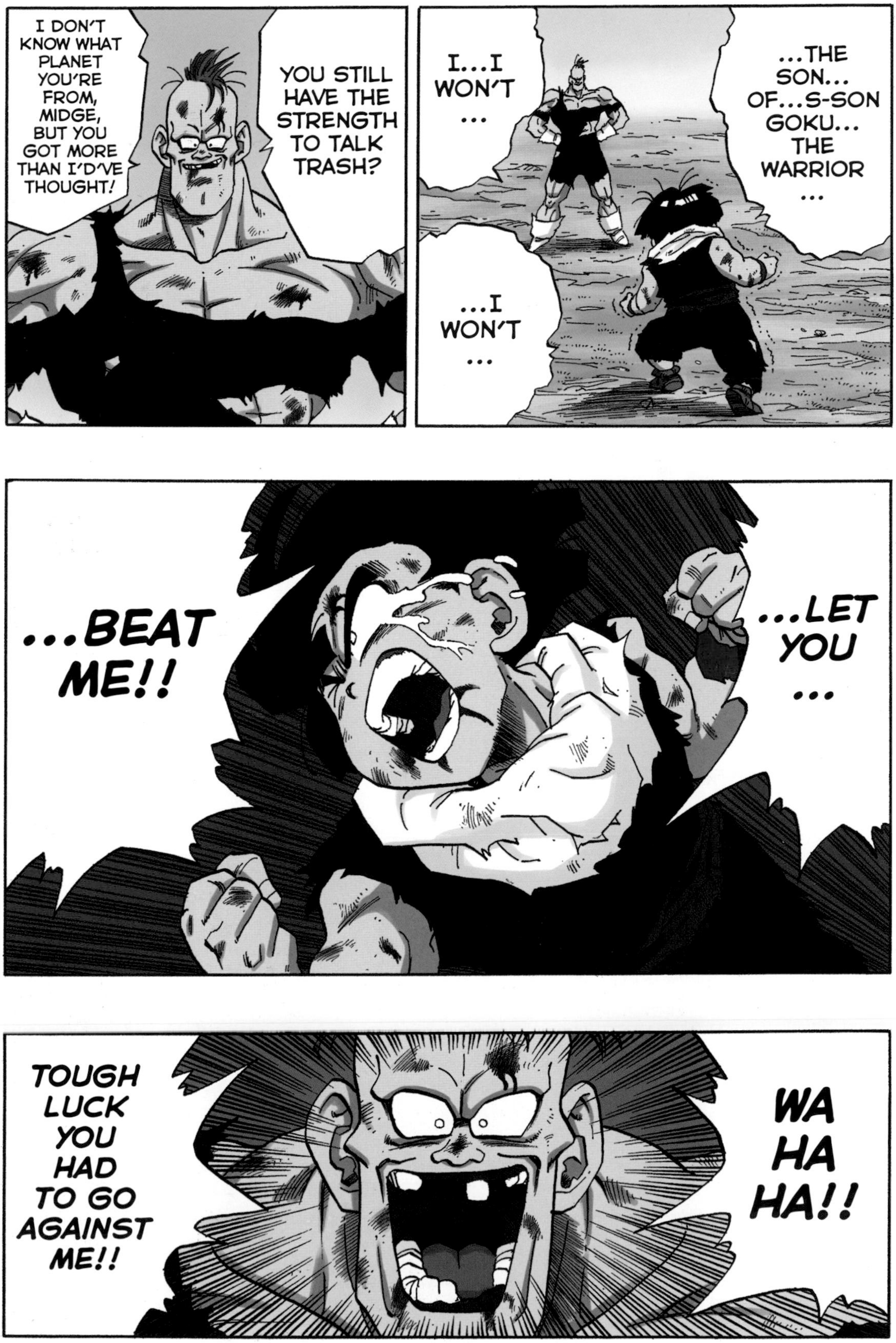

...THE SON... OF...S-SON GOKU... THE WARRIOR ...
I...I WON'T ...
...I WON'T ...
YOU STILL HAVE THE STRENGTH TO TALK TRASH?
I DON'T KNOW WHAT PLANET YOU'RE FROM, MIDGE, BUT YOU GOT MORE THAN I'D'VE THOUGHT!
...LET YOU ...
...BEAT ME!!
WA HA HA!!
TOUGH LUCK YOU HAD TO GO AGAINST ME!!

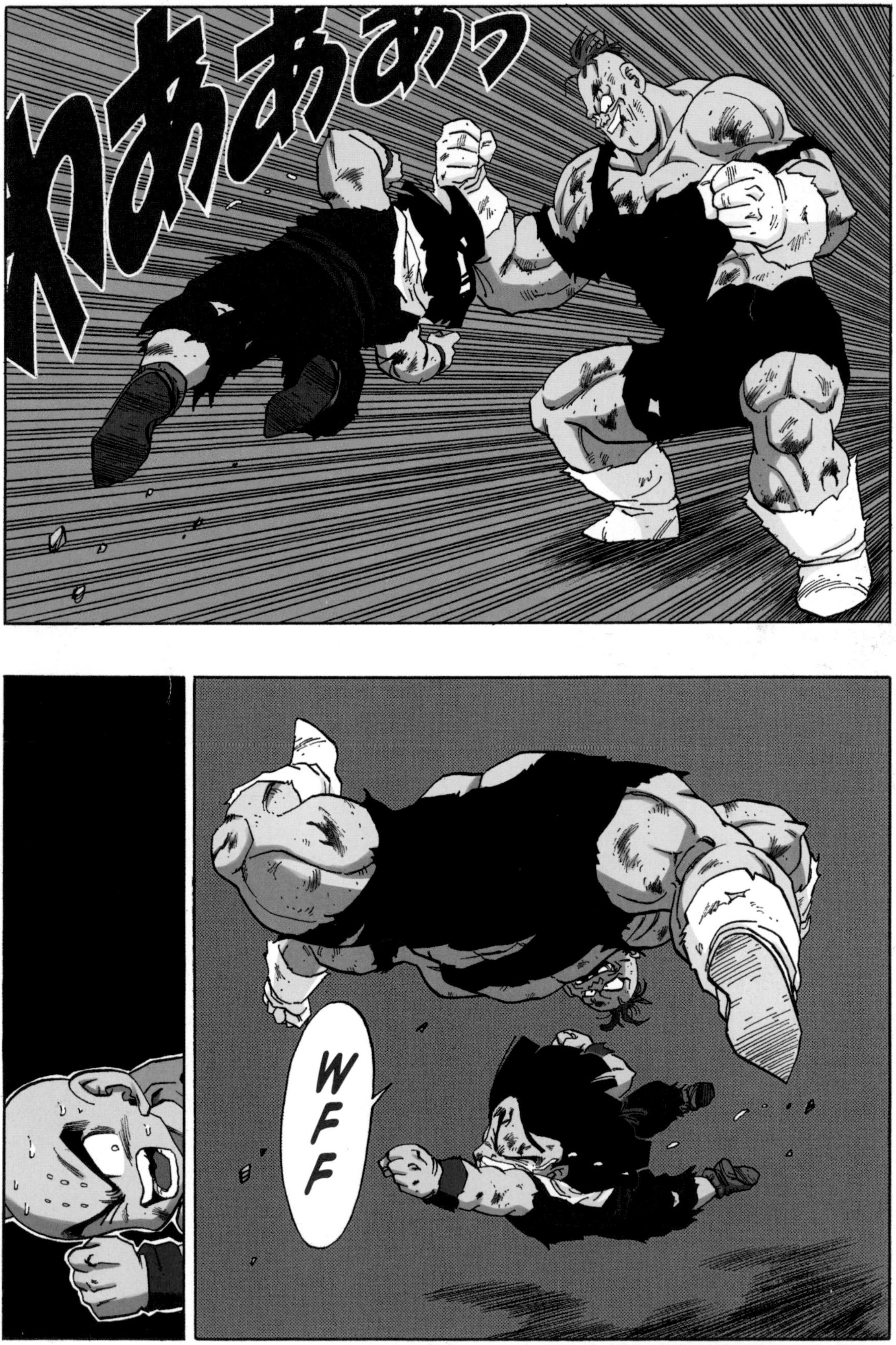
わあああっ
WFF

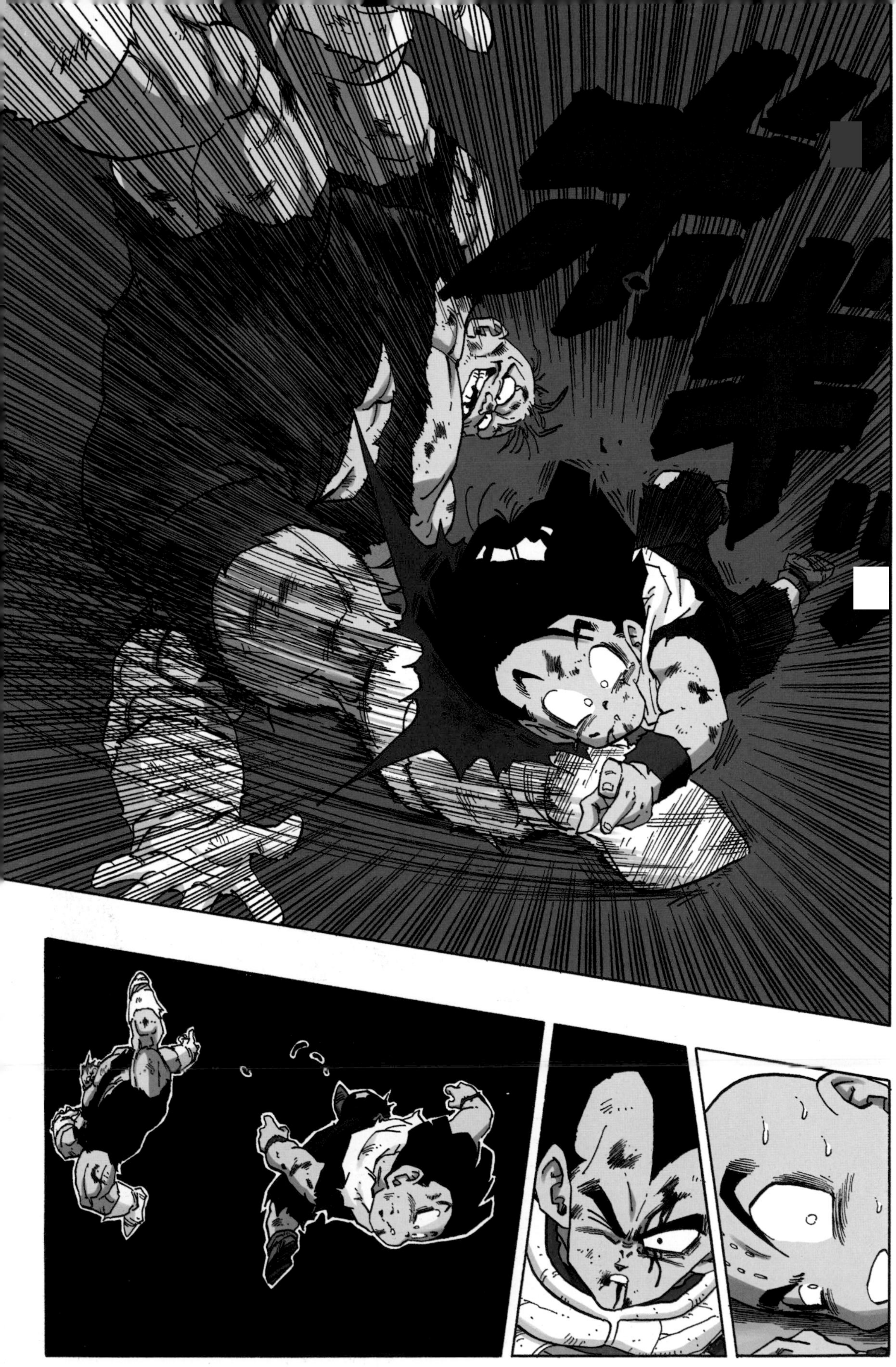

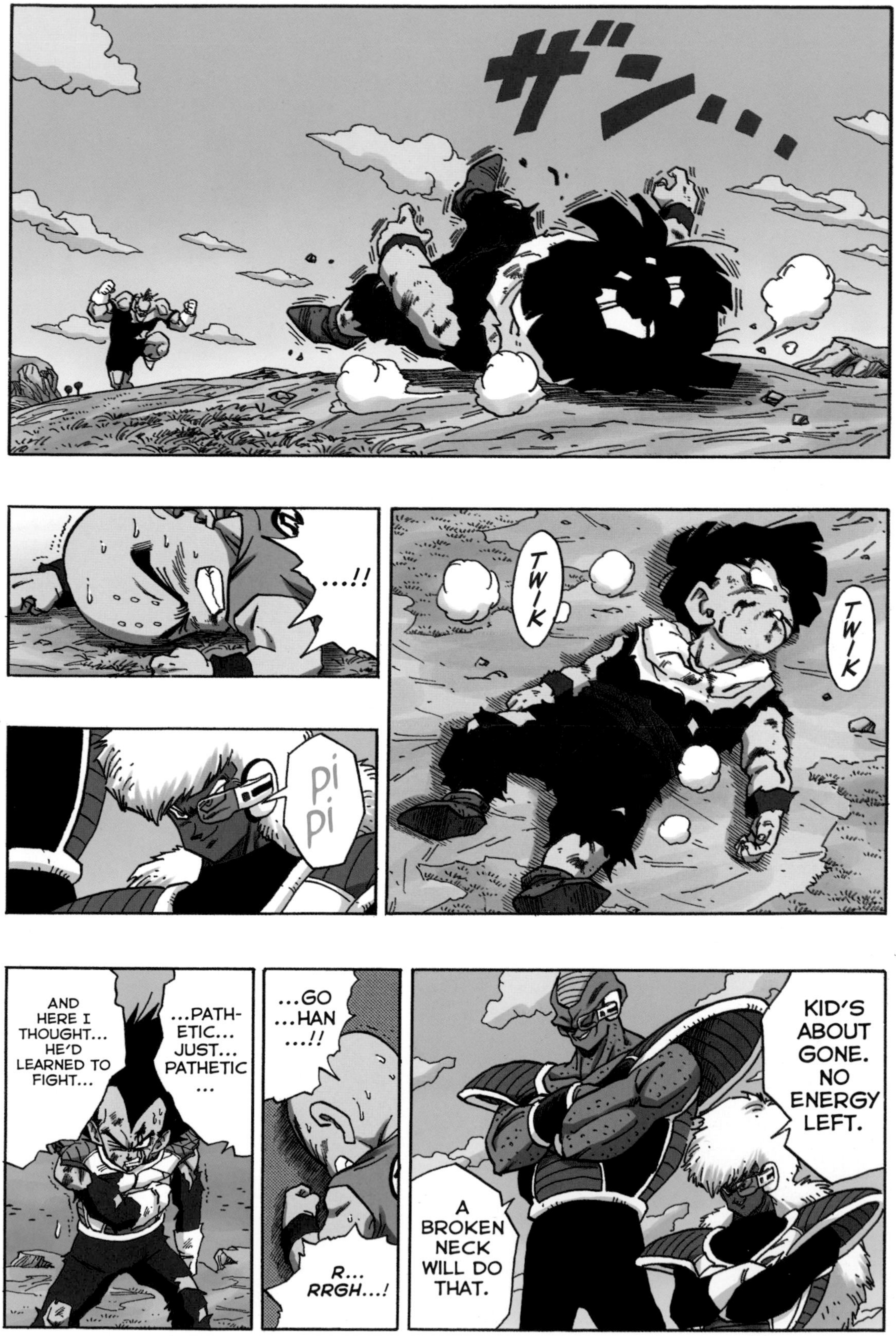
ザン…
TWIK
TWIK
...!!
pi pi
KID'S ABOUT GONE. NO ENERGY LEFT.
A BROKEN NECK WILL DO THAT.
...GO ...HAN ...!!
R... RRGH...!
...PATH-ETIC... JUST... PATHETIC ...
AND HERE I THOUGHT... HE'D LEARNED TO FIGHT...

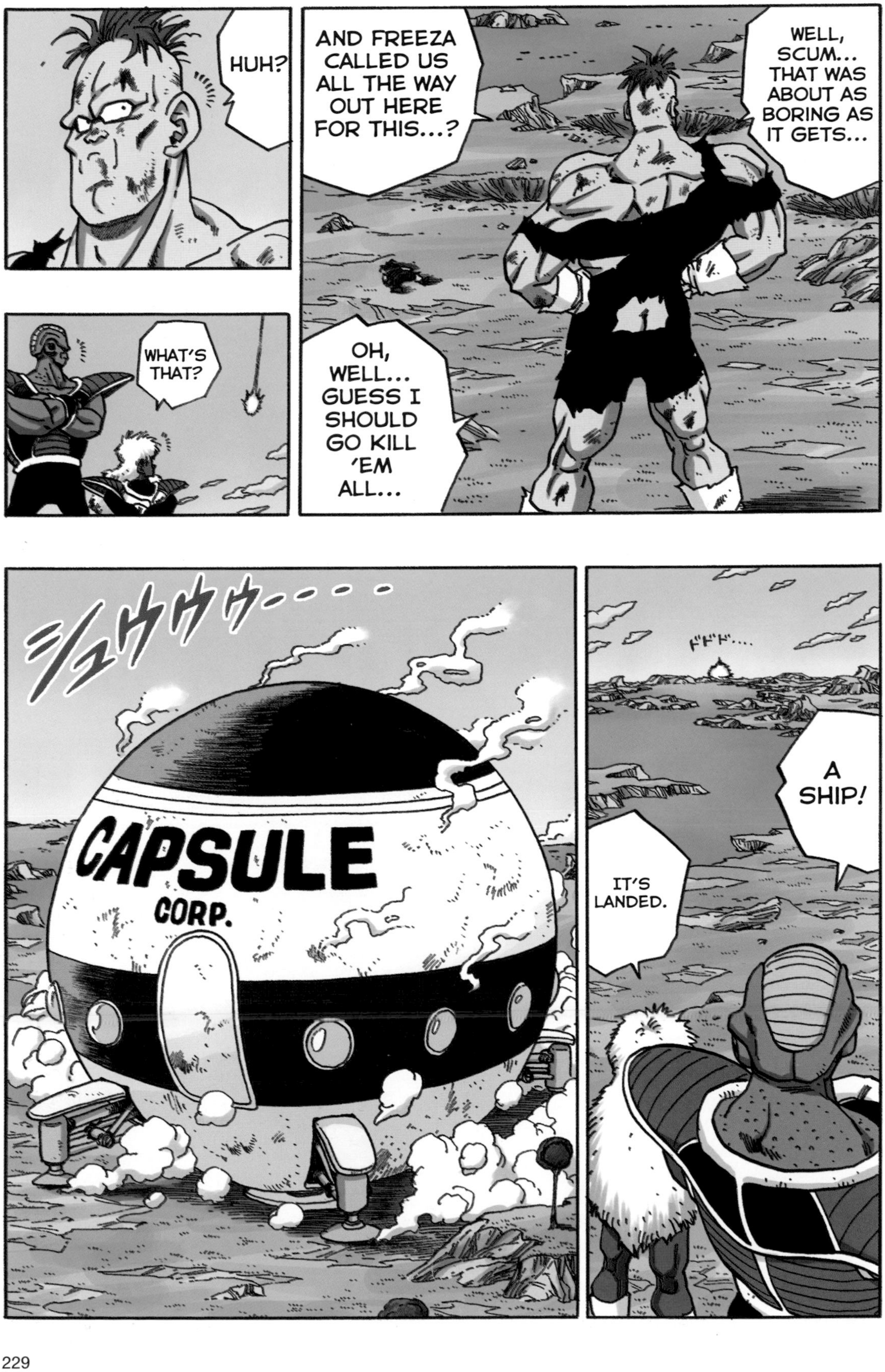
WELL, SCUM... THAT WAS ABOUT AS BORING AS IT GETS...
AND FREEZA CALLED US ALL THE WAY OUT HERE FOR THIS...?
OH, WELL... GUESS I SHOULD GO KILL 'EM ALL...
HUH?
WHAT'S THAT?
ドドド....
A SHIP!
IT'S LANDED.
シュウウウ-----
CAPSULE CORP.

Chapter 34 • Son Goku Has Landed!

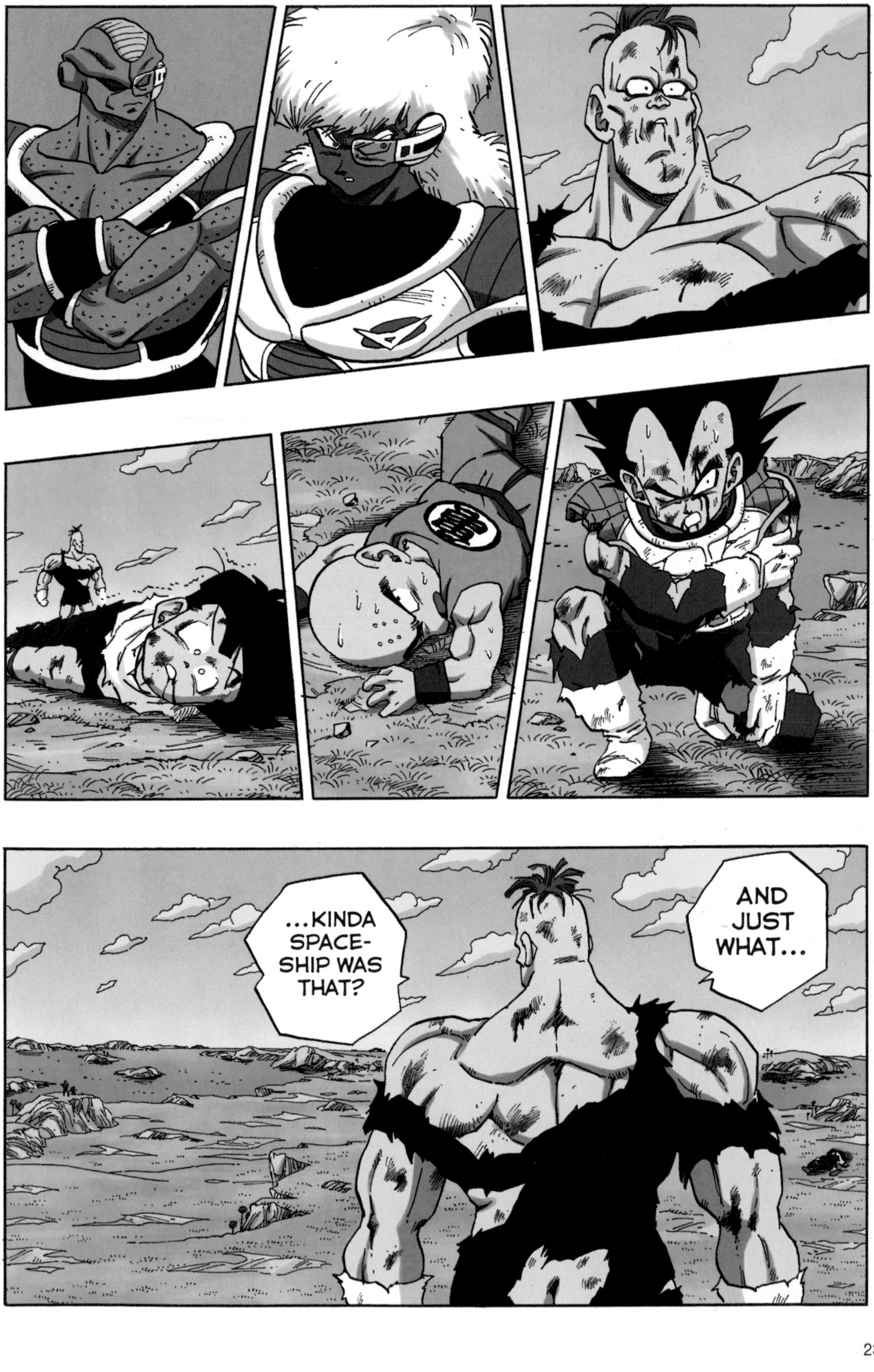
AND JUST WHAT...
...KINDA SPACE-SHIP WAS THAT?

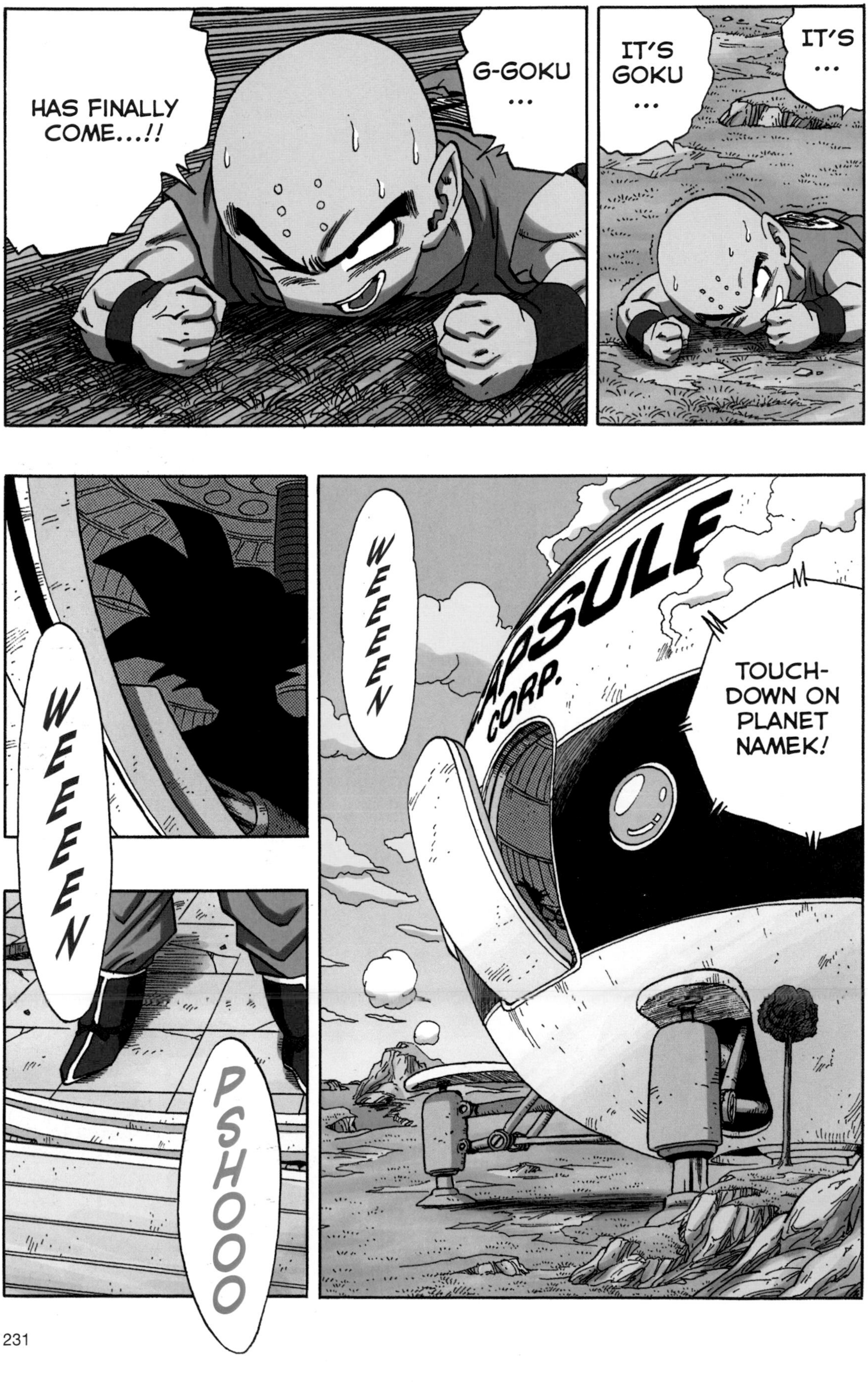
IT'S ...
IT'S GOKU ...
G-GOKU ...
HAS FINALLY COME...!!
CAPSULE CORP.
TOUCH-DOWN ON PLANET NAMEK!
WEEEEN
WEEEEN
PSHOOOO

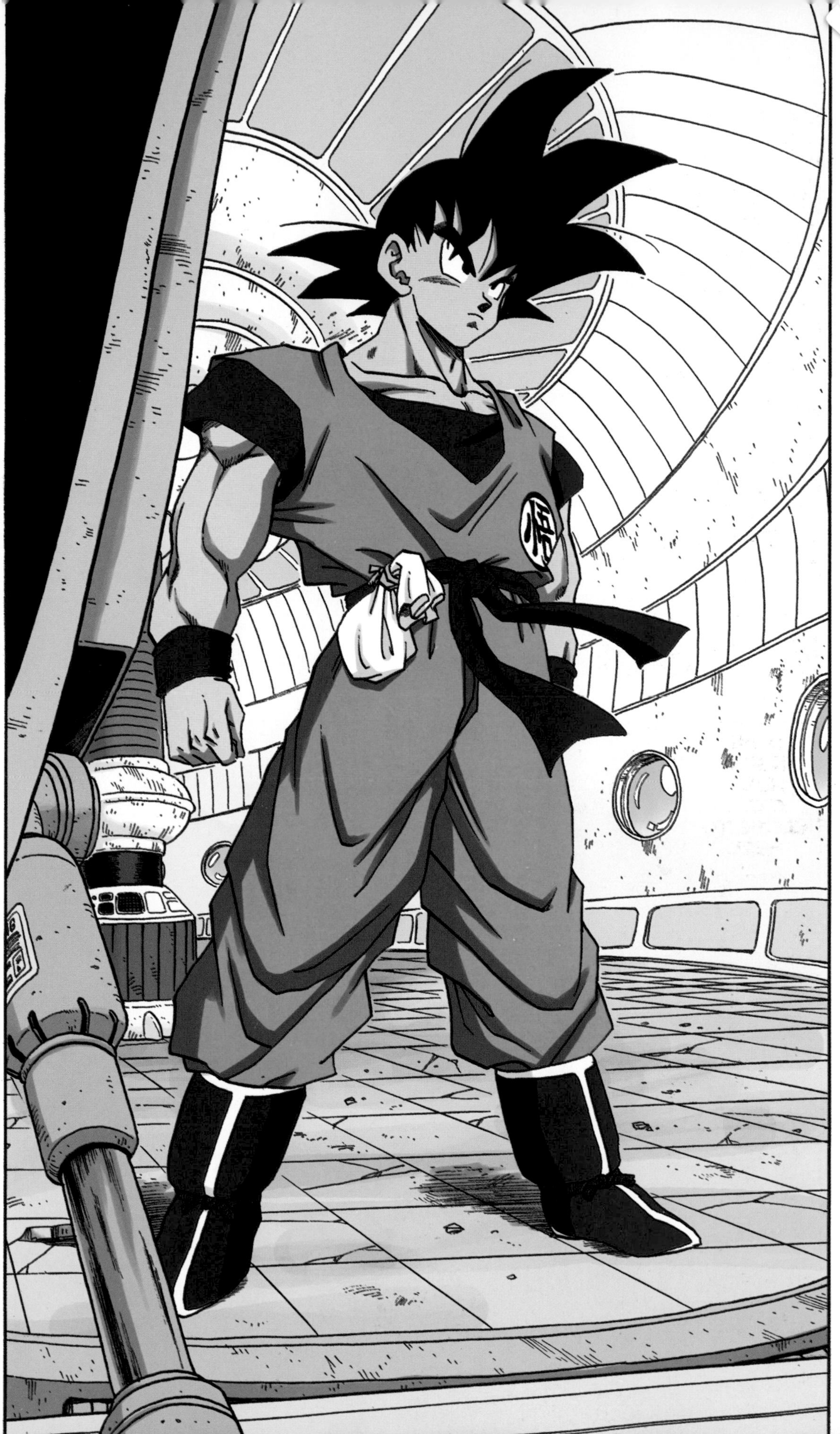

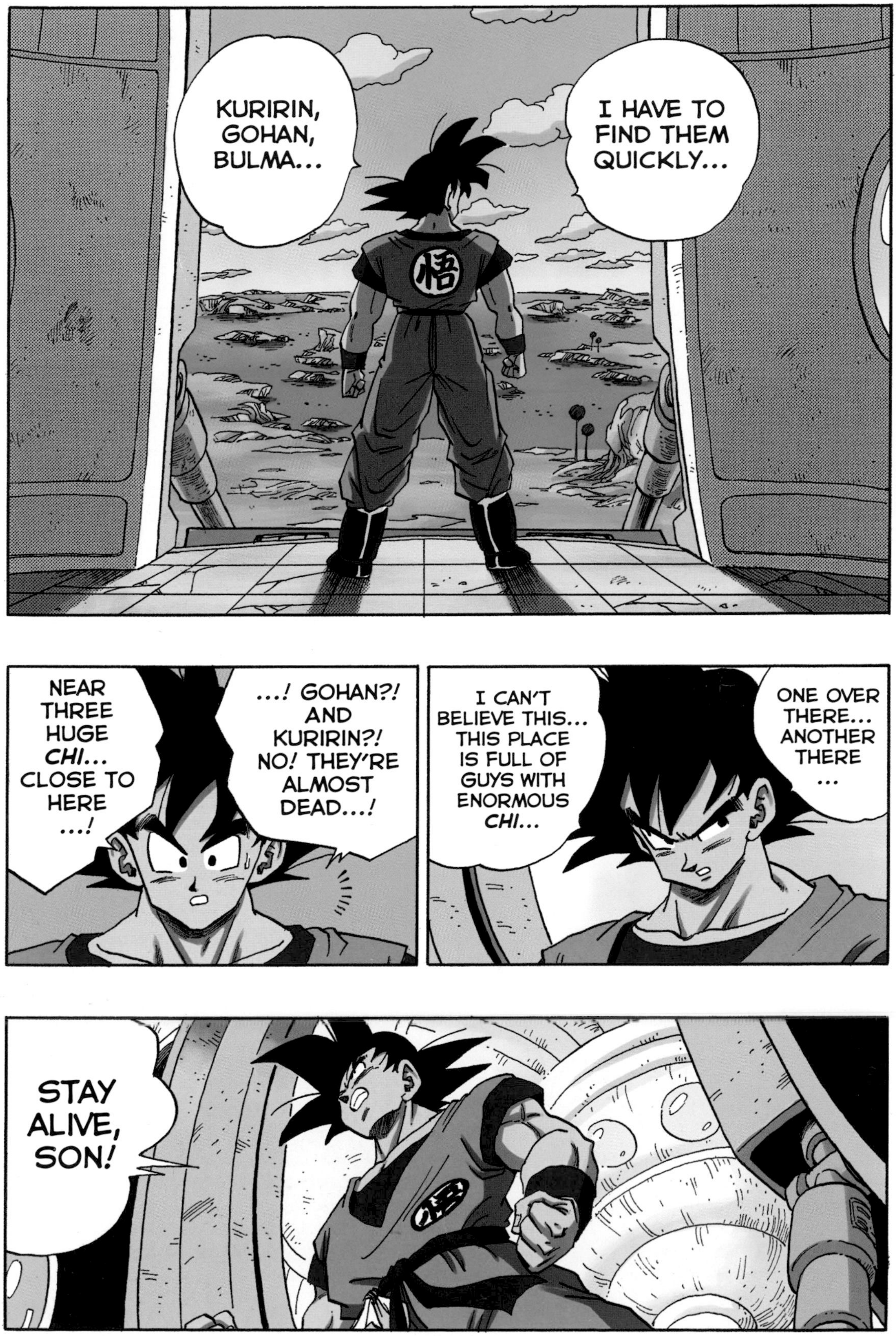
I HAVE TO FIND THEM QUICKLY...
KURIRIN, GOHAN, BULMA...
ONE OVER THERE... ANOTHER THERE ...
I CAN'T BELIEVE THIS... THIS PLACE IS FULL OF GUYS WITH ENORMOUS *CHI*...
...! GOHAN?! AND KURIRIN?! NO! THEY'RE ALMOST DEAD...!
NEAR THREE HUGE *CHI*... CLOSE TO HERE ...!
STAY ALIVE, SON!

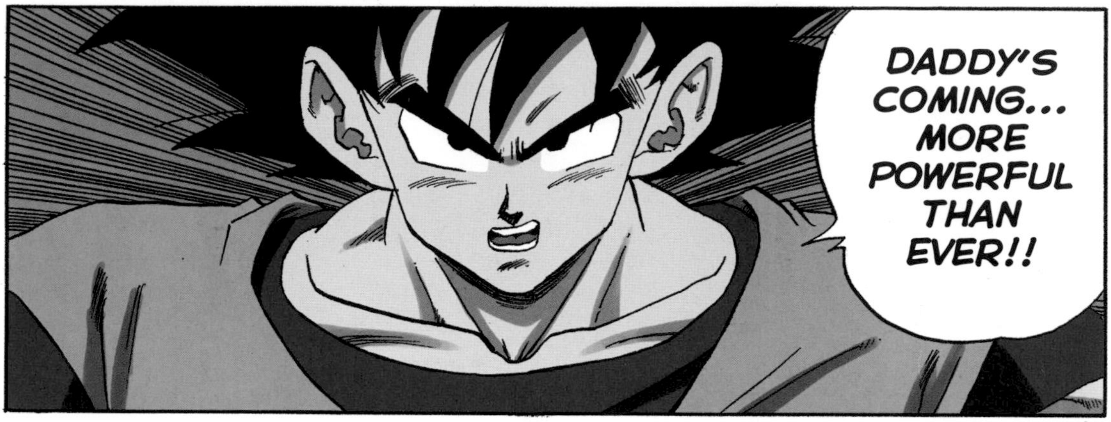
DADDY'S COMING... MORE POWERFUL THAN EVER!!

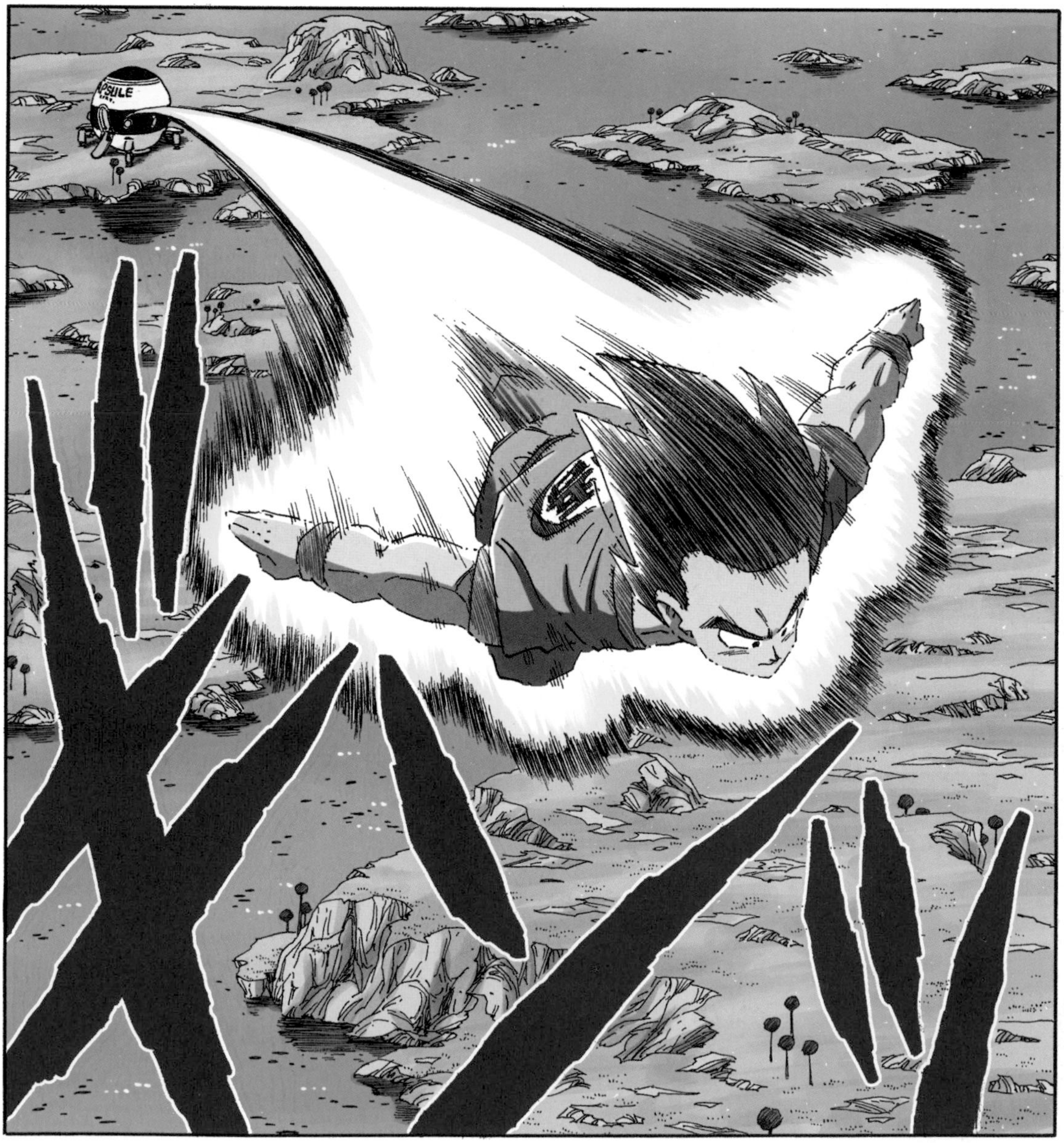

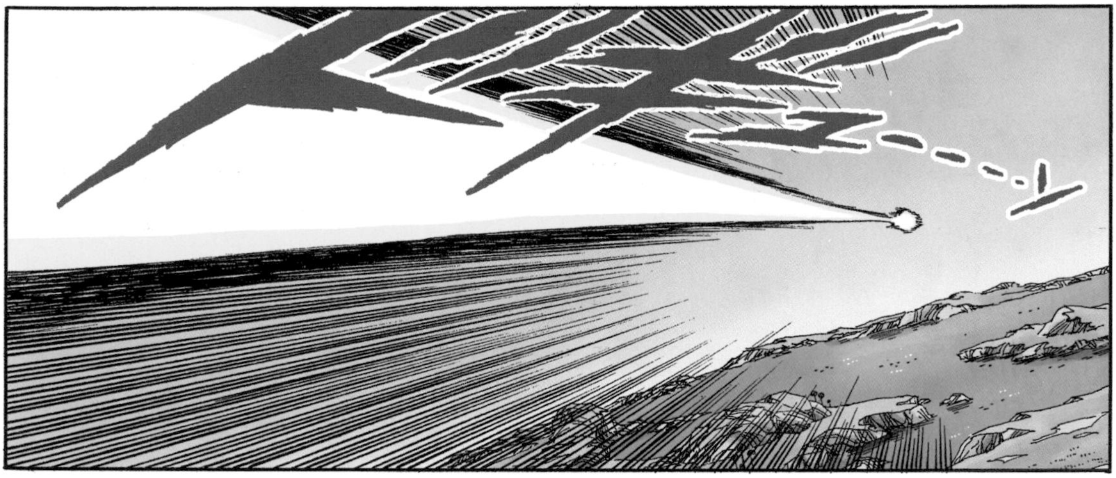

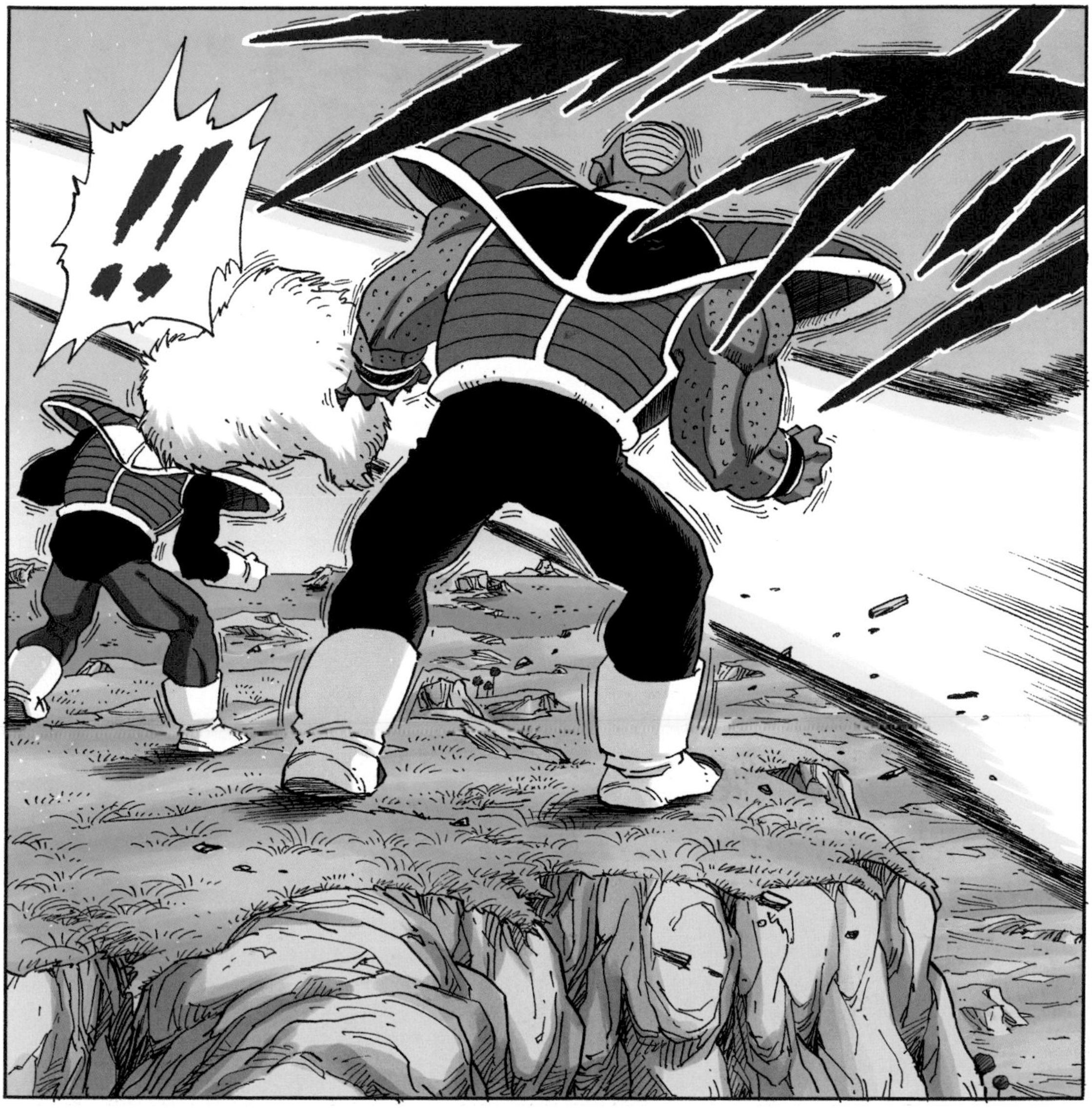
!!

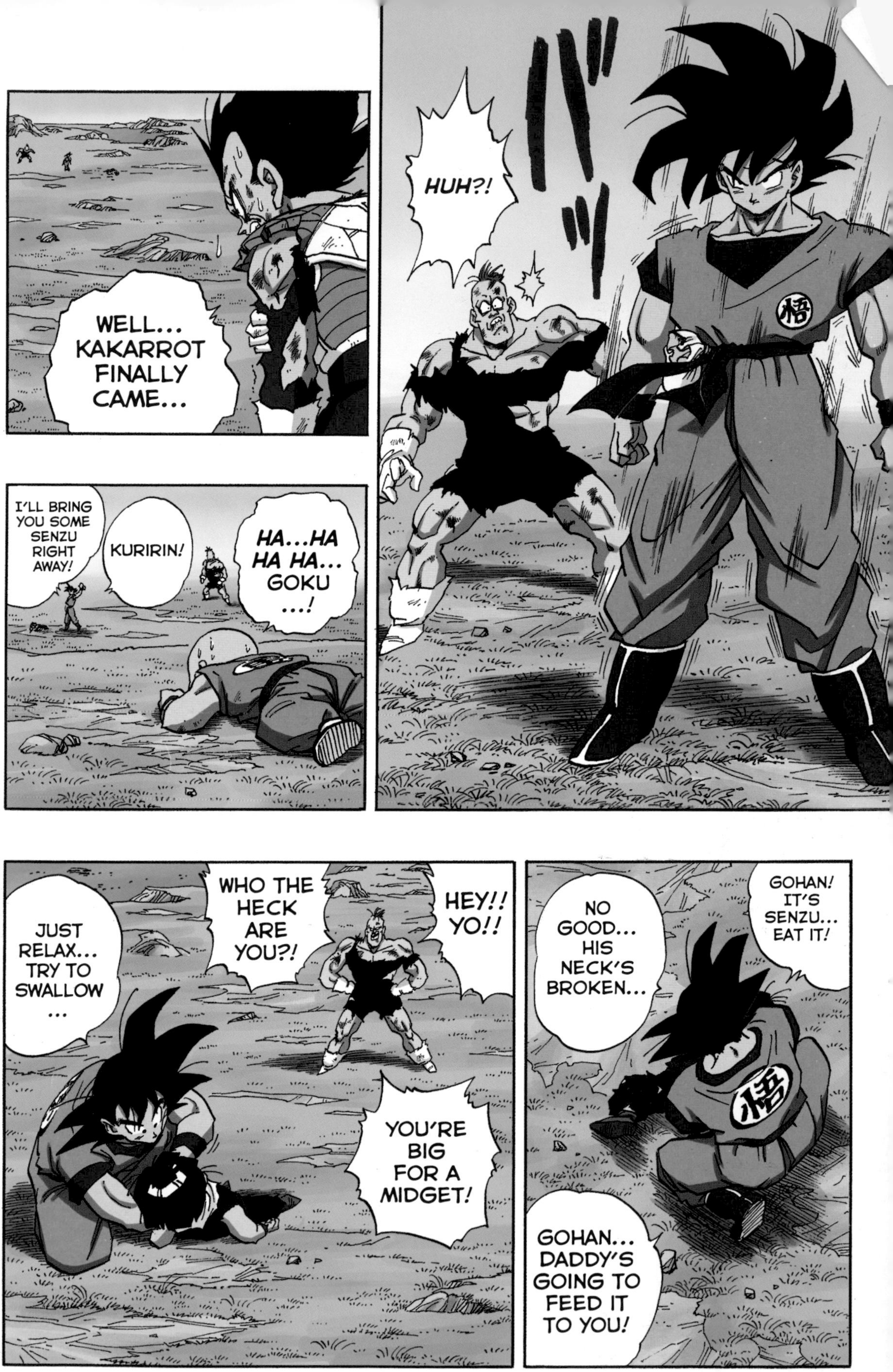
バッ
HUH?!
WELL... KAKARROT FINALLY CAME...
HA...HA HA HA... GOKU ...!
KURIRIN!
I'LL BRING YOU SOME SENZU RIGHT AWAY!
GOHAN! IT'S SENZU... EAT IT!
NO GOOD... HIS NECK'S BROKEN...
GOHAN... DADDY'S GOING TO FEED IT TO YOU!
HEY!! YO!!
WHO THE HECK ARE YOU?!
JUST RELAX... TRY TO SWALLOW ...
YOU'RE BIG FOR A MIDGET!

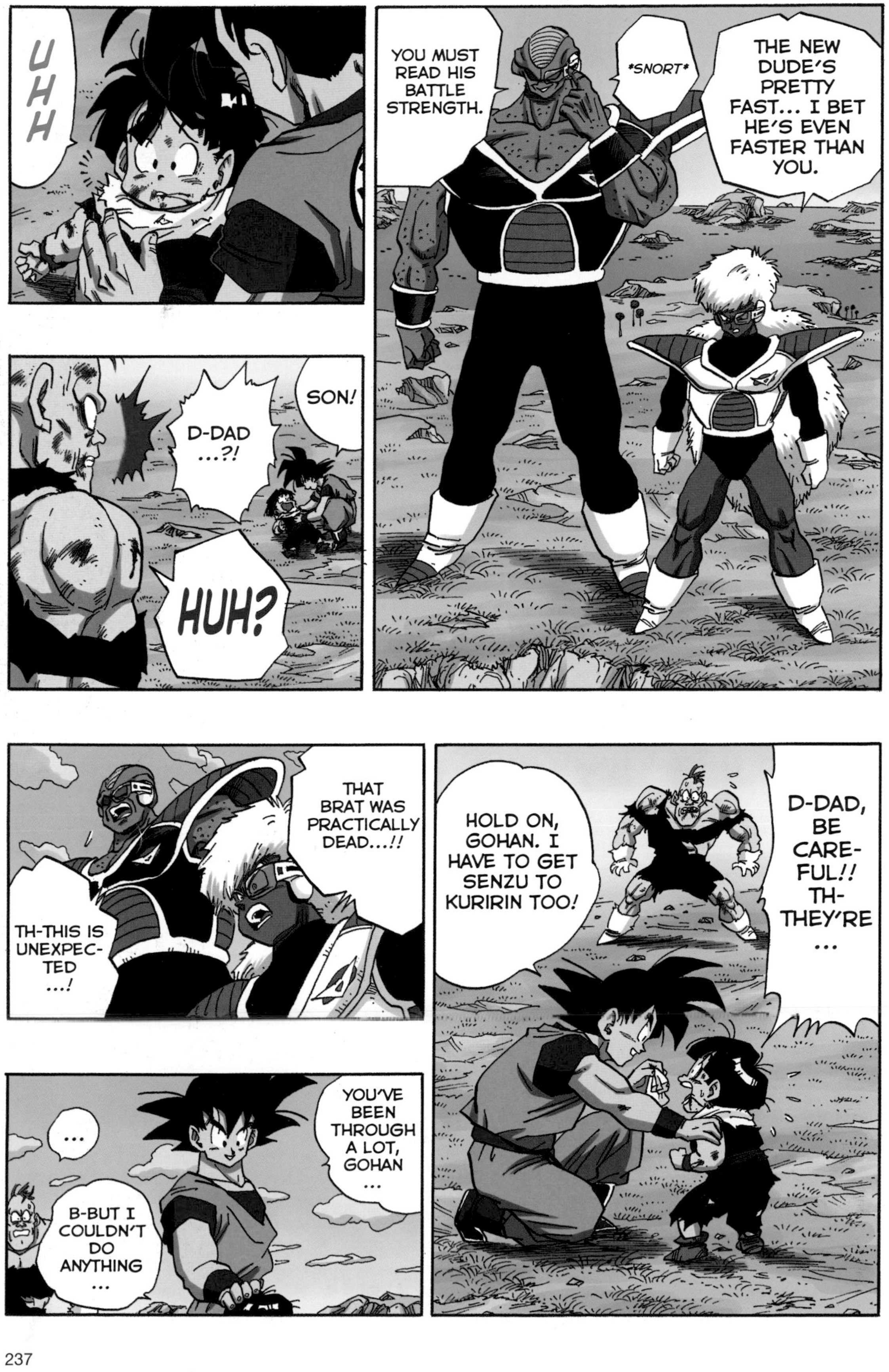
THE NEW DUDE'S PRETTY FAST... I BET HE'S EVEN FASTER THAN YOU.
SNORT
YOU MUST READ HIS BATTLE STRENGTH.
UHH
SON!
D-DAD ...?!
HUH?
D-DAD, BE CARE-FUL!! TH-THEY'RE ...
HOLD ON, GOHAN. I HAVE TO GET SENZU TO KURIRIN TOO!
THAT BRAT WAS PRACTICALLY DEAD...!!
TH-THIS IS UNEXPEC-TED ...!
YOU'VE BEEN THROUGH A LOT, GOHAN ...
...
B-BUT I COULDN'T DO ANYTHING ...

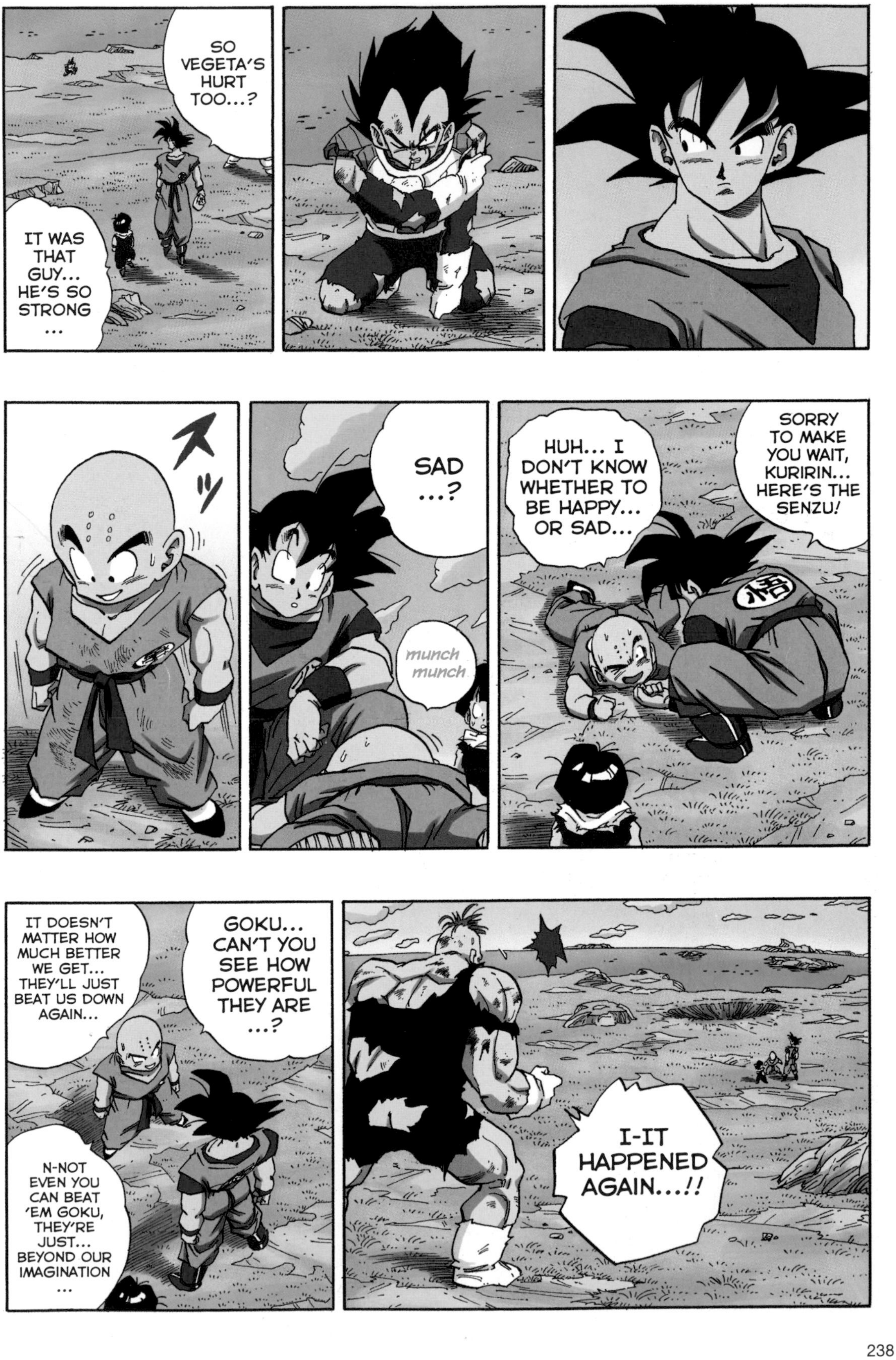
SO VEGETA'S HURT TOO...?
IT WAS THAT GUY... HE'S SO STRONG...
SORRY TO MAKE YOU WAIT, KURIRIN... HERE'S THE SENZU!
HUH... I DON'T KNOW WHETHER TO BE HAPPY... OR SAD...
SAD...?
munch munch
スッ
I-IT HAPPENED AGAIN...!!
GOKU... CAN'T YOU SEE HOW POWERFUL THEY ARE...?
IT DOESN'T MATTER HOW MUCH BETTER WE GET... THEY'LL JUST BEAT US DOWN AGAIN...
N-NOT EVEN YOU CAN BEAT 'EM GOKU, THEY'RE JUST... BEYOND OUR IMAGINATION...

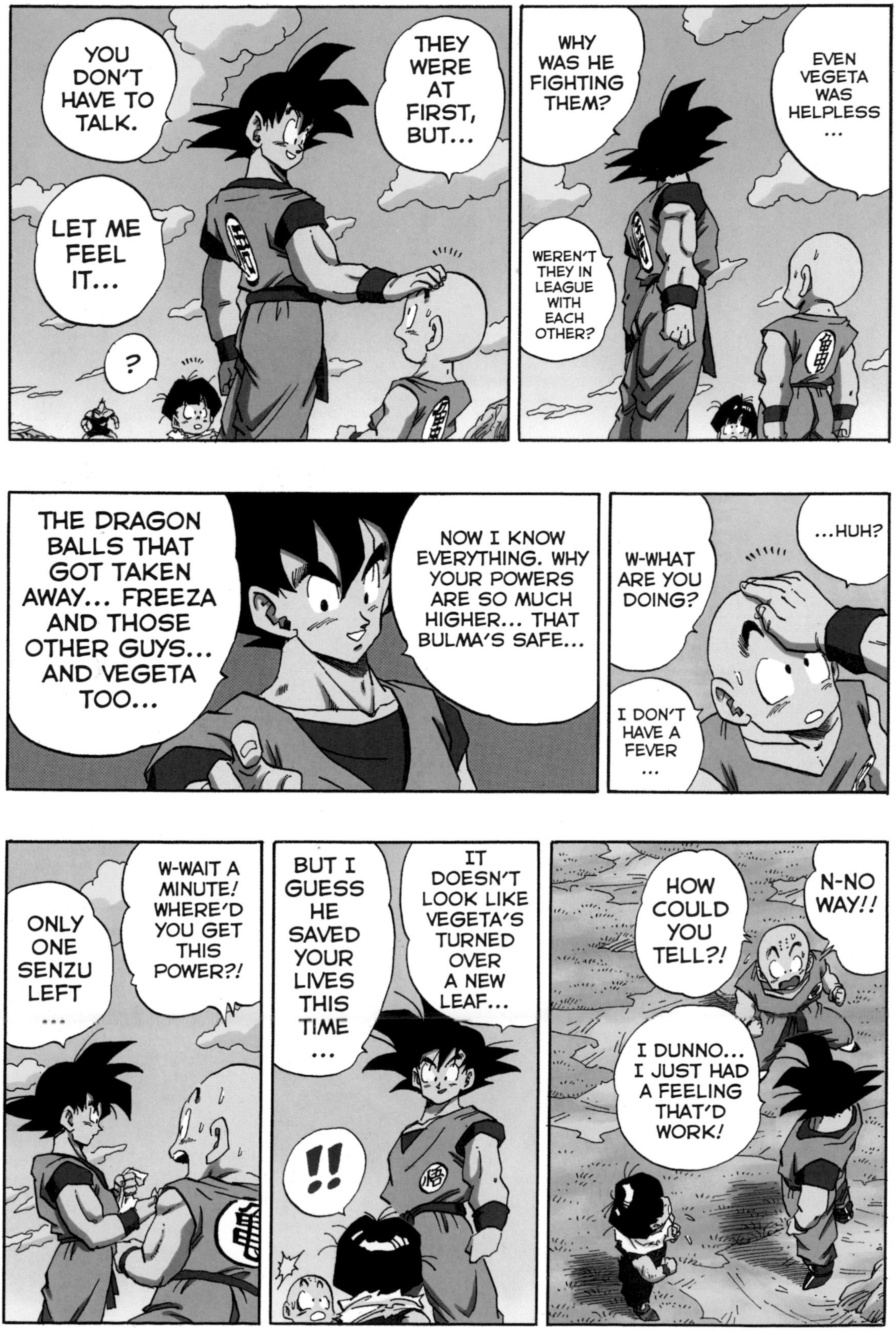

EVEN VEGETA WAS HELPLESS ...
WHY WAS HE FIGHTING THEM?
WEREN'T THEY IN LEAGUE WITH EACH OTHER?
THEY WERE AT FIRST, BUT...
YOU DON'T HAVE TO TALK.
LET ME FEEL IT...
?
...HUH?
W-WHAT ARE YOU DOING?
I DON'T HAVE A FEVER ...
NOW I KNOW EVERYTHING. WHY YOUR POWERS ARE SO MUCH HIGHER... THAT BULMA'S SAFE...
THE DRAGON BALLS THAT GOT TAKEN AWAY... FREEZA AND THOSE OTHER GUYS... AND VEGETA TOO...
N-NO WAY!!
HOW COULD YOU TELL?!
I DUNNO... I JUST HAD A FEELING THAT'D WORK!
IT DOESN'T LOOK LIKE VEGETA'S TURNED OVER A NEW LEAF...
BUT I GUESS HE SAVED YOUR LIVES THIS TIME ...
!!
W-WAIT A MINUTE! WHERE'D YOU GET THIS POWER?!
ONLY ONE SENZU LEFT ...

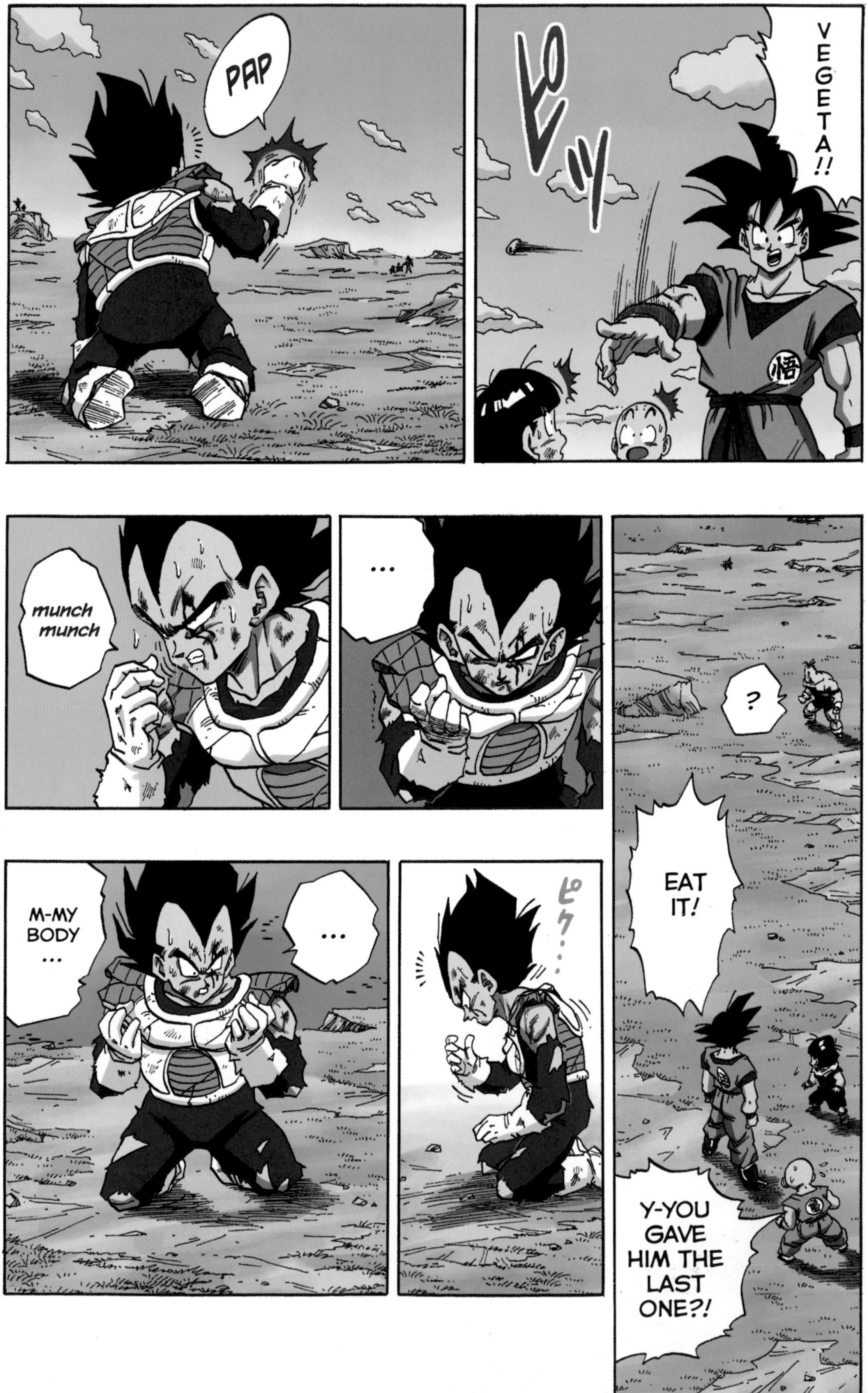
ピッ
VEGETA!!
PAP
?
EAT IT!
Y-YOU GAVE HIM THE LAST ONE?!
...
munch munch
ピク...
...
M-MY BODY ...

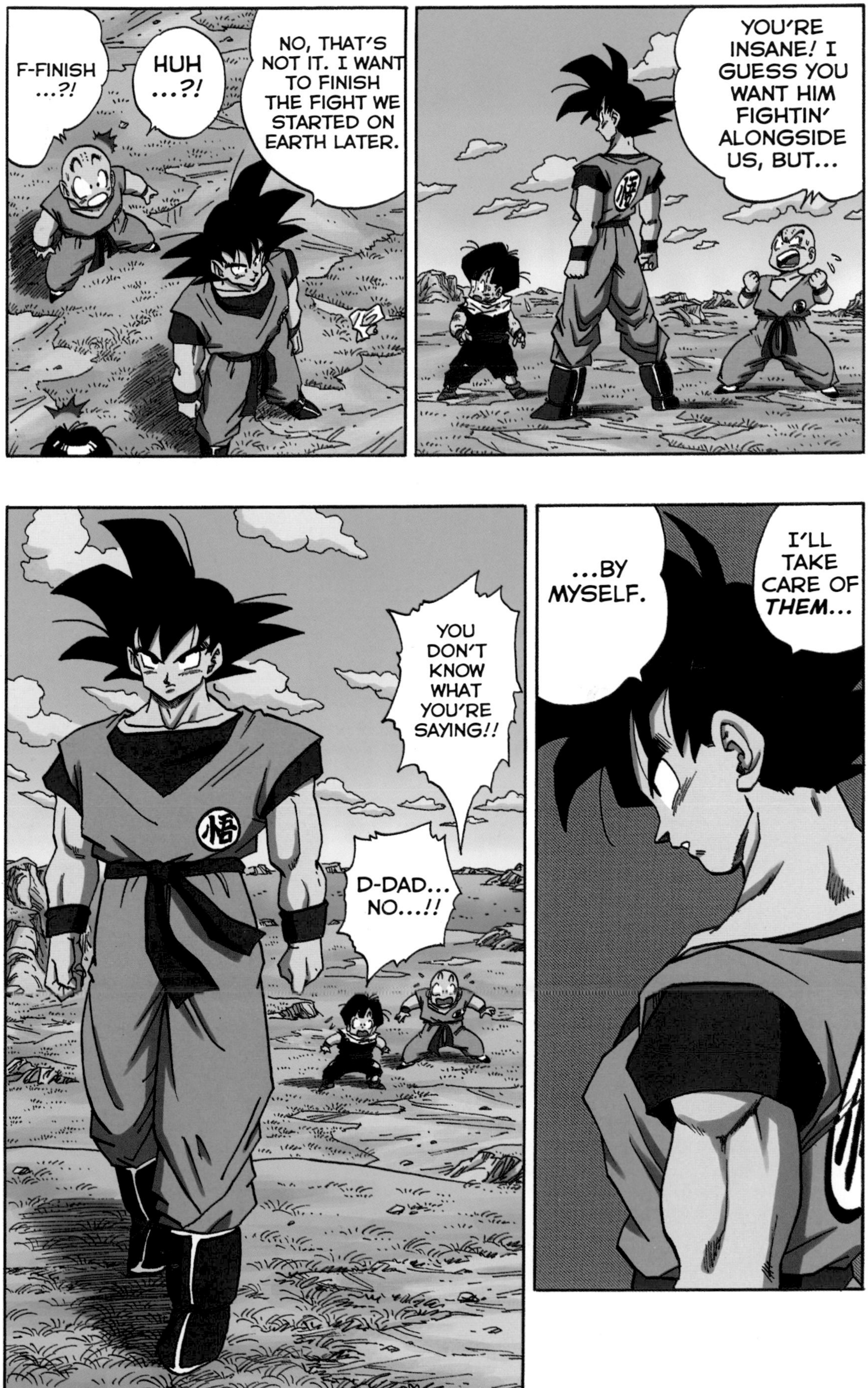
YOU'RE INSANE! I GUESS YOU WANT HIM FIGHTIN' ALONGSIDE US, BUT...
NO, THAT'S NOT IT. I WANT TO FINISH THE FIGHT WE STARTED ON EARTH LATER.
HUH ...?!
F-FINISH ...?!
I'LL TAKE CARE OF *THEM*...
...BY MYSELF.
YOU DON'T KNOW WHAT YOU'RE SAYING!!
D-DAD... NO...!!

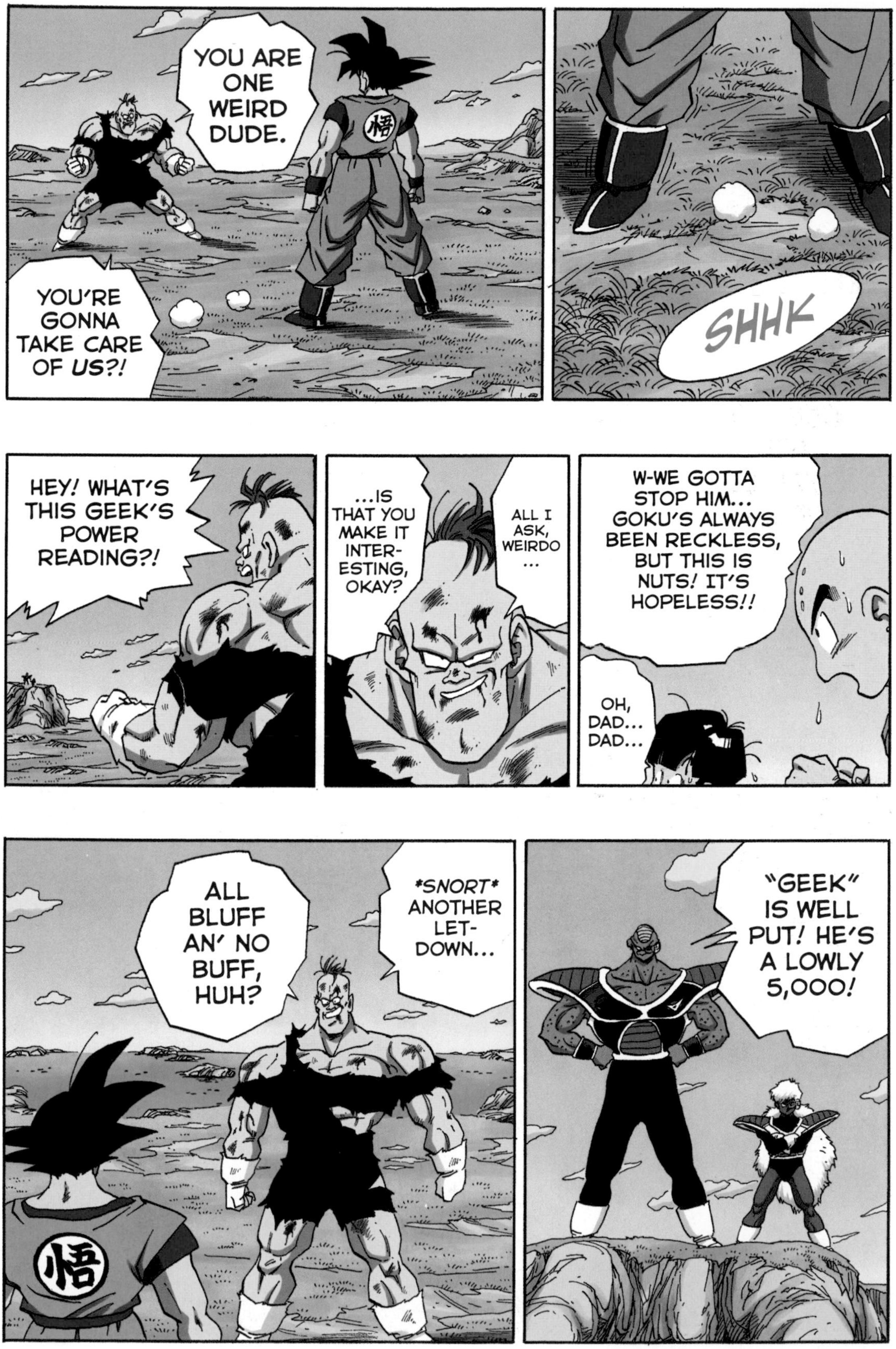
SHHK
YOU ARE ONE WEIRD DUDE.
YOU'RE GONNA TAKE CARE OF *US*?!
W-WE GOTTA STOP HIM... GOKU'S ALWAYS BEEN RECKLESS, BUT THIS IS NUTS! IT'S HOPELESS!!
OH, DAD... DAD...
ALL I ASK, WEIRDO...
...IS THAT YOU MAKE IT INTERESTING, OKAY?
HEY! WHAT'S THIS GEEK'S POWER READING?!
"GEEK" IS WELL PUT! HE'S A LOWLY 5,000!
SNORT ANOTHER LET-DOWN...
ALL BLUFF AN' NO BUFF, HUH?

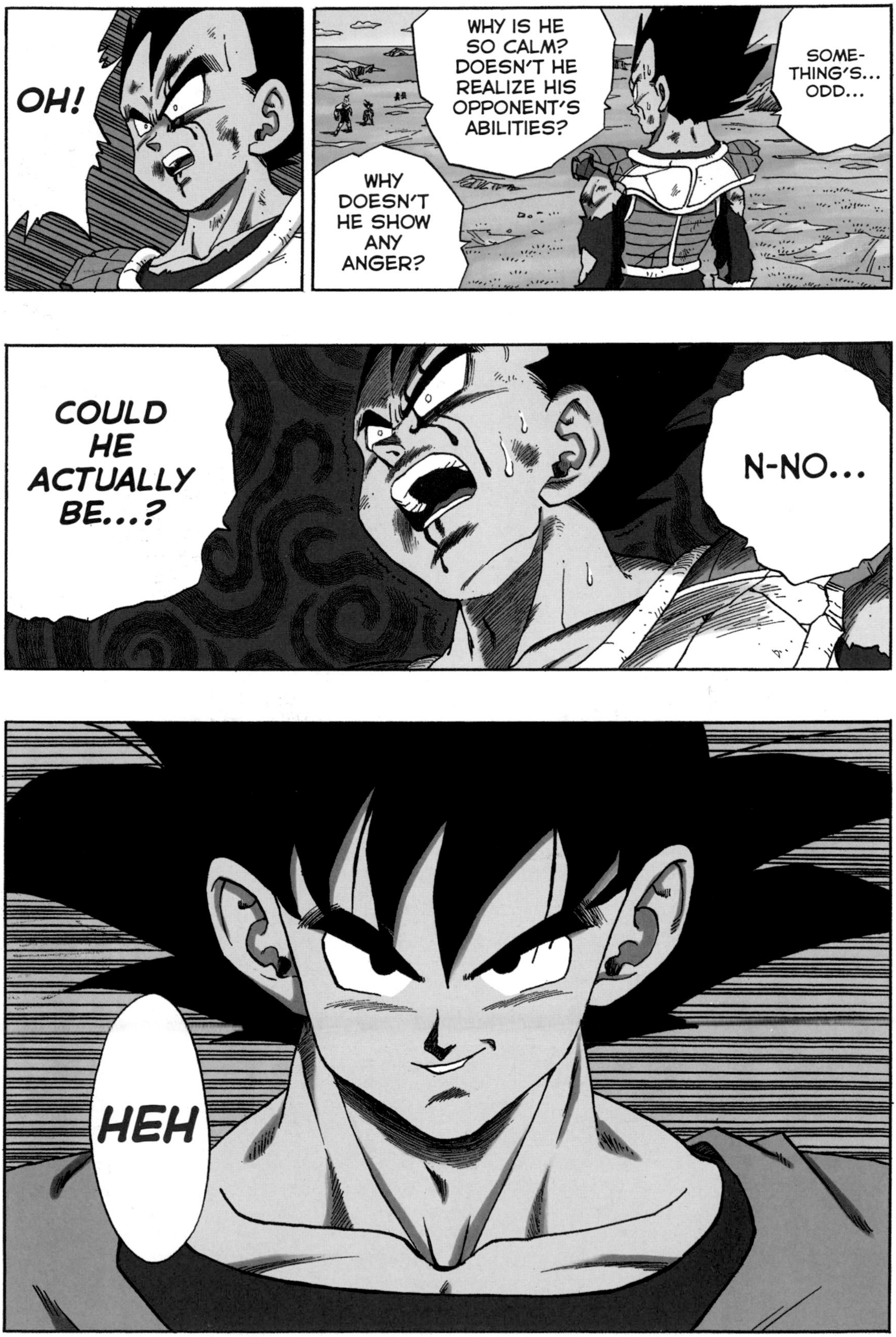
SOME-THING'S... ODD...
WHY IS HE SO CALM? DOESN'T HE REALIZE HIS OPPONENT'S ABILITIES?
WHY DOESN'T HE SHOW ANY ANGER?
OH!
N-NO...
COULD HE ACTUALLY BE...?
HEH

AKIRA TORIYAMA

Renowned worldwide for his playful, innovative storytelling and humorous, distinctive art style, Akira Toriyama burst onto the manga scene in 1980 with the wildly popular ***Dr. Slump***. His hit series ***Dragon Ball*** (published in the U.S. as ***Dragon Ball*** and ***Dragon Ball Z***) ran from 1984 to 1995 in Shueisha's ***Weekly Shonen Jump*** magazine. He is also known for his design work on video games such as ***Dragon Quest***, ***Chrono Trigger***, ***Tobal No. 1*** and ***Blue Dragon***. His recent manga works include ***COWA!***, ***Kajika***, ***Sand Land***, ***Neko Majin***, ***Toccio the Angel*** and ***Jaco the Galactic Patrolman***. He lives with his family in Japan.

SOUND EFFECTS GLOSSARY

The sound effects in this color edition of Dragonball have been preserved in their original Japanese format. To avoid additional lettering cluttering up the panels, a list of the sound effects (FX) is provided here. Each FX is listed by page and panel number, so for example 6.1 would mean the FX is on page 6 in panel 1. If there is a third number, it means there is more than one FX in the panel—6.1.1 and 6.1.2 for example.

44.1	BAKOOM		6.1	DOOM
45.4	FSSH		6.3	DOOM
46.1	HYUUUUUN		6.4	HAF
48.1	SPLOOOSH		7.1	KYOWW
51.4	ZMMM		8.2	GOM
52.1	DOOM		8.3	KANG
52.2	WHRRR		9.1	VNN
52.3	TM		9.3	KUWW
52.4	POW		9.5	BAM
52.5	ZIP		10.2	DOOM
53.2	VVVN		11.1	HWOO
53.3	VVVN VVVN		11.2	FCH
54.1	HYUN HYUN HYUN		11.3	KRI
54.2	SSSH		11.4	KRI
54.3	VSH		13.1	ZUUU
55.2	FWA		13.2	FA
57.1	BLASH		13.3	VIP
58.5	FYOOOOO		13.4	GMP
59.1	HYUUUUN		14.2	VOOOON
59.6	HYUUUN		14.3	KIIIIN
60.2	FLASSSHH		14.4	VM
61.2	HYUUUUN HYUUN		15.1	D-BOOM
62.1	HYOOO		15.2	SHHHH
63.1	SHOOM		16.4	PF
63.3	HYUUN		17.2	SHFFFF
63.5	HYUUN		17.5	SPLASH
63.7	HYUUN		18.4	HYUUUN
64.6	HYUUUUN		23.3	FYOOOO
64.7	TMP		24.5	KIIIII—N
66.2	SHPAA		24.7	TMP
66.5	TMP		25.3	VMM
68.3	KIIIIN		26.1	HYUUU
68.4	WVOOSH		26.3	PFT
70.1	BWOOM		26.4	BA BA BA BA BAAA
71.2	HWA		26.5	BAM
71.2	VWOON		26.6	DMM
71.2	SSHH		29.3	VIIIIN
71.3	FYOOO		36.2	ZHH
72.1	DOMM		38.4	HYUUUU
72.4	VMMM		39.1	HOOOOM
73.2	SSHHH		39.2	SHOWWWW
73.3	BRAK		43.7	TMMM

74.1	BRAK
74.3	DOOM
74.4	VASSSHHH
75.1	GWOM
75.2	KIIIINN
75.3	ZBLOOSH
76.2	DM DM DM DM DM
77.1	DA BA BA
	DA BA BA BA BA
	DA BA BA
77.2	DA BA BA BA BA...
78.3	BR-AAAAT
78.4	Z-BOOM-BOOM
79.3	BOOM
80.1	BOOSH BOOSH
80.2	TM TM
82.2	DOOM
83.1	GA BAM DAM BAM
	BAM DAM BAM DAM
83.2	SLAM BAM
83.2	GWOM GOOM
83.3	MOOSH
85.1	DOOM
85.5	D-BOOOOSH
87.7	HWOOSH
89.1	HYOOOOON
89.5	BOOM
90.3	VVVOWWW
90.4	ZIP
91.4	SSS
91.7	SSSHHH
93.7	DOOM
94.2	WOOOO
95.3	VIIIIIN
98.1	BLOOSH
98.2	KONNNG
99.1	ZYOOOOOM
99.3	DOM
100.1	KROOM
102.2	MUNCH MUNCH
105.2	VIIIIIIN
105.3	VWOOOSH
106.3	BAM BAM BAM
107.1	SSS
107.1	HWOOOOO
107.2	DM DM DM
108.1	DOM
108.2	DRAG...
108.9	SHAH
110.2	BAM
110.5	BIIII BI-BIII
111.1	PSSHHHH
111.6	VOONNN
111.7	SSHHH
111.8	PWAP
112.2	FYOOOO
112.3	CHOOOM
113.2	SHK SHK
113.5	VYOOOO
115.7	SSHH
116.4	DMM
117.3	VOOOSH
118.5	KIII—N
119.4	HWOOOSH
120.4	SKREE
120.5	FSSSH...
122.1	VOOSH
122.1	VWINNG
122.2	VANNNG
123.4	DM
124.2	ZZZUUU
125.1	TM
125.2	SHK
128.4	DWOOO DWOO DWOO
129.6	HOON HOON HOON
131.1	VYOOO
131.2	DM DOOM DOOM
132.3-2	VIIIING
132.4	TMP
133.1	VOOOSH
134.1	SHK
135.1	BOING BOING
135.2	SHTP
135.3	SHTP
135.4	SHTP
136.1	HYAH
136.3	HYAH
136.5	HYAH
137.1	HYAH
137.3	HYAH
140.5	SH-SHOOOOM
141.1	KIII—N
141.3	VWOOO
142.2	MOOF
144.2	TM TM
144.3	SWOO
145.1	SHTP SHTP
148.4	VOON
149.2	FOW
149.3	PSSH
151.1	PING
151.3	SHFF
154.5	HYOOOO
156.3	SHK
158.1	DOMM
158.3	pi pi pi---
158.5	FASSSH
159.1	WHOOOM
160.1	HWOOOOO
160.3	PING

195.1	ZUDDD		160.3	SHMMM
195.3	GLOM		161.1	SHK
196.1	FFF		162.3	ZWOOOO
196.2	VOOOOM		163.4	PING
196.6	DBAM		165.1	VOOON VOOON
197.2	ZOOOP		167.3	TMP TMP TMP
197.4	BOM		168.3	KRAK
198.1	BLAM		169.4	VYOOO
198.2	ZUMM		170.1	ZASH
198.2	DOMF		170.2	TWIK
199.1	BOMM		171.1	SSHHH
200.3	VSH		171.3	ROLLL ROLLL
201.3	KII—IIN		172.2	BMM
203.1	HOOSH		172.3	DOOM
203.2	HHHSSSS		175.4	CLAP
203.4	TMMM		176.2	VNNN
204.2	GGK		176.4	HWOOO
205.2	KAK		177.2	DOMM
205.3	D-GOOOM		178.1	BWAK...
206.1	HWOOO		178.2	BOM
206.3	TAKA TAKA		178.3	DM
207.1	ZZZWRRRB		179.1	THOK
208.3	HWOKK		179.2	ZUBB
209.2	VNN		180.2	BKOOM
209.3	DMM		181.1	VPP
209.3	TMM		181.2	WOOM
211.2	BAK		182.2	KWOOOM
211.3	TMP		183.1	DM DM DM DM
212.1	DOM		183.2	ZAM DOOM
212.2	VIIIIN		184.1	HYOOOO
212.4	VNN		184.1	HST
213.2	GOOM		184.5	HYOOOO
213.3	SSHHH		186.4	KRAK
213.4	VISH		187.2	TOOONG
220.5	VOOSH		188.1	ZOOOSH
221.2	VVNN		188.3	BONG
222.1	DM DM DM		188.4	DOM
223.1	DM DM		189.2	BLACH
223.2	FSSH		189.3	GNG
223.2	WAKK		190.1	WOKKA WOKKA
223.3	BAM		190.1	BOK BOK
224.2	STAGGER		190.2	BM BM BM DM DM DM
224.3	TMM		190.3	GONK
226.1	SHHHH		191.1	BWAK
227.2	SNAP		191.2	HWAH
228.1	DMMM		191.4	VMM
229.4	BOOM		191.5	PSHOOO
229.5	SSHHHH		192.1	VWSSSH
236.2	ZOOM		192.2	FYOO
237.1	GYOOOOON		192.3	VIIIIN
237.2	VWOO		193.2	BWAK
238.1	TMM		193.3	BLOOSH
238.6	ZIP		194.1	SLUSSSHHH
240.1	FLING		194.3	PSHOOOO
240.6	FLINCH		194.4	BOMF

DRAGON BALL FULL COLOR FREEZA ARC Volume 2
SHONEN JUMP Edition

STORY & ART BY **AKIRA TORIYAMA**

Translation **Mari Morimoto**
English Adaptation **Gerard Jones**
Lettering **Zack Turner**
Cover & Interior Design **Shawn Carrico**
Editor **Mike Montesa**

DRAGON BALL © 1984 by BIRD STUDIO
All rights reserved. First published in Japan in 1984 by SHUEISHA Inc., Tokyo.
English translation rights arranged by SHUEISHA Inc.

The stories, characters and incidents mentioned in this
publication are entirely fictional.

Printed in China.

Published by VIZ Media, LLC
P.O. Box 77010
San Francisco, CA 94107

10 9 8 7 6 5 4 3 2 1
First printing, July 2016

www.viz.com

www.shonenjump.com